PLASHET

GONE, BUT NOT FORGOTTEN

1896-1900

PLASHET

GONE, BUT NOT FORGOTTEN

1896-1900

Transcribed, edited and photographed by

MIRIAM POLLAK

PLASHET – GONE, BUT NOT FORGOTTEN: 1896-1900

First published in September 2013 by Plashet Services.
(03)-8763 2686. International +61-3-8763 2686.
111 Walls Road, Werribee, Victoria 3030, Australia
www.plashet.com

Transcribed, edited and photographed by Miriam Pollak

National Library of Australia Cataloguing-in-Publication entry

Title: Plashet - gone, but not forgotten. 1896-1900 / transcribed and edited by Miriam Pollak.

ISBN: 978-0-9875610-0-8 (hardback) / 978-0-9875610-1-5 (paperback)

Notes: Includes bibliographical references and index.

Subjects: Plashet Jewish Cemetery (London, England)
Register of births, etc.--England--London.
Jewish epitaphs--England--London.
Inscriptions, Jewish--England--London.
Jewish cemeteries--England--London.
Jewish sepulchral monuments--England--London.
London (England)--Genealogy

Cover and text design by The Mixing Bowl Gaphic Design
www.mixing-bowl.com.au

Illustrations by Miriam Pollak and The Mixing Bowl Graphic Design

Website by Potent Web Design
www.potent.com.au

Printed in Australia, UK and USA.

This book is dedicated to my ancestors who must have passed on to me a cluster of genes that allow for tenacity and downright 'pig-headedness'. The number of people who have said that what I wanted to do was not only impossible but stupid is endless. Yet through it all I have stuck to my guns. Thanks for ancestors who have worked and slaved against the grain. Here's to you!

CONTENTS

FOREWARD	I
INTRODUCTION	II
BACKGROUND	IV
HOW TO USE THIS BOOK	V
1896	1
1897	11
1898	93
1899	195
1900	335
NAME INDEX	454
MARRIAGE INDEX - GROOM	459
MARRIAGE INDEX - BRIDE	462
BIBLIOGRAPHY	466
ACKNOWLEDGEMENTS	468

FOREWARD

With the growth of additional aids to research available on the Internet, many researchers have experienced the temptation to expand a data source to include more detailed information. Few, however, have followed up on this urge. We are fortunate to have one such enthusiastic colleague take up the challenge for the burials in Plashet Cemetery. Documenting old cemeteries is a valuable project but Miriam Pollak has not just listed many who are buried there but has expanded the records to include personal information from other references.

Many of us have found family members from Miriam's exceptionally useful Jewish Chronicle's Personal Announcements Collection and, with the many references to 'Australian and South African papers please copy' in this latest project, there will be many more finds.

Rieke Nash
Past President
Australian Jewish Genealogical Society

INTRODUCTION

Plashet Cemetery is situated on High Street North in East Ham, a suburb within the Newnham Council area of eastern London. Most people in the area are totally unaware that there is a cemetery in their midst, as the cemetery is surrounded on all sides by housing and shops. There is only a small gated entrance on High Street North into the cemetery itself. In the past there was also a larger back entrance from Bristol Road, which is now locked.

From the United Synagogue's web-page about Plashet Cemetery, the Cemetery has been known as the "Trade Unionist Cemetery" because a number of past secretaries of the cigars union and costermongers union are buried in the cemetery.

According to the Jewish Chronicle published on 6 July 1883, during the meeting of the Executive Committee of the United Synagogue, Mr J. Magnus submitted a report from the Burial Committee to the Executive Committee to the effect that West Ham Cemetery was "rapidly filling up and that with every economy of space the ground will not last longer than ten years". It was decided that a Special Sub-Committee should be formed "to inquire into the capacity of the present cemetery at West Ham, whether it is desirable to secure a site at a distance from London, and whether any special site is procurable".

It wasn't until the Executive Committee's meeting in April 1887 that the Cemetery Sub-Committee reported on the capacity of the West Ham cemetery. The Sub-Committee reported that, "allowing for increases of population, enough ground was left in January (1887) to last ten years; and it was their opinion that any new cemetery should be as near London as possible." The Committee examined several sites and had found a piece of land at Plashet, one mile from the present West Ham Cemetery. The parcel of land was 17 acres – the owner wanted £500 per acre but might be willing to take £420 per acre – being £7,140 for the total parcel of land. Mr N.S. Joseph, the Honorary Architect, was given the authorization to continue negotiations with the land-owner for the purchase of the land *(Jewish Chronicle, 8 April 1887).*

In May 1888 the public were made aware that the United Synagogue had entered a contract for the purchase of land at Plashet. Because of a shortage of available funds for this purchase it was planned to institute a public subscription in the hope that members of the various Jewish congregations would help with funds to defray the cost of the Cemetery. The expenses needed for the purchase had now grown to £8,500, which included the cost of walling in the land *(Jewish Chronicle, 25 May 1888).*

In the Jewish Chronicle on 2 October 1888 it was noted that the land had now been purchased for the new cemetery at East Ham. "The result of the appeal to the public does not appear to have been successful. Messrs Rothschild and Sons gave £2,000, and in addition Lord Rothschild lent the Plashet Account £3,500 for several months, free of interest." Further donations to the value of £1,979 were received and other funds had been made available for the purchase. "A large sum of money will be required to enclose the land with a wall, but of course, as the ground will not be required for some eight years, this is not a pressing necessity" *(Jewish Chronicle 2 October 1888).*

In an article called 'New Cemetery at Plashet' *(Jewish Chronicle 8 November 1895),* Mr Joseph Magnus presented a report from the Burial Committee stating that "West Ham Cemetery will shortly be full, and in consequence interments will have to take place in the ground already acquired at Plashet for the purposes of a cemetery". At that time, the site at Plashet was let to a market gardener. The Honorary Officers then made arrangements with the tenant to give up possession of the land at the end of the current year for the payment of one hundred pounds. The total cost of getting the site ready for use as a cemetery was approximately £3000.

In the Jewish Chronicle (26 June 1896) the Burial Committee of the United Synagogue advertised for a Groundskeeper for Plashet Cemetery. For the sum of £100 per annum including residence, rates and taxes, gas and coals free, the applicant was required to devote his whole time to the services of the United Synagogue. He was also required to be able to read and write English and Hebrew fluently.

By the 3rd of July, the Burial Committee of the United Synagogue had unanimously resolved to recommend to the Council the election of Mr Morris A. Solomon as keeper of the new cemetery at Plashet. Mr Solomon was at that time employed as an Investigating Officer to the Jewish Board of Guardians *(Jewish Chronicle, 3 July 1896).*

In its edition of the 9 October 1896, the Jewish Chronicle devoted nearly two columns of the newspaper to the consecration of the new cemetery at Plashet by the Chief Rabbi, together with the cream of London's Jewry. The paper included the service verbatim for those members of the public who had been unable to attend. At the end of the service the Chief Rabbi announced that the Cohanim would assemble at the Burial ground on the occasion of the first interment therein, to dig the grave in accordance with time honoured custom *(Jewish Chronicle, 9 October 1896).*

The first interment took place on 7 November when a gathering of Cohanim, including the Chief Rabbi and Dayan Susman Cohen, partly dug the first grave at Plashet Cemetery *(Jewish Chronicle, 13 November 1896).*

BACKGROUND

Plashet Cemetery is one of twelve cemeteries that are owned and run by the United Synagogue's Burial Society. The cemeteries are:

Alderney Road Cemetery –the oldest Askenazi cemetery in the UK (opened 1697; closed 1852)
Aldershot Cemetery – A small cemetery in Hampshire
Bancroft Road Cemetery – Closed to burials in 1907
Brady Street Cemetery – Opened in 1761 and closed in 1857
Bushey Cemetery – Opened 1947 - open for burials
Dover Cemetery – Opened 1864 – open for burials
East Ham Cemetery – Opened 1919, no longer taking burials
Lauriston Road Cemetery – Opened 1788; closed in 1886
Plashet Cemetery – Opened in 1896; no longer taking burials
Waltham Abbey Cemetery – Opened in 1960 - open for burials
West Ham Cemetery – Opened in 1857; no longer taking burials
Willesden Cemetery – Opened in 1873; no longer taking burials

The United Synagogue (US) is an organisation that was founded in 1870 against the 'background of the mass immigration of foreign-born Jews at the end of the nineteenth century'. [The United Synagogue 1870-1970 by Aubrey Newman, London, 1976.] At the time of the creation of the US (as an organisation) contained just three Ashkenazi Synagogues (the Great Synagogue, Hambro' Synagogue, and the New Synagogue). By 1939 the US comprised 52 communities and during the period 1945 to 1955 thirty more communities joined the organisation. According the US website, the US now comprises over 60 communities. (http://www.theus.org.uk/the_united_synagogue/about_the_us/our_history/ . 17/09/2011).

HOW TO USE THIS BOOK

Each and every entry in this book is about an individual who is buried at Plashet Cemetery. Each entry is made up of the following items:

- **The person's name and nickname (if known); then the cemetery reference which is made up of three items** – the section in alphabetical order (B-); the row (42-) and the plot number (5) making a cemetery reference of B-42-5.
- **Death date** – this has been obtained either from the tombstone itself or from an entry in the Jewish Chronicle newspaper.
- **Date buried** – this date is from the United Synagogue's Burial Office database (which can be found at http://www.theus.org.uk/support_services/find_your_family/burial_records).
- **Partner's Name** – information from either the Jewish Chronicle entry or from census records (especially if a partner died before the deceased). I have tried to include information about the partner's death to complete the data.
- **Age at Death** – mostly obtained from either the Jewish Chronicle entry (where the information may be incorrect as dates were not nearly as important in the past as they are today), or from Births, Marriages and Deaths registers for the deceased. This information was provided to the registrar by an informant who may have just guessed the age.

The next section contains the Death Notice placed in the Jewish Chronicle. The date beside the name Jewish Chronicle is the date of publication. A second entry from the Jewish Chronicle contains the Tombstone Setting information. Occasionally there is also an Obituary or other information.

The next group of data is from the Births, Marriages & Deaths (BMD) in the following format: quarter of the year (1-4), year (in full), age at death (in square brackets), registration district (where the death was registered, for instance London City, Mile End, Whitechapel, etc.), volume number (i.e. 1c for the city; 1b for Hackney, 4a for West Ham, etc.), and a page number. This information is vital if a person wishes to obtain a certificate for the registered event – i.e. Birth, Marriage, or Death.

The next section contains information taken from the Census records. These entries contain a street address, followed by a list of residents. I have not included if married or single for the entries, as most entries mention a husband or wife, plus children. Entries include data about the year born and where, the current age of the residents, and occupation.

Marriage information is available when it has been found (in a number of cases it is clear that the couple were married outside England). For instance, if a husband dies, there is sometimes a new marriage, which has been included for completeness.

Some entries also include information about the deceased parents (information has been taken from census records).

Other information that may appear includes details of Nationality and Naturalisation from The National Archives. Occasionally information also appears in *The Jewish Victorian: Genealogical Information from Jewish Newspapers 1871-1880* which was transcribed and edited by Doreen Berger. Page numbers for entries that appear in this book are included.

The last item of an entry is the death of a partner. This included the BMD reference and a statement of where the person is buried. Burials in the late 1890s took place in a number of cemeteries – Plashet, West Ham, East Ham or Willesden Cemetery. Included in this entry is the cemetery reference for a partner, and the date of burial. For some partners the Death Notice from the Jewish Chronicle has also been included

Every source used in this book is available to the general public, either on the Internet or in book format. The internet sources include The Jewish Chronicle (for appearances in the newspaper), The National Archives (for information about naturalisations etc.), Findmypast.com (for Births, Marriages, Deaths, Census records and travel documentation), United Synagogue (for Burial Records) and FreeBMD as a form of backup if a record could not be found.

Please note that the information contained in the book may not be 100% accurate. Names changed over the years, often becoming anglicised. A person would often choose a name to use that was not so Jewish or foreign sounding. First names changed with time, for instance the name Louis became Lewis, Harris became Harry or Henry. It was not just first names that changed over time. For example, consider the surname Levy. There were a number of different spellings for this name – Levi, Levy and Levey. Sometimes the changes were due to the enumerators who took down the data for the census in the first place. They had to deal with strange and wonderful accents and possibly no one at home who could speak English. Sometimes a neighbour was called in to help gather the information, so naturally errors slipped in. Ages seem to change in every 'census' rather than decade which is ambiguous.

1896

BERLINSKY, Israel Joseph – B-1-19

BERLINSKY, Israel Joseph – B-1-19

Died: 05 Nov 1896
Buried: 17 Nov 1896
Hebrew Name: Israel Yosef bar Avraham Yehuda
Partner: Clara Berlinsky (d. 1922)
Aged: 45th year

Jewish Chronicle – 20 Nov 1896

BERLINSKY – On the 15th of November, at his residence, 27, Loraine Road, Holloway, Israel J. Berlinsky, in his 45th year, after a long and painful illness, borne with pious resignation. The beloved son-in-law of Mr and Mrs Louis Van Praagh. Deeply mourned by his sorrowing wife and children, and a numerous circle of friends. Australian, Cape, and American papers please copy.

Jewish Chronicle – 08 Jan 1897

The tombstone to the memory of the late Mr I.J. Berlinsky, will be set on Sunday next (10 Jan 1897), at 3 o'clock, at Plashet Cemetery. Relatives and friends please accept this, the only intimation – 27, Loraine Road, Holloway.

Death:

Q4 1896 [44] ISLINGTON 1b 250.

1891 Census

Address:

18 Mountford Street, Whitechapel

Residents:

Israel BERLINSKY – Head – b. 1852 Poland – aged 39 – Tailor
Clara BERLINSKY – Wife – b. 1852 Whitechapel – aged 39
Leah BERLINSKY – Daughter – b. 1877 Whitechapel – aged 14 – Cigar Maker
Kate BERLINSKY – Daughter – b. 1879 Whitechapel – aged 12 – Scholar
Rebecca BERLINSKY – Daughter – b. 1883 Whitechapel – aged 8 – Scholar
Mark BERLINSKY – Son – b. 1885 Whitechapel – aged 6 – Scholar
Abraham BERLINSKY – Son – b. 1887 Whitechapel – aged 4 – Scholar
Amelia BERLINSKY – Daughter – b. 1889 Whitechapel – aged 2
Rachael BERLINSKY – Mother – Widow – b. 1835 Poland – aged 56 – Supported by family
Harry BERLINSKY – Brother – b. 1867 Poland – aged 24 – Tailor
Annie SEAGER – Domestic Servant

1881 Census

Address:

10 Dock Street, Whitechapel

Residents:

Isiah BERLINSKI – Head – b. 1854 Poland – aged 27 – Tailor
Clara BERLINSKI – Wife – b. 1852 Whitechapel – aged 29
Leah BERLINSKI – Daughter – b. 1877 Whitechapel – aged 4 – Scholar
Catherine BERLINSKI – Daughter – b. 1879 Whitechapel – aged 2
Coleman BERLINSKI – Son – b. 1881 Whitechapel – aged 0
Ellen FITZGERALD – Domestic Servant

Marriage:

Israel BERLINSKY to Clara VAN PRAAG – Q4 1876 LONDON CITY 1c 178.

1901 Census

Address:

12 West Arbour Street, Mile End Old Town

Residents:

Clara BERLINSKY – Head – Widow – b. 1846 London – aged 55 – Living on own means
Rebecca BERLINSKY – Daughter – b. 1878 London – aged 23 – Cap Packer
Mark BERLINSKY – Son – b. 1882 London – aged 19 – Warehouseman
Abraham BERLINSKY – Son – b. 1885 London – aged 16 – Office Boy
Millie BERLINSKY – Daughter – b. 1887 London – aged 14
Esther BERLINSKY – Daughter – b. 1889 London – aged 12

1911 Census

Address:

28 Brunswick Buildings, Aldgate

Residents:

Clara BERLINSKY – Head – Widow – b. 1852 London – aged 59
Jack BERLINSKY – Son – b. 1893 London – aged 18 – Brass Engraver
Esther BERLINSKY – Daughter – b. 1895 London – aged 16 – Tailoress

Death:

Clara BERLINSKY – Q1 1922 [70] WHITECHAPEL 1c 338.
Buried at East Ham Cemetery – G-10-8 on 03 Jan 1922.

Jewish Chronicle – 06 Jan 1922

BERLINSKY – On the 1st of January, 1922, corresponding with 1st Tebeth, at 28, Brunswick Buildings, Aldgate, Clara, aged 70, relict of the late Israel Berlinsky. Devoted mother of Lily Barzilay, 122, Ernest Street, Mile End; Rebecca Barnett, 67, Brunswick Buildings; Abraham Berlinsky, 58, Sunbury Buildings, Shoreditch; Hetty Berlinsky; and Mark Berlinsky, Katie Aarons, and Jack Berlinsky, of Australia. Deeply mourned by her sorrowing children, sons-in-law, daughters-in-law, grandchildren, and a numerous circle of friends. Shiva at 28, Brunswick

Buildings. God rest her dear soul in peace. Australian and African papers please copy. BERLINSKY – On the 1st of January at 28, Brunswick Buildings, Aldgate, Clara, beloved sister of Mrs Sidney Aarons, 12, Montpelier Road, Brighton; Mrs Hannah Solomons, 4, British Street, Bow; Mrs David Isaacs, 53, St. Philip Street, Battersea; and Mrs Michael Abrahams, 1, Newcastle Street, Aldgate. Deeply mourned. Shiva at respective addresses.

HYAM, David – B-2-16

Died: 21 Dec 1896
Buried: 24 Dec 1896
Parents: Benjamin & Lucy Hyam
Aged: 30 years

Jewish Chronicle – 25 Dec 1896

HYAM – On the 21st of December, at 21, Church Crescent, South Hackney, David Hyam, aged 30, son of Mrs Benjamin Hyam, of 21, Gascony Avenue, N.W. Deeply lamented by his sorrowing mother, brothers and sister. Shiva at 45, Brondesbury Road, Kilburn.

Jewish Chronicle – 09 Jul 1897

The tombstone in memory of David, son of Lucy and the late Benjamin Hyam, will be set at Plashet Cemetery, East Ham, on Sunday next, July 11th, at 3 o'clock. Friends will please accept this intimation.

Death:

Q4 1896 [30] HACKNEY 1b 365.

Birth:

Q4 1865 SWANSEA 11a 558 – David Louis HYAM

1881 Census

Address:

41 Houndsditch, St. Botolph Without Aldgate

Residents:

Lucy HYAM – Head – Widow – b. 1833 London – aged 48 – Dressmaker
Hyrum (Hyam) L. HYAM – Son – b. 1858 Swansea – aged 23 – Stock Brokers Clerk
Sarah HYAM – Daughter – b. 1861 Swansea – aged 20 – Dressmaker
Abraham HYAM – Son – b. 1862 Swansea – aged 19 – Watchmaker
Joseph Cosman HYAM – Son – b. 1864 Swansea – aged 17 – Wood Carver
Mark HYAM – Son – b. 1869 Swansea – aged 12 – Scholar
Solomon AMOS – Boarder – b. 1833 Morocco – aged 48 – General Merchant
Habib AMOS – Boarder – b. 1839 Morocco – aged 42 – General Merchant

1871 Census

Address:

Aldgate, St. Katharine Cree, London

Residents:

Lucy HYAM – Head – Widow – b. 1831 Middlesex – aged 40 – Dressmaker
Hyam HYAM – Son – b. 1858 Swansea – aged 13 – Scholar
Jacob HYAM – Son – b. 1859 Swansea – aged 12 – Scholar
Sarah HYAM – Daughter – b. 1860 Swansea – aged 11 – Scholar
Joseph HYAM – Son – b. 1864 Swansea – aged 7 – Scholar
Mark HYAM – Son – b. 1869 Swansea – aged 2

Death:

Benjamin HYAM – Q3 1870 [52] SWANSEA 11a 311.

1861 Census

Address:

22 Clothier, Castle Street, Swansea

Residents:

Benjamin HYAM – Head – b. 1817 London – aged 44 – Clothier
Lucy HYAM – Wife – b. 1828 London – aged 33
Hyam L. HYAM – Son – b. 1858 Swansea – aged 3
Jacob J. HYAM – Son – b. 1859 Swansea – aged 2
Sarah HYAM – Daughter – b. 1861 – 10 months
Maureen BASS – General Servant
Alice AUGUSTUS – Nurse/Domestic Servant

Marriage:

Benjamin HYAM to Lucy HADIDA – Q4 1856 LONDON CITY 1c 292.

1901 Census

Address:

36 St. Julian's Road, Willesden

Residents:

Lucy HYAM – Head – Widow – b. 1832 London – aged 69
Sara HYAM – Daughter – b. 1861 Swansea – aged 40 – Fancy Needleworker
Mark L. HYAM – Son – b. 1869 Swansea – aged 32 – Clerk for Fruit Brokers

Death:

Lucy HYAM – Q1 1913 [82] WILLESDEN 3a 336.
Buried at Willesden Jewish Cemetery – AX-20-18 on 07 Feb 1913.

ISRAEL, Rebecca – B-1-44

ISRAEL, Rebecca – B-1-44

Died: 27 Dec 1896
Buried: 29 Dec 1896
Partner: Abraham Israel (d. 1915)
Aged: 53rd year

Jewish Chronicle – 01 Jan 1897

ISRAEL – On the 27th of December, at No. 9, Bow Road, E., Rebecca, dearly loved wife of Abraham Israel, in her 53rd year. Dearly loved and deeply mourned. May her soul rest in peace. Mother of Mr Alfred Israel, of 6, Russell Street, Covent Garden, and Mr David Israel, of 31, Grafton Street, E., and sister of Mrs Sarah Solomons, of 28, Calverley Street, E. Shiva a 9, Bow Road, E. South African papers please copy.

Jewish Chronicle – 10 Sep 1897

The tombstone in memory of the lamented Mrs Rebecca Israel, of 9 Bow Road, E., will be set on Sunday next, September 19th, at Plashet Cemetery at 1.30 p.m. Relatives and friends kindly accept this, the only intimation.

Death:

Q4 1896 [52] POPLAR 1c 358.

1891 Census

Address:

7 Bow Road, Bow or Stratford Le Bow, Bow & Bromley the Tower Hamlets

Residents:

Abraham ISRAEL – Head – b. 1849 Aldgate – aged 42 – Carman Contractor
Rebecca ISRAEL – Wife – b. 1846 Aldgate – aged 45
Abraham A. ISRAEL – Son – b. 1872 Aldgate – aged 19 – Carman Contractor
David ISRAEL – Son – b. 1874 Aldgate – aged 17 – Carman Contractor
John ISRAEL – Son – b. 1875 Aldgate – aged 16 – Clerk Carman Contractor
Rebecca ISRAEL – Daughter – b. 1876 Aldgate – aged 15
Nancy A. ISRAEL – Daughter – b. 1881 Mile End – aged 10 – Scholar
Elizabeth ISRAEL – Daughter – b. 1883 Mile End – aged 8 – Scholar
Emma SULLIVAN – General Domestic Servant
Lucy MCCARTHY – General Domestic Servant

1881 Census

Address:

1 Buckeridge Street, Mile End Old Town

Residents:

Abraham ISRAEL – Head – b. 1848 London – aged 33 – Carman

Rebecca ISRAEL – Wife – b. 1845 London – aged 36
Abraham ISRAEL – Son – b. 1872 London – aged 9 – Scholar
David ISRAEL – Son – b. 1874 London – aged 7 – Scholar
John ISRAEL – Son – b. 1875 London – aged 6 – Scholar
Rebecca ISRAEL – Daughter – b. 1876 London – aged 5 – Scholar
Henry ISRAEL – Son – b. 1878 London – aged 3
Michael ISRAEL – Son – b. 1880 London – aged 1
Ann ISRAEL – Daughter – b. 1881 London – aged 0
Ann TREADWELL – General Servant
Mary Ann WHALE – Nursemaid

1871 Census

Address:
Bull Court, Christ Church, Whitechapel

Residents:
Abraham ISRAEL – Head – b. 1848 Middlesex – aged 23 - Fruiterer
Rebecca ISRAEL – Wife – b. 1845 Spitalfields – aged 26
Elizabeth ISRAEL – Daughter – b. 1871 Middlesex – aged 5 months

Marriage:
Abraham ISRAEL to Rebecca ISRAEL – Q2 1869 LONDON CITY 1c 156.

1901 Census

Address:
18 Kilburn Priory, Hampstead

Residents:
Abraham ISRAEL – Head – Widower – b. 1848 Bow – aged 53 – Fruit Merchant
Michael ISRAEL – Son – b. 1880 Bow – aged 21 – Assistant Merchant
Nancy ISRAEL – Daughter – b. 1881 Bow – aged 20
Elizabeth ISRAEL – Daughter – b. 1883 Bow – aged 18
Fanny ISRAEL – Sister-in-law – b. 1854 Bow – aged 47
Isaac C. JACKSON – Cousin – b. 1869 Bow – aged 32 – Tailor
Emma WICKER – Domestic Servant
Susan MORAN – Domestic Servant

1911 Census

Address:
38 Gordon Mansions, St. Pancras

Residents:
Abraham ISRAEL – Head – Widower – b. 1848 London – aged 63 – Fruit Merchant
Nancy ISRAEL – Daughter – b. 1881 London – aged 30
Henry ISRAEL – Son – b. 1878 London – aged 33 – Fruit Merchant
May Clara HOWARD – General Domestic Servant

Death:

Abraham ISRAEL – Q4 1915 [67] PANCRAS 1b 55.
Buried at Willesden Cemetery – CX-14-28 on 25 Nov 1915.

Jewish Chronicle – 26 Nov 1915

ISRAEL – On the 24th of November, at 38, Gordon Mansions, W.C., Abraham Israel, the beloved father of Alfred Israel, 40, Brondesbury Road, N.W.; David Israel, 15, Stockwell Park Road, S.W.; John Israel, 5, Garlinge Road, N.W.; Mrs John Joel, 110, High Street, Sutton; Henry Israel, 46, Wymering Mansions, W.; Michael Israel, 2, River Court Road, Hammersmith, W.; Mrs M. Bonn, 24, Gordon Mansions, W.C.; and Miss Nancy Israel. Deeply mourned by his sorrowing children, daughters-in-law, sons-in-law, and grandchildren. May his dear soul rest in everlasting peace. Amen. Shiva at 38, Gordon Mansions, Gower Street, W.C.

SCHREIBERG, Woolf (Lewis) – B-1-1

Died: **05 Nov 1896**
Buried: **08 Nov 1896**
Aged: **62 years**

Jewish Chronicle – 13 Nov 1896

PLASHET CEMETERY (p. 9) – The first interment at the new Jewish cemetery at Plashet took place on Sunday last, when Mr Lewis Schreiber(g), of Bedford Street, Commercial Road, was buried. In accordance with time-honoured custom, the first grave was partly dug by the Cohanim. The Chief Rabbi and Dayan Susman Cohen were among the Cohanim who attended on the occasion.

Death:

Woolf SHRIEBERG - Q4 1896 [62] MILE END OLD TOWN 1c 299.

1897

In Memory of
LOUISA,
BELOVED WIFE OF
JOHN ABRAHAMS,
OF 9 EXCHANGE BUILDINGS,
HOUNDSDITCH,
WHO DIED 25TH MAY 1897,
AGED 28.
MY LOVED ONES DEAR MY TIME IS PAST,
I LOVED YOU WHILE MY LIFE DID LAST,
MOURN NOT FOR ME NOR SORROW TAKE,
AND LOVE EACH OTHER FOR MY SAKE.

ABRAHAMS, Louisa – A-7-28

ABRAHAMS, Louisa – A-7-28

Died: 25 May 1897
Buried: 27 May 1897
Partner: Jack/John Abrahams
Aged: 28th year

Jewish Chronicle – 28 May 1897

ABRAHAMS – On the 25th of May, Louisa the beloved wife of Mr Jack Abrahams of 9, Exchange Buildings, Cutler Street, Houndsditch, in her 28th year. Deeply lamented by her sorrowing husband, children, relatives, and friends.

Jewish Chronicle – 01 Apr 1898

The tombstone in memory of the late Louisa, the beloved wife of Jack Abrahams, of 9, Exchange-buildings, Houndsditch, and daughter of Solomon Joel, late of Mitre-street, will be set on Sunday next, the 3rd of April, at 4 o'clock at Plashet Cemetery. Relatives and friends please accept this, the only intimation.

Death:
Q2 1897 [27] LONDON CITY 1c 2.

1891 Census

Address:
7 Bury Street, St. Katherine Cree, London

Residents:
John ABRAHAMS – Head – b. 1867 London – aged 24 – Dealer
Louisa ABRAHAMS – Wife – b. 1870 Mile End – aged 21

Marriage:
Jack ABRAHAMS to Louisa JOEL – Q1 1891 LONDON CITY 1c 102.

Marriage:
John ABRAHAMS to Elizabeth Betsy COHEN – Q1 1899 LONDON CITY 1c 86.

1901 Census

Address:
3 & 4 Cutler Street, St. Botolph Without Aldgate

Residents:
John ABRAHAMS – Head – b. 1867 City – aged 34 – Licensed Victualler
Elizabeth ABRAHAMS – Wife – b. 1871 City – aged 30
Maria ABRAHAMS – Daughter – b. 1893 City – aged 8
Benjamin ABRAHAMS – Son – b. 1894 City – aged 7
Anne ABRAHAMS – Daughter – b. 1900 City – aged 1

Rose COURTNAY – Domestic Servant
Rose McGUIRE – Domestic Servant

1911 Census

Address:

33 Carlton Mansions, Portsdown Road, Paddington W.

Residents:

John ABRAHAMS – Head – b. 1866 Aldgate – aged 45 – General Dealer
Elizabeth ABRAHAMS – Wife (12 years) – b. 1871 – Aldgate
Benjamin ABRAHAMS – Son – b. 1894 Aldgate – aged 17 – Barman
Marie ABRAHAMS – Daughter – b. 1893 Aldgate – aged 18
Annie ABRAHAMS – Daughter – b. 1900 Aldgate – aged 11 – at School
Monti ABRAHAMS – Son b. 1902 Aldgate – aged 9
Janie MANCHIP – Domestic Servant

ABRAHAMS, Rebecca – A-6-27

Died: **24 Feb 1897**
Buried: **26 Feb 1897**
Parents: **Benjamin & [Dinah] Abrahams**
Aged: **27 years**

Jewish Chronicle – 05 Mar 1897

ABRAHAMS – On the 24th of February, at 115, Houndsditch, Rebecca, second daughter of B. Abrahams, aged 27 years. God rest her soul. Johannesburg papers please copy.

Jewish Chronicle – 04 Mar 1898

The tombstone in memory of Benjamin Abrahams of 115, Houndsditch, and his daughter Rebecca, will be set on Sunday, March the 6th, at Plashet at 4 o'clock. Relatives and friends will accept this only intimation.

Death:

Q1 1897 [27] LONDON CITY 1c 2.

1891 Census

Address:

115 Houndsditch, Aldgate, London

Residents:

Benjamin ABRAHAM – Head – Widower – b. 1843 Spitalfields – Clothes Dealer
Jane ABRAHAM – Daughter – b. 1866 London – aged 25
Rebecca ABRAHAM – Daughter – b. 1868 London – aged 23

1881 Census

Address:

18 Carter Street, St. Botolph Without Aldgate

Residents:

Benjamin ABRAHAM – Head – Widower – b. 1843 Spitalfields – Government Contractor
Ada ABRAHAM – Sister – b. 1854 Spitalfields – aged 27
Moss ABRAHAM – Brother – b. 1856 Spitalfields – aged 25 – Government Contractor
Alfred ABRAHAM – Brother – b. 1858 Spitalfields – aged 23 – Merchant
Elizabeth ABRAHAM – Sister – b. 1859 Spitalfields – aged 22
Jane ABRAHAM – Niece – b. 1865 Aldgate – aged 16
John ABRAHAM – Nephew – b. 1867 Aldgate – aged 14
Rebecca ABRAHAM – Niece – b. 1868 Aldgate – aged 13 – Scholar
Rebecca PARKER – Visitor – b. 1860 Spitalfields – aged 21
Maria ABRAHAMS – Niece – b. 1874 Aldgate – aged 7 – Scholar

1871 Census

Address:

12 White Street, Aldgate, City of London, London

Residents:

Benjamin ABRAHAMS – Head – b. 1842 London – aged 29
Jane ABRAHAMS – Daughter – b. 1865 London – aged 6
John ABRAHAMS – Son – b. 1866 London – aged 5
Rebecca ABRAHAMS – Daughter – b. 1868 London – aged 3

1861 Census

Address:

12 White Street, St. Botolph Without Aldgate, London

Residents:

John ABRAHAMS – Head – b. 1816 Childerditch – aged 45 – Dealer
Jane ABRAHAMS – Wife – b. 1813 Whitechapel – aged 48
Benjamin ABRAHAMS – Son – b. 1841 Christchurch – aged 20 – General Dealer
Ann ABRAHAMS – Daughter – b. 1843 Christchurch – aged 18 – Waistcoat Maker
Sarah ABRAHAMS – Daughter – b. 1845 Christchurch – aged 16 – Waistcoat Maker
Rebecca ABRAHAMS – Daughter – b. 1847 Christchurch – aged 14
Moss ABRAHAMS – Grandson – b. 1848 Christchurch – aged 13 – Scholar
Rachael ABRAHAMS – Daughter – b. 1850 Christchurch – aged 11 – Scholar
Abraham ABRAHAMS – Son – b. 1852 Christchurch – aged 9 – Scholar
Samuel ABRAHAMS – Son – b. 1854 Christchurch – aged 7 – Scholar
Elizabeth ABRAHAMS – Daughter – b. 1856 Christchurch – aged 5 – Scholar
Sarah ABRAHAMS – Mother-in-Law – b. 1816 Middlesex – aged 45

Marriage:

Benjamin ABRAHAMS to Dinah JOEL – Q3 1897 LONDON CITY 1c 112.

Death:

Benjamin Abrahams – Q1 1898 [56] LONDON CITY 1c 2.
Buried at Plashet Cemetery – A-11-15 on 27 Jan 1898.

Jewish Chronicle – 28 Jan 1898

ABRAHAMS – On the 25th of January, at 115, Houndsditch, Benjamin Abrahams, husband of Dinah Abrahams, formerly Mrs Joel, of Kimberley and Johannesburg, father of Jack Abrahams, of 9, Exchange Buildings, Houndsditch, and brother of Lizzie and Alfred Abrahams, and Mrs H.S. Parker, late of the "White Swan", Islington. Shiva at 115, Houndsditch. Kimberley and Johannesburg papers please copy.

BENJAMIN, Hyman – B-3-1

Died: **12 May 1897**
Buried: **14 May 1897**
Hebrew Name: **Ephraim ben Yaakov**
Partner: **Jane Benjamin (d. 1934)**
Aged: **47th year**

Jewish Chronicle – 14 May 1897

BENJAMIN – On the 12th of May, at 10, St. Mark Street, Goodman's Fields, Hyman Benjamin, in his 47th year. Deeply lamented by his sorrowing wife, children, mother and family. May his soul rest in peace.

Jewish Chronicle – 10 Sep 1897

The tombstone in loving memory of the late Mr Hyman Benjamin, of 10, St. Mark's Street, Goodman's Fields, will be set on Sunday, the 12th inst., at Plashet Cemetery at 4 o'clock. Train leaves Liverpool Street, at 3.4 p.m. Relatives and friends please accept this, the only intimation.

Death:

Q2 1897 [47] WHITECHAPEL 1c 202.

1891 Census

Address:

10 St. Marks Street, St. Mary Whitechapel, London, Tower Hamlets

Residents:

Joel WOOLF – Head – Widower – b. 1829 Whitechapel – aged 62 – Baker
Hyman BENJAMIN – Son-in-law – b. 1852 Aldgate – aged 39 – Hotel Manager
Jane BENJAMIN – Daughter – b. 1852 Aldgate – aged 39

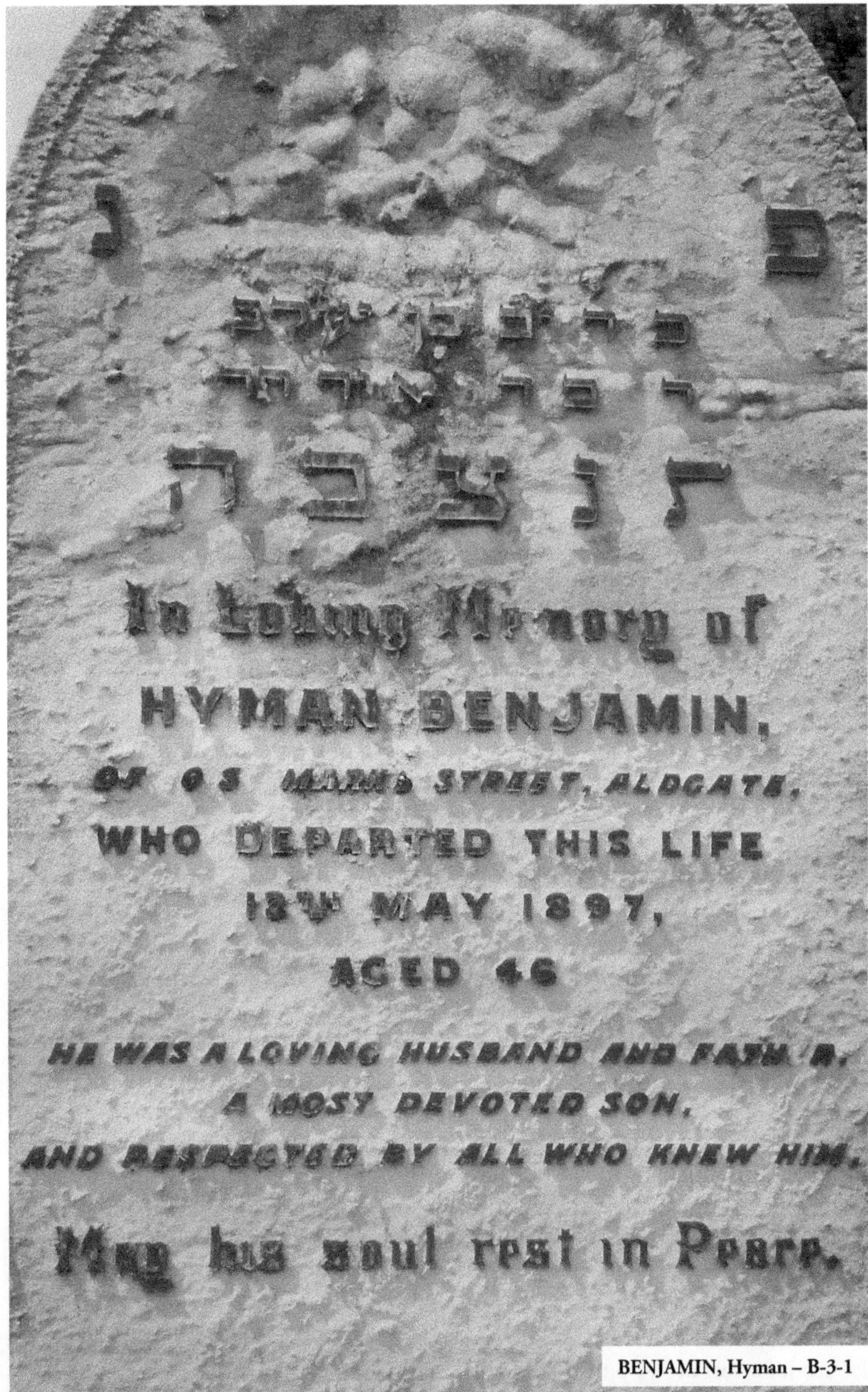

BENJAMIN, Hyman – B-3-1

Rosetta WOOLF – Daughter – b. 1869 Aldgate – aged 22 – Assistant Baker
Ellen BENJAMIN – Granddaughter – b. 1879 Spitalfields – aged 12 – Scholar
Angel BENJAMIN – Grandson – b. 1882 Whitechapel – aged 9 – Scholar
Susan TAYLOR – Domestic Servant

1881 Census

Address:
72 Commercial Street, Spitalfields

Residents:
Adolphus HARRIS – Head – b. 1852 Prussia – aged 29 – Baker
Sarah HARRIS – Wife – b. 1858 London – aged 23 – Baker
Michael HARRIS – Son – b. 1880 London – aged 1
Hyman BENJAMIN – Brother – b. 1850 London – aged 31 – Billiard Maker
Jane BENJAMIN – Sister-in-law – b. 1853 London – aged 28
John BENJAMIN – Nephew – b. 1877 London – aged 4
Helen BENJAMIN – Niece – b. 1878 London – aged 3
Rebecca YOUNG – Domestic Servant
Helen YOUNG – Domestic Servant

Marriage:
Hyman BENJAMIN to Jane WOOLF – Q3 1875 LONDON CITY 1c 189.

Death:
Jane BENJAMIN – Q2 1934 [81] HAMMERSMITH 1a 244.
Buried at East Ham Cemetery – XC-2-87 on 03 May 1934.

BOSS, Gumpert – A-8-6

Died: **03 Jun 1897**
Buried: **04 Jun 1897**
Hebrew Name: **Ephraim ben Aahron**
Partner: **Mina Boss (d. 1905)**
Aged: **77 years**

Jewish Chronicle – 11 Jun 1897

BOSS – On Thursday, the 3rd of June, at 88, Stepney Green, E., Gumpert Boss, husband of Mrs M. Boss. Mourned by his sorrowing wife, sons and daughters.

Jewish Chronicle – 03 Sep 1897

The tombstone in loving memory of Gumpert Boss, of 88, Stepney Green, will be set at Plashet Cemetery at 4 o'clock on Sunday, September 5th. Train leaves Liverpool-street at 3.4 p.m.

BOSS, Gumpert – A-8-6

Death:

Q2 1897 [77] MILE END 1c 269.

1891 Census

Address:

88 Stepney Green, Mile End Old Town

Residents:

Gumpert BOSS – Head – b. 1817 Germany – aged 74 – Retired Traveller
Mina BOSS – Wife – b. 1825 Germany – aged 66
Annie BOSS – Daughter – b. 1864 London – aged 27 – Dressmaker
Esther BOSS – Daughter – b. 1866 London – aged 25 – Dressmaker
Charlotte BOSS – Daughter – b. 1874 London – aged 17

1881 Census

Address:

11 Turner Street, Mile End Old Town

Residents:

Mina BOSS – Head – b. 1831 Prussia – aged 50 – Needle Worker
Maria BOSS – Daughter – b. 1857 Hull – aged 24 – Needle Worker
Annie BOSS – Daughter – b. 1863 London – aged 18 – Needle Worker
Esther BOSS – Daughter – b. 1865 London – aged 16 – Needle Worker
Solomon BOSS – Son – b. 1870 London – aged 11 – Scholar
Charlotte BOSS – Daughter – b. 1872 London – aged 9 – Scholar

1871 Census

Address:

Hooper Square, St. Mary Whitechapel

Residents:

Mina BOSS – Head – b. 1831 Germany – aged 40
Aaron BOSS – Son – b. 1855 Yorkshire – aged 16
Nathan BOSS – Son – b. 1858 Yorkshire – aged 13
Annie BOSS – Daughter – b. 1863 London – aged 8
Moses BOSS – Son – b. 1864 London – aged 7
Esther BOSS – Daughter – b. 1867 London – aged 4
Solomon BOSS – Son – b. 1870 London – aged 1

1861 Census

Address:

3 Winter Street, Manchester

Residents:

Gumpert BOSS – Head – b. 1822 Prussia – aged 39 – Traveller
Mina BOSS – Wife – b. 1829 Prussia – aged 32
Rachael BOSS – Daughter – b. 1853 Lincolnshire – aged 8 – Scholar

Aaron BOSS – Son – b. 1855 Yorkshire – aged 6 – Scholar
Mary BOSS – Daughter – b. 1857 Yorkshire – aged 4 – Scholar
Matthew BOSS – Son – b. 1858 Yorkshire – aged 3 – Scholar
Rebecca BOSS – Daughter b. 1860 Yorkshire – aged 1

Death:
Mina BOSS – Q1 1905 [76] WEST HAM 4a 176.
Buried at Plashet Cemetery – F-3-19 on 25 Jan 1905.

Jewish Chronicle – 27 Jan 1905

BOSS – On the 24th of January – 18th Shebat, at 99, Colworth Road, Leytonstone, Mina, widow of the late Gumpert Boss, dearly loved mother of Mrs D.L. Rynveld, Mrs Joseph Meller, Mrs L. Klein, and Annie and Charlotte Boss, also of Arthur A. Boss, of Johannesburg, Nathan Boss of Port Elizabeth, and Harry and Solomon Boss, of San Francisco. Shiva at 99, Colworth Road.

Jewish Chronicle – 20 Oct 1905

The tombstone to the memory of Mina Boss (widow of the late Gumpert Boss), will be set at Plashet Cemetery, on Sunday, October 29th, at 2.30 p.m.

BRIGMAN, Simon – B-2-43

Died: **13 Feb 1897**
Buried: **16 Feb 1897**
Partner: **Annie Brigman**
Aged: **44 years**

Jewish Chronicle – 19 Feb 1897

BRIGMAN – On the 13th of February, at his residence, 94 and 96, Barking Road, Canning Town, Simon Brigman (trading in the name of Brig), aged 44, Vice-President of the Poplar Synagogue. Deeply lamented by his sorrowing wife, children and family. May his soul rest in peace.

Jewish Chronicle – 17 Sep 1897

The tombstone in loving memory of S. Brigman, of Barking Road, will be set at Plashet Cemetery, on Sunday next, September 19th, at 3.30 p.m.

Death:
Q1 1897 [44] WEST HAM 4a 64.

1901 Census

Address:
94 and 96 Baking Road, West Ham

Residents:

Abraham MANDLESTAN – Head – b. 1857 Russia – aged 44 – Tailor
Caroline MANDELSTAN – Wife – b. 1858 Aldgate – aged 32
Morris MANDELSTAN – Son – b. 1881 St Lukes – aged 20 – Tailor's Assistant
Annie BRIGMAN – Sister-in-law – Widow – b. 1856 Aldgate – aged 45
Minnie BRIGMAN – Niece – b. 1882 St Lukes – aged 19
Solomon BRIGMAN – Nephew – b. 1888 West Ham – aged 13

1891 Census

Address:

164, Barking Road, West Ham

Residents:

Simon BRIGMAN – Head – b. 1854 Warsaw – aged 37 – Tailor
Annie BRIGMAN – Wife – b. 1856 Shoreditch – aged 35
Minnie BRIGMAN – Daughter – b. 1882 Shoreditch – aged 9
Solomon M. BRIGMAN – Son – b. 1888 Canning Town – aged 3
Josephine SUMMERS – Domestic Servant

Marriage:

Simon BRIGMAN to Annie MORRIS – Q3 1878 LONDON CITY 1c 176.

COOK, Fanny – A-6-6

Died: **18 Jan 1897**
Buried: **19 Jan 1897**
Hebrew Name: **Faigel bat Yehuda**
Partner: **Barnett Cook (d. 1903)**
Aged: **28 years**

Jewish Chronicle – 22 Jan 1897

COOK – On the 18th of January, at 72, Cable-street, E., Fanny, the beloved wife of Barnett Cook and sister of Jacob Rosenberg of 75, High-street, Whitechapel. Deeply mourned by her sorrowing husband, children, relatives and friends. May her dear soul rest in peace. Shiva at 72, Cable-street.

Jewish Chronicle – 26 Nov 1897

The tombstone in loving memory of Fanny, wife of Barnett Cook, of 72, Cable-street, E., will be set at the Plashet Cemetery on Sunday next, November 28th, at 3 o'clock. Relatives and friends accept this intimation.

Death:

Q1 1897 [28] ST. GEORGE IN THE EAST 1c 224.

COOK, Fanny – A-6-6

1891 Census

Address:

60 Cable Street, St. George in the East

Residents:

Barnett COOK – Head – b. 1853 Poland – aged 38 – Bootmaker
Fanny COOK – Wife – b. 1868 St. Georges – aged 23
Morris COOK – Son – b. 1876 St. Georges – aged 15 – Apprentice Bootmaker
Solly COOK – Son – b. 1884 St. Georges – aged 7
Annie COOK – Daughter – b. 1889 St. Georges – aged 2
Rosie COOK – Daughter – b. 1891 St. Georges – aged 7 months
Emma FIELD – Domestic Servant

Marriage:

Barnet COOK to Fanny ROSENBERG – Q1 1888 LONDON CITY 1c 85.

1881 Census

Address:

60 Cable Street, St. George in the East

Residents:

Barnett COOK – Head – b. 1853 Poland – aged 28 – Master Shoe Maker
Fanny COOK – Wife – b. 1855 Poland – aged 26
Morris COOK – Son – b. 1876 London – aged 5
Sarah TOBIAS – Visitor – b. 1861 Poland – aged 20 – Machinist (sewing)
Henry PORTER – Visitor – b. 1842 London – aged 39 – Vice Man (Whitesmith)
Elizabeth PORTER – Visitor – b. 1841 London – aged 40 – wife of above
Alfred JONES – Boarder – b. 1821 London – aged 60 – Printer
John JONES – Boarder – b. 1864 London – aged 17 – Dock Labourer
Edward ANCELL – Boarder – b. 1848 London – aged 33 – Carpenter

Death:

Fanny COOK – Q3 1883 [25] LAMBETH 1d 257.
Place of burial unknown.

Marriage:

Barnett COOK to Rosa LESOLSKY – Q2 1899 MILE END OLD TOWN 1c 829.

1901 Census

Address:

106 Matthias Road, Stoke Newington

Residents:

Barnett COOK – Head – b. 1851 Poland – aged 50 – Boot Maker
Jane COOK – Wife – b. 1856 Poland – aged 45 (? Rosa)
Maurice COOK – Son – b. 1876 St. Georges – aged 25 – Boot Maker

Solomon COOK – Son – b. 1884 St. Georges – aged 17 – Butcher's Apprentice
Philip COOK – Son – b. 1897 St. Georges – aged 4

Death:

Barnett COOK – Q4 1903 [52] HACKNEY 1b 241.
Buried at Plashet Cemetery – E-23-10 on 17 Nov 1903.

Jewish Chronicle – 20 Nov 1903

COOK – On the 13th of November, at 106, Matthias Road, Newington Green, Barnett Cook, in his fifty-third year. Deeply mourned by his sorrowing wife, children and a large circle of friends. God rest his dear soul in peace.

DAVIS, Sarah Queenie – C-2-33

Died: **01 Dec 1897**
Buried: **03 Dec 1897**
Parents: **Solomon and Sylvia Davis**
Aged: **15 months**

Jewish Chronicle – 03 Dec 1897

DAVIS – On the 1st of December, at 303, Mile End Road, Sarah Queenie, dearly beloved infant of Sol and Sylvia Davis, aged fifteen months. May her dear soul rest in peace.

Jewish Chronicle – 26 Aug 1898

The tombstone in loving memory of Sarah (Queenie), the darling daughter of Sol. and Sylvia Davis, 303, Mile End Road, will be set at Plashet Cemetery on Sunday next, August 28th, at 4 o'clock. Relatives and friends accept this, the only intimation.

Death:

Sara Sadi Q DAVIS - Q4 1897 [1] MILE END 1c 364.

Birth:

Sara Sadi Q DAVIS – Q3 1896 MILE END OLD TOWN 1c 536.

1891 Census

Address:

303 Mile End Road, Mile End Old Town

Residents:

Solomon DAVIS – Head – b. 1853 London – aged 38 – Fish Merchant
Lydia DAVIS – Wife – b. 1858 London – aged 33
David DAVIS – Son – b. 1879 London – aged 12
Judah DAVIS – Son – b. 1880 London – aged 11

DAVIS, Sarah Queenie – C-2-33

Benjamin DAVIS – Son – b. 1882 London – aged 9
Arthur DAVIS – Son – b. 1883 London – aged 8
Bessie DAVIS – Daughter – b. 1885 London – aged 6
Sidney DAVIS – Son – b. 1888 London – aged 3
Lewis DAVIS – Son – b. 1889 London – aged 2
Ernest DAVIS – Son – b. 1890 London – aged 1
Jane BONS – General Servant
Annie BONS – General Servant

1901 Census

Address:
303 Mile End Road, Mile End Old Town

Residents:
Solomon DAVIS – Head – b. 1852 London – aged 49 – Fish Merchant
Thypo (Sylvia) DAVIS – Wife – b. 1857 London – aged 44
David DAVIS – Son – b. 1879 London – aged 22 – Fish Merchant
Judah DAVIS – Son – b. 1880 London – aged 21 – Fish Merchant
Benjamin DAVIS – Son – b. 1882 London – aged 19 – Clerk
Abraham DAVIS – Son – b. 1884 Mile End – aged 17 – Fish Porter
Betsy DAVIS – Daughter – b. 1886 Mile End – aged 15 – Shop Assistant
Sidney S. DAVIS – Son – b. 1888 Mile End – aged 13
Louis DAVIS – Son – b. 1889 Mile End – aged 12
Elias DAVIS – Son – b. 1891 Mile End – aged 10
Joseph DAVIS – Son – b. 1893 Mile End – aged 8
Angel DAVIS – Son – b. 1895 Mile End – aged 6
Kate DAVIS – Daughter – b. 1898 Mile End – aged 3
Jane BALLS – General Servant
Anne BALLS – Domestic Servant
Ada BALLS – Domestic Servant

1911 Census

Address:
303 Mile End Road

Residents:
Sylvia DAVIS – Head – Widow – b. 1857 Spitalfields – aged 54
Benjamin DAVIS – Son – b. 1882 Mile End – aged 29 – Commission Agent
Arthur DAVIS – Son – b. 1884 Spitalfields – aged 27 – Fish Porter
Sidney DAVIS – Son – b. 1886 Mile End – aged 25 – Fish Porter
Louis DAVIS – Son – b. 1888 Mile End – aged 23 – Fish Porter
Elias Ernest DAVIS – Son – b. 1890 Mile End – aged 21 – Clothers Manager
Joseph DAVIS – Son – b. 1893 Mile End – aged 18 – Clothers Assistant
Angel DAVIS – Son – b. 1894 Mile End – aged 17 – Clerk

Katie DAVIS – Daughter – b. 1898 Mile End – aged 13
Milly JACOBS – Domestic Servant

Marriage:

Solomon DAVIS to Sylvia GREEN – Q3 1877 LONDON CITY 1c 182.

Grandparents:

Sylvia Green – parents: Judah & Elizabeth Green (1871 Census)
Solomon Davis – parents: David & Elizabeth Davis (1871 Census)

Death:

Solomon Davis – Q1 1909 [56] MILE END OLD TOWN 1c 339
Buried at Plashet Cemetery - J-10-39 on 01 Apr 1909.

Jewish Chronicle – 02 Apr 1909

DAVIS – On the 30th of March, at 303, Mile End Road, after a long and painful illness, Sol., the dearly beloved and devoted husband of Sylvia Davis, aged 56. Affectionate father of Ben, Arthur, Sid, Lew, Ernie, Joe, Angel and Katie. May his dear soul rest in peace.

DAVIS – On the 30th of March, at 303, Mile End Road, after a long illness borne with great fortitude, Sol, devoted father of Dave Davis, of 139, Evering Road, N., aged 56. Deeply mourned by his affectionate son, daughter-in-law and grandsons. May God rest his soul in everlasting peace. Shiva at 303, Mile End Road.

DAVIS – On the 30th of March, at 303, Mile End Road, after a long and painful illness, Sol, the loving and devoted father of Bob Davis, 16, Grand Parade, Green Lanes, Harringay, aged 56. Deeply mourned by his affectionate son, daughter-in-law, and granddaughter. May his dear soul rest in peace. Shiva at 303, Mile End Road.

DAVIS – On the 30th of March, at 303, Mile End Road, after a long and painful illness, Sol, the loving father of Mrs Isidore Hyman (nee Bessie Davis), 292, Camden Road, N., aged 56. Deeply mourned by his sorrowing daughter and son-in-law. May his dear soul rest in peace. Shiva at 303, Mile End Road.

DAVIS – On the 30th of March, at 303, Mile End Road, after a long and painful illness, Sol, the loving brother of Lew Davis, of 11, Litchfield Road, Bow, aged 56. May his soul rest in peace. Shiva at 303, Mile End Road.

Death:

Sylvia DAVIS – Q2 1928 [70] STEPNEY 1c 276.
Buried at Willesden Cemetery – LX-4-4 on 14 Jun 1928.

Jewish Chronicle – 15 Jun 1928

DAVIS – On the 12th of June, at 303, Mile End Road, E., Sylvia Davis, aged 70. Devoted darling mother of Benjamin, Sidney, Lewis, Ernest and Joseph. Deeply mourned by her heartbroken sons. May her angel soul rest in peace. Shiva at the above address.

DAVIS – On the 12th of June, Sylvia Davis, darling devoted mother of Mrs Isidore Hyman, 25, West Bank, Stamford Hill. Deeply mourned and sadly missed by her heart-broken daughter, son-in-law and grandchildren. God rest her angel soul in everlasting peace. Shiva at 303, Mile End Road.

DAVIS – On the 12th of June, Sylvia Davis, the beloved mother of Arthur Davis, of 22a, Warrington Crescent, Maida Vale. Deeply mourned by her heart-broken son, daughter-in-law and grandchildren. God rest her dear soul in peace. Shiva at 303, Mile End Road.

DAVIS – On the 12th of June, Sylvia Davis, the darling and devoted mother of Mrs John Kaye (Katie), of 48, St. Gabriel's Road, Cricklewood. Deeply mourned by her grief-stricken daughter, son-in-law and grandchildren. God rest her angel soul in peace. Shiva at 303, Mile End Road.

DAVIS – On the 12th of June, Sylvia Davis, beloved sister of Mrs Kate Levy, Mrs Sarah Marks, Mr Sol. Green, of Melbourne. Deeply mourned. God rest her soul in peace. Shiva at 17, Carlton Vale, Maida Vale.

DAVIS – On the 12th of June, Sylvia, aged 70, the beloved and devoted mother of David Davis, 21, West Bank, Stamford Hill. Deeply mourned by her son, daughter-in-law and grandchildren. The blessed Almighty has called her angel soul to rest in everlasting peace. Shiva at 303, Mile End Road.

DAVIS – On the 12th of June, Sylvia, aged 70, the devoted and beloved mother of Robert (Bob) Davis, of 16, Grand Parade, Harringay. Deeply mourned by her devoted son, daughter-in-law and grandchildren. The sweetest of mothers. God rest her dear soul in peace. Shiva at 303, Mile End Road.

DAVIS – On Tuesday, the 12th of June, Sylvia Davis, the beloved mother of Angel Davis, 222, Finchley Road, N.W.3. Deeply mourned by her son, daughter-in-law and grandchildren. Shiva at 303, Mile End Road.

DAVIS – On Tuesday, the 12th of June, Sylvia Davis, the devoted friend of Mr and Mrs Edward Ellis – 222, Finchley Road, N.W.3.

Jewish Chronicle – 28 Jun 1929

DAVIS – The tombstone in memory of the late Sylvia Davis, formerly of 303, Mile End Road, will be consecrated at Willesden Cemetery on Sunday, June 30th, 1 p.m. – 207, Maida Vale, W.

GLENSNICK, Augusta – A-7-3

GLENSNICK, Augusta – A-7-3

Died: 01 May 1897
Buried: 03 May 1897
Hebrew Name: Gittel bat Avraham
Partner: Jacob Glensnick (d. 1914)
Aged: 64 years

Jewish Chronicle – 07 May 1897

GLENSNICK – On the 1st of May, at the residence of her daughter, 16, Strathblaine Road, Clapham Junction, S.W., Augusta, the dearly beloved wife of Jacob Glensnick, of 92 Houndsditch, E.C., aged 64 years. Deeply mourned by her sorrowing family and friends. God rest her soul. Shiva at 16, Strathblaine Road.

GLENSNICK – On the 1st of May at 16, Strathblaine Road, Clapham Junction, Mrs J. Glensnick, beloved mother of Abraham Woolf Glensnick, 32, Gorst Road, Wandsworth Common, S.W. God rest her soul. Shiva at 16, Strathblaine Road, S.W.

GLENSNICK – On the 1st of May, at 16, Strathblaine Road, Clapham Junction, S.W., Mrs J. Glensnick, the beloved mother of Mrs H. Berlinsky, aged 64. May her soul rest in peace. Shiva at above address.

Jewish Chronicle – 03 Sep 1897

The tombstone in loving memory of the late Mrs Augusta Glensnick, of 92, Houndsditch, E.C. will be set at Plashet Cemetery on Sunday next, September 5th, at 4 o'clock. Relatives and friends please accept this, the only intimation.

Death:

Q2 1897 [64] WANDSWORTH 1d 317.

1881 Census

Address:

5 Anne Street, Whitechapel

Residents:

Jacob GLENSNICK – Head – b. 1835 Russia – aged 46 – Tailor
Augusta GLENSNICK – Wife – b. 1835 Russia – aged 46
Abraham GLENSNICK – Son – b. 1859 Russia – aged 22 – Printer
Philip GLENSNICK – Son – b. 1860 Russia – aged 21 – Tailor
Esther GLENSNICK – Daughter – b. 1864 Spitalfields – aged 17 – Tailoress
Mordecai GLENSNICK – Son – b. 1866 Spitalfields – aged 15 – Jeweller
Newman GLENSNICK – Son – b. 1868 Bethnal Green – aged 13 – Butcher

1871 Census

Address:

High Street, St. Mary Whitechapel

Residents:

Jacob GLENSNICK – Head – b. 1836 Russia – aged 35
Augusta GLENSNICK – Wife – b. 1834 Russia – aged 37
Abraham GLENSNICK – Son – b. 1859 Russia – aged 12
Philip GLENSNICK – Son – b. 1860 Russia – aged 11
Esther GLENSNICK – Daughter – b. 1865 Russia – aged 6
Montague GLENSNICK – Son – b. 1866 Middlesex – aged 5
Newman GLENSNICK – Son – b. 1868 Middlesex – aged 3

1901 Census

Address:

92 Houndsditch, St. Botolph Without Bishopsgate

Residents:

Jacob GLENSNICK – Head – Widower – b. 1836 Poland – aged 65 – Tailor Machinist
Philip GLENSNICK – Son – b. 1862 Poland – aged 39 – Tailor Machinist
Mordecai GLENSNICK – Son – b. 1865 Spitalfields – aged 36 – General Dealer
Betsy GLENSNICK – Daughter-in-law – b. 1873 Spitalfields – aged 28
Joseph FRENCHMAN – Boarder – b. 1879 Spitalfields – aged 22 – Dealer in Cigars

Death:

Jacob GLENSNICK – Q4 1914 [79] LONDON CITY 1c 2.
Buried at Plashet Cemetery – A-7-2 on 27 Oct 1914.

Jewish Chronicle – 30 Oct 1914

GLENSNICK - On the 25th of October, at 92, Houndsditch, E.C., Jacob Glensnick, in his 79th year, the dearly beloved father of Abraham W. Glensnick, 266, Edgware Road. God rest his dear soul. Shiva at Edgware Road.
GLENSNICK – On the 25th of October, at 92, Houndsditch, E.C., Jacob Glensnick, the dearly beloved father of Philip Glensnick, of 9, Farleigh Road, Stoke Newington, and Newman Glensnick of Ipswich. God rest his dear soul. Shiva at Farleigh Road.
GLENSNICK – On the 25th of October, at 92, Houndsditch, E.C., Jacob Glensnick, the dearly beloved father of Esther Berlin, of 72, Sudbourne Road, Brixton Hill. Deeply lamented by his son-in-law, Harry Berlin. God rest his dear soul.
GLENSNICK – On the 25th of October, at 92, Houndsditch, E.C., Jacob Glensnick, the dearly beloved father of Mordecai (Bob) Glensnick of 92, Houndsditch. Deeply lamented by all his relatives and friends. God rest his dear soul. Shiva at above address.

Jewish Chronicle – 02 Jul 1915

The tombstone in loving memory of Mr J. Glensnick, 92, Houndsditch, E.C., will be consecrated on Sunday next, the 4th of July, at 3.30 at Plashet Cemetery. Relatives and friends kindly accept this, the only intimation.

GOLDBERG, Morris – A-6-59

Died: 14 Apr 1897
Buried: 15 Apr 1897
Hebrew Name: Moshe Avigdor ben Harar Morini Me'ir
Partner: Leah Goldberg (d. 1905)
Aged: 61 years

Jewish Chronicle – 16 Apr 1897

GOLDBERG – On the 14th of April, at 84, Greenfield Street, Commercial Road, Morris Goldberg, the dearly beloved husband of Leah Goldberg, aged 61 years. Deeply mourned by his sorrowing son, daughters and grandchildren. God rest his soul in peace.

Jewish Chronicle – 14 May 1897

The tombstone in loving memory of the late Morris Goldberg, of 84, Greenfield Street, E., will be set at Plashet Cemetery on Sunday next, May 16th, at 3.30. Relatives and friends please accept this, the only intimation.

Death:

Q2 1897 [61] MILE END OLD TOWN 1c 260.

1891 Census

Address:

84 Greenfield Street, Mile End Old Town

Residents:

Morris GOLDBERG – Head – b. 1837 Olzkior Poland – aged 54 – Tailor
Leah GOLDBERG – Wife – b. 1839 Olzkior Poland – aged 52
Annie GOLDBERG – Daughter – b. 1875 London – aged 16 – Student
Marsden GOLDBERG – Son – b. 1877 London – aged 14 – Tailor's Apprentice
Simon GOLDBERG – Boarder – b. 1871 Russia – aged 20 – Tailor
Abraham TAWBER – Boarder – b. 1869 Russia – aged 22 – Printer
Hyman ILLANSNER – Lodger – b. 1868 Krakow – aged 23 – Cap Maker
Davis NEEDLESTICH – Lodger – b. 1871 Marilch Poland – aged 20 – Tailor

1881 Census

Address:

84 Greenfield Street, Mile End Old Town

Residents:

Morris GOLDBERG – Head – b. 1837 Poland – aged 44 – Tailor
Leah GOLDBERG – Wife – b. 1839 Poland – aged 42
Miriam GOLDBERG – Daughter – b. 1867 Whitechapel – aged 14 – Pupil Teacher
Rachel GOLDBERG – Daughter – b. 1869 Whitechapel – aged 12 – Scholar

GOLDBERG, Morris – A-6-59

Annie GOLDBERG – Daughter – b. 1875 Whitechapel – aged 6 – Scholar
Mordecai GOLDBERG – Son – b. 1876 Whitechapel – aged 5 – Scholar

1871 Census

Address:
Plumber's Row, or Skye's Buildings

Residents:
Morris GOLDBERG – Head – b. 1837 Russia – aged 34
Dina GOLDBERG – Wife – b. 1839 Russia – aged 32
Miriam GOLDBERG – Daughter – b. 1867 Russia – aged 4
Rachel GOLDBERG – Daughter – b. 1869 London – aged 2
Kate GOLDBERG – Daughter – b. 1871 London – aged 0

Death:
Leah Dinah GOLDBERG – Q4 1905 [66] HACKNEY 1b 344.
Buried at Plashet Cemetery – A-6-60 on 12 Nov 1905.

Jewish Chronicle – 17 Nov 1905

GOLDBERG – On the 10th of November, 1905, at the residence of her daughter, 103, King Edward Road, Hackney, Leah, relict of the late Morris Goldberg, of 84, Greenfield Street, Commercial Road, the beloved mother of Mrs John Lazarnick, Mrs S.G. Tuchman, Mrs Charles Lazarnick and Mr Mark Goldberg, of New York. Sadly missed and mourned by her beloved daughters, son, sons-in-law and grandchildren. American and African papers please copy. God rest her dear soul in peace. Amen.

Jewish Chronicle – 08 Nov 1907

The tombstone in loving memory of our dear mother, Mrs Goldberg, late of 84 Greenfield Street, and her grandchild, Pearlier, the beloved daughter of Charles and Annie Lazarnick, will be set at Plashet Cemetery on Sunday, November 10th at 3 p.m.

HART, Gershon – B-2-26

Died: 09 Jan 1897
Buried: 12 Jan 1897
Partner: Rosetta (Rosa) Hart (d. 1921)
Parents: Michael & Sarah Hart
Aged: 51 years

Jewish Chronicle – 15 Jan 1897

HART – On the 9th of January, at the London Hospital, Gershon Hart, of 20, Carter Street, Houndsditch, 51 years of age. Deeply lamented by his sorrowing wife, children, sister and a large circle of friends. May his soul rest in peace.

Jewish Chronicle – 25 Jun 1897

The tombstone in loving and fond memory of the late Gershon Hart, of 20, Carter Street, Houndsditch, will be set at the Plashet Cemetery, at 4.30, on Sunday next. Relatives and friends please accept this, the only intimation.

Death:

Q1 1897 [51] WHITECHAPEL 1c 186. [George Hart]

1891 Census

Address:

10 Garden Court, Aldgate, London

Residents:

Jereboam HART – Head – b. 1846 London – aged 45 – General Dealer
Rose HART – Wife – b. 1845 London – aged 46
Sarah HART – Daughter – b. 1870 London – aged 21 – Dressmaker
Rachael HART – Daughter – b. 1872 London – aged 19 – Assistant to Father
Simon HART – Son – b. 1881 London – aged 10 – Scholar
Elizabeth HART – Daughter – b. 1883 London – aged 8 – Scholar
Michael HART – Son – b. 1884 London – aged 7 – Scholar
Phoebe HART – Daughter – b. 1885 London – aged 6 – Scholar
Kate HART – Daughter – b. 1887 London – aged 4 – Scholar
Hyman HART – Son – b. 1889 London – aged 2

1881 Census

Address

10 Ellison Street, St. Botolph Without Aldgate

Residents:

George HART – Head – b. 1847 Spitalfields – aged 34 – Dealer in Unredeemed Pledges
Rosa HART – Wife – b. 1849 Spitalfields – aged 32
Sarah HART – Daughter – b. 1870 Aldgate – aged 11 – Scholar
Rachael HART – Daughter – b. 1871 Aldgate – aged 10 – Scholar
Michael HART – Son – b. 1873 Aldgate – aged 8 – Scholar
Emanuel HART – Son – b. 1875 Aldgate – aged 6 – Scholar
Simeon HART – Son – b. 1881 Aldgate – aged 0

1871 Census

Address:

Cook's Buildings, Aldgate, London

Residents:

Gershon HART – Head – b. 1847 Spitalfields – aged 24
Rosa HART – Wife – b. 1847 Whitechapel – aged 24

Sarah HART – Daughter – b. 1871 Aldgate – aged 0
Julia SOLOMONS - Servant

Marriage:
Gershon HART to Rosetta HYAMS – Q3 1869 LONDON CITY 1c 183.

1901 Census

Address:
20 Cutler Street, St. Botolph Without Aldgate

Residents:
Rose HART – Head – Widow – b. 1847 Whitechapel – aged 54
Michael HART – Son – b. 1874 Whitechapel – aged 27 – Clothes Repairer
Simon HART – Son – b. 1881 London – aged 20 – Carman
Betsy HART – Daughter – b. 1883 London – aged 18
Phoebe HART – Daughter – b. 1886 London – aged 15 – Cigar Maker
Katie HART – Daughter – b. 1888 London – aged 13
Jack HART – Son – b. 1892 London – aged 9
Esther HART – Granddaughter – b. 1897 Mile End – aged 4
Miriam HART – Granddaughter – b. 1900 Whitechapel – aged 1

1911 Census

Address:
25 Queens Block, Stoney Lane, Houndsditch

Residents:
Rosetta HART – Head – Widow – b. 1846 Whitechapel – aged 65 – Supported by family
Jack HART – Son – b. 1892 London – aged 19 – Market Porter in Old Clothing

Death:
Rose HART – Q4 1921 [96] WHITECHAPEL 1c 296.
Buried at East Ham Jewish Cemetery – E-9-20 on 12 Dec 1921.

Jewish Chronicle – 16 Dec 1921

HART – On the 9th of Kislev, 10th day of December, after a short illness, Rose Hart, relict of the late Gershon Hart, of Carter Street, Houndsditch, and beloved mother of Michael Hart. Deeply mourned by her daughter-in-law (Annie), and grandchildren. God rest her dear soul. Shiva at "Tyssen Arms", Dalston Lane.

HART – On the 9th of Kislev, 10th day of December, after a short illness, Rose Hart, relict of the late Gershon Hart, of Carter Street, Houndsditch, beloved mother of Emanuel Hart (Whippets), of 3, Wellington Street, Canton, Cardiff, South Wales. Deeply mourned by her daughter-in-law (Lizzie), and grandchildren. May her dear soul rest in peace. Shiva at above address.

HART – On the 10th of December, after a short and painful illness, Rose, widow

of the late Gershon Hart. Deeply mourned and sadly missed by her daughters, Mrs L. Myers, Ray Hart and Mrs G. Barnett, Quincey, USA. Shiva at 170, Osbaldestone Road, N.16.
HART – On the 9th of Kislev, 10th day of December, after a short illness, Rose Hart, relict of the late Gershon Hart, of Carter Street, Houndsditch, beloved mother of Simeon Hart (Barney), of "The Lamb", Wilmot Street, Bethnal Green. Deeply mourned by her daughter-in-law (Florrie) and grandchildren. God rest her dear soul. Shiva at "Tyssen Arms", Dalston Lane.
HART – On the 9th of Kislev, 10th day of December, after a short illness, Rose Hart, relict of the late Gershon Hart, of Carter Street, Houndsditch; beloved mother of Betsy Jacobs (Bessie), of 27, Magdalen Street, Norwich. Deeply mourned by her son-in-law (Angel). May her dear soul rest in peace.

ISAACS, Joseph – B-3-6

Died: **10 Apr 1897**
Buried: **13 Apr 1897**
Hebrew Name: **Yossef ben Yehuda**
Partner: **Mary Isaacs (d. 1882)**
Aged: **66 years**

Jewish Chronicle – 16 Apr 1897

ISAACS – On the 10th of April, at 90, Hoxton Street, Hoxton, Joseph Isaacs, aged 66 years. Deeply mourned by his bereaved children, relatives and friends. American papers please copy.

Jewish Chronicle – 10 Sep 1897

The tombstone to the memory of the late Joseph Isaacs, of 90, Hoxton Street, N., will be set at Plashet Cemetery on Sunday next (19/9/1897), at 3.30. Relatives and friends please accept this, the only intimation.

Death:

Q2 1897 [66] SHOREDITCH 1c 34.

1891 Census

Address:

90 Hoxton Street, Shoreditch

Residents:

Joseph ISAACS – Head – Widower – b. 1831 London – aged 60 – Tailor
Lewis ISAACS – Son – b. 1863 London – aged 28
Mary ISAACS – Son's wife – b. 1866 London – aged 25
Joseph ISAACS – Son – b. 1887 London – aged 4

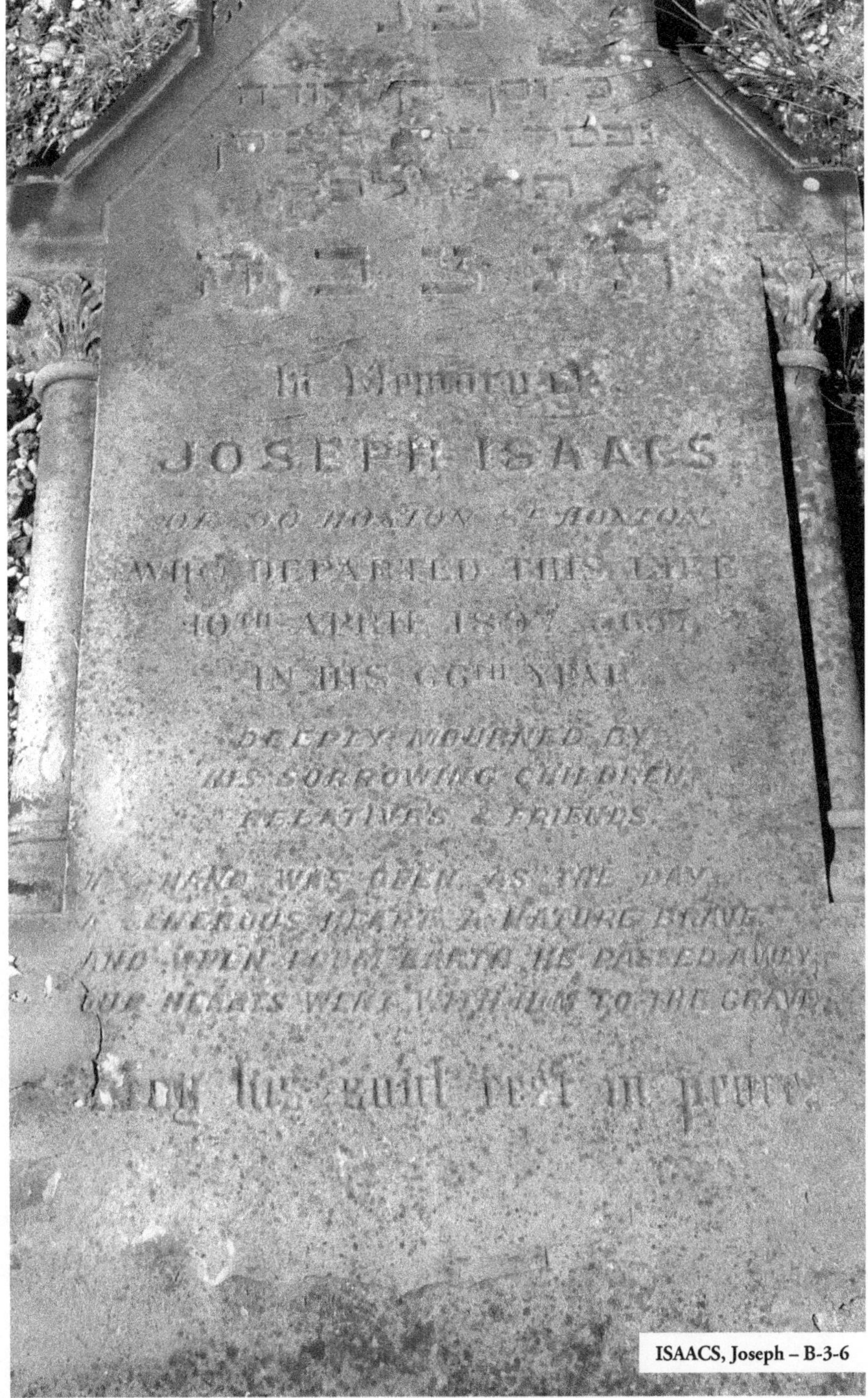

ISAACS, Joseph – B-3-6

Gilda DAFRIES – Niece – b. 1876 London – aged 15 – Cigar Maker
Anna FENTON – General Servant

1881 Census

Address:
90 Hoxton Street, Shoreditch

Residents:
Joseph ISAACS – Head – b. 1833 London – aged 48 – Clothier
Mary ISAACS – Wife – b. 1839 London – aged 42 – Clothier Tailor
Barnett ISAACS – Son – b. 1868 Shoreditch – aged 13 – Clerk

1871 Census

Address:
Hoxton Street, Shoreditch

Residents:
Joseph ISAACS – Head – b. 1832 Middlesex – aged 39 – Clothier
Mary ISAACS – Wife – b. 1838 Middlesex – aged 33
Hannah ISAACS – Daughter – b. 1857 Middlesex – aged 14 – Scholar
Amelia ISAACS – Daughter – b. 1859 Middlesex – aged 12 – Scholar
Lewis ISAACS – Son – b. 1863 Middlesex – aged 8 – Scholar
Barnett ISAACS – Son – b. 1867 Middlesex – aged 4 – Scholar

1861 Census

Address:
16 New Street, St. Botolph Aldgate, City of London

Residents:
Joseph ISAACS – Head – b. 1832 Poland – aged 29 – Tailor
Mary ISAACS – Wife – b. 1838 London – aged 23
Hannah ISAACS – Daughter – b. 1857 London – aged 4
Amelia ISAACS – Daughter – b. 1859 London – aged 2
Bridget HIGGINS – Domestic Servant

Marriage:
Joseph ISAACS to Mary EMANUEL – Q1 1856 LONDON CITY 1c 235.

Death:
Mary ISAACS – Q4 1882 [47] SHOREDITCH 1c 52.
Place of burial unknown.

ISAACS, Michael – A-8-32

Died: 10 Aug 1897
Buried: 12 Aug 1897
Hebrew Name: Michael ben Eliyahu
Partner: Amelia Isaacs (d. 1893)
Aged: 47th year

Jewish Chronicle – 13 Aug 1897

ISAACS – On the 10th of August, at 124, Stepney Green, Michael Isaacs (for many years with M. Angel and Sons, Shaftesbury Avenue) in his 47th year. May his soul rest in peace.

Jewish Chronicle – 21 Jan 1898

The tombstone erected to the memory of the late Michael Isaacs, of 124, Stepney Green, E., will be set on Sunday next, the 23rd inst., at Plashet Cemetery at 2.30. Relatives and friends will accept this, the only intimation.

Death:
Q3 1897 [46] MILE END 1c 338.

1891 Census

Address:
4 Cecil Street, Mile End Old Town

Residents:
Michael ISAACS – Head – b. 1853 London – aged 38 – Clothiers Assistant
Amelia ISAACS – Wife – b. 1855 London – aged 36
Elias ISAACS – Son – b. 1875 London – aged 16 – Bootmaker
Louis ISAACS – Son – b. 1877 London – aged 14 – Bootmaker Apprentice
Amelia ISAACS – Daughter – b. 1879 London – aged 12 – Scholar
Maurice ISAACS – Son – b. 1881 London – aged 10 – Scholar
Moss ISAACS – Daughter – b. 1883 London – aged 8 – Scholar
Elizabeth ISAACS – Daughter – b. 1885 Mile End – aged 6 – Scholar
Sarah ISAACS – Daughter – b. 1886 Mile End – aged 5 – Scholar
Annie ISAACS – Daughter – b. 1888 Mile End – aged 3
Elizabeth BORAN – Domestic Servant

1881 Census

Address:
6 Cath. W. Alley, St. Botolph Without Bishopsgate

Residents:
Michael ISAACS – Head – b. 1851 London – aged 30 – Tailors Assistant

SACRED
TO THE MEMORY OF
MICHAEL ISAACS,
WHO DIED 10TH AUGUST 1897,
IN HIS 47TH YEAR.
DEEPLY LAMENTED BY HIS FAMILY,
AND A LARGE CIRCLE OF FRIENDS.

ISAACS, Michael – A-8-32

Amelia ISAACS – Wife – b. 1855 London – aged 26
Elias ISAACS – Son - b. 1875 London – aged 6
Lewis ISAACS – Son – b. 1877 London – aged 4
Amelia ISAACS – Daughter – b. 1878 London – aged 3
Morris ISAACS – Son – b. 1880 London – aged 1
Agnes PRENE – Domestic Servant

Marriage:
Michael ISAACS to Amelia JACOBS – Q4 1874 LONDON CITY 1c 191.

Death:
Amelia ISAACS – Q1 1893 [41] MILE END OLD TOWN 1c 386.
Buried at West Ham Cemetery – F-11-22 on 22 Mar 1893.

Jewish Chronicle – 24 Mar 1893

On the 20th of March, at 4, Cecil Street, Mile End, after a long and painful illness, Amelia, the dearly beloved wife of Michael Isaacs, in her 40th year. Deeply lamented by her family and a very large circle of friends.

Jewish Chronicle – 09 Jun 1893

The tombstone of the late Mrs Amelia Isaacs, of 4, Cecil Street, Mile End Road, will be set at West Ham Cemetery, on Sunday, June 11th, at 4 o'clock. Relatives and friends please accept this invitation.

JACOBS, Solomon – A-7-40

Died: **14 Jun 1897**
Buried: **16 Jun 1897**
Hebrew Name: **Shlomo ben Yehuda**
Partner: **Rachel Jacobs (d. 1900)**
Aged: **64 years**

Jewish Chronicle – 18 Jun 1897

JACOBS – On the 14th of June, Solomon Jacobs, the dearly beloved brother of Mrs Hyam Levy, 20, Mile End Road, E. May his dear soul rest in peace.
JACOBS – On Monday, 14th of June, Solomon Jacobs, brother of Mrs Elizabeth Lesser, 102, Stepney Green, E. May his soul rest in peace.

Jewish Chronicle – 01 Oct 1897

The tombstone to the memory of the late Solomon Jacobs, of 134, Mile End Road, E., brother of Elias Jacobs, Esq., of London and Johannesburg, South Africa, will be set on Sunday next, October 3rd, at 3.30 at Plashet Cemetery.

JACOBS, Solomon – A-7-40

Death:

Q2 1897 [64] MILE END 1c 271.

1891 Census

Address:

6 Drum Yard, Whitechapel

Residents:

Solomon JACOBS – Head – b. 1837 Whitechapel – aged 54 – Hawker
Rachel JACOBS – Wife – b. 1835 Whitechapel – aged 56
Leah JACOBS – Daughter – b. 1868 Whitechapel – aged 23 – Cigar Maker
Sarah JACOBS – Daughter – b. 1870 Whitechapel – aged 21 – Cigar Bundler
Esther JACOBS – Daughter – b. 1874 Whitechapel – aged 17 – Cigar Maker
Abraham JACOBS – Son – b. 1871 Whitechapel – aged 20 – Boot Laster

1881 Census

Address:

54 Brady Street, Whitechapel

Residents:

Solomon JACOBS – Head – b. 1837 London – aged 44 – Traveller (Walking sticks)
Rachel JACOBS – Wife – b. 1838 London – aged 43
Dinah JACOBS – Daughter – b. 1864 London – aged 17 – Tailoress
Leah JACOBS – Daughter – b. 1866 London – aged 15 – Scholar
Abraham JACOBS – Son – b. 1871 London – aged 10 – Scholar
Sarah JACOBS – Daughter – b. 1869 London – aged 12 – Scholar
Esther JACOBS – Daughter – b. 1874 London – aged 7

1871 Census

Address:

Swan Court, Whitechapel

Residents:

Saul JACOBS – Head – b. 1834 Middlesex – aged 37
Rachel JACOBS – Wife – b. 1835 Middlesex – aged 36
Louis JACOBS – Son – b. 1857 Middlesex – aged 14
Joseph JACOBS – Son – b. 1861 Middlesex – aged 10
Dinah JACOBS – Daughter – b. 1864 Middlesex – aged 7
Leah JACOBS – Daughter – b. 1868 Middlesex – aged 3
Sarah JACOBS – Daughter – b. 1870 Middlesex – aged 1

1861 Census

Address:

15 Swan Court, Middlesex Street, Whitechapel, London

Residents:

Solomon JACOBS – Head – b. 1837 Whitechapel – aged 24 – General Dealer

Rachel JACOBS – Wife – b. 1835 Whitechapel – aged 26
Lewis JACOBS – Son – b. 1858 Whitechapel – aged 3 – Scholar
Joseph JACOBS – Son – b. 1861 Whitechapel – aged 8 months

Marriage:
Solomon JACOBS to Rachel JOSEPH, Q4 1856 LONDON CITY 1c 296.

1851 Census
Address:
Fishers Alley, Spitalfields, Tower Hamlets
Residents:
Joseph HYAMS – Head – b. 1806 Aldgate – aged 45 – Shoe Manufacturer
Sarah HYAMS – Wife – b. 1816 Chelmsford – aged 35
Solomon JACOBS – Step-son – b. 1837 Spitalfields – aged 14
Michael HYAMS – Son – b. 1838 Aldgate – aged 13
Elizabeth JACOBS – Step-daughter – b. 1839 Spitalfields – aged 12
Elizabeth HYAMS – Daughter – b. 1840 Whitechapel – aged 11
Elias JACOBS – Step-son – b. 1842 Spitalfields – aged 9
David HYAMS – Son – b. 1843 Spitalfields – aged 8
Louisa JACOBS – Step-daughter – b. 1844 Spitalfields – aged 7
Catharine HYAMS – Daughter – b. 1850 Spitalfields – aged 1

1841 Census
Address:
Three Tun Alley, St. Mary Whitechapel, Tower Hamlets
Residents:
Lewis JACOBS – Head – b. 1813 Middlesex – aged 28
Sarah JACOBS – Wife – b. 1818 Middlesex – aged 23
Solomon JACOBS – Son – b. 1836 Middlesex – aged 5
Betsey JACOBS – Daughter – b. 1839 Middlesex – aged 2
Lawrence JACOBS – Son – b. 1841 Middlesex – aged 6 days
Sarah SMITH – General help

Marriage:
Sarah JACOBS to Joseph HYAMS – Q3 1849 WHITECHAPEL 2 593.

Death:
Rachel JACOBS – Q4 1900 [65] WHITECHAPEL 1c 207.
Buried at Plashet Cemetery – B-11-3 on 02 Oct 1900.

JOEL, Harry – B-3-8

Died: 05 Apr 1897
Buried: 07 Apr 1897
Partner: Amelia Sarah Joel (d. 1911)
Aged: 56th year

Jewish Chronicle – 09 Apr 1897

JOEL – On the 5th of April, at his residence, 25, Offley Road, Brixton, S.W., after a long and painful illness, Harry, beloved husband of Amy Joel, in his 56th year, late of Newcastle-on-Tyne and "The Princes'", Wardour Street, W.C. May his dear soul rest in peace.
JOEL – On the 5th of April, at 25, Offley Road, Brixton, after a long illness, Harry Joel, brother of Mrs Lewis Leapman, 165, Kennington Park Road, S.E.

Jewish Chronicle – 10 Sep 1897

The tombstone in loving memory of the late Mr Harry Joel, of London and Newcastle-on-Tyne, will be set at Plashet Cemetery at 3 o'clock on Tuesday next, September 14th. Relatives and friends please accept this intimation.

Death:
Q2 1897 [55] LAMBETH 1d 231 [Henry Leopold]

1891 Census

Address:
15 Canonbury Road, Islington, London

Residents:
Henry JOEL – Head – b. 1838 Shoreditch – aged 53 – Glass Cutter
Sarah A. JOEL – Wife – b. 1837 Clerkenwell – aged 54
Henry J. JOEL – Son – b. 1867 Shoreditch – aged 24 – Cab Driver

1881 Census

Address:
45 Buckland Street, Shoreditch

Residents:
Henry JOEL – Head – b. 1833 Shoreditch – aged 48 – Glass Fitter
Amelia JOEL – Wife – b. 1837 Clerkenwell – aged 44
Henry JOEL – Son – b. 1866 Shoreditch – aged 15 – Boot Maker
Amelia JOEL – Daughter – b. 1867 Poplar – aged 14

1871 Census

Address:
29 Libra Road, Bow

Residents:

Henry JOEL – Head – b. 1838 Middlesex – aged 33 – Looking Glass Fitter
Amelia Sarah JOEL – Wife – b. 1837 Middlesex – aged 34
Ann Esther JOEL – Daughter – b. 1865 Middlesex – aged 6
Henry Isaac JOEL – Son – b. 1867 Middlesex – aged 4
Amelia Harriet JOEL – Daughter – b. 1868 Middlesex – aged 3

Marriage:

Henry JOEL to Amelia Sarah HULBERT - Q4 1863 ISLINGTON 1b 352.

Parents:

Harry/Henry's parents - Isaac & Sarah Jane JOEL (1851 Census)

Death:

Amelia JOEL - Q1 1911 [72] MILE END OLD TOWN 1c 301.
Buried at Plashet Cemetery – I-22-18 on 05 Mar 1911.

JONAS, Esther – A-9-13

Died: **04 Nov 1897**
Buried: **07 Nov 1897**
Hebrew Name: **Ester bat Gerson**
Partner: **Samuel Jonas (d. 1909)**
Aged: **40 years**

Jewish Chronicle – 12 Nov 1897

JONAS – On the 4th of November, Esther, the dearly beloved wife of Samuel Jonas, of 226, Oxford Street, Stepney, and daughter of Mr and Mrs G. Sloman, aged 40. Gone, but never to be forgotten. May her dear soul rest in peace. Dutch and Australian papers please copy.

Jewish Chronicle – 10 Dec 1897

The tombstone in loving memory of Esther, the beloved wife of Samuel Jonas, of 226, Oxford Street, Stepney, will be set at Plashet Cemetery on Sunday next, December 12th, at 3 o'clock. Relatives and friends please accept this intimation.

Death:

Q4 1897 [40] WHITECHAPEL 1c 236.

1891 Census

Address:

1 Morgan Street, St. George in the East, St. George East

JONAS, Esther – A-9-13

Residents:

Samuel JONAS – Head – b. 1850 Spitalfields – aged 41 – Butcher
Esther JONAS – Wife – b. 1859 Amsterdam – aged 32
Nerby LEVY – Visitor

Marriage:

Samuel JONAS to Esther DE ROSE – Q1 1888 MILE END OLD TOWN 1c 687.

Death:

Abraham DE ROSE – Q3 1882 [33] WHITECHAPEL 1C 208.

Marriage:

Abraham DE ROSE to Esther SOESAN – Q3 1876 LONDON CITY 1c 175.

1881 Census

Address:

10 Princes Street, Spitalfields

Residents:

Abraham DE ROSE – Head – b. 1850 Netherlands – aged 31 – Cigar Maker
Esther DE ROSE – Wife – b. 1857 Netherlands – aged 24
Hellena DE ROSE – Mother – Widow – b. 1813 Netherlands – aged 68

Death:

Samuel JONAS – Q1 1909 [54] MILE END OLD TOWN 1c 318.
Buried at Plashet Cemetery – K-8-3 on 26 Jan 1909.

JOSEPH, Mary – A-8-12

Died: 22 Jun 1897
Buried: 24 Jun 1897
Partner: John (Jacob) Joseph (d. 1916)
Aged: 53 years

Jewish Chronicle – 25 Jun 1897

JOSEPH – On the 22nd of June, at 102, Sandringham Road, Dalston, Mary, the beloved wife of John Joseph, and mother of Mrs J. Goldhill of 97, Mile End Road, and Mr L. Joseph, 90, Sandringham Road. God rest her soul. Shiva at 102, Sandringham Road.

JOSEPH – On the 22nd of June, at 102, Sandringham Road, Dalston, Mary Joseph, aged 53, sister of Mrs L. Cohen of 12, Well Street, London Dock. May her soul rest in peace.

Jewish Chronicle – 29 Oct 1897

The tombstone in memory of the late Mary Joseph, beloved wife of John Joseph of 102, Sandringham Road, Dalston, will be set at Plashet Cemetery on Sunday, October the 31st at 3 o'clock. Relatives and friends please accept this, the only intimation.

Death:

Q2 1897 [53] HACKNEY 1b 304.

1891 Census

Address:

102 Sandringham Road, Hackney

Residents:

John JOSEPH – Head – b. 1844 Borough – aged 47 – Chair Maker
Marie JOSEPH – Wife – b. 1845 Borough – aged 46
Ray JOSEPH – Daughter – b. 1869 Whitechapel – aged 22
Louis JOSEPH – Son – b. 1872 Whitechapel – aged 19 – Wood Carver
John JOSEPH – Son – b. 1874 Whitechapel – aged 17 – Upholsterer
Benjamin JOSEPH – Son – b. 1876 Whitechapel – aged 15 – Piano Stringer
Elizabeth JOSEPH – Daughter – b. 1878 Whitechapel – aged 13 – Scholar
Maurice JOSEPH – Son – b. 1880 Whitechapel – aged 11 – Scholar
Sarah JOSEPH – Daughter – b. 1882 Whitechapel – aged 9 – Scholar
Samuel JOSEPH – Son – b. 1883 Whitechapel – aged 8 – Scholar
Hannah JOSEPH – Daughter – b. 1885 Whitechapel – aged 6 – Scholar
Maria JOSEPH – Daughter – b. 1887 Dalston – aged 4 – Scholar

1881 Census

Address:

113 Leman Street, Whitechapel

Residents:

John JOSEPH – Head – b. 1844 St. Georges – aged 37 – Cabinet Maker
Mary JOSEPH – Wife – b. 1846 Newington – aged 35
Rachel JOSEPH – Mother – b. 1822 – aged 59
Rachel JOSEPH – Daughter – b. 1869 Shoreditch – aged 12 – Scholar
Louis JOSEPH – Son – b. 1872 Whitechapel – aged 9 – Scholar
John JOSEPH – Son – b. 1874 Whitechapel – aged 7 – Scholar
Benjamin JOSEPH – Son – b. 1876 Whitechapel – aged 5 – Scholar
Elizabeth JOSEPH – Daughter – b. 1878 Whitechapel – aged 3 – Scholar
Morris JOSEPH – Son – b. 1880 Whitechapel – aged 1
Katherine MALONEY – Domestic Housemaid

Marriage:

John (Jacob) JOSEPH to Mary JACOBS – Q2 1868 LONDON CITY 1c 189.

1901 Census

Address:

102 Sandringham Road, Hackney

Residents:

John JOSEPH – Head – Widower – b. 1845 Bow – aged 56 – Cabinet Maker
Maurice JOSEPH – Son – b. 1880 Whitechapel – aged 21 – Clerk to Cabinet Maker
Elizabeth JOSEPH – Daughter – b. 1878 Whitechapel – aged 23
Sarah JOSEPH – Daughter – b. 1882 Whitechapel – aged 19
Hannah JOSEPH – Daughter – b. 1885 Whitechapel – aged 16
Marie JOSEPH – Daughter – b. 1887 Dalston – aged 14 – Dressmaker

Marriage:

John JOSEPH to Mary Ann van COEVORDEN – Q2 1901 LONDON C 1c 93.

1911 Census

Address:

102 Sandringham Road, London N.E.

Residents:

John JOSEPH – Head – b. 1844 Camberwell – aged 67 – Chair Manufacturer
Marion JOSEPH – Wife (11 years) – b. 1867 Bethnal Green – aged 44
Anna JOSEPH – Daughter – b. 1886 Whitechapel – aged 25 – Telephone Operator
Maria JOSEPH – Daughter – b. 1888 Dalston – aged 23 – Post Card Artist
Elizabeth NELLY – Domestic Servant

Death:

John (Jacob) JOSEPH – Q2 1916 [72] ST. MARTIN 1a 588.
Buried at Plashet Cemetery – O-4-37 on 27 Jun 1916.

Jewish Chronicle – 30 Jun 1916

JOSEPH – On the 24th of June, John, the dearly beloved husband of Miriam Joseph, of 15, Linley Road, Bruce Grove, Tottenham, aged 72. Shiva at above address. God rest his dear soul.

JOSEPH – On the 24th of June, John, the dearly beloved father of John Joseph, 2, Broadway, Streatham S.W. Shiva at above address.

JOSEPH – On the 24th of June, John, the dearly beloved father of Mrs Raie Goldhill, Mrs Sarah Cutts, Misses Hannah and Marie Joseph, of 44, Cazenove Road, Stoke Newington; Mrs Elizabeth Joseph of 53, Perrymead Street, Fulham; Lewis Joseph of 18, Burnfoot Avenue, Fulham; Maurice Joseph, 145, Sandringham Road, Dalston; and Samuel Joseph, of Adelaide, South Australia. Shiva at 44, Cazenove Road.

LEVY, Minnie – A-7-19

Died: 11 May 1897
Buried: 13 May 1897
Hebrew Name: Binna bat Yish'i
Partner: Aaron Levy (d. 1915)
Aged: 58 years

Jewish Chronicle – 14 May 1897

LEVY – On the 11th of May, at 109, Rutland Street, E., Minnie, the beloved wife of Aaron Levy, aged 58. Deeply mourned by her husband and daughters.

Jewish Chronicle – 13 Aug 1897

The tombstone in loving memory of Minnie, the beloved wife of A. Levy, of 109, Rutland Street, E., will be set on Sunday next, August 15th, at 4 p.m. at the Plashet Cemetery. Friends please accept this, the only intimation.

Death:

Q2 1897 [54] MILE END 1c 266.

1891 Census

Address:

109 Rutland Street, Mile End Old Town

Residents:

Aaron LEVY – Head – b. 1846 Russian Poland – aged 45 – Cap Maker
Minnie LEVY – Wife – b. 1842 Germany – aged 49
Caroline LEVY – Daughter – b. 1872 London – aged 19 – Cap Maker
Julia LEVY – Daughter – b. 1873 London – aged 18 – Tailoress
Esther LEVY – Daughter – b. 1877 London – aged 14
Sarah LEVY – Daughter – b. 1879 London – aged 12 – Scholar
Fanny LEVY – Mother – Widow – b. 1816 Russian Poland – aged 75
Harriet EDWARDS – Domestic Servant

1881 Census

Address:

56 Pelham Street, Mile End New Town

Residents:

Aaron LEVY – Head – b. 1847 Russia – aged 34 – Cap Maker
Minna LEVY – Wife – b. 1849 Prussia – aged 32
Caroline LEVY – Daughter – b. 1872 Middlesex – aged 9 - Scholar
Julia LEVY – Daughter – b. 1873 Middlesex – aged 8 – Scholar
Esther LEVY – Daughter – b. 1877 Middlesex – aged 4 – Scholar

LEVY, Minnie – A-7-19

Sarah LEVY – Daughter – b. 1879 Middlesex – aged 2
Fanny LEVY – Mother – b. 1817 Russia – aged 64
Betsy SEELIG – General Servant

1871 Census

Address:

Church Street, Stepney

Residents:

Aaron LEVY – Head – b. 1846 Poland – aged 25
Minnie LEVY – Wife – b. 1847 Germany – aged 24

Marriage:

Aaron LEVY to Minnie BLUMENTHAL – Q3 1870 LONDON CITY 1c 193.

Death:

Aaron LEVY – Q4 1915 [68] GREENWICH 1d 1207
Buried at Plashet Cemetery – N-35-8 on 14 Oct 1915.

Jewish Chronicle – 15 Oct 1915

LEVY – On the 12th of October, at 53, Amersham Road, New Cross, Aaron Levy, the dearly beloved husband of the late Jane Levy, and father of George Levy. Shiva at above address. May his dear soul rest in peace. S. African papers please copy.

LIMBURG, Abraham – B-3-7

Died: **09 Apr 1897**
Buried: **11 Apr 1897**
Partner: **Sophia Limburg (d. 1902)**
Aged: **66 years**

Jewish Chronicle – 16 Apr 1897

LIMBURG – On the 9th of April, at 131, Victoria Park Road, Abraham, the dearly beloved husband of Sophia Limburg, aged 66. Deeply mourned by his sorrowing wife, children, grandchildren and a large circle of friends. May his dear soul rest in peace.

Jewish Chronicle – 16 Jul 1897

The tombstone in loving memory of Abraham Limburg, late of 131, Victoria Park Road, N.E., will be set on Sunday next, the 18th inst., at Plashet Cemetery, at 4 o'clock. Relatives and friends please accept this intimation.

Death:

Q2 1897 [66] HACKNEY 1b 310.

1891 Census

Address:

131 Victoria Park Road, Hackney

Residents:

Abraham LIMBURG – Head – b. 1831 Holland – aged 60 – Boot Manufacturer
Sophia LIMBURG – Wife – b. 1839 Amsterdam – aged 52
David LIMBURG – Son – b. 1868 Spitalfields – aged 23
Adelaide LIMBURG – Daughter – b. 1870 Spitalfields – aged 21
Jane LIMBURG – Daughter – b. 1872 Spitalfields – aged 19
Emmanuel LIMBURG – Son – b. 1874 Spitalfields – aged 17
Henry LIMBURG – Son – b. 1877 Spitalfields – aged 14
Emelia LIMBURG – Daughter – b. 1879 Spitalfields – aged 12
Mary LANGLEY – General Domestic Servant

1881 Census

Address:

21 Whites Row, Spitalfields

Residents:

Abraham LIMBURG – Head – b. 1831 Netherlands – aged 50 – Boot Manufacturer
Sophia LIMBURG – Wife – b. 1839 Netherlands – aged 42
Elizabeth LIMBURG – Daughter – b. 1862 London – aged 19 – Teacher
Lewis LIMBURG – Son – b. 1864 London – aged 17 – Boot Clicker
Joseph LIMBURG – Son – b. 1866 London – aged 15 – Diamond Polisher
David LIMBURG – Son – b. 1868 London – aged 13 – Errand Boy
Adelaide LIMBURG – Daughter – b. 1870 London – aged 11 – at School
Jane LIMBURG – Daughter – b. 1872 London – aged 9 – at School
Emanuel LIMBURG – Son – b. 1874 London – aged 7 – at School
Henry LIMBURG – Son – b. 1877 London – aged 4 - at School
Amelia LIMBURG – Daughter – b. 1879 London – aged 2
Emma WINDER – Domestic Servant

1871 Census

Address:

21 Whites Row, Spitalfields

Residents:

Abraham LIMBURG – Head – b. 1841 Netherlands – aged 40 – Boot Maker
Sophia LIMBURG – Wife – b. 1835 Netherlands – aged 36
Elizabeth LIMBURG – Daughter – b. 1859 Middlesex – aged 12
Louis LIMBURG – Son – b. 1864 Middlesex – aged 7
Joseph LIMBURG – Son – b. 1866 Middlesex – aged 5
David LIMBURG – Son – b. 1868 Middlesex – aged 3
Adelaide LIMBURG – Daughter – b. 1870 Middlesex – aged 1

Kate BURROWS – General Servant

Marriage:

Abraham LIMBURG to Sophia GOLDSTEIN – Q4 1859 LONDON CITY 1c 262.

1901 Census

Address:

18 High Street, Norton Folgate

Residents:

Sophia LIMBURG – Head – Widow – b. 1840 Amsterdam – aged 61
Henry LIMBURG – Son – b. 1877 Spitalfields – aged 24 – Shoe Manufacturer
Amelia LIMBURG – Daughter – b. 1879 Spitalfields – aged 22
Ann GUTTRIGE – General Domestic Servant

Naturalisation:

Certificate A4662 issued 15 July 1886 for Abraham Limburg, from Holland Resident in London.
Reference: HO 144/172/A43808.

Death:

Sophia Phoebe LIMBURG - Q1 1902 [62] HACKNEY 1b 395.
Buried at Plashet Cemetery – B-22-33 on 16 Mar 1902.

Jewish Chronicle – 21 Mar 1902

LIMBURG – On the 13th of March, after a serious operation, Sophia, widow of the late Abraham Limburg, aged 62. Deeply mourned by her loving children, grandchildren, brothers and sisters, and a large circle of friends. – 18, Norton Folgate, E.C.
LIMBURG – On the 14th of March, at the German Hospital, after a short and painful illness, Sophia (Phoebe) Limburg, of 18, Norton Folgate, Bishopsgate, in her 63rd year. Deeply mourned by her sorrowing sisters and brothers, Mrs J. De Haan, 14, Rothschild Buildings; Mrs H. Melhado, 55, Wellesley Street, Stepney; Mrs A. Ducker, 53, Brook Street, Ratcliff; Jacob Goldstein, 38, Rothschild Buildings, and Morris Goldstein, 26, Shepherd Street, Spitalfields. God rest her dear soul.

Jewish Chronicle – 26 Sep 1902

The tombstone erected in memory of our dear mother, the late Sophia Limburg, will be set on Sunday next, September 28th, at 4 o'clock. Relatives and friends please accept this, the only intimation.

MANHEIM, Catherine – B-3-28

Died: 02 May 1897
Buried: 04 May 1897
Partner: Herman Manheim (d. 1927)
Aged: 60th year

Jewish Chronicle – 07 May 1897

MANHEIM – On Sunday, the 2nd of May, at 7, Emanuels Buildings, Wellclose Square, (late of 69, Great Prescot Street), Kate, the dearly beloved wife of Herman Manheim, in her 60th year. Deeply mourned by her sorrowing husband, son, granddaughter, sisters and relatives and friends. May her soul rest in peace.

Jewish Chronicle – 13 Aug 1897

The tombstone to the memory of the late Catherine Manheim, beloved wife of Herman Manheim, of Emanuels-buildings, Wellclose Square, E., will be set on Sunday next, August 15th, at Plashet Cemetery, at 3.30 p.m. Relatives and friends kindly accept this, the only intimation.

Jewish Chronicle – 22 Apr 1898

In loving and affectionate memory of our dear wife, mother, grandmother and sister, Catherine (nee Kitty) Manheim, who died 1st of Iyar 5657, corresponding with May 2nd, 1897. Ever fondly remembered and sadly missed. Peace to her dear soul. Amen.

Death:

Q2 1897 [60] STEPNEY 1c 232 [Catherine Mannheim]

1891 Census

Address:

69 Great Prescot Street, Whitechapel, London, Tower Hamlets

Residents:

Herman MANHEIM – Head – b. 1839 Germany – aged 52 – Tailor
Catherine MANHEIM – Wife – b. 1839 London – aged 52

1881 Census

Address:

69 Great Prescot Street, Whitechapel

Residents:

Herman MANHEIM – Head – b. 1839 Prussia – aged 42 – Tailor
Catherine MANHEIM – Wife – b. 1838 London – aged 43
Benjamin MANHEIM – Son – b. 1861 Whitechapel – aged 20 – Tailor

MANHEIM, Catherine – B-3-28

Marriage:

Herman MANHEIM to Catherine BARNETT – Q1 1857 LONDON CITY 1c 219.

1901 Census

Address:

7, Emanuel Alms Houses, Wapping

Resident:

Herman MANNHEIM - Widower – b. 1838 (? Scotland) – aged 63

1911 Census

Address:

19 Joel Emanuel Alms Houses, Egerton Road, Stanford Hill, N.

Resident:

Herman MANHEIM – Widower – b. 1839 Germany – aged 72

Death:

Herman MANHEIM – Q2 1927 [86] HACKNEY 1b 418.
Buried at Plashet Cemetery – B-3-29 (date not given).

MARTIN, Esther Rachel – A-6-2

MARTIN, Esther Rachel – A-6-2

Died: 02 Jan 1897
Buried: 04 Jan 1897
Hebrew Name: Ester Rikael bat David
Partner: Morris Martin (d. 1898)
Aged: 61 years

Jewish Chronicle – 15 Jan 1897

MARTIN – On the 2nd of January, after a long illness, at 15, Nottingham Place, London, E., Esther, the beloved wife of Morris Martin, and sister of H. [Hyam] Davis of 100, Cannon Street Road, aged 61. Deeply mourned by her husband, children, relations and friends. African and American papers please copy.

Jewish Chronicle –17 Sep 1897

The tombstone in loving memory of our dear wife, mother and sister, Esther Martin, late of 15, Nottingham Place, will be set on Sunday, September 19th, at 3 p.m. at Plashet Cemetery. Relations and friends please accept this only intimation.

Death:

Q1 1897 [61] MILE END 1c 281.

1891 Census

Address:

15 Nottingham Place, Mile End Old Town

Residents:

Morris MARTIN – Head – b. 1838 Poland – aged 53 - Tailor
Esther MARTIN – Wife – b. 1836 Poland – aged 55
Samuel MARTIN – Son – b. 1865 Poland – aged 26 – Tailor
Dora MARTIN – Daughter – b. 1863 Poland – aged 28 – Tailoress
Joseph MARTIN – Son – b. 1869 Poland – aged 22 – Tailor
David MARTIN – Visitor – b. 1869 Poland – aged 22 – Tailor

1881 Census

Address:

22 Talford Street, Mile End Old Town

Residents:

Morris MARTIN – Head – b. 1832 Poland – aged 49 – Tailor
Esther MARTIN – Wife – b. 1836 Poland – aged 45
David MARTIN – Son – b. 1959 Poland – aged 22 – Tailor
Emanuel MARTIN – Son – b. 1861 Poland – aged 20 – Tailor
Dora MARTIN – Daughter – b. 1864 Poland – aged 17 – Tailoress

Joseph MARTIN – Son – b. 1867 Poland – aged 14 – Tailor
Samuel MARTIN – Son – b. 1869 Poland – aged 12 – Scholar

Death:

Morris MARTIN – Q3 1898 [67] MILE END OLD TOWN 1c 327.
Buried at Plashet Cemetery – D-5-1 on 18 Aug 1898.

Jewish Chronicle – 26 Aug 1898

MARTIN – On Tuesday, the 16th of August, at 15, Nottingham Place, Morris Martin, the beloved husband of the late Esther Martin. Deeply mourned by his loving children, grandchildren, relatives and friends. May his soul rest in peace. African papers please copy.

MOSES, Emanuel Frederick – A-9-35

Died: 21 Nov 1897
Buried: 23 Nov 1897
Partner: Esther Moses (d. 1887)
Aged: 73rd year

Jewish Chronicle – 26 Nov 1897

MOSES – On the 21st of November, at 23, Rectory Square, E., after a long illness, Emanuel F. Moses, formerly of Swansea, South Wales, brother of Mrs Seline, 9, Grove Place, Swansea, Mrs L. Cohen, Bridgend, Mrs Fonseca, 49, Westbourne Park Crescent, W., in his 73rd year. Deeply mourned by his sons, daughters and relatives.

Jewish Chronicle – 03 Jun 1898

The tombstone in memory of the late lamented Emanuel F. Moses, of 23, Rectory Square, Stepney Green, late of Swansea, will be set on Sunday, June 5th, at Plashet Cemetery, London, E., at 4 p.m. Relatives and friends please accept this intimation.

Death:

Q4 1897 [72] MILE END 1c 334.

1891 Census

Address:

378 Mile End Road, Mile End Old Town

Residents:

Emanuel F. MOSES – Head – Widower – b. 1825 Swansea – aged 66 – Coal Merchant – Partially Blind
Rachel MOSES – Daughter – b. 1865 Swansea – aged 26 – Wood Steel Coverer
Flora MOSES – Daughter – b. 1866 Swansea – aged 25 – Wood Steel Coverer
Harriett MOSES – Daughter – b. 1869 Swansea – aged 22 – School Teacher

In
Loving Memory of
EMANUEL FREDERICK MOSES,
DIED 21ST NOVEMBER 1897,
27TH MARCHESHVAN 5658,
AGED 71.
May his dear Soul rest in Peace.
ת נ צ ב ה

MOSES, Emanuel Frederick – A-9-35

1881 Census

Address:

65 White Horse Lane, Mile End Old Town

Residents:

Emmanuel F. MOSES – Head – b. 1825 Swansea – aged 56 – Coal & Coke Agent
Esther MOSES – Wife – b. 1827 London – aged 54
James MOSES – Son – b. 1857 Swansea – aged 24
Harriett MOSES – Daughter – b. 1869 Swansea – aged 12 – Scholar

1871 Census

Address:

College Street, Swansea

Residents:

Emmanuel F. MOSES – Head – b. 1825 Glamorgan – aged 46
Esther MOSES – Wife – b. 1829 Middlesex – aged 42
Julia MOSES – Daughter – b. 1854 Glamorgan – aged 17
James MOSES – Son – b. 1858 Glamorgan – aged 13
Moses MOSES – Son – b. 1859 Glamorgan – aged 12
Selin MOSES – Son – b. 1860 Glamorgan – aged 11
Isabella M. MOSES – Daughter – b. 1863 Glamorgan – aged 8
Rachel H. MOSES – Daughter – b. 1865 Glamorgan – aged 6
Flora MOSES – Daughter – b. 1866 Glamorgan – aged 5
Harriett MOSES – Daughter – b. 1866 Glamorgan – aged 2
Martha RICHARDS – Domestic Servant

1861 Census

Address:

26 College Street, Swansea

Residents:

Emanuel Fred MOSES – Head – b. 1825 Swansea – aged 36 – Pawnbroker
Esther MOSES – Wife – b. 1827 London – aged 34
Bertram James MOSES – Son – b. 1851 Swansea – aged 10 – Scholar
Hannah MOSES – Daughter – b. 1853 Swansea – aged 8 – Scholar
Julia MOSES – Daughter – b. 1854 Swansea – aged 7 – Scholar
Henry MOSES – Son – b. 1856 Swansea – aged 5 – Scholar
James MOSES – Son – b. 1858 Swansea – aged 3
Moss MOSES – Son – b. 1859 Swansea – aged 2
Salim MOSES – Son – b. 1860 Swansea – aged 1
Sarah Ann HUGHES – Nursemaid

1851 Census

Address:

45 Oxford Street, Swansea

Residents:

Emanuel F. MOSES – Head – b. 1825 Swansea – aged 26 – Travelling Jeweller
Esther MOSES – Wife – b. 1827 Westminster – aged 24
Brahane MOSES – Son – b. 1851 Swansea – aged 3 months
Harriet MOSES – Sister – b. 1829 Swansea – aged 22 – Dressmaker
Anne EATON – Domestic Servant

1841 Census

Address:

Strand, Swansea

Residents:

Michael MOSES – b. 1823 Glamorgan – aged 18
Emanuel MOSES – b. 1822 Glamorgan – aged 19

Marriage:

Emanuel Frederick MOSES to Esther KISCH - Q2 1849 ST. JAMES WESTMINSTER 1 127.

Death:

Esther MOSES – Q3 1887 [61] MILE END OLD TOWN 1c 394
Buried at West Ham Cemetery – J-7-33 on 27 Sep 1887.

Jewish Chronicle – 7 Oct 1887

On Kol Nidre night, at 10, Emmott Street, Mile End Road, Esther, the beloved and devoted wife of E.F. Moses, late of Swansea, and daughter of the late Abraham Kisch, of St. Alban's Place Synagogue, Haymarket, in her 62nd year, after a long and painful illness, borne with great resignation. Her passing was peace!

MYERS, Abraham – A-9-5

Died: 24 Aug 1897
Buried: 26 Aug 1897
Hebrew Name: Avraham ben Me'ir Ephraim
Partner: Elizabeth Myers (d. 1903)
Aged: 85th year

Jewish Chronicle – 27 Aug 1897

MYERS – On Tuesday morning, the 24th of August, after a long illness borne with great patience, Abraham Myers, of 78, Amhurst Park, Stamford Hill, in his 85th

MYERS, Abraham – A-9-5

year. Deeply mourned by his sorrowing wife and children. Australian, Californian and American papers please copy.
MYERS – On Tuesday morning, the 24th of August, after a long illness borne with great patience, Abraham Myers, of 76, Amhurst Park, Stamford Hill, in his 85th year, the dearly beloved father of Mrs A. Mendes. Deeply mourned by all who knew him.

Jewish Chronicle – 29 Oct 1897

The tombstone in loving memory of Abraham Myers, late of 76, Amhurst Park, N., will be set at the Plashet Cemetery on Sunday next, October 31st, at 3 o'clock precisely. Relatives and friends please accept this intimation.

Death:
Q3 1897 [85] HACKNEY 1b 283.

1891 Census

Address:
14 Spital Square, Spitalfields, London, Whitechapel
Residents:
Abraham MYERS – Head – b. 1816 Aldgate – aged 75 – Commercial Traveller – Cigars
Elizabeth MYERS – Wife – b. 1821 Bethnal Green – aged 70
Rachel MYERS – Daughter – b. 1856 Whitechapel – aged 35
Isaac MYERS – Son – b. 1861 Stepney – aged 30 – Cigar Manufacturer
Louisa HEAD – Domestic Servant

1881 Census

Address:
425 Liverpool Road, Islington
Residents:
Abraham MYERS – Head – b. 1813 London – aged 68 – Commercial Traveller
Elizabeth MYERS – Wife – b. 1818 London – aged 63
Rachael MYERS – Daughter – b. 1855 London – aged 26 – Pianoforte Teacher
Dinah MYERS – Daughter – b. 1857 London – aged 24 – Forewoman (Manager)
Isaac MYERS – Son – b. 1859 London – aged 22 – Cigar Manufacturer
Rebecca BARNETT – Niece – b. 1857 London – aged 24
Jane EDWARDS – Granddaughter – b. 1875 London – aged 6 – Scholar
Rose BINGHAM – General Domestic Servant

1871 Census

Address:
Leman Street, Whitechapel

Residents:

Abraham MYERS – Head – b. 1814 Middlesex – aged 57
Elizabeth MYERS – Wife – b. 1819 Middlesex – aged 52
Rachel MYERS – Daughter – b. 1854 Middlesex – aged 17
Dinah MYERS – Daughter – b. 1856 Middlesex – aged 15
Isaac MYERS – Son – b. 1858 Middlesex – aged 13
Joseph LEIGH – Father-in-law
Rebecca BARNETT – Niece – b. 1856 Middlesex – aged 15
Ellen TENNYSON – Domestic Servant

1861 Census

Address:

21 Maria Terrace, Stepney

Residents:

Abraham MYERS – Head – b. 1815 Whitechapel – aged 46 – Cigar Maker
Elizabeth MYERS – Wife – b. 1819 Bethnal Green – aged 42
Ephraim MYERS – Son – b. 1840 Beck Row – aged 21 – Cigar Maker
M. Harry MYERS – Son – b. 1842 Whitechapel – aged 19 – Cigar Maker
Sarah MYERS – Daughter – b. 1851 Whitechapel – aged 10
Nathaniel MYERS – Son – b. 1850 Whitechapel – aged 11 – Scholar
Clara MYERS – Daughter – b. 1849 Whitechapel – aged 12 – Scholar
Alexander MYERS – Son – b. 1851 Whitechapel – aged 10 – Scholar
Rachael MYERS – Daughter – b. 1853 Whitechapel – aged 8 – Scholar
Dinah MYERS – Daughter – b. 1855 Whitechapel – aged 6 – Scholar
Isaac MYERS – Son – b. 1861 Stepney – aged 6 months
Joseph LEIGH – Father-in-law – Pensioner – b. 1796 Shoreditch – aged 65

1901 Census

Address:

141 Graham Road, Hackney

Residents:

Elizabeth MYERS – Head – Widow – b. 1820 Mile End – aged 81
Isaac MYERS – Son – b. 1861 Stepney – aged 40 – Cigar Manufacturer
Ray MYERS – Daughter – b. 1859 Whitechapel – aged 42
Sarah CHESTERMAN – Domestic Servant

Death:

Elizabeth MYERS – Q2 1903 [85] HACKNEY 1b 288.
Buried at Plashet Cemetery – E-9-47 on 26 Jun 1903.

Jewish Chronicle – 26 Jun 1903

MYERS – On the 24th of June, at 141, Graham Road, the beloved mother of Mrs A. Mendes, of 15, Shore Road, South Hackney. Shiva at 141, Graham Road,

Dalston. Beloved by all who knew her.
MYERS – On the 24th of June, at 141, Graham Road, Elizabeth, the beloved aunt of Mrs D. Sasserath, of 20, Northholme Road, Highbury New Park, N.
MYERS – On the 24th of June, at 141, Graham Road, Dalston, Elizabeth, relict of the late Abraham Myers, after a long and painful illness, borne with great fortitude. Deeply mourned by her loving children, grandchildren, great-grandchildren, relatives and friends. American, Australian and Californian papers please copy.
MYERS – On the 24th of June, at 141, Graham Road, Dalston, Elizabeth Myers, aged 85, the beloved mother of Mrs Albert Calman, of 132, Graham Road. Beloved by all who knew her. Shiva at 141, Graham Road, Dalston.

NASCH, Augusta Esther – A-9-21

Died: **08 Nov 1897**
Buried: **11 Nov 1897**
Partner: **Isidor Nasch**
Aged: **61st year**

Jewish Chronicle – 19 Nov 1897

NASCH – On the 8th of November, 1897, at 251, Whitechapel Road, E., Augusta, the dearly beloved wife of Isidor Nasch, in her 61st year. Deeply regretted by her affectionate husband and nephew, and a large circle of relatives and friends. May her soul rest in peace.

Jewish Chronicle – 14 Oct 1898

The tombstone in memory of Augusta, dearly loved wife of Isidor Nasch, will be set at Plashet Cemetery, at 1.30 o'clock on Sunday, the 16th of October. Friends please accept this, the only intimation.

Death:
Q4 1897 [61] WHITECHAPEL 1c 237.

1891 Census

Address:
251 Whitechapel Road, Whitechapel

Residents:
Isidore NASH – Head – b. 1835 Berlin – aged 56 – Mechanical Engineer
Augusta NASH – Wife – b. 1839 Berlin – aged 52
William NASH – Nephew – b. 1864 Berlin – aged 27 – Engineer

Jewish Chronicle – 21 Jan 1898

NASCH, Augusta Esther – A-9-21

Article:

The Sewing Machine in Germany

We quote the following from the current issue of the *Journal of Domestic Appliances*: - "We regret to have to announce the death of Mrs Nasch, wife of Mr Isidor Nasch, the well-known sewing machine inventor. This lady has been identified with the sewing machine from its earliest days. Indeed, it was largely through her faith in it that the machine made such rapid progress in the German mantle and tailoring trades. Mr Isidor Nasch and his cousin, Mr Julius Gutmann, were the first to introduce a sewing machine into Germany – a "Thomas" in 1857. At this time Miss Augusta Laubrich (Mrs Nasch's maiden name) was employed in a mantle factory in Berlin, and her future husband not only persuaded her to adopt the machine, but also himself, in a partnership which lasted until death. As most of our readers are aware, Mr Nasch has been a prolific inventor, largely in connection with button-hole and book-sewing machines, and he has always desired it to be known by the trade that the assistance rendered by his wife in completing his various inventions was of the highest value."

NATHAN, Esther – A-7-5

Died: 26 Apr 1897
Buried: 28 Apr 1897
Parents: Nathan & Sarah Nathan
Aged: 22nd year

Jewish Chronicle – 30 Apr 1897

NATHAN – On the 26th of April, at 431, Mile End Road, E., Esther, the dearly beloved daughter of Nathan and Sarah Nathan, in her 22nd year. God rest her soul.

Jewish Chronicle – 15 Jul 1898

The tombstone in memory of Esther, the beloved daughter of Sarah and Nathan Nathan, of 431, Mile End Road, will be set on Sunday next, July 17th, at Plashet Cemetery at 4 p.m. Relatives and friends please accept this, the only intimation.

Death:

Q2 1897 [21] MILE END OLD TOWN 1c 282.

Birth:

Esther NATHAN – Q3 1876 WHITECHAPEL 1c 357.

1891 Census

Address:

431 Mile End Road, Mile End Old Town

Residents:

Nathan NATHAN – Head – b. 1838 Spitalfields – aged 53 – Traveller
Sarah NATHAN – Wife – b. 1844 Spitalfields – aged 47
Hanah NATHAN – Daughter – b. 1869 Aldgate – aged 22 – Machinist
Rebecca NATHAN – Daughter – b. 1870 Aldgate – aged 21
David NATHAN – Son – b. 1870 Aldgate – aged 21
Milly NATHAN – Daughter – b. 1869 Aldgate – aged 22 – Cap Maker
Louisa NATHAN – Daughter – b. 1872 Aldgate – aged 19 – Shoe Trimmer
Kate NATHAN – Daughter – b. 1874 Aldgate – aged 17 – Dressmaker
Esther NATHAN – Daughter – b. 1877 Aldgate – aged 14 – Dressmaker
Lewis NATHAN – Son – b. 1878 Aldgate – aged 13 – Clickers Apprentice
Nathan NATHAN – Son – b. 1879 Bow – aged 12 – Scholar
Rose NATHAN – Daughter – b. 1881 Bow – aged 10 – Scholar
Harry NATHAN – Son – b. 1883 Bow – aged 8 – Scholar
Hannah NATHAN – Mother – Widow – b. 1813 Bow – aged 78
Bessy LEARY – Aunt – Widow – b. 1811 Spitalfields – aged 80 – Deaf & Dumb
Clara MAIDDLE – Domestic Servant

1881 Census

Address:

69, Lincoln Street, Mile End Old Town

Residents:

Nathan NATHAN – Head – b. 1839 Spitalfields – aged 42 – Sportsman
Sarah NATHAN – Wife – b. 1843 Aldgate – aged 38
Rebecca NATHAN – Daughter – b. 1870 Whitechapel – aged 11 – Scholar
David NATHAN – Son – b. 1870 Whitechapel – aged 11 – Scholar
Amelia NATHAN – Daughter – b. 1871 Whitechapel – aged 10 – Scholar
Louisa NATHAN – Daughter – b. 1873 Whitechapel – aged 8 – Scholar
Kate NATHAN – Daughter – b. 1874 Whitechapel – aged 7 – Scholar
Esther NATHAN – Daughter – b. 1876 Whitechapel – aged 5 – Scholar
Louis NATHAN – Son – b. 1878 Whitechapel – aged 3
Nathan NATHAN – Son – b. 1879 Whitechapel – aged 2
Rose NATHAN – Daughter – b. 1871 Mile End – aged 10
Davis MOSES – Nephew – b. 1857 Middlesex – aged 24 – Elementary Teacher
Elizabeth LEVY – Aunt – Widow – b. 1813 Whitechapel – aged 68 – Deaf & Dumb
Elizabeth COLLISON – Domestic Servant
Rose ABBOT – Nurse Maid

Marriage:

Nathan NATHAN to Sarah ISAACS – Q2 1866 LONDON CITY 1c 225.

NATHAN, Matilda – A-6-37

Died: 07 Mar 1897
Buried: 08 Mar 1897
Partner: Barnet Davis Nathan
Aged: 87 years

Jewish Chronicle – 12 Mar 1897

NATHAN – On the 7th of March, at 14, Freeman Street, Spitalfields, Matilda, dearly beloved widow of the late B.D. Nathan (Chiropodist). Deeply mourned by her sorrowing sons, daughters, grandchildren and great-grandchildren, and a large circle of friends. May her dear soul rest in peace. American and Dutch papers please copy.

Jewish Chronicle – 30 Jul 1897

The tombstone in loving memory of the late Matilda Nathan, of 14, Freeman Street, Spitalfields, will be set on Sunday next, August 1st, at Plashet Cemetery, East Ham, at 4.30. Friends please accept this intimation.

Death:
Q1 1897 [87] WHITECHAPEL 1c 165.

1891 Census

Address:
14 Freeman Street, Spitalfields, London

Residents:
Matilda NATHAN – Head – Widow – b. 1810 Holland – aged 81
Hannah NATHAN – Daughter – b. 1850 Spitalfields – aged 41 – Ostrich Feather Curler
Harriett NATHAN – Daughter – b. 1858 Spitalfields – aged 33
Rebecca NATHAN – Daughter – b. 1859 Spitalfields – aged 32 – Buyer
Hyman NATHAN – Son – b. 1872 Spitalfields – aged 19 – Hawker

1881 Census

Address:
13 Freeman Street, Spitalfields

Residents:
Martha NATHAN – Head – Widow – b. 1810 Netherlands – aged 71
Hannah NATHAN – Daughter – b. 1843 Spitalfields – aged 38 – Charwoman
Harriet NATHAN – Daughter – b. 1853 Spitalfields – aged 28 – Feather Curler (Dresser)
Rebecca NATHAN – Daughter – b. 1855 Spitalfields – aged 26 – Tailoress
Hyman MOORE – Grandson – b. 1872 Spitalfields – aged 9 - Scholar

NATHAN, Matilda – A-6-37

1871 Census

Address:

Freeman Street, Christ Church Spitalfields

Residents:

Mathilda NATHAN – Head – b. 1811 Netherlands – aged 60
Anna NATHAN – Daughter – b. 1843 Middlesex – aged 28
Louis NATHAN – Son – b. 1847 Middlesex – aged 24
Esther NATHAN – Daughter – b. 1849 Middlesex – aged 22
Nathan NATHAN – Son – b. 1851 Middlesex – aged 20

1851 Census

Address:

14 Freeman Street, Christchurch, Tower Hamlets

Residents:

Barnes Davis NATHAN – Head – b. 1810 Hanover – aged 41 - Chiropodist
Matilda NATHAN – Wife – b. 1815 Amsterdam – aged 36
Deborah NATHAN – Daughter – b. 1836 Spitalfields – aged 15 – Tailoress
Jesse NATHAN – Daughter – b. 1837 Spitalfields – aged 14 – Cap Maker
Phoebe NATHAN – Daughter – b. 1841 Spitalfields – aged 10 – Scholar
Hannah NATHAN – Daughter – b. 1842 Spitalfields – aged 8 – Scholar
Lewis NATHAN – Son – b. 1847 Spitalfields – aged 4 – Scholar
Esther NATHAN – Daughter – b. 1849 Spitalfields – aged 2
Nathan NATHAN – Son – b. 1851 Spitalfields – aged 1 month

ROSENTHAL, Isaac – B-2-32

Died: 20 Jan 1897
Buried: 24 Jan 1897
Partner: Hannah Rosenthal (d. 1909)
Aged: 67 years

Jewish Chronicle – 29 Jan 1897

ROSENTHAL – On the 20th of January, suddenly, Isaac Rosenthal, of 4, Mansell Street, Aldgate, aged 67. Deeply regretted.

Jewish Chronicle – 28 May 1897

The tombstone in loving memory of the late Isaac Rosenthal, of 4, Mansell Street, Aldgate, will be set on Sunday, May 30th, at 3.30, at Plashet Cemetery. Relatives and friends will kindly accept this, the only intimation.

Death:

Q1 1897 [67] LONDON CITY 1c 11.

1891 Census

Address:

52 Great Prescot Street, Whitechapel, London, Tower Hamlets

Residents:

Isaac ROSENTHAL – Head – b. 1829 Poland – aged 62 – Boot Maker
Hannah ROSENTHAL – Wife – b. 1832 London – aged 59
Maurice ROSENTHAL – Son – b. 1865 London – aged 26 – Boot Maker / Deaf from childhood

1881 Census

Address:

16 Swan Street, Whitechapel

Residents:

Isaac ROSENTHAL – Head – b. 1829 Poland – aged 52 – Boot Manufacturer
Hannah ROSENTHAL – Wife – b. 1832 Strand – aged 49
Lewis ROSENTHAL – Son – b. 1861 London – aged 20 – Schoolmaster
Maurice ROSENTHAL – Son – b. 1865 Whitechapel – aged 16 – Bootmaker / Deaf from Birth
Emma SMITH – Domestic Servant

1871 Census

Address:

16 Swan Street South Side, Whitechapel

Residents:

Isaac ROSENTHAL – Head – b. 1831 Poland – aged 40 – Boot Maker
Hannah ROSENTHAL – Wife – b. 1832 Middlesex – aged 39
Louis ROSENTHAL – Son – b. 1861 Middlesex – aged 10 - Scholar
Israel ROSENTHAL – Son – b. 1862 Middlesex – aged 9 - Scholar
Maurice ROSENTHAL – Son – b. 1865 Middlesex – aged 6 – Scholar

Marriage:

Isaac ROSENTHAL to Evaline MAISONPIERRE – Q2 1858 LONDON CITY 1c 258.

1901 Census

Address:

4 Mansell Street, St. Botolph Without Aldgate

Residents:

Hannah ROSENTHAL – Head – Widow – b. 1832 St. Clements – aged 69 – Shoe Dealer

Maurice ROSENTHAL – Son – b. 1865 Whitechapel – aged 36 – Boot Maker

Death:

Hannah ROSENTHAL – Q4 1908 [76] LONDON CITY 1c 2.
Buried at Plashet Cemetery – K-7-4 on 03 Jan 1909.

Jewish Chronicle – 08 Jan 1909

ROSENTHAL – On the 31st of December, at 39, New Street, Houndsditch (late of Mansell Street), Hannah, relict of the late I. Rosenthal; beloved mother of L.I. Rosenthal, 38, Portland Road, Finsbury Park, Maurice Rosenthal, and sister of S.L. Hickman, 20a, Albion Road, Newington Green, aged 77. God rest her soul.

SAMPSON, Rose / Rosetta – A-11-1

Died: 08 Dec 1897
Buried: 10 Dec 1897
Hebrew Name: Ritza bat Michael
Partner: Nathan Sampson (d. 1928)
Aged: 42 years

Jewish Chronicle – 12 Dec 1897

SAMPSON – On the 8th of December, after a long and painful illness, borne with great fortitude, Rosie, the dearly loved wife of Nathan Sampson, of 126, Hoxton Street, N., aged 42. May her dear soul rest in peace.
SAMPSON – On the 8th of December, after a long and painful illness, Rosie Sampson, mother of Mrs Jack Zealander, and Mr Michael Sampson. Shiva at 126, Hoxton Street, N. May her dear soul rest in peace.

Jewish Chronicle – 22 Jul 1898

The tombstone in memory of Rose, dearly loved wife of Nathan Sampson, of 126, Hoxton Street, Hoxton, will be set at Plashet Cemetery at 3 o'clock on Sunday, 24th of July. Relatives and friends please accept this, the only intimation.

Death:

Q4 1897 [42] MARYLEBONE 1a 396.

1891 Census

Address:

126 Hoxton Street, Shoreditch

Residents:

Nathan SAMPSON – Head – b. 1853 Poland – aged 38 – Boot Manufacturer
Rose SAMPSON – Wife – b. 1857 London – aged 34
Amelia SAMPSON – Daughter – b. 1873 London – aged 18 – Assistant in Business

Michael SAMPSON – Son – b. 1875 London – aged 16
Marion SAMPSON – Daughter – b. 1876 London – aged 15
Clara SAMPSON – Daughter – b. 1878 London – aged 13 – Scholar
Jack SAMPSON – Son – b. 1879 London – aged 12 – Scholar
Baron SAMPSON – Son – b. 1881 London – aged 10 – Scholar
Abigail SAMPSON – Daughter – b. 1882 London – aged 9 – Scholar
Frank SAMPSON – Son – b. 1884 London – aged 7 – Scholar
Louis SAMPSON – Son – b. 1886 London – aged 5 – Scholar
Sarah SAMPSON – Daughter – b. 1888 London – aged 3
Harry SAMPSON – Son – b. 1890 London – aged 1
Sarah STOOKER – Domestic Servant

1881 Census

Address:

7 Ton Alley, Whitechapel

Residents:

Nathan SAMPSON – Head – b. 1853 Poland – aged 28 - Bootmaker employing 4 boys
Rosetta SAMPSON – Wife – b. 1855 Whitechapel – aged 26
Amelia SAMPSON – Daughter – b. 1873 Whitechapel – aged 8 – Scholar
Michael SAMPSON – Son – b. 1875 Whitechapel – aged 6 – Scholar
Mary SAMPSON – Daughter – b. 1876 Whitechapel – aged 5 – Scholar
Clara SAMPSON – Daughter – b. 1878 Whitechapel – aged 3 – Scholar
Jacob SAMPSON – Son – b. 1879 Whitechapel – aged 2
Baron SAMPSON – Son – b. 1881 Whitechapel – aged 0
Julia COCKLING – Domestic Servant

Marriage:

Nathan SAMPSON to Rosetta LEVY – Q2 1872 LONDON CITY 1c 182.

1901 Census

Address:

126 Hoxton Street, Shoreditch

Residents:

Nathan SAMPSON – Head – b. 1853 Poplar – aged 48 – Boot Manufacturer
Millie SAMPSON – Wife – b. 1863 London – aged 38
Jacob SAMPSON – Son – b. 1879 Spitalfields – aged 22 – Assistant
Benn SAMPSON – Son – b. 1881 Spitalfields – aged 20
Frank SAMPSON – Son – b. 1883 Bethnal Green – aged 18
Sarah SAMPSON – Daughter – b. 1889 Hoxton – aged 12
Annie SAMPSON – Daughter – b. 1891 Hoxton – aged 10
Moss SAMPSON – Son – b. 1893 Hoxton – aged 8
Doris SAMPSON – Daughter – b. 1901 Hoxton – 5 months

Isabel JEFFRIES – Domestic Servant
Maggie McGANE – Domestic Servant

1911 Census

Address:

68 Highbury New Park, Highbury, London N.

Residents:

Nathan SAMPSON – Head – b. 1853 Poland – aged 58 – Managing Director of Boot and Shoe Retailer
Milly SAMPSON – Wife (12 years) – b. 1863 London – aged 48
Lewis SAMPSON – Son – b. 1886 Shoreditch – aged 25 – Boot and Shoe Salesman
Sarah SAMPSON – Daughter – b. 1889 Shoreditch – aged 22 – Assistant in Mantle and Dress Warehouse
Hyman SAMPSON – Son – b. 1890 Shoreditch – aged 21 – Assistant in Boot and Shoes
Annie SAMPSON – Daughter – b. 1892 Shoreditch – aged 19 – Dressmaker
Moss SAMPSON – Son – b. 1893 Shoreditch – aged 18 – Tailor
Doris Dinah SAMPSON – Daughter – b. 1901 Shoreditch – aged 10
Alexander Lazarus SAMPSON – Son – b. 1906 Islington – aged 5
Louie Maud BECKETT – Domestic Servant
Annie Maud FLETCHER – Domestic Servant

Marriage:

Nathan SAMPSON to Millie ALEXANDER – Q3 1899 LONDON CITY 1c 93.

Death:

Nathan SAMPSON – Q3 1928 [76] HACKNEY 1b 292.
Buried at Willesden Jewish Cemetery – LX-9-45 on 19 Jul 1928.

Jewish Chronicle – 20 Jul 1928

SAMPSON – On Wednesday, the 18th of July, Nathan Sampson, aged 76, late of Hoxton Street. May his soul rest in peace. No Shiva.
SAMPSON – On the 18th of July, 1928, at "The Lodge", Finsbury Park Road, N.4., Nathan Sampson (Nate), aged 76. Dearly beloved husband of Millie Sampson and father of Alex. Sampson and Mrs Norman Cohen. God rest his soul.

SAUNDERS, Annie – B-2-31

Died: 21 Jan 1897
Buried: 22 Jan 1897
Partner: Nathan Saunders (d. 1905)
Aged: 65 years

Jewish Chronicle – 29 Jan 1897

SAUNDERS – On the 21st of January, at Half Moon Passage, Whitechapel, suddenly, Annie, the beloved wife of Nathan Saunders, aged 65 years.

Jewish Chronicle – 19 Feb 1897

The tombstone in memory of Anna, the beloved wife of Nathan Saunders, will be set on Sunday next (21 Feb 1897), at Plashet Cemetery, at 2 o'clock.

Death:

Q1 1897 [65] WHITECHAPEL 1c 217.

1891 Census

Address:

3a Halfmoon Passage, Whitechapel

Residents:

Nathan SAUNDERS – Head – b. 1816 Poland – aged 75 – Hotel Keeper
Anna SAUNDERS – Wife – b. 1831 Poland – aged 60
Rose SAUNDERS – Sister – Widow – b. 1821 Poland – aged 70
Leah FRANKENSTEIN – Servant
Ester STIRLING – Servant
John WASSERMAN – Boarder – b. 1846 Austria – aged 45 – School Teacher
Frederick FRIEDMAN – Boarder – b. 1859 Russia – aged 32 – Horse Dealer
Thomas COLER – Boarder – b. 1865 Hull – aged 26 – Jeweller
Fred HASSELL – Boarder – b. 1863 Hungary – aged 28 – Wine Merchant
Sarah POLNER – Granddaughter – b. 1884 Whitechapel – aged 7

1881 Census

Address:

Camperdown House, Half Moon Passage, Whitechapel

Residents:

Nathan SAUNDERS – Head – b. 1815 Poland – aged 66 – Restaurant Proprietor
Hannah SAUNDERS – Daughter – b. 1856 Middlesex – aged 25
Leah SAUNDERS – Daughter – b. 1858 Middlesex – aged 23 – Tailoress
Rosa SAUNDERS – Daughter – b. 1860 Portsea – aged 21 – Domestic cook
Michael SAUNDERS – Son – b. 1861 Hampshire – aged 20 – Clothes Cutter

SAUNDERS, Annie – B-2-31

Mary TAYLOR – Domestic Servant
Joseph FEBERMAN – Hotel Porter
Joseph COHEN – Visitor – b. 1859 Hull – aged 22 – Commercial Traveller
Isaac GOLDMAN – Visitor – b. 1836 Middlesex – aged 45 – Jewellery Commercial Traveller
Hyman ASH – Visitor – b. 1838 Poland – aged 43 – Jewellery Commercial Traveller

1871 Census

Address:

Leman Street, Whitechapel

Residents:

Nathan SAUNDERS – Head – b. 1815 Poland – aged 56 - Tailor
B. SAUNDERS – Wife – b. 1825 Poland – aged 46
Anna SAUNDERS – Daughter – b. 1849 London – aged 22
Phillip SAUNDERS – Son – b. 1851 London – aged 20
Rosey SAUNDERS – Daughter – b. 1858 Hampshire – aged 13
Michael H. SAUNDERS – Son – b. 1861 Hampshire – aged 10

Marriage:

Nathan SAUNDERS to Annie NEWMAN – Q4 1882 MILE END OLD TOWN 1c 1147.

1901 Census

Address:

Camperdown House, Half Moon Passage, Whitechapel

Residents:

Abraham ISAACS – Head – b. 1847 Stepney – aged 54 – Restaurant & Hotel Proprietor
Maria ISAACS – Wife – b. 1848 Tower Hamlets – aged 53
Michael ISAACS – Son – b. 1877 Tower Hamlets – aged 24 – Watchmaker
Solomon ISAACS – Son – b. 1879 Tower Hamlets – aged 22 – Warehouseman
Aaron ISAACS – Son – b. 1880 Tower Hamlets – aged 21 – Silver Mounter
Lazarus ISAACS – Son – b. 1887 Tower Hamlets – aged 14
Hannah ISAACS – Daughter – b. 1875 Tower Hamlets – aged 26 – Dressmaker
Kate ISAACS – Daughter – b. 1881 Tower Hamlets – aged 20 – School Teacher
Isabel ISAACS – Daughter – b. 1883 Tower Hamlets – aged 18
Rebecca ISAACS – Daughter – b. 1886 Tower Hamlets – aged 15 – Dressmaker
Nathan SAUNDERS – Father-in-law – Widower – b. 1817 Russia – aged 84 – Retired Hotel Proprietor
Sarah POSNER – Niece – b. 1885 Bethnal Green – aged 16 – Dressmaker
David HENRIQUES – Boarder – b. 1871 Holland – aged 30 – Diamond Broker

Death:

Nathan SAUNDERS - Q1 1905 [91] ISLINGTON 1b 229
Buried at Plashet Cemetery – F-2-36 on 02 Jan 1905.

Jewish Chronicle – 06 Jan 1905

SAUNDERS – On the 1st of January, corresponding with 24th Tebet, at 46, Poet's Road, Nathan Saunders, late of Half Moon Passage, in his 90th year, beloved father of P. Saunders, of Johannesburg, Mrs Isaacs, of above address, Mrs Barnett, 30, Aldgate, Mrs Kemp, 89, Leconfield Road, N., and Mrs Fredman, of Norwich, and brother of Mrs Comer, 9, Percy Street, W.C. Deeply mourned by his sister, children, grandchildren, sons-in-law, relatives and friends. African and American papers please copy.

SOLOMONS, Fanny – B-2-29

Died: 18 Jan 1897
Buried: 15 Jan 1897
Partner: Abraham Solomons (d. 1903)
Aged: 64 years

Jewish Chronicle – 22 Jan 1897

SOLOMONS – On Wednesday, the 18th of January, at 116, Cannon Street Road, London, after a long and painful illness, Fanny, aged 64, beloved wife of Abraham Solomons, mother of Mrs I. Ehrenberg, 84, Battle Street, Elias Solomons, Reading, Mrs B. Cohen, Mrs Z. Crown, London, Mrs A. Kartz, Sydney. Deeply mourned by her sorrowing husband, sons, daughters, relatives and a large circle of friends. May her dear soul rest in peace. Australian and American papers please copy.

Jewish Chronicle – 11 Jun 1897

The tombstone in loving memory of the late Fanny Solomons, wife of Abraham Solomons, 116, Cannon Street Road, E., will be set at Plashet Cemetery on Sunday next, the 13th, at 3 o'clock. Relatives and friends are cordially invited to attend.

Death:
Q1 1897 [64] HACKNEY 1b 332 [Annie Marie Solomons].

1891 Census

Address:
116 Cannon Street Road, St. George in the East, London

Residents:
Abraham SOLOMONS – Head – b. 1831 Russian Poland – aged 60 – Tailor
Fanny SOLOMONS – Wife – b. 1832 Russian Poland – aged 59
John SOLOMONS – Son – b. 1872 Russian Poland – aged 19 – Tailor
Isaac SOLOMONS – Son – b. 1876 Russian Poland – aged 15 – Tailor

1881 Census

Address:
124 Cannon Street Road, St. George in the East

Residents:
Abraham SOLOMONS – Head – b. 1833 Poland – aged 48 – Tailor
Francis SOLOMONS – Wife – b. 1834 Poland – aged 47 - Tailoress
Kate SOLOMONS – Daughter – b. 1864 Whitechapel – aged 17 – Tailoress
Mark SOLOMONS – Son – b. 1865 Whitechapel – aged 16 – Tailor
Elias SOLOMONS – Son – b. 1867 Whitechapel – aged 14 – Tailor
Eve SOLOMONS – Daughter – b. 1870 Whitechapel – aged 11 – Scholar

SOLOMONS, Fanny – B-2-29

John SOLOMONS – Son – b. 1873 Whitechapel – aged 8 – Scholar
Isaac SOLOMONS – Son – b. 1876 Whitechapel – aged 5 – Scholar

1871 Census

Address:
4 New Road, Mile End Old Town

Residents:
Abraham SOLOMONS – Head – b. 1832 Poland – aged 39 – Tailor
Fanny SOLOMONS – Wife – b. 1835 – aged 36
Caroline SOLOMONS – Daughter – b. 1855 – aged 16
Maria SOLOMONS – Daughter – b. 1858 – aged 13
Kate SOLOMONS – Daughter – b. 1863 Middlesex – aged 8
Mark SOLOMONS – Son – b. 1865 Middlesex – aged 6
Elias SOLOMONS – Son – b. 1867 Middlesex – aged 4
Eve SOLOMONS – Daughter – b. 1870 Middlesex – aged 1
Mary A. FRANCIS – Domestic Servant

Death:
Abraham SOLOMONS – Q3 1903 [75] MILE END 1c 265.
Buried at Plashet Cemetery – E-11-49 on 24 Sep 1903.

VAN PRAAGH, Moses – A-11-3

Died: 27 Dec 1897
Buried: 28 Dec 1897
Hebrew Name: Moshe bar Ya'akov
Partner: Hannah van Praagh (d. 1892)
Aged: 69 years

Jewish Chronicle – 31 Dec 1897

VAN PRAAGH – On the 27th of December, Moses Van Praagh, of 30, Scarborough Street, Goodman's Fields, E., aged 69. Deeply mourned by his sorrowing sons, daughter, brothers, relatives and friends. May his soul rest in peace. Dutch papers please copy.

Jewish Chronicle – 18 Nov 1898

The tombstone in loving memory of Moses Van Praagh, late of 30, Scarborough Street, E., will be set at Plashet Cemetery on Sunday next, November 20th, at 3 o'clock.

Death:
Q4 1897 [70] HACKNEY 1b 379.

VAN PRAAGH, Moses – A-11-3

1891 Census

Address:

30 Scarborough Street, St. Mary Whitechapel, Tower Hamlets

Residents:

Moses VAN PRAAGH – Head – b. 1829 Amsterdam – aged 62 – Cigar Maker
Hannah VAN PRAAGH – Wife – b. 1827 Amsterdam – aged 64
Jacob VAN PRAAGH – Son – b. 1860 Whitechapel – aged 31 – Teacher

1881 Census

Address:

10 Commercial Road, Whitechapel

Residents:

Moses VAN PRAAGH – Head – b. 1831 Amsterdam – aged 50 – Cigar Maker
Hannah VAN PRAAGH – Wife – b. 1828 Amsterdam – aged 53
Jacob VAN PRAAGH – Son – b. 1854 Whitechapel – aged 27 – Scholar
Clara VAN PRAAGH – Daughter – b. 1861 Whitechapel – aged 20 – Scholar
Abraham VAN PRAAGH – Son – b. 1864 Whitechapel – aged 17 – Engraver

1871 Census

Address:

Tewkesbury Buildings, St. Mary Whitechapel

Residents:

Moses VAN PRAAGH – Head – b. 1829 Netherlands – aged 42
Hannah VAN PRAAGH – Wife – b. 1827 Netherlands – aged 44
Jacob VAN PRAAGH – Son – b. 1860 Netherlands – aged 11
Clara VAN PRAAGH - Daughter – b. 1861 London – aged 10
Abraham VAN PRAAGH – Son – b. 1862 London – aged 9

Death:

Hannah VAN PRAAGH – Q2 1892 [66] WHITECHAPEL 1c 222.
Buried at West Ham Cemetery – E-8-2 on 17 Apr 1892.

Jewish Chronicle – 22 Apr 1892

On the 14th of April, at 30, Scarborough Street, Goodman's Fields, Hannah, wife of Moses van Praagh, and beloved mother of Jacob van Praagh, Clara Wynschenk and Abraham van Praagh, of 14, Saint Mark Street, E., aged 66. Deeply mourned by her sorrowing husband, children, brothers and sisters – May her dear soul rest in peace.

WEINRABE, Esther – B-2-28

Died: 12 Jan 1897
Buried: 14 Jan 1897
Partner: Abraham Maurice Weinrabe (d. 1908)
Aged: 39 years

Jewish Chronicle – 15 Jan 1897

WEINRABE – On the 12th of January, after a long and painful illness, borne with great patience, aged 39, Esther, the beloved wife of Maurice Weinrabe, 37, Argyle Road, Mile End, and sister of Mrs George Solomon, 29, Amhurst Road, Hackney. Deeply mourned by her husband, children and friends. May her dear soul rest in peace. Amen. Shiva at both addresses. Australian papers please copy.

Jewish Chronicle – 17 Nov 1899

The tombstone in memory of the late Mrs Esther Weinrabe and Mrs Sarah Weinrabe [D-7-8] will be consecrated at 3.30 on Sunday, November 19th at Plashet Cemetery. Friends and relatives please accept this, the only intimation.

Death:

Q1 1897 [40] WHITECHAPEL 1c 187.

1891 Census

Address:

14 Burdett Road, Mile End Old Town

Residents:

Abraham Maurice WEINRABE – Head – b. 1852 London – aged 39 – Traveller
Esther WEINRABE – Wife – b. 1855 Birmingham – aged 36
Leah WEINRABE – Daughter – b. 1878 London – aged 13 – Scholar
Jacob WEINRABE – Son – b. 1882 London – aged 9 – Scholar
Solomon WEINRABE – Son – b. 1886 London – aged 5 – Scholar
Joseph WEINRABE – Son – b. 1887 London – aged 4 - Scholar
Jennie WEINRABE – Daughter – b. 1883 London – aged 8 – Scholar
Harry WEINRABE – Son – b. 1874 London – aged 17
Arabella – Domestic Servant

1881 Census

Address:

28 Turner Street, Mile End Old Town

Residents:

Abraham Maurice WEINRABE – Head – b. 1853 Whitechapel – aged 28 –Traveller
Esther WEINRABE – Wife – b. 1855 Birmingham – aged 26
Leah WEINRABE – Daughter – b. 1878 Mile End – aged 3

Louis WEINRABE – Son – b. 1880 Mile End – aged 1
Jane WEST – General Domestic Servant

Marriage:
Abraham Maurice WEINRABE to Esther SIMONDS – Q3 1875 LONDON CITY 1c 172.

1901 Census

Address:
8 Gotha Street, Hackney

Residents:
Maurice WEINRABE – Head – Widower – b. 1853 Whitechapel – aged 48 – Commercial Traveller
Leah WEINRABE – Daughter – b. 1879 Mile End – aged 22
Jennie WEINRABE – Daughter – b. 1883 Mile End – aged 18
Joseph WEINRABE – Son – b. 1887 Mile End – aged 14
Francis WEINRABE – Niece – b. 1898 Mile End – aged 3

Marriage:
Maurice WEINRABE to Annie KEYS – Q3 1906 WEST HAM 4a 686.

1911 Census

Address:
168a Romford Road, Forest Gate, London E.

Residents:
Anna Maria WEINRABE – Head – Widow – b. 1863 London – aged 48 – Manageress of a Public House
Clara EDMUNDS – Sister – b. 1872 London – aged 39 – Barmaid
Jennie WEINRABE – Stepdaughter – b. 1883 London – aged 28

Death:
Abraham M. WEINRABE – Q4 1908 [56] WEST HAM 4a 28.
Buried at Plashet Cemetery – I-11-15 on 16 Dec 1908.

Jewish Chronicle – 18 Dec 1908

WEINRABE – On the 14th of December, at 1, Windsor Road, Forest Gate, Maurice, the dearly beloved husband of Nance, and father of Jennie, Jacob, Solomon and Joseph Weinrabe, and brother of Harry Weinrabe. Deeply mourned by his loving wife and children. God rest his soul in peace. Amen. Australian and American papers please copy. Shiva as above.
WEINRABE – On the 14th of December, at his residence, 1, Windsor Road, Forest Gate, Maurice Weinrabe, brother of Solly. Deeply mourned by his brother. Shiva at 50, Grafton Street, Mile End.
WEINRABE – On the 14th of December, at his residence, 1, Windsor Road,

Forest, Gate, Maurice Weinrabe, suddenly, aged 59. Deeply mourned by his son Louis, daughter Leah, and grandchildren. May his dear soul rest in peace. Shiva at 20, Mossford Street, Mile End.

Jewish Chronicle – 26 Feb 1909

WEINRABE – The tombstone in loving memory of the late Abraham Maurice Weinrabe will be consecrated at Plashet Cemetery on Sunday next, February 29th, at 4 p.m.

WOOLF, Sarah – A-9-7

Died: 29 Sep 1987
Buried: 30 Sep 1897
Partner: Raphael Woolf (d. 1912)
Parents: Elizabeth & Solomon Lazarus
Aged: 42 years

Jewish Chronicle – 01 Oct 1897

WOOLF – On the 29th of September, at 7, Pretoria Avenue, Walthamstow, Sarah Woolf, the dearly beloved daughter of Elizabeth and the late Solomon Lazarus, and sister of Mrs H. Wybrow, Birmingham, and Mrs Lewis Levy, 101, Highbury New Park, N., aged 42. God rest her dear soul.
WOOLF – On the 29th of September, at 7, Pretoria Avenue, Walthamstow, Sarah, wife of Raphael Woolf, aged 42. Deeply mourned.

Jewish Chronicle – 19 Aug 1898

The tombstone in memory of the late Sarah Woolf, of 21, Princes Square, will be set at the Plashet Cemetery on Sunday next, the 21st inst., at 4 o'clock.

Death:

Q3 1897 [42] WEST HAM 4a 233.

Marriage:

Raphael WOOLF to Sarah LAZARUS – Q3 1878 LONDON CITY 1c 182.

1881 Census

Address:

201 Kentish Town Road, St. Pancras

Residents:

Raphael I. WOOLF – Head – b. 1850 London – aged 31 – Tailor & Outfitter
Sara WOOLF – Wife – b. 1856 Bethnal Green – aged 25
Phoebe WOOLF – Daughter – b. 1880 St. Pancras – aged 1
Solomon S. WOOLF – Son – b. 1881 St. Pancras – aged 0

Margaret METCALF – General Domestic Servant

1901 Census

Address:

7 Pretoria Avenue, Walthamstow – registered as WOLF

Residents:

Raphael WOOLF – Head – Widower – b. 1850 London – Aged 51 - Tailors Cutter
Phoebe WOOLF – Daughter – b. 1880 St. Pancras – aged 21
Sydney WOOLF – Son – b. 1881 St. Pancras – aged 20 – Elementary School Teacher
Alfred WOOLF – Son – b. 1883 St. Pancras – aged 18 – Pupil Teacher in Elementary School
Lewis WOOLF – Son – b. 1887 Stoke Newington – aged 14
Harry A. WOOLF – Son – b. 1889 Tottenham – aged 12
Rebecca PARKER – General Domestic Servant

Death:

Raphael Isaac WOOLF – Q1 1912 [63] WEST HAM 4a 401.
Buried at Plashet Cemetery – K-30-8 on 01 Feb 1912.

1898

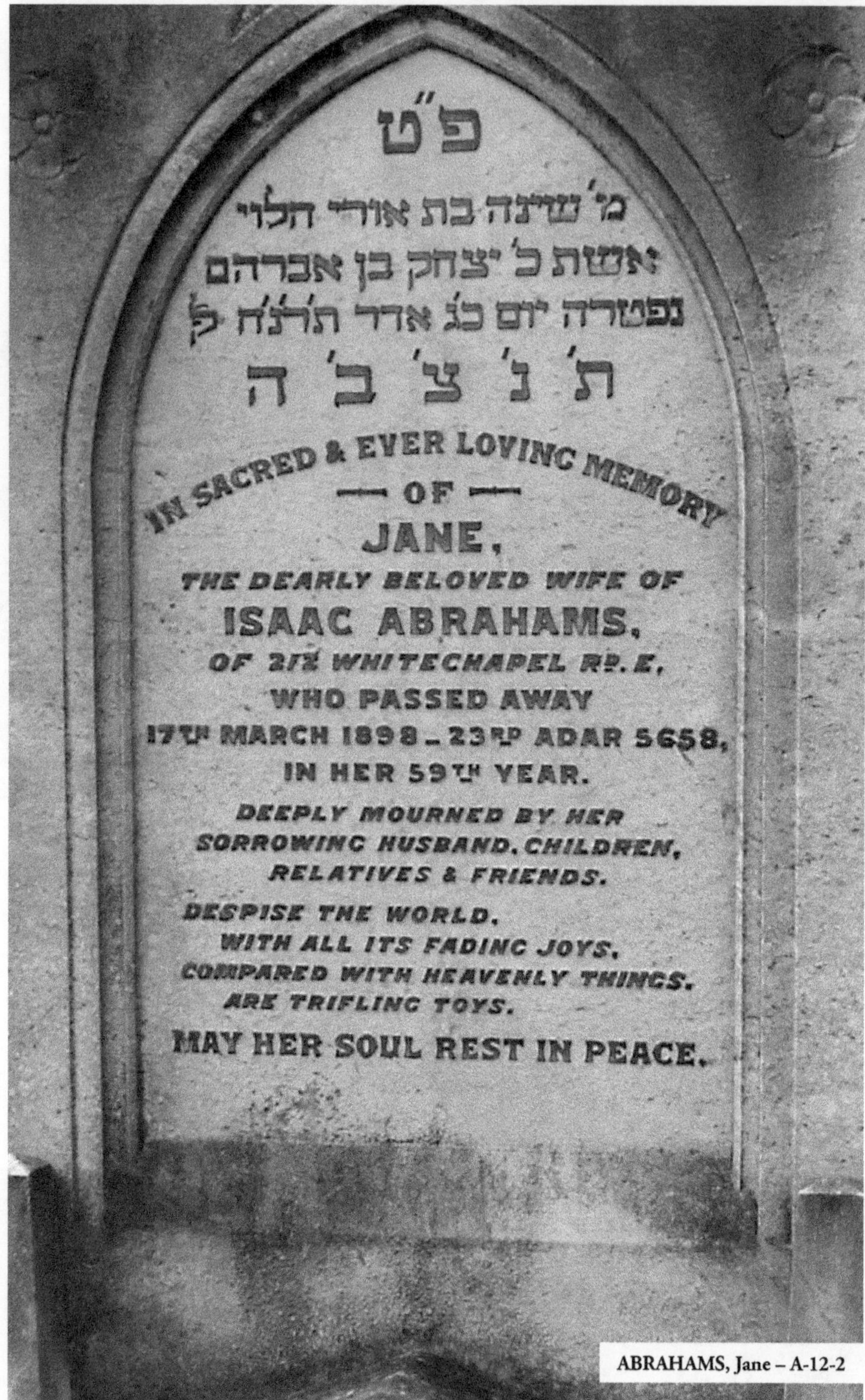

ABRAHAMS, Jane – A-12-2

ABRAHAMS, Jane – A-12-2

Died: 17 Mar 1898
Buried: 20 Mar 1898
Hebrew Name: Sheena bat Uri Halevi
Partner: Isaac Abrahams (d. 1921)
Aged: 59th year

Jewish Chronicle – 18 Mar 1898

ABRAHAMS – on the 17th of March, at 212, Whitechapel Road, Jane, the dearly beloved wife of Isaac Abrahams, in her 59th year. Deeply mourned by her sorrowing husband and children – Funeral will leave the above address Sunday next, the 20th inst.at 1.30 p.m. Friends and relatives kindly accept this, the only intimation. No flowers by request.

Jewish Chronicle – 03 Mar 1899

The tombstone in memory of Jane, the beloved wife of Isaac Abrahams, of 212, Whitechapel Road, will be set at Plashet Cemetery, on Sunday next, the 5th March (Jahrzeit), at 4 p.m. Friends and relatives kindly accept this, the only intimation.

Death:
Q1 1898 [54] WHITECHAPEL 1c 257.

1891 Census

Address:
212 Whitechapel Road, Whitechapel

Residents:
Isaac ABRAHAM – Head – b. 1840 London – aged 51 – Cigar Manufacturer
Jane ABRAHAM – Wife – b. 1840 London – aged 51
Philip ABRAHAM – Son – b. 1869 Whitechapel – aged – 22 – Commercial Traveller
Lawrence ABRAHAM – Son – b. 1870 London – aged 21 - Tobacconists Assistant
Abraham ABRAHAM – Son – b. 1872 Whitechapel – aged 19 – Tobacconists Warehouseman
Joshua ABRAHAM – Son – b. 1874 Whitechapel – aged 17 – Cigar Maker
Julia ABRAHAM – Daughter – b. 1875 Whitechapel – aged 16 – Cigar Sorter
John ABRAHAM – Son – b. 1876 Whitechapel – aged 15 – Opticians Assistant
Ellen BULL – Domestic Servant

1881 Census

Address:
16 Newcastle Street, Whitechapel

Residents:

Isaac ABRAHAMS – Head – b. 1841 Godston – aged 40 – Cigar Maker
Jane ABRAHAMS – Wife – b. 1840 London – aged 41
Philip ABRAHAMS – Son – b. 1869 Whitechapel – aged 12 – Scholar
Laurence ABRAHAMS – Son – b. 1870 Aldgate – aged 11 – Scholar
Abraham ABRAHAMS – Son – b. 1872 Whitechapel – aged 9 – Scholar
Joshua ABRAHAMS – Son – b. 1874 Whitechapel – aged 7 – Scholar
Julia ABRAHAMS – Daughter – b. 1875 Whitechapel – aged 6 – Scholar
John ABRAHAMS – Son – b. 1877 Whitechapel – aged 4 – Scholar
Ann MURPHY – Domestic Servant

1871 Census

Address:

Angel Court, Aldgate, London

Residents:

Isaac ABRAHAMS – Head – b. 1838 Middlesex – aged 33
Jane ABRAHAMS – Wife – b. 1838 Middlesex – aged 33
Philip ABRAHAMS – Son – b. 1869 Middlesex – aged 2
Lawrence ABRAHAMS – Son – b. 1870 Middlesex – aged 1
Ann CANNORAN – Servant
Kate LEONARD – Servant

Marriage:

Isaac ABRAHAMS to Jane LEVY – Q3 1866 LONDON CITY 1c 218.

1901 Census

Address:

136 Whitechapel Road, Whitechapel

Residents:

Isaac ABRAHAMS – Head – Widower – b. 1840 London – aged 61 – Cigar Manufacturer
Joshua ABRAHAMS – Son – b. 1874 London – aged 27 – Commercial Traveller
Julia ABRAHAMS – Daughter – b. 1875 London – aged 26
John ABRAHAMS – Son – b. 1877 London – aged 24 – Commercial Traveller

1911 Census

Address:

68 Gloucester Road, Finsbury Park, N.

Residents:

Alfred ABRAHAMS – Head – b. 1877 Aldgate – aged 34 – Warehouseman
Julia ABRAHAMS – Wife (of 9 years) – b. 1876 Whitechapel – aged 35
Hilda ABRAHAMS – Daughter – b. 1904 Finsbury Park – aged 7

Cyril ABRAHAMS – Son – b. 1906 Finsbury Park – aged 5
Nancy ABRAHAMS – Daughter – b. 1910 Finsbury Park – aged 1
Isaac ABRAHAMS – Father-in-law – b. 1840 Walworth – aged 71 – Retired
John ABRAHAMS – Brother-in-law – b. 1877 Whitechapel – aged 34 – Manufacturers Agent
Mary MARSHALL – General Domestic Servant
Susan SILCOCK – Domestic Nurse

Death:

Isaac ABRAHAMS – Q1 1921 [80] HACKNEY 1b 404.
Buried at Willesden Cemetery – MX-7-23 on 11 Jan 1921.

Jewish Chronicle – 14 Jan 1921

ABRAHAMS – On the 8th of January, at 68, Gloucester Road, Finsbury Park, N.4, Isaac Abrahams, in his 81st year. Deeply mourned.
ABRAHAMS – On the 8th of January, Isaac Abrahams, beloved father of Joshua Abrahams, of "The Duke's Head", Whitechapel Road, E. Shiva at 3, Wilbury Avenue, Hove.
ABRAHAMS – On the 8th of January, at 68, Gloucester Road, Finsbury Park, N.4, Isaac Abrahams, brother of Mrs Zalic Cohen, 3, Turner's Road, Burdett Road, E.

ABRAHAMS, Kate – A-11-20

Died: **21 Apr 1898**
Buried: **24 Apr 1898**
Hebrew Name: **Gaula bat Yehuda**
Partner: **Henry Abrahams (d. 1893)**
Aged: **51 years**

Jewish Chronicle – 29 Apr 1898

ABRAHAMS – On the 21st of April, after a few days illness, Mrs Kate Abrahams, aged 51. Beloved daughter of the late Lewis and Hannah Samuels, 1 and 2 Ellison Street, Aldgate. Deeply regretted by her sorrowing daughter, brothers, sisters, nieces and nephews and a large circle of friends. God rest her deal soul.

Jewish Chronicle – 03 Jun 1898

The tombstone of Mrs Kate Abrahams (Kate Samuels) will be set on Sunday next, June 5th, at Plashet Cemetery, at 4.30. Relatives and friends please accept this intimation.

Death:

Q2 1898 [49] WHITECHAPEL 1c 172.

ABRAHAMS, Kate – A-11-20

1891 Census

Address:

13 Wentworth Court, Spitalfields, London

Residents:

Harry ABRAHAMS – Head – b. 1843 London – aged 48 – Fish Salesman
Kate ABRAHAMS – Wife – b. 1847 London – aged 44
Isaac ABRAHAMS – Son – b. 1876 London – aged 15 – Scholar
Maria ABRAHAMS – Daughter – b. 1881 London – aged 10 – Scholar
Hannah ABRAHAMS – Daughter – b. 1888 London – aged 3
Margaret ABRAHAMS – Domestic servant

1881 Census

Address:

13 Wentworth Street, Wentworth Court, Spitalfields

Residents:

Henry ABRAHAMS – Head – b. 1843 Whitechapel – aged 38 – Fishmonger
Elizabeth ABRAHAMS – Wife – b. 1848 Whitechapel – aged 33
Harriett ABRAHAMS – Daughter – b. 1871 Whitechapel – aged 10
Benjamin ABRAHAMS – Son – b. 1873 Whitechapel – aged 8
Isaac ABRAHAMS – Son – b. 1875 Whitechapel – aged 6
Abraham ABRAHAMS – Son – b. 1878 Whitechapel – aged 3
Maria ABRAHAMS – Daughter – b. 1881 – aged 0

Marriage:

Harry ABRAHAMS to Kate SAMUELS – Q4 1885 LONDON CITY 1c 173.

Marriage:

Henry ABRAHAMS to Elizabeth MEDCALF – Q2 1869 MILE END 1c 1027.

Death:

Elizabeth ABRAHAMS – Q1 1885 [33] WHITECHAPEL 1c 204.

Death:

Harry ABRAHAMS – Q4 1893 [50] WHITECHAPEL 1c 221.
Buried at West Ham Cemetery – I-10-30 on 18 Jan 1894.

ANGEL, Coleman – A-14-12

Died: 13 Aug 1898
Buried: 15 Aug 1898
Partner: Jane Angel (d. 1911)
Aged: 66th year

ANGEL, Coleman – A-14-12

Jewish Chronicle – 18 Aug 1898

ANGEL – On Saturday the 13th of August at 61 Parkholme Road, Dalston, after 5 days' illness, Coleman Angel, the beloved husband of Jane Angel, in his 66th year, and beloved father of Mark Angel, 28, Colvestone Crescent, Dalston, Mrs Sarah Zimmerman, 3, Albert Square, E., Mrs Esther Nathan, 245, Roman Road, Bow, Mrs Louie Goldhill, 264, Dalston Lane, Hackney, Mrs Rebecca Myers, 88, Spencer Street, Liverpool, and of Moss Angel. Deeply mourned by his sorrowing wife, loving children, grandchildren and a large circle of friends. God rest his dear soul – Shiva at 61 Parkholme Road. Australian and American papers please copy.

Jewish Chronicle – 21 Apr 1899

The tombstone in loving memory of Coleman Angel, late of 61, Parkholme-road, Dalston, will be set at the Plashet Cemetery, on Sunday next, April 23rd, at 3 o'clock. Relatives and friends will please accept this, the only intimation.

Death:

Q3 1898 [65] HACKNEY 1b 343.

1891 Census

Address:

7 St. Marks Road, Hackney

Residents:

Coleman ANGEL – Head – b. 1836 Russia – aged 55 – Importer and Exporter of Mouldings
Jane ANGEL – Wife – b. 1836 Germany – aged 55
Mark J. ANGEL – Son – b. 1867 London – aged 24 – Traveller in Mouldings
Louise ANGEL – Daughter – b. 1869 London – aged 22 – Clerk
Rebecca B. ANGEL – Daughter – b. 1872 London – aged 19
Moss J. ANGEL – Son – b. 1873 London – aged 18 – Shop Assistant
Alice TAYLOR – General Servant

1881 Census

Address:

116 Commercial Street, Spitalfields

Residents:

Coleman ANGEL – Head – b. 1836 Poland – aged 45 – Glass Cutter
Jane ANGEL – Wife – b. 1836 Germany – aged 45
Sarah ANGEL – Daughter – b. 1862 Middlesex – aged 19 – Buttonhole Maker (Tailor)
Esther ANGEL – Daughter – b. 1864 Middlesex – aged 17 – Teacher
Barnett ANGEL – Son – b. 1866 Middlesex – aged 15 – Assist in business
Mark ANGEL – Son – b. 1867 Middlesex – aged 14 – Assist in business
Louisa ANGEL – Daughter – b. 1869 Middlesex – aged 12 – Scholar

Rebecca ANGEL – Daughter – b. 1872 Middlesex – aged 9 – Scholar
Mossy ANGEL – Son – b. 1876 Middlesex – aged 5
Margaret CALANS – General Servant

1871 Census

Address:
Commercial Street, Christ Church Spitalfields

Residents:
Coleman ANGEL – Head – b. 1833 Poland – aged 38
Jane ANGEL – Wife – b. 1833 Germany – aged 38
Kitty L. ANGEL – Daughter – b. 1858 Middlesex – aged 13
Sarah ANGEL – Daughter – b. 1861 Middlesex – aged 10
Esther ANGEL – Daughter – b. 1863 Middlesex – aged 8
Barnet ANGEL – Son – b. 1866 Middlesex – aged 5
Mark ANGEL – Son – b. 1867 Middlesex – aged 4
Louisa ANGEL – Daughter – b. 1869 Middlesex – aged 2
Mary AURE – Domestic Servant

1861 Census

Address:
Anns Street, Wentworth Street, Whitechapel

Residents:
Coleman ANGEL – Head – b. 1832 Poland – aged 29 – Glass cutter
Jane ANGEL – Wife – b. 1833 Whitechapel – aged 28
Jessie ANGEL – Daughter – b. 1857 Whitechapel – aged 4
Sarah ANGEL – Daughter – b. 1861 Whitechapel – aged 1 month
Annah SCHAT – Domestic Servant

Marriage:
Coleman ANGEL to Jane SAMUELS – Q1 1856 LONDON CITY 1c 258.

Nationality and Naturalisation:
Angel, Coleman from Russia, Resident in London
Certificate A4888 issued 16 Sep 1886
Reference: HO 144/179/A44558.

Death:
Jane ANGEL – Q3 1911 [81] HACKNEY 1b 462.
Buried at Plashet Cemetery – A-14-13 on 29 Aug 1911.

Jewish Chronicle – 01 Sep 1911

ANGEL – On the 27th of August, at 18, Ravensdale Road, Stamford Hill, Jane, relict of the late Coleman Angel, in her 82nd year; mother of Mrs S. Zimmerman,

58, Linthorpe Road, N.; Mrs Joe Nathan, 256, Upper Tooting Road, S.W., Mrs Shirley Goldhill, 45, Amhurst Park, N., Mrs S.J. Myers, 65, Cazenove Road, N. Shiva at 58, Linthorpe Road, Stamford Hill.
ANGEL – On Sunday, the 27th of August, Jane, relict of the late Coleman Angel, beloved mother of Mrs Henry Zender, Zender Lodge, 64, Upper Clapton Road. Shiva at above address.
ANGEL – On the 27th of August, at 18, Ravensdale Road, N., Jane, mother of Mark and Moss Angel. May her deal soul rest in peace. Shiva, 109, Clapton Common, N.
ANGEL – On the 27th of August, at 18, Ravensdale Road, Stamford Hill, Jane Angel, beloved sister of Mrs Betsy Crook. Shiva, 58, Sandringham Road, Dalston.

Jewish Chronicle – 15 Mar 1912

The tombstone in memory of the late Jane Angel will be set at Plashet Cemetery next Sunday, March 17th, at 3.30.

BARDER, Hannah – A-13-25

Died: **07 Jul 1898**
Buried: **10 Jul 1898**
Husband: **Lewis/Louis Barder (d. 1906)**
Aged: **73 years**

Jewish Chronicle – 16 Jul 1898

BARDER – On the 7th of July at 40, Horton-road, Hackney, Hannah, the beloved wife of Lewis Barder, and mother of Isaac Barder of 41, Elizabeth Street, Manchester, of Levy Barder, 111, Brondesbury Villas, Kilburn, and of Jack Barder, Greencroft Gardens, Hampstead, of Mrs Shonman, of 213, Richmond-road, Hackney, of Arnold Barder, of 1, Callcott-road, Kilburn, of Phillip Barder, of 223, Richmond-road, Hackney, of Albert Barder, 156, Bethune Road, Stamford Hill, of Sam Barder, of 25, College Green, Bristol, and of Esther and Sarah Barder of Horton Road, Hackney. May her dear soul rest in peace.

Jewish Chronicle – 09 Jun 1899

The tombstone in loving memory of Hannah, the beloved wife of Louis Barder, of 40, Horton Road, Hackney, will be set at the Plashet Cemetery on Sunday, June 11th, at 4 o'clock. Relatives and friends will please accept this, the only intimation.

Death:

Q3 1898 [73] HACKNEY 1b 334.

1891 Census

Address:

40 Horton Road, Hackney

Residents:

Louis BARDER – Head - b. 1827 Austria – aged 64 – Fancy Trims Maker
Hannah BARDER – Wife – b. 1828 Austria – aged 63
Esther BARDER – Daughter – b. 1865 London – aged 26 – Milliner
Samuel BARDER – Son – b. 1867 London – aged 24 – Furrier
Sarah BARDER – Daughter – b. 1870 Manchester – aged 21
Emma SHEARSBY – Domestic Servant (deaf)

1901 Census

Address:

40 Horton Road, Hackney

Residents:

Louis BARDER – Head – Widower – b. 1827 Germany – aged 74 – Furrier
Sarah BARDER – Daughter – b. 1873 Manchester – aged 28 – Drapers Saleswoman
Sarah WATSON – General Domestic Servant

Death:

Louis BARDER – Q3 1906 [81] FYLDE 8e 420.
Buried at Willesden Cemetery – G-K-28 on 08 Jul 1906.

Jewish Chronicle – 13 Jul 1906

BARDER – On the 5th of July, in his 82nd year, Louis Barder, of 111, Brondesbury Villas, Kilburn. Deeply mourned by his sorrowing children, Isaac Barder, 14, Bignor Street, Cheetham, Manchester, Levy Barder, 111, Brondesbury Villas, N.W., Jack Barder, 2, William Street, S.W., Arnold Barder, 1, Callcott Road, N.W., Phillip Barder, 17, Lordship Park, N., Albert Barder, 7, Garlinge Road, N.W., Sam Barder, 26, College Green, Bristol, Mrs Shonman, 10, Gloucester Road, N., Mrs Fainlight, 16, St. Margarets Avenue, Hornsey, Mrs Sherman, 16, Bridge Street, Greenwich, also by his grandchildren and great grandchildren. May his dear soul rest in peace.

BARNETT, Nancy – A-13-4

Died: 20 May 1898
Buried: 22 May 1898
Hebrew Name: Itznota bat Avraham
Partner: Joshua Barnett (d. 1873)
Aged: 75 years

BARNETT, Nancy – A-13-4

Jewish Chronicle – 27 May 1898

BARNETT –On Friday, the 20th of May, at 104A, Bridge-street, Burdett-road, Nancy, relict of the late Joshua Barnett, of Harrow Alley, in her 75th year; mother of Baron Barnett, 12-1/2, Artillery-passage, E.C., Elias Barnett, 26, Cutler-street, City, Mrs White, 5, Tenter-street North, Mrs Taylor, 120, Antil-road, Bow, Mrs Wolfers, 104D, Bridge-street, Mark Barnett, 60, Landseer-road, N., Mrs Benabo, 17, White Horse-lane, Sam Barnett, No. 1, Upper Montague-street, Bow, Abraham Barnett and Mrs J. Simmonds, 12, Ormside Street, S.E. Deeply mourned by her loving children, sisters, grandchildren, relatives and a large circle of friends. May her dear soul rest in peace. Amen. Foreign papers please copy.

Jewish Chronicle – 11 Nov 1898

The tombstone in loving memory of the late Nancy Barnett of Bridge-street, Burdett-road, relict of Joshua Barnett of Harrow-alley, will be set on Sunday next, 13th inst., at Plashet Cemetery, at 3 p.m.

Death:

Q2 1898 [74] MILE END 1c 287.

1891 Census

Address:

77 Bancroft Road, Mile End Old Town

Residents:

Nancy BARNETT – Head – Widow – b. 1824 London – aged 67
Elias BARNETT – Son – b. 1854 London – aged 37 – Dealer in 2nd Hand Clothes

1881 Census

Address:

14 Swan Street, Whitechapel

Residents:

Nancy BARNETT – Head – Widow – b. 1824 London – aged 57 – Dealer in Lady's 2nd Hand Old Clothes
Mary BARNETT – Daughter – b. 1852 London – aged 29
Elias BARNETT – Son – b. 1854 London – aged 27 – Dealer in 2nd Hand Clothes
Fanny BARNETT – Daughter – b. 1855 London – aged 26 – Tailoress
Asher BARNETT – Son – b. 1857 London – aged 24 – General Dealer
Lizzie BARNETT – Daughter – b. 1859 London – aged 22 – Tailoress
Samuel BARNETT – Son – b. 1862 London - aged 19 – Tailor Cutter
Rebecca BARNETT – Daughter – b. 1864 London – aged 17 – Feather Trade
Isabella BARNETT – Daughter – b. 1867 London – aged 14 – Feather Trade

1871 Census

Address:

9 Harrow Alley, Aldgate, London

Residents:

Joshua BARNETT – Head – b. 1816 Middlesex – aged 55
Nancy BARNETT – Wife – b. 1824 Middlesex – aged 47
Baron BARNETT – Son – b. 1849 Middlesex – aged 22
Abraham BARNETT – Son – b. 1850 Middlesex – aged 21
Mary BARNETT – Daughter – b. 1851 Middlesex – aged 20
Elias BARNETT – Son – b. 1852 Middlesex – aged 19
Fanny BARNETT – Daughter – b. 1855 Middlesex – aged 16
Asher BARNETT – Son – b. 1857 Middlesex – aged 14
Elizabeth BARNETT – Daughter – b. 1859 Middlesex – aged 12
Mark BARNETT – Son – b. 1860 Middlesex – aged 11
Samuel BARNETT – Son – b. 1862 Middlesex – aged 9
Rebecca BARNETT – Daughter – b. 1864 Middlesex – aged 7
Isabella BARNETT – Daughter – b. 1867 Middlesex – aged 4

1861 Census

Address:

9 Harrow Alley, St. Botolph Aldgate, City of London

Residents:

Joshua BARNETT – Head – b. 1820 London – aged 41 - General Dealer
Nancy BARNETT – Wife – b. 1824 London – aged 37
Lewis BARNETT – Son – b. 1845 London – aged 16 – General Dealer
Baron BARNETT – Son – b. 1849 London – aged 12
Abraham BARNETT – Son – b. 1850 London – aged 11
Mary BARNETT – Daughter – b. 1851 London – aged 10
Elias BARNETT – Son – b. 1853 London – aged 8
Fanny BARNETT – Daughter – b. 1855 London – aged 6
Asher BARNETT – Son – b. 1856 London – aged 5
Elizabeth BARNETT – Daughter – b. 1859 London – aged 2
Mark BARNETT – Son – b. 1860 London – aged 1
Hannah BATTEY – General Servant

1851 Census

Address:

11 Ebenezer Square, St. Botolph Aldgate, London

Residents:

Joshua BARNETT – Head – b. 1816 Spitalfields – aged 35 – General Dealer
Mary BARNETT – Wife – b. 1824 Whitechapel – aged 27 – General Dealer
Lewis BARNETT – Son – b. 1845 Aldgate – aged 6

Baron BARNETT – Son – b. 1849 Aldgate – aged 2
Abraham BARNETT – Son – b. 1850 Aldgate – aged 1
Mary BARNETT – Daughter – b. 1851 Aldgate – aged 3 months
Ellen MURPHY – Domestic Servant

Marriage:
Joshua BARNETT to Nancy BENJAMIN – Q2 1844 LONDON CITY 2 177.

Death:
Joshua BARNETT – Q4 1873 [58] LONDON CITY 1c 9.
Buried at West Ham Cemetery (cemetery reference unknown).

Jewish Chronicle – 26 Dec 1873

On the 20th inst., at 9, Harrow Alley, Houndsditch, after a protracted illness, Joshua Barnett, in his 59th year. May his soul rest in peace. Cape, Australian and American papers please copy.

Jewish Chronicle – 29 May 1874

Mrs Barnett, of 9, Harrow Alley, Houndsditch, before to inform her relatives and friends that the tombstone of her late lamented husband, Josh Barnett, will be set at the West Ham Cemetery, on Sunday next, 31st inst., at 4 o'clock.

COHEN, Elias – A-12-7

Died: **25 Mar 1898**
Buried: **28 Mar 1898**
Partner: **Kitty Cohen (d. 1915)**
Aged: **64 years**

Jewish Chronicle – 01 Apr 1898

COHEN – On Friday, the 25th March, at 9, Great Prescot Street, Goodman's Fields, Elias (Eiley) Cohen, beloved husband of Kitty Cohen, and beloved uncle of Henry and Eiley Cohen. God rest his soul. Shiva at above.
COHEN – On the 25th of March, at 9, Great Prescot Street, Elias (Eiley) Cohen, brother of Isaac Cohen, 48, Nicholas Street, St. Peter's Road, Mile End. May his soul rest in peace.
COHEN – On Friday, the 25th of March, at 9 Great Prescot Street, Elias Cohen, the beloved brother of Mrs Michael Isaacs and Mrs Simeon Levy. Shiva at 307, Mile End Road, E. God rest his soul.

COHEN, Elias – A-12-7

Jewish Chronicle – 22 Jul 1898

The tombstone in memory of Elias Cohen, late of 9, Great Prescot Street, is to be set on Sunday next, July 24th, at Plashet Cemetery, at 4 pm. Relatives and friends please accept this, the only intimation.

Death:

Q1 1898 [64] WHITECHAPEL 1c 268.

1891 Census

Address:

9 Great Prescot Street, Whitechapel, London, Tower Hamlets

Residents:

Elias COHEN – Head – b. 1836 London – aged 55 – Tailor
Kate COHEN – Wife – b. 1835 London – aged 56
Moss LEVY – Uncle – b. 1814 London – aged 77 – General Dealer
Esther CONSTABLE – Domestic Servant
Henry COHEN – Nephew – b. 1876 London – aged 15 – Manager
Elias COHEN – Nephew – b. 1878 London – aged 13 – Clerk

1881 Census

Address:

4 Hutchinson Street, St. Botolph Without Aldgate

Residents:

Elias COHEN – Head – b. 1836 London – aged 45 – Tailor
Kate COHEN – Wife – b. 1835 London – aged 46
Moss LEVY – Uncle – b. 1813 London – aged 58 – General Dealer
Henry COHEN – Nephew – b. 1876 London – aged 5
Helen HOLLAND – Domestic Servant

1871 Census

Address:

Cobb's Yard, Christ Church

Residents:

Elias COHEN – Head – b. 1835 Middlesex – aged 36
Catherine COHEN – Wife – b. 1836 Middlesex – aged 35
Moss LEVY – Uncle – b. 1814 Middlesex – aged 57
Maria LEVY – Sister-in-law – b. 1842 Middlesex – aged 29
Henry LEVY – Brother-in-law – b. 1844 Middlesex – aged 27
Bridget MORRIS – Domestic Servant

1861 Census

Address:

13, Cobb's Yard, Spitalfields

Residents:

Elias COHEN – Head – b. 1837 Spitalfields – aged 24 – General Dealer
Catherine COHEN – Wife – b. 1838 Spitalfields – aged 23
Maria LEVY – Sister-in-law – b. 1841 Spitalfields – aged 20
Elizabeth LEVY – Sister-in-law – b. 1843 Spitalfields – aged 18 – Tailoress
Henry LEVY – Brother-in-law – b. 1845 Spitalfields – aged 16 – General Dealer

Marriage:

Elias COHEN to Catherine LEVY – Q1 1859 LONDON CITY 1c 269.

Parents:

Elias Cohen – Parents = Levy & Esther Cohen (1851 Census)
Catherine Levy – Parents = Lewis & Sarah Levy (1851 Census)

Death:

Catherine COHEN – Q2 1915 [76] LONDON C 1c 1.
Buried at Plashet Cemetery – K-48-2 on 23 Apr 1915

Jewish Chronicle – 23 Apr 1915

COHEN – On the 21st of April, at 12, Brushfield Street, Bishopsgate, Catherine (Kitty) Cohen, aged 76. Deeply mourned by her children, grandchildren, great-grandchildren and intended son-in-law.
COHEN – On the 21st of April, at 12, Brushfield Street, Bishopsgate, Catherine (Kitty) Cohen, the beloved mother of Mrs J.J. Woolley and Betsy Cohen, of 32, Cazenove Road, Stamford Hill, N.
COHEN – On the 21st of April, at 12, Brushfield Street, Bishopsgate, Catherine (Kitty) Cohen, the beloved mother of Louis Cohen, of 28, Leswin Road, Stoke Newington. Shiva at 12, Brushfield Street.

COWEN, Samuel – A-11-62

Died: 01 Apr 1898
Buried: 04 Apr 1898
Hebrew Name: Shmuel bar Yehuda Hacohen
Partner: Annie Cowen (d. 1921)
Aged: 63 years

Jewish Chronicle – 08 Apr 1898

COWEN – On the 1st of April, at 120, Hackney Road, N.E., Samuel Cowen, aged 63, many years resident in W.C. district. May his soul rest in peace.

Jewish Chronicle – 21 Oct 1898

The tombstone in loving memory of the late Samuel Cowen will be set at Plashet

COWEN, Samuel – A-11-62

Cemetery on Sunday next, the 23rd inst., at 3.30 p.m. Please accept this, the only intimation. – 120, Hackney Road.

Death:

Q2 1898 [63] BETHNAL GREEN 1c 84.

1891 Census

Address:

39 Fitzroy Street, St. Pancras, London

Residents:

Samuel COWEN – Head – b. 1839 Poland – aged 52 – Tailor
Annie COWEN – Wife – b. 1843 Poland – aged 48
Bessie COWEN – Daughter – b. 1871 Poland – aged 20
Rose COWEN – Daughter – b. 1874 Whitechapel – aged 17
Ray COWEN – Daughter – b. 1876 Whitechapel – aged 15 – Scholar
Benjamin COWEN – Son – b. 1877 Whitechapel – aged 14 – Scholar
Harriet SCHMITT – Domestic Servant
Jane CLIFFORD – Visitor – b. 1868 – aged 23 – Dressmaker

Death:

Adele Anna COWEN – Q1 1921 [84] HACKNEY 1b 416.
Buried at Plashet Cemetery – N-55-2 on 25 Feb 1921.

Jewish Chronicle – 04 Mar 1921

COWEN – On the 23rd of February, at 149, Queen's Road, Finsbury Park, Adele Anna, relict of the late Samuel Cowen, in her 84th year. Deeply mourned by her children, Mrs Charles Phillips, Mrs M. Linton, Lewis I. Cowen, M. Cowen (Kimberley), Ben S. Cowen (Johannesburg), sons-in-law, daughters-in-law, grandchildren and great-grandsons.

DAVIS, Leah – A-13-8

Died: 03 May 1898
Buried: 04 May 1898
Hebrew Name: Masha bat Zvi
Partner: Morris Davis (d. 1905)
Aged: 60 years

Jewish Chronicle – 06 May 1898

DAVIS – On the 3rd of May, at 42, Grove Road, Bow, Leah, the beloved wife of Morris Davis. Deeply mourned.

פ ט

אשה ישרה מרת לאה
אשת משה בן צבי
שהלכה לעולמה יום ג׳ י״א אי״ר
תרנ״ח ל׳פק
ת׳נ״צ״ב״ה

In Loving Memory of

LEAH,

WIFE OF MORRIS DAVIS,

WHO DEPARTED THIS LIFE

ON THE

3RD MAY 1898. 11TH IYAR 5658.

A LOVING WIFE AN AFFECTIONATE MOTHER
AND A KIND FRIEND.

DAVIS, Leah – A-13-8

Jewish Chronicle – 22 Jul 1898

The tombstone in memory of Mrs Leah Davis, loving wife of Mr Morris Davis, of 42, Grove Road, Bow, will be set at 3 o'clock on Sunday next, July 24th, at Plashet Cemetery. Friends will please accept this intimation.

Death:
Q2 1898 [60] MILE END 1c 282.

1891 Census

Address:
42 Grove Road, Mile End Old Town

Residents:
Morris DAVIS – Head – b. 1839 Manchester – aged 52 – Commission Agent
Leah DAVIS – Wife – b. 1844 Holland – aged 47
Sarah DAVIS – Daughter – b. 1866 Bow – aged 25
Rebecca DAVIS – Daughter – b. 1865 Bow – aged 26 – Elementary School Teacher
Solomon DAVIS – Son – b. 1872 Bow – aged 19 – Journalist
Annie DAVIS – Daughter – b. 1876 Bow – aged 15 – Elementary School Teacher
Margaret RAHMAN – General Servant

1881 Census

Address:
42 Grove Road, Mile End Old Town

Residents:
Morris DAVIS – Head – b. 1838 Manchester – aged 43 – General Dealer in Toys & Fancy Goods
Leah DAVIS – Wife – b. 1838 Amsterdam – aged 43
David DAVIS – Son – b. 1863 Shoreditch – aged 18 – Working Jeweller
Sarah DAVIS – Daughter – b. 1865 Shoreditch – aged 16
Louis DAVIS – Son – b. 1869 Shoreditch – aged 12 – Scholar
Rebecca DAVIS – Daughter – b. 1871 Hackney – aged 10 – Scholar
Solomon DAVIS – Son – b. 1874 Hackney – aged 7 – Scholar
Annie DAVIS – Daughter – b. 1876 Hackney – aged 5 – Scholar
Elizabeth HARVEY – Domestic Servant

1871 Census

Address:
Leslie Street, Mile End Old Town

Residents:
Morris DAVIS – Head – b. 1839 Lancashire – aged 32
Leah DAVIS – Wife – b. 1839 Netherlands – aged 32
Henry DAVIS – Son – b. 1861 Middlesex – aged 10
David DAVIS – Son – b. 1862 Middlesex – aged 9

Sarah DAVIS – Daughter – b. 1865 Middlesex – aged 6
Louis DAVIS – Son – b. 1869 Middlesex – aged 2
Elizabeth DOWNING – Domestic Servant
Samuel CHURCH – Lodger – b. 1835 Netherlands – aged 36

1861 Census

Address:
34 New Castle Street, Whitechapel

Residents:
Morris DAVIS – Head – b. 1839 – aged 22 – Hawker
Leah DAVIS – Wife – b. 1838 – aged 23
Henry DAVIS – Son – b. 1861 Middlesex – aged 7 months
Judith DAVIS – Lodger – Widow – b. 1786 Hampshire – aged 75
Martha SAMUELS – Lodger – b. 1831 – aged 30

Marriage:
Morris DAVIS to Leah CHURCH – Q4 1859 MANCHESTER 8d 731.

Marriage:
Morris DAVIS to Isabella GOLDBERG – Q2 1899 WHITECHAPEL 1c 545.

Death:
Morris DAVIS – Q3 1905 [68] WHITECHAPEL 1c 182.
Buried at Plashet Cemetery – F-9-23 on 03 Sep 1905.

Jewish Chronicle – 08 Sep 1905

DAVIS – On the 31st of August, at the London Hospital, after a painful illness borne with great fortitude, Morris Davis, aged 68, dearly beloved husband of Betsy Davis, 17, Ford Square, Commercial Road, E., and beloved father of Mrs Bloomah Goodman, 28, Cursitor Street, W., Fanny Weinberg, and E.L. Davis, of 12, Huntington Street, Kingsland Road, N. Deeply mourned and sadly missed by his sorrowing wife, sons, daughters, daughters-in-law, sons-in-law, grandchildren and a large circle of friends. A loving husband, kind father and good friend, beloved and respected by all who knew him. May his dear soul rest in peace. Amen. Shiva at 12, Huntington Street, Kingsland Road, N.

DAVIS – On the 31st of August, at the London Hospital, after a painful illness born with great fortitude, Morris Davis, aged 68, beloved father of Sol. Davis, 11, Montague Place, Poplar, E., Jack Davis, 33, Woodstock Road, Poplar, E. and beloved brother of Mrs Samuel Tenser, 43, Pell Street, Reading. Deeply mourned and sadly missed by his sons, daughters-in-law, grandchildren, sister and a large circle of friends. Beloved and respected by all who knew him, a loving husband, kind father and good friend. May his dear soul rest in peace. Amen. Shiva at 11, Montague Place, Poplar, E.

DE FRIES, Hannah – D-6-15

Died: 07 Nov 1898
Buried: 10 Nov 1898
Partner: Harry De Fries (d. 1906)
Aged: 72 years

Jewish Chronicle – 11 Nov 1898

DE FRIES – On the 7th of November, after a long and painful illness, borne with fortitude, Hannah, the beloved wife of Harry De Fries, and loving mother of Messrs. Harry, Daniel, John, Alf, Michael and George De Fries, and of Mrs Ben Mills, Joseph Jacobs (of Plymouth), George Pollock, Lewis Rosenthal and John Solomons. Shiva at Middlesex Street, Grafton Road, E., Sandringham Road and the "Eagle", Andle Street, W.

Jewish Chronicle – 16 Jun 1899

The tombstone in memory of the lamented Mrs Hannah Defries, beloved wife of Henry Defries, Senior, of Middlesex Street, will be set on Sunday next, June 18th, at Plashet, at 4.30 p.m. Relatives and friends please accept this, the only intimation.

Death:

Q4 1898 [72] LONDON CITY 1c 1.

1891 Census

Address:

318 Mile End Road, Mile End Old Town

Residents:

Henry DEFRIES – Head – b. 1825 Shoreditch – aged 66 – Gas Fitter
Hannah DEFRIES – Wife – b. 1826 Spitalfields – aged 65
Alfred DEFRIES – Son – b. 1858 Aldgate – aged 33
Elizabeth DEFRIES – Daughter – b. 1860 Bishopsgate – aged 31
Isaac DEFRIES – Son – b. 1868 Bishopsgate – aged 23
Henrietta DEFRIES – Daughter – b. 1872 Whitechapel – aged 19

1881 Census

Address:

11 and 12 Bateman Street, Shoreditch, London

Residents:

Henry DEFRIES – Head – b. 1824 London – aged 57 – Licensed Victualler
Hannah DEFRIES – Wife – b. 1826 London – aged 55
John DEFRIES – Son – b. 1849 London – aged 32 – Jeweller
Rebecca DEFRIES – Daughter – b. 1858 London – aged 23 – Barmaid

Alfred DEFRIES – Son – b. 1859 London – aged 22 – Gas Fitter
Elizabeth DEFRIES – Daughter – b. 1860 London – aged 21 – Tailoress
Mary DEFRIES – Daughter – b. 1861 London – aged 20 – Tailoress
Ada DEFRIES – Daughter – b. 1863 London – aged 18 – Tailoress
Mara DEFRIES – Daughter – b. 1865 London – aged 16 – Tailoress
Michael DEFRIES – Son – b. 1866 London – aged 15 – Furrier
Isaac DEFRIES – Son – b. 1868 London – aged 13 – Gas Fitter
Henrietta DEFRIES – Daughter – b. 1871 London – aged 10 – Scholar

1861 Census

Address:
1, Three Tun Alley, Whitechapel

Residents:
Henry DEFRIES – Head – b. 1821 London – aged 40 – Gas Fitter
Hannah DEFRIES – Wife – b. 1823 London – aged 38
Henry DEFRIES – Son – b. 1849 London – aged 12 – Scholar
John DEFRIES – Son – b. 1851 London – aged 10 – Scholar
Daniel DEFRIES – Son – b. 1854 London – aged 7 – Scholar
Rebecca DEFRIES – Daughter – b. 1855 London – aged 6 – Scholar
Abraham DEFRIES – Son – b. 1857 London – aged 4 – Scholar
Elizabeth DEFRIES – Daughter – b. 1859 – aged 2
Mary DEFRIES – Daughter – b. 1861 London – aged 4 months

1851 Census

Address:
2 Petticoat Lane, Saint Mary Whitechapel, Tower Hamlets

Residents:
Henry DEFRIES – Head – b. 1826 Middlesex – aged 25 – Brass Founder
Hannah DEFRIES – Wife – b. 1829 Middlesex – aged 22
Henry DEFRIES – Son – b. 1850 Middlesex – aged 1
Leah HARRIS – Visitor – b. 1834 Middlesex – aged 17 - Servant
Kitty TOPES – Lodger – b. 1814 Middlesex – aged 37 - Needlewoman
Kitty ARIGAN – Lodger – b. 1830 Middlesex – aged 21 – Laundress

Marriage:
Henry DE FRIES to Hannah HARRIS – Q1 1849 ST. LUKES 2 258.

1901 Census

Address:
55 Middlesex Street, St. Botolph Without, Aldgate

Residents:
Henry DEFRIES – Head – Widower – b. 1824 Shoreditch – aged 77 – Gas Fitter
Alfred DEFRIES – Son – b. 1857 London – aged 44 – Gas Fitter

George DEFRIES – Son – b. 1873 Mile End – aged 28 – Cabman

Death:

Henry DEFRIES – Q1 1906 [78] HACKNEY 1b 313.
Buried at Plashet Cemetery – F-16-39 on 20 Feb 1906.

Jewish Chronicle – 23 Feb 1906

DEFRIES – On Sunday, the 18th of February, after a long and painful illness, Henry Defries, aged 85, at the residence of his son, 13, Ellingfort Road, Mare Street, Hackney, husband of the late Hannah Defries, 55, Middlesex Street, Aldgate; beloved father of John Defries and Mrs Joseph Jacobs, of Wharf House, Plymouth. Deeply mourned. May his soul rest in peace. Shiva at 7, Leslie Street, Mile End

DEFRIES – On Sunday, the 18th of February, 1906, at 13, Ellingfort Road, Hackney, Henry Defries, aged 85, beloved father of Mrs L.I. Rosenthal, 38, Portland Road, Finsbury Park, N.

DEFRIES – On Sunday, the 18th of February, at 13, Ellingfort Road, Hackney, Henry Defries, aged 78 years, the dearly beloved father of Daniel Defries. Shiva at 32, Coborn Street, Bow. May his soul rest in peace. Amen.

DEFRIES – On the 18th of February, after a long and painful illness, at 13, Ellingfort Road, Hackney, Henry Defries, Senior, late of 55, Middlesex Street, Aldgate. Dearly beloved father of Mrs B. Mills, Mrs G. Pollock and Mrs. J. Selman. Shiva at the Manchester Arms, Baker Street, W. May his soul rest in peace.

FRESCO, Levy – D-5-23

Died: **12 Oct 1898**
Buried: **14 Oct 1898**
Partner: **Sarah Fresco (d. 1911)**
Aged: **78th year**

Jewish Chronicle – 14 Oct 1898

FRESCO – On the 12th of October, Levy Fresco, of 11, Gate Street, Holborn, in his 78th year. God rest his soul – 68, Lincolns Inn.

FRESCO – On Wednesday, the 12th of October, at 11, Gate Street, Holborn, Levy Fresco, aged 78 years, beloved father of Sam Fresco, of Duke's Place, Aldgate. God rest his soul in peace.

Jewish Chronicle – 26 May 1899

The tombstone in affectionate remembrance of the late Mr Levy Fresco, will be set on Sunday, May 28th, at 3 o'clock, at Plashet – 11, Gate Street, Holborn.

Death:

Q4 1898 [77] ST. GILES 1b 359.

1891 Census

Address:

11 Gate Street, Bloomsbury, London

Residents:

Levy FRESCO – Head – b. 1822 The Hague – aged 69 – General Dealer
Sarah FRESCO – Wife – b. 1827 The Hague – aged 64
John FRESCO – Son – b. 1859 Spitalfields – aged 32 – Commercial Traveller
Bertha FRESCO – Daughter – b. 1861 Spitalfields – aged 30
Kate FRESCO – Daughter – b. 1867 Goodmans Fields – aged 24
Dora FRESCO – Daughter – b. 1871 Aldgate – aged 20
Sarah FRESCO – Granddaughter – b. 1880 The Hague – aged 11 – Scholar
Nellie SAUNDERS – Domestic Servant

1881 Census

Address:

4 and 3, Half Moon Passage, Whitechapel

Residents:

Levy FRESCO – Head – b. 1823 The Hague – aged 58 – General Dealer
Sarah FRESCO – Wife – b. 1828 The Hague – aged 53
John FRESCO – Son – b. 1858 Spitalfields – aged 23 – General Dealer
Rebecca FRESCO – Daughter - b. 1861 Spitalfields – aged 20 – Cigar Maker
Kate FRESCO – Daughter – b. 1865 Goodmans Fields – aged 16 – Cigar Maker
Dora FRESCO – Daughter – b. 1867 London – aged 14
John FRESCO – Grandson – b. 1874 The Hague – aged 7 – Scholar
E. BARRY – Lodger – b. 1846 Shoreditch – aged 35 – Seamstress
Emily BARRY – Lodgers daughter – b. 1878 Whitechapel – aged 3

1861 Census

Address:

10 Whites Row, Spitalfields

Residents:

Levy FRESCO – Head – b. 1822 Rotterdam – aged 39 – General Dealer
Sarah FRESCO – Wife – b. 1827 Rotterdam – aged 34
Samuel FRESCO – Son – b. 1845 Rotterdam – aged 16 – Cigar Maker
Aaron FRESCO – Son – b. 1848 Rotterdam – aged 13 – Cigar Maker
Israel FRESCO – Son – b. 1852 Rotterdam – aged 9 – Scholar
Myer FRESCO – Son – b. 1854 Spitalfields – aged 7 – Scholar
Jonas FRESCO – Son – b. 1856 Spitalfields – aged 5 – Scholar
Rebecca FRESCO – Daughter – b. 1858 Spitalfields – aged 3 – Scholar

Dora FRESCO – Daughter – b. 1861 Spitalfields – aged 9 months
Anna KLEINBANK – Domestic Servant

1901 Census

Address:
11 Gate Street, St. Giles in the Fields, and St. George Bloomsbury

Residents:
Sara FRESCO – Head – Widow – b. 1826 Holland – aged 75
Kate FRESCO – Daughter – b. 1868 London – aged 33 – Furniture Dealer
Cherrie FRESCO – Granddaughter – b. 1880 Holland – aged 21 – Commercial Clerk
Nellie SAUNDERS – Domestic Servant

1911 Census

Address:
11 Gate Street, London

Residents:
Sarah FRESCO – Head – Widow – b. 1825 Holland – aged 86
Kate FRESCO – Daughter – b. 1868 London – aged 43 – Antique Dealer
Dora HEUVEL – Daughter (15 yrs married) – b. 1870 London – aged 41
Jacques HEUVEL – Son-in-law – b. 1870 Holland – aged 41 – Orchestral Violinist
Samuel FRESCO – Nephew – b. 1858 Holland – aged 53 – Dealer in Furniture
Sara FRESCO – Granddaughter – b. 1880 Holland – aged 31 – Typist
Cats FRESCO – Granddaughter – b. 1887 Holland – aged 24 – Mothers Help/ Domestic
Bertha HEUVEL – Granddaughter – b. 1897 London – aged 14 – at School
Sadie HEUVEL – Granddaughter – b. 1901 London – aged 10 – at School
Jack HEUVEL – Grandson – b. 1903 London – aged 8 – at School
Nelly SAUNDERS – General Domestic Servant

Death:
Sarah FRESCO – Q2 1911 [81] ST. GILES 1b 292.
Buried at Plashet Cemetery – I-23-24 on 22 May 1911.

Jewish Chronicle – 26 May 1911

FRESCO – On Saturday, the 20th of May, at 11, Gate Street, Kingsway, Sarah, relict of the late Levy Fresco, in her 81st year. Deeply mourned by her sorrowing sons, daughters, sons-in-law, daughters-in-law, and grandchildren. May her soul rest in everlasting peace.

GELBERG, Abraham – D-7-1

GELBERG, Abraham – D-7-1

Died: 24 Nov 1898
Buried: 27 Nov 1898
Hebrew Name: Avraham ben Moshe Yehuda
Parents: Morris & Amelia Gelberg
Age: 33 years

Jewish Chronicle – 02 Dec 1898

GELBERG – On the 24th of November, after a long and painful illness, Abraham Gelberg, aged 33, the dearly beloved brother of Mrs B. Sussman, of 3, Beresford Road, Canonbury. May his dear soul rest in peace.

Jewish Chronicle – 09 Jun 1899

The tombstone to the memory of the late Abraham Gelberg, will be set on Sunday next, June 11th, at 4 p.m., at Plashet Cemetery. Relatives and friends please accept this, the only intimation.

Death:
Q4 1898 [33] HASTINGS 2b 26.

1891 Census

Address:
22 Graham Road, Hackney

Residents:
Morris GELBERG –Head – b. 1829 Austria – aged 62 – Commercial Traveller
Amelia GELBERG – Wife – b. 1841 Poland – aged 50
Benjamin GELBERG – Son – b. 1868 Scotland – aged 23 – Commercial Traveller
Simon GELBERG – Son – b. 1871 Whitechapel – aged 20 – Theology Student
William FERGUSON – Boarder – b. 1846 Scotland – aged 45 – Clerk

1891 Census

Address:
67 Milton Road, Hornsey

Residents:
Albert SEPRO – Head – b. 1860 Russia – aged 31 – Commercial Traveller
Ree SEPRO – Wife – b. 1862 Liverpool – aged 29
Lena SEPRO – Daughter – b. 1887 Dublin – aged 4
Abraham GELBERG – Boarder – b.1865 Scotland – aged 26 – Commercial Traveller
Esther SMITH – Domestic Servant

1871 Census

Address:

Cannon Place, Mile End Old Town

Residents:

Morris GELBERG – Head – b. 1830 Austria – aged 41 - Jeweller
Amelia GELBERG – Wife – b. 1841 Poland – aged 30
Bertha GELBERG – Daughter – b. 1860 Lancashire – aged 11
Isaac GELBERG – Son – b. 1862 Scotland – aged 9
Abraham GELBERG – Son – b. 1866 Scotland – aged 5
Benjamin GELBERG – Son – b. 1868 Scotland – aged 3
Simon GELBERG – Son – b. 1871 London – aged 0

1901 Census

Address:

22 Graham Road, Hackney

Residents:

Amelia GELBERG – Head – Widow – b. 1841 Poland – aged 60
Benjamin GELBERG – Son – b. 1868 Edinburgh – aged 33 – Traveller in Jewellery

Death:

Morris GELBERG – Q4 1900 [71] HACKNEY 1b 311.
Buried at Plashet Cemetery – D-24-3 on 06 Dec 1900.

Amelia GELBERG – Q2 1922 [81] HACKNEY 1b 465.
Buried at Willesden Cemetery – MX-10-11 on 18 May 1922.

GOLDSTEIN, Simeon – A-14-26

Died: **11 Oct 1898**
Buried: **13 Oct 1898**
Hebrew Name: **Simeon bar Michael**
Partner: **Charlotte Goldstein (d. 1891)**
Aged: 75 years

Jewish Chronicle – 14 Oct 1898

GOLDSTEIN – On the 11th of October, at 16, James Street, Long Acre, W.C., Simeon Goldstein, beloved father of Mr M.H. Goldstein, Mr Alf Goldstein, Mr Maurice Goldstein, Miss Sadie Goldstein, Miss Rebecca Goldstein and Miss Ray Goldstein. God rest his dear soul.

Jewish Chronicle – 28 Jul 1899

The tombstone in loving memory of Simon Goldstein, late of Long Acre, will be

GOLDSTEIN, Simeon – A-14-26

set at Plashet Cemetery Sunday next, July 30th, at 4 o'clock. Will friends kindly accept this intimation.

Death:

Q4 1898 [75] STRAND 1b 371.

1891 Census

Address:

21 St. Peters Road, Mile End Old Town

Residents:

Simon GOLDSTEIN – Head – b. 1828 Austria Krakan – aged 63 – Jeweller
Charlotte GOLDSTEIN – Wife – b. 1831 Austria Krakan – aged 60
Lazarus GOLDSTEIN – Son – b. 1859 Whitechapel – aged 32 – Jeweller
Sarah GOLDSTEIN – Daughter – b. 1861 Whitechapel – aged 30 – Burlesque Actress and Vocalist
Morris GOLDSTEIN – Son – b. 1865 Whitechapel – aged 26 – Jeweller
Rebecca GOLDSTEIN – Daughter – b. 1868 Whitechapel – aged 23
Rachel GOLDSTEIN – Daughter – b. 1872 Whitechapel – aged 19 – Teacher of Piano Forte

1881 Census

Address:

77 St. Peters Road, Mile End Old Town

Residents:

Simon GOLDSTEIN – Head – b. 1830 Austria – aged 51 – Commercial Traveller
Leah GOLDSTEIN – Wife – b. 1831 Austria – aged 50
Sarah GOLDSTEIN – Daughter – b. 1858 Bow – aged 23 – Tailoress
Lazarus GOLDSTEIN – Son – b. 1859 Bow – aged 22 – Commercial Traveller
Morris GOLDSTEIN – Son – b. 1862 Bow – aged 19 – Working Jeweller
Katie GOLDSTEIN – Daughter – b. 1865 Bow – aged 16 – Tailoress
Rebecca GOLDSTEIN – Daughter – b. 1867 Bow – Dress Maker
Rachel GOLDSTEIN – Daughter – b. 1871 Bow – aged 10 – Scholar

1871 Census

Address:

Wagener's Buildings, Whitechapel

Residents:

Simon GOLDSTEIN – Head – b. 1831 Austria – aged 40
Leah GOLDSTEIN – Wife – b. 1833 Austria – aged 38
Michael GOLDSTEIN – Son – b. 1854 Middlesex – aged 17
Sarah GOLDSTEIN – Daughter – b. 1856 Middlesex – aged 15
Lazarus GOLDSTEIN – Son – b. 1858 Middlesex – aged 13
Morris GOLDSTEIN – Son – b. 1862 Middlesex – aged 9

Kate GOLDSTEIN – Daughter – b. 1866 Middlesex – aged 5
Rebecca GOLDSTEIN – Daughter – b. 1868 Middlesex – aged 3
Rachel GOLDSTEIN – Daughter – b. 1870 Middlesex – aged 1

1861 Census

Address:
15 Wageners Building, Whitechapel

Residents:
Simon GOLDSTEIN – Head – b. 1827 Poland – aged 34 – Cigar Maker
Charlotte GOLDSTEIN – Wife – b. 1832 Poland – aged 29
Michael GOLDSTEIN – Son – b. 1853 Poland – aged 8 – Scholar
Sarah GOLDSTEIN – Daughter – b. 1855 Whitechapel – aged 6 – Scholar
Lazarus GOLDSTEIN – Son – b. 1857 Whitechapel – aged 4 – Scholar
Morris GOLDSTEIN – Son – b. 1860 Whitechapel – aged 1

Death:
Charlotte GOLDSTEIN – Q3 1891 [62] MILE END OLD TOWN 1c 318.
Buried at West Ham Cemetery – E-6-8 on 21 Aug 1891.

Jewish Chronicle – 28 Aug 1891

Mr Simeon Goldstein, sons and daughters, return their sincere thanks for visits and many kind expressions of sympathy tendered to them during the week of mourning for their late lamented darling wife and mother. Peace be to her dear soul – 21, St. Peter's Road, Mile End, E.

GOODMAN, Rosa/Rose – A-14-14

Died: 19 Aug 1898
Buried: 21 Aug 1898
Hebrew Name: Masha bat Naphtali
Partner: Woolf Goodman (d. 1932)
Aged: 52nd year

Jewish Chronicle – 26 Aug 1898

GOODMAN – On the 19th of August suddenly, at 288, Commercial Road, E., Rose, the beloved wife of Woolf Goodman, in her 52nd year, mother of H. Goodman, Dalston, Mrs L. Bloom, 257, Commercial Road, E. and Mrs M. Phillips, 19, Mansell Street, Aldgate. Deeply mourned by her bereaved husband, children, relatives and friends.

GOODMAN, Rosa/Rose – A-14-14

Jewish Chronicle – 09 Dec 1898

The tombstone in memory of Rosa, the dearly beloved wife of Woolf Goodman of 288, Commercial Road, will be set on Sunday, December 11th at 2.30 at Plashet Cemetery. Relatives and friends please accept this, the only intimation.

Death:

Q3 1898 [52] ST. GEORGE IN THE EAST 1c 253.

1891 Census

Address:

28 Hanbury Street, Spitalfields, London, Tower Hamlets

Residents:

Woolf GOODMAN – Head – b. 1845 Russia – aged 46 – Hat & Cap Manufacturer
Rose GOODMAN – Wife – b. 1846 Russia – aged 45
Sarah GOODMAN – Daughter – b. 1868 Aldgate – aged 23 – Cap Machinist
Leah GOODMAN – Daughter – b. 1870 Aldgate – aged 21
Abraham GOODMAN – Son – b. 1872 Whitechapel – aged 19 – Cap Cutter
Morris GOODMAN – Son – b. 1874 Whitechapel – aged 27 – Cap Packer
Dorah GOODMAN – Daughter – b. 1877 Lancashire – aged 14
Rachel GOODMAN – Daughter – b. 1880 London – aged 11
Esther GOODMAN – Daughter – b. 1885 Bethnal Green – aged 6
Victor GOODMAN – Son – b. 1884 London – aged 7
Lawrence GOODMAN – Son – b. 1888 Spitalfields – aged 3
David GOODMAN – Son – b. 1889 Spitalfields – aged 2
Elizabeth GREENER – Domestic Servant

1881 Census

Address:

7 Fairclough Street, St. George in the East

Residents:

Wolf GOODMAN – Head – b. 1844 Poland – aged 37 – Cap Maker
Rachel GOODMAN – Wife – b. 1845 Poland – aged 36
Harris GOODMAN – Son – b. 1866 Poland – aged 15 – Cap Maker
Sarah GOODMAN – Daughter – b. 1868 Bishopsgate – aged 13 – Scholar
Leah GOODMAN – Daughter – b. 1870 Whitechapel – aged 11
Abraham GOODMAN – Son – b. 1872 Whitechapel – aged 9
Phineas GOODMAN – Son – b. 1874 Whitechapel – aged 7
Dora GOODMAN – Daughter – b. 1876 Manchester – aged 5
Rachel GOODMAN – Daughter – b. 1881 St. Geo E. – aged 0

1871 Census

Address:

Commercial Place, Whitechapel

Residents:

Woolf GOODMAN – Head – b. 1845 Poland – aged 26
Rachel GOODMAN – Wife – b. 1848 Poland – aged 23
Harris GOODMAN – Son – b. 1865 Poland – aged 6
Sarah GOODMAN – Daughter – b. 1867 London – aged 4
Leah GOODMAN – Daughter – b. 1870 London – aged 1

Marriage:

1. No information found in England in first marriage
2. Woolf GOODMAN to Leah BARNETT – Q1 1900 LONDON CITY 1c 89.

1901 Census

Address:

67 Greenwood Road, Hackney

Residents:

Woolf GOODMAN – Head – b. 1846 Russia – aged 55 – Cap Maker
Leah GOODMAN – Wife – b. 1851 Russia – aged 50
Morris GOODMAN – Son – b. 1875 Whitechapel – aged 26 – Cap Maker
Dora GOODMAN – Daughter – b. 1878 Manchester – aged 23
Rachel GOODMAN – Daughter – b. 1881 Manchester – aged 20
Lawrence GOODMAN – Son – b. 1887 Whitechapel – aged 14
David GOODMAN – Son – b. 1889 Whitechapel – aged 12
Hester GOODMAN – Daughter – b. 1885 Whitechapel – aged 16
Dora BRESKAL – Step-daughter – b. 1884 Spitalfields – aged 17
Deborah BRESKAL – Step-daughter – b. 1889 Spitalfields – aged 12
Kate BRESKAL – Step-daughter – b. 1894 Spitalfields – aged 7
Morris BRESKAL – Step-son – b. 1890 Spitalfields – aged 11
Annie CHAPPEL – Housemaid / Domestic Servant

[Death – Lazarus BRESKAL [43] Q1 1897 WHITECHAPEL 1c 163.]

1911 Census

Address:

67 Greenwood Road, Dalston, London N.E.

Residents:

Woolf GOODMAN – Head – b. 1845 Russia – aged 66 – Cap Manufacturer
Leah GOODMAN – Wife – b. 1855 Russia – aged 56
Lawrence GOODMAN – Son – b. 1887 Whitechapel – aged 24 – Cap Assistant
Morris BEISHAL – Step-son – b. 1891 Whitechapel – aged 20 – Clerk

Katy BEISHAL – Step-daughter – b. 1895 Whitechapel – aged 16 – Milliner's Assistant
Phoebe LEWIS – Visitor – b. 1879 Poland – aged 32
Annie ALEXANDER – General Domestic Servant

Death:
Woolf GOODMAN – Q3 1932 [83] HACKNEY 1b 304.
Place of burial not found.

Jewish Chronicle – 12 Aug 1932

GOODMAN – On the 7th of August, at 1, Kyverdale Road, N.16, Woolf Goodman, beloved father of Mrs L.J. Bloom, Mrs M. Phillips, Mrs J.M. Sonenfield, Mrs H.M. Matthews, Mrs D. Schneiders, Abraham, Phineas (Plin), Lawrie and George. Deeply mourned by his sons, daughters, sons-in-law, daughter-in-law, grandchildren, great-grandchildren, relatives and friends. God rest his soul in peace. Shiva at above address.

HOSE, Esther – A-13-24

Died: **04 Jul 1898**
Buried: **05 Jul 1898**
Partner: **Joseph Barnett Hose (d. 1917)**
Aged: **36 years**

Jewish Chronicle – 08 Jul 1898

HOSE – On the 4th of July, Esther, the dearly beloved wife of Joseph B. Hose, of 13, Lidfield Road, Green Lanes, N., and only beloved sister of Mrs M. Joel, of 61, Great Prescot Street. May she rest in peace. Shiva at 13, Lidfield Road.

Jewish Chronicle – 10 Feb 1899

The tombstone in loving memory of Esther Hose, lamented wife of Joseph Barnett Hose, of 13, Lidfield Road, Green Lanes, N., will be set on Sunday, the 12th of February, at 3 o'clock at the Plashet Cemetery. Friends and relatives will please accept this, the only intimation.

Death:
Q3 1898 [36] WESTMINSTER 1a 375.

1891 Census

Address:
13 Lidfield Road, Stoke Newington

Residents:
Joseph B. HOSE – Head – b. 1859 Spitalfields – aged 32 – Teacher of Hebrew & Scripture

HOSE, Esther – A-13-24

Esther HOSE – Wife – b. 1860 Spitalfields – aged 31
Barnett J. HOSE – Son – b. 1887 Spitalfields – aged 4
Phillip HOSE – Son – b. 1888 Spitalfields – aged 3
Sarah HOSE – Daughter – b. 1889 Spitalfields – aged 2
Alice SMITH – General Domestic Servant

Marriage:
Joseph Barnett HOSE to Esther JACOBS – Q1 1885 LONDON CITY 1c 121.
Joseph Barnett HOSE to Flora ISAACS – Q3 1899 ISLINGTON 1b 924.

1901 Census

Address:
13 Lidfield Road, Stoke Newington

Residents:
Joseph HOSE – Head – b. 1858 Spitalfields – aged 43 – Private Tutor
Flora HOSE – Wife – b. 1868 London – aged 33
Barnet J. HOSE – Son – b. 1887 Spitalfields – aged 14
Phillip HOSE – Son – b. 1888 Spitalfields – aged 13
Sarah HOSE – Daughter – b. 1890 Spitalfields – aged 11
Victor J. HOSE – Son – b. 1901 Spitalfields – aged 3 months

1911 Census

Address:
13 Lidfield Road, London N.
Joseph Barnett HOSE – Head – b. 1858 Spitalfields – aged 53 – Private Tutor
Flora HOSE – Wife (12 years) – b. 1866 Spitalfields – aged 45
Sarah HOSE – Daughter – 1890 Spitalfields – aged 21 – Certified Teacher
Victor HOSE – Son – b. 1901 Stoke Newington – aged 10 – Scholar
Cyril HOSE – Son – b. 1906 Stoke Newington – aged 5 – Scholar

Death:
Joseph Barnett HOSE – Q1 1917 [59] HACKNEY 1b 655.
Buried at Plashet Cemetery – O-8-42 on 08 Jan 1917.

Flora HOSE – Q1 1925 [56] ISLINGTON 1b 404.
Buried at East Ham Cemetery – C-19-42 on 12 Jan 1925.

HOUTMAN, Judah – A-11-24

HOUTMAN, Judah – A-11-24

Died: 06 Mar 1898
Buried: 08 Mar 1898
Hebrew Name: Yehuda ben Yaakov
Partner: Flora Houtman
Aged: 26 years

Jewish Chronicle – 11 Mar 1898

HOUTMAN – On the 6th of March, Judah Houtman, beloved brother of Elizabeth Beever (nee Houtman), aged 26. Deeply mourned. May his soul rest in peace. Shiva 72, Greenfield Street, Commercial Road, E.
HOUTMAN – On the 6th of March, at the North London Hospital, Mount Vernon, Judah, the beloved husband of Flora Houtman (nee Cohen) and dearly beloved son of Jacob and Deborah Houtman, aged 26. Deeply mourned by his sorrowing wife, parents, sisters, brothers and large circle of friends. May his soul rest in peace. Shiva at 20, Newark Street, New Road. Amsterdam papers please copy

Jewish Chronicle – 20 May 1898

The tombstone in memory of the late lamented Judah Houtman, of 61, Wellesley Street, will be set on Sunday next, May 22nd, at the Plashet Cemetery, at 5 o'clock. Relatives and friends will please accept this, the only intimation.

Death:
Q1 1898 [25] HAMPSTEAD 1a 542.

Marriage:
Judah HOUTMAN to Flora COHEN – Q4 1896 MILE END OLD TOWN 1c 955.

1901 Census

Address:
24 Newmark Street, Mile End Old Town

Residents:
Jane HOUTMAN – Head – Widow – b. 1873 London – aged 28 – Mantle Machinist
Jacob HOUTMAN – Son – b. 1898 Spitalfields – aged 3
Deborah WOOLF – Niece – b. 1890 England – aged 11

1911 Census

Address:
26 Stayners Road, Mile End

Residents:

Flora HOUTMAN – Head – Widow – b. 1873 Spitalfields – aged 38 – Mantle Machinist

Jacob HOUTMAN – Son – b. 1898 Stepney – aged 13

Parents:

Judah HOUTMAN – parents are Jacob & Deborah Houtman of 20, Newmark Street, Mile End Old Town (Census 1901).

Flora COHEN – parents are Marcus & Henrietta Cohen of 10, Spital Square, Spitalfields, London (1891 Census). Marcus is a Beadle at the Germany Synagogue, New Broad Street in the City - 1881 census) and comes from Cleve in Prussia, while Henrietta comes from Utrecht in Holland.

Marriage:

Flora HOUTMAN to Solomon LEE – Q2 1915 WHITECHAPEL 1c 592.

HUMPHREYS, Rosetta – D-7-2

Died: 26 Nov 1898
Buried: 29 Nov 1898
Hebrew Name: Tizba bat Asher
Parents: Henry Jacob & Sophia Humphreys
Age: 56 years

Jewish Chronicle – 02 Dec 1898

HUMPHREYS – On the 26th of November, at her residence, 142, Turner's Road, Burdett Road, E., Rosetta Humphreys, daughter of the late Henry Jacob Humphreys, of 37, Prince's Square, St. George's, E. Deeply lamented by her brothers (Mr M. Humphreys, Barking, Mr L. Humphreys, Poplar) and sisters (Mrs S. Weber, Forest Gate, Mrs S. Weber, Prince's Square, E., Mrs J. Humphreys, Turner's Road, E., Mrs M. Hilkowits, Plummer's Row, E.) and all her friends. May her soul rest in peace. Shiva at 142, Turner's Road, E. American papers please copy.

Death:

Q4 1898 [56] MILE END 1c 319.

1891 Census

Address:

142 Turners Road, Mile End Old Town

Residents:

Rosetta HUMPHREYS – Head – b. 1843 Sydney – aged 48 – Piano Teacher

Charlotte HUMPHREYS – Sister – b. 1863 London – aged 28 – Tailoress

HUMPHREYS, Rosetta – D-7-2

Rosetta WEBER – Niece – b. 1882 London – aged 9 – Scholar

1881 Census

Address:

8 Helmsley Terrace, Hackney

Residents:

Albert IVIMEY – Head – b. 1847 Bow – aged 34 – Carpet Salesman
Kate IVIMEY – Wife – b. 1846 St Lukes – aged 35
Chas Thomas IVIMEY – Son – b. 1870 Bow – aged 11 – Scholar
Albert E. IVIMEY – Son – b. 1872 Bow – aged 9 – Scholar
Kate F. IVIMEY – Daughter – b. 1874 Hackney – aged 7 – Scholar
Elizabeth M. IVIMEY – Daughter – b. 1876 Hackney – aged 5 – Scholar
Maud IVIMEY – Daughter – b. 1878 Hackney – aged 3
Amy L. IVIMEY – Daughter – b. 1880 Hackney – aged 1
Sarah M. DORE – Sister-in-law – b. 1849 Battersea – aged 32 – Machinist
Rosetta HUMPHREYS – Visitor – b. 1843 Sydney – aged 38 – Pianoforte Teacher

1871 Census

Address:

8 Princes Square, St. George, East

Residents:

Henry J. HUMPHREYS – Head – b. 1813 Middlesex – aged 58 – Tailor
Sophia HUMPHREYS – Wife – b. 1821 Middlesex – aged 50
Rose HUMPHREYS – Daughter – b. 1843 Sydney – aged 28
Saul HUMPHREYS – Son – b. 1845 Sydney – aged 26 – Book Maker
Mark HUMPHREYS – Son – b. 1847 Sydney – aged 24 – General Dealer
Rachel HUMPHREYS – Daughter – b. 1849 Sydney – aged 22
William HUMPHREYS – Son – b. 1852 Sydney – aged 19 – Cigar Maker
Sarah HUMPHREYS – Daughter – b. 1854 Sydney – aged 17
Lewis HUMPHREYS – Son – b. 1858 Whitechapel – aged 13 – Scholar
Katherine HUMPHREYS – Daughter – b. 1859 Whitechapel – aged 12 – Scholar
Charlotte HUMPHREYS – Daughter – b. 1862 Whitechapel – aged 9 – Scholar

1861 Census

Address:

8 Princes Square, St. Georges East

Residents:

Henry J. HUMPHREYS – Head – b. 1814 Wapping – aged 47 – Tailor
Sophia HUMPHREYS – Wife – b. 1820 St. Georges E – aged 41
Henry HUMPHREYS – Son – b. 1841 Sydney – aged 20 – Traveller
Rosetta HUMPHREYS – Daughter – b. 1843 Sydney – aged 18
Saul HUMPHREYS – Son – b. 1845 Sydney – aged 16 – Book Maker

Mordecai HUMPHREYS – Son – b. 1847 Sydney – aged 14 – Scholar
Rachel HUMPHREYS – Daughter – b. 1849 Sydney – aged 12 – Scholar
Joseph HUMPHREYS – Son – b. 1850 Sydney – aged 11 – Scholar
William HUMPHREYS – Son – b. 1852 Sydney – aged 9 – Scholar
Sarah HUMPHREYS – Daughter – b. 1854 Sydney – aged 7 – Scholar
Leon HUMPHREYS – Son – b. 1858 St. Georges E – aged 3
Catherine HUMPHREYS – Daughter – b. 1859 St. Georges E – aged 2
Charlotte HUMPHREYS – Daughter – b. 1861 St. Georges E – aged 2 months

Marriage:

Henry Jacob HUMPHREYS to Sophia COHEN – Q3 1840 LONDON CITY 2 175.

ISRAEL, Caroline – A-11-43

Died: 25 Mar 1898
Buried: 27 Mar 1898
Partner: Elkin Israel (d. 1881)
Aged: 80 years

Jewish Chronicle – 01 Apr 1898

ISRAEL – On Friday, the 25th of March, at 5, Arthur Street, W.C., Caroline, widow of the late Elkan Israel, and mother of Misses Esther and Maria Israel, and Mr Andrew Israel. Deeply lamented by her sorrowing children and family, and a large circle of friends. American papers please copy. May her soul rest in peace.

Jewish Chronicle – 07 Apr 1899

The tombstone of the late Rachel Israel (A-14-23) of 11, Wentworth Street, Spitalfields and also of the late Caroline Israel of 5, Arthur Street, Oxford Street, will be set at Plashet Cemetery, on Sunday, April 9th, at 4 o'clock. The only intimation.

Death:

Q1 1898 [80] ST. GILES 1b 463.

1891 Census

Address:

8 Bury Street, St. Katherine Cree, London

Residents:

Caroline ISRAEL – Head – Widow – b. 1817 Portsmouth – aged 74 – Cook
Esther ISRAEL – Daughter – b. 1859 London – aged 32 – Assistant
Annie DUSKIN – Domestic Servant
Annie COLLINS – Domestic Servant

1881 Census

Address:

3 St. James Place, St. James Dukes Place

Residents:

Joseph RAPHAEL – Head – b. 1807 Portsmouth – aged 74
Elizabeth RAPHAEL – Wife – b. 1818 Liverpool – aged 63 – Club Proprietor
Lizzie STEIN – Granddaughter – b. 1853 London – aged 28
Annie ARTHURST – Domestic Servant
Mary HUNEY – Domestic Servant
George BALLARD – General Servant
Caroline ISRAEL – Cook – Widow – b. 1821 London – aged 60
Jane HART – Aunt – b. 1793 Portsmouth – aged 88

1871 Census

Address:

Angel Court, Aldgate, London

Residents:

Elkin ISRAEL – Head – b. 1823 Middlesex – aged 48
Caroline ISRAEL – Wife – b. 1821 Hampshire – aged 50
Esther ISRAEL – Daughter – b. 1853 Middlesex – aged 18
Maria ISRAEL – Daughter – b. 1855 Middlesex – aged 16
Martha ISRAEL – Daughter – b. 1857 Middlesex – aged 14
Sarah ISRAEL – Daughter – b. 1859 Middlesex – aged 12
Barnett ISRAEL – Son – b. 1861 Middlesex – aged 10
Andrew ISRAEL – Son – b. 1863 Middlesex – aged 8

1861 Census

Address:

12 Angel Court, St. Botolph Aldgate, City of London

Residents:

Elkan ISRAEL – Head – b. 1825 Spitalfields – aged 36 – General Dealer
Caroline ISRAEL – Wife – b. 1822 Portsmouth – aged 39 – General Dealer
Rebecca ISRAEL – Daughter – b. 1849 Aldgate – aged 12
Esther ISRAEL – Daughter – b. 1851 Aldgate – aged 10
Mary ISRAEL – Daughter – b. 1856 Aldgate – aged 5
Matilda ISRAEL – Daughter – b. 1855 Aldgate – aged 6
Sarah ISRAEL – Daughter – b. 1857 Aldgate – aged 4
Barnett ISRAEL – Son – b. 1861 Aldgate – aged 0

Marriage:

Elkin ISRAEL to Caroline LYONS – Q1 1850 ST. LUKE 2 258.

Death:

Elkin ISRAEL – Q1 1881 [54] WHITECHAPEL 1c 260.
Buried at West Ham Jewish Cemetery – M-6-6 on 07 Feb 1881.

ISRAEL, Lazarus – A-13-36

Died: **12 Jun 1898**
Buried: **13 Jun 1898**
Hebrew Name: **Eliezer ben Moshe Hacohen**
Partner: **Miriam Israel (d. 1915)**
Aged: **53 years**

Jewish Chronicle – 17 Jun 1898

ISRAEL – On the 12th of June, at 31, Cambridge Road, Mile End, Lazarus Israel, aged 53. Deeply mourned by his loving wife, children, relatives and friends. God rest his dear soul.
ISRAEL – On the 12th of June, at his residence, 31, Cambridge Road, Mile End, Lazarus Israel, dearly beloved father of Mrs B. Hyman, of 13, Bermondsey New Road, S.E. May his soul rest in peace.
ISRAEL – On the 12th of June at 31, Cambridge Road, E., Lazarus Israel, the dearly beloved brother of Mrs B. Kauffmann, 28, Goodge Street, W. God rest his dear soul.

Jewish Chronicle – 28 Oct 1898

The tombstone in memory of Lazarus Israel of Cambridge Heath Road, will be set on Sunday next, 30th inst., at Plashet Cemetery at 3 o'clock. Relatives and friends please accept this intimation.

Death:

Q2 1898 [53] BETHNAL GREEN 1c 139.

1891 Census

Address:

59 Cambridge Road, Bethnal Green, London

Residents:

Lazarus ISRAEL – Head – b. 1845 Aldgate – aged 46 – Fishmonger
Miriam ISRAEL – Wife – b. 1850 Aldgate – aged 41 – Clothier
Nancy ISRAEL – Daughter – b. 1867 Aldgate – aged 24 – Domestic Servant
Hannah ISRAEL – Daughter – b. 1871 Aldgate – aged 20 – Feather Curler
Benjamin ISRAEL – Son – b. 1873 Whitechapel – aged 18 – Fishmonger
Elias ISRAEL – Son – b. 1875 Whitechapel – aged 16 – Clothiers Assistant
Samuel ISRAEL – Son – b. 1877 Mile End – aged 14 – Pupil Teacher
Joseph ISRAEL – Son – b. 1882 Mile End – aged 9 – Scholar

ISRAEL, Lazarus – A-13-36

Esther ISRAEL – Daughter – b. 1885 Mile End – aged 6 – Scholar
Betsy ISRAEL – Daughter – b. 1887 Mile End – aged 4 – Scholar
Bernhard ISRAEL – Son – b. 1889 Mile End – aged 2
William ISRAEL – Son – b. 1891 Mile End – aged 3 months
Margaret DANBY – Domestic Servant

1881 Census

Address:
71 Cambridge Road, Bethnal Green

Residents:
Lazarus ISRAEL – Head – b. 1846 London – aged 35 – Clothier
Mary ISRAEL – Wife – b. 1850 Fishmonger's Alley – aged 31 – Clothier
Annie ISRAEL – Daughter – b. 1867 Middlesex St – aged 14 – Clothier
Maurice ISRAEL – Son – b. 1868 Harrow Alley – aged 13 – Clothier
Hannah ISRAEL – Daughter – b. 1871 Swan St – aged 10 – Scholar
Benjamin ISRAEL – Son – b. 1873 George Yard – aged 8 – Scholar
Elias ISRAEL – Son – b. 1875 George Yard – aged 6 – Scholar
Samuel ISRAEL – Son – b. 1877 Bethnal Green – aged 4 – Scholar
Ellen WHITE – Domestic Servant

1871 Census

Address:
Harrow Alley, Aldgate, London

Residents:
Lazarus ISRAEL – Head – b. 1846 London – aged 25
Mary ISRAEL – Wife – b. 1849 London – aged 22
Nancy ISRAEL – Daughter – b. 1866 London – aged 5
Moses ISRAEL – Son – b. 1868 London – aged 3
Hannah ISRAEL – Daughter – b. 1870 London – aged 1

Marriage:
Lazarus ISRAEL to Mary Ann JOSEPH – Q1 1867 EAST LONDON 1c 47.

Death:
Miriam ISRAEL – Q3 1915 [66] MILE END OLD TOWN 1c 423.
Buried at Plashet Cemetery – L-24-10 on 11 Aug 1915.

Jewish Chronicle – 13 Aug 1915

ISRAEL – On the 9th of August, at 10, Bancroft Road, E., Miriam (Polly), wife of the late Lazarus Israel. Dearly beloved mother of Benjamin, Joseph, Bernhard, Willie, David, Mrs Mark Morris, 10, Bancroft Road, E.; Mrs Isaac Beber, 86, Grafton Street, E. Deeply mourned by her sons, daughters, sons-in-law, daughters-in-law, grandchildren, and a large circle of relatives and friends.

May her dear soul rest in peace. Gone but never to be forgotten. Shiva at 10, Bancroft Road.

ISRAEL – On the 9th of August, at 10, Bancroft Road, E., Miriam (Polly), the dearly loved and loving mother of Moss Israel, 19, Chaucer Road, Forest Gate. Deeply mourned by her son, daughter-in-law, and grandchildren. God rest her dear soul. Shiva at 19, Chaucer Road.

ISRAEL – On the 9th of August, at 10, Bancroft Road, E., Miriam (Polly), the dearly loved and loving mother of Elias Israel, 49, Romford Road, Forest Gate. Deeply mourned by her son, daughter-in-law and grandchildren. God rest her dear soul. Shiva at 49, Romford Road.

ISRAEL – On the 9th of August, at 10, Bancroft Road, E., Miriam (Polly), the dearly loved mother of Mrs Barney Hyman, 87, St. Stephen's Road, Upton Park. Deeply mourned by her daughter, son-in-law, and grandchildren. God rest her dear soul. Shiva at 87, St. Stephen's Road.

ISRAEL – On the 9th of August, at 10, Bancroft Road, Miriam, beloved sister of Mrs Joseph Lyons, 79, Wellesley Street. Shiva at 79, Wellesley Street.

ISRAEL, Nancy – A-14-16

Died: 20 Aug 1898
Buried: 22 Aug 1898
Parents: Lazarus & Miriam Israel
Aged: 32 years

Jewish Chronicle – 26 Aug 1898

ISRAEL – On the 20th of August, at 31, Cambridge Road, Mile End, E., Nancy, the eldest daughter of the late Lazarus Israel (A-13-36), and sister of Mr Moss Israel, of 46, Beaumont Square, E., of Mr Elias Israel, of 2, Eastbury Terrace, E. and of Mrs B. Hyman, of 13, Bermondsey New Road, S.E., aged 32. Deeply mourned by family and friends. May her dear soul rest in peace.

Jewish Chronicle – 02 Sep 1899

The tombstones in loving memory of Nancy and Samuel Isaac (A-14-39), son and daughter of Polly (L-24-10) and the late Lazarus Israel (A-13-36) of 31, Cambridge Road, E., will be set at Plashet Cemetery on Sunday next, September 3rd, at 4 o'clock.

Death:

Q3 1898 [32] BETHNAL GREEN 1c 164.

Birth:

Q3 1866 LONDON 1c 310.

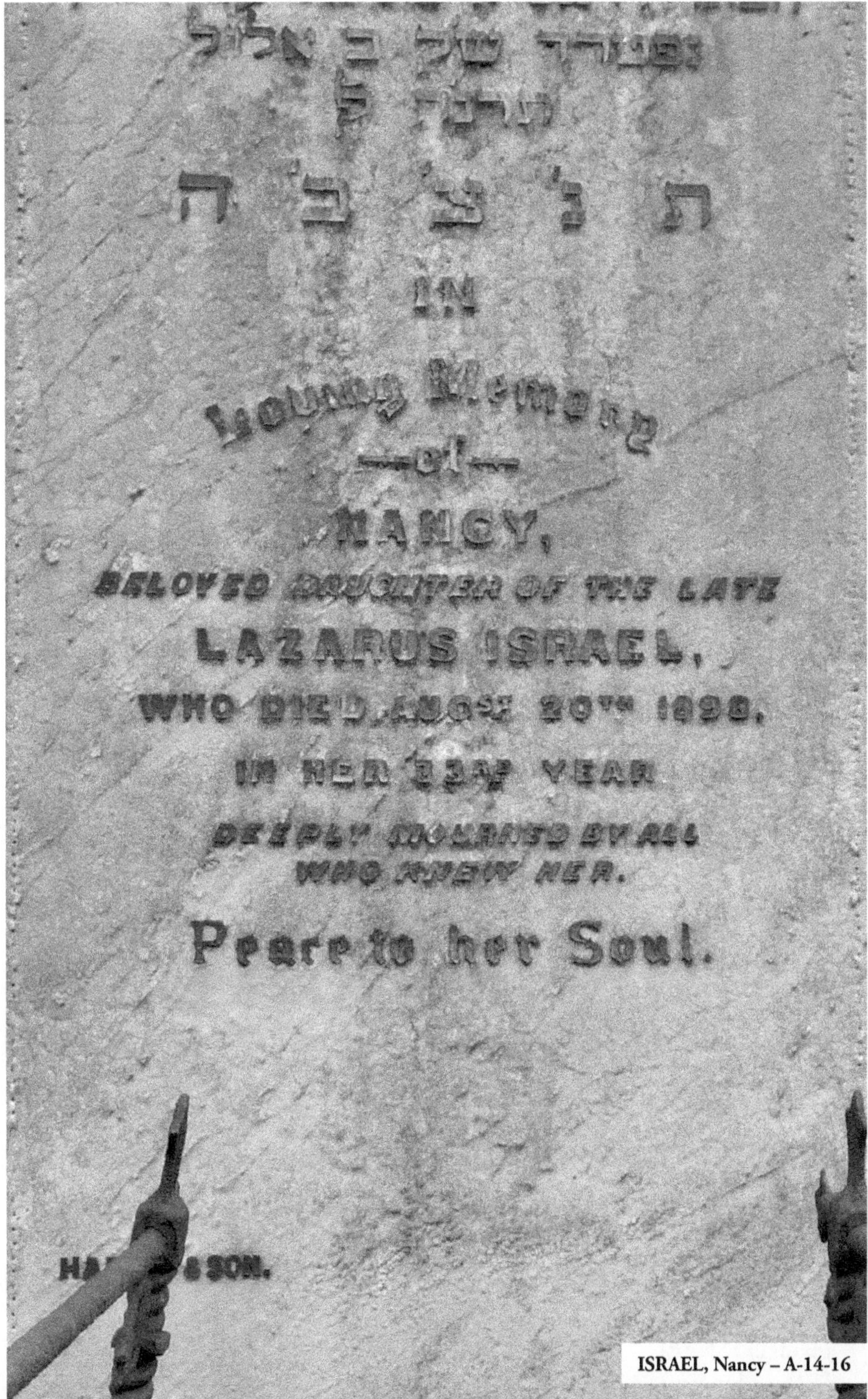

ISRAEL, Nancy – A-14-16

1891 Census

Address:

59 Cambridge Road, Bethnal Green, London

Residents:

Lazarus ISRAEL – Head – b. 1845 Aldgate – aged 46 – Fishmonger
Miriam ISRAEL – Wife – b. 1850 Aldgate – aged 41 – Clothier
Nancy ISRAEL – Daughter – b. 1867 Aldgate – aged 24 – Domestic Servant
Hannah ISRAEL – Daughter – b. 1871 Aldgate – aged 20 – Feather Curler
Benjamin ISRAEL – Son – b. 1873 Whitechapel – aged 18 – Fishmonger
Elias ISRAEL – Son – b. 1875 Whitechapel – aged 16 – Clothiers Assistant
Samuel ISRAEL – Son – b. 1877 Mile End – aged 14 – Pupil Teacher
Joseph ISRAEL – Son – b. 1882 Mile End – aged 9 – Scholar
Esther ISRAEL – Daughter – b. 1885 Mile End – aged 6 – Scholar
Betsy ISRAEL – Daughter – b. 1887 Mile End – aged 4 – Scholar
Bernhard ISRAEL – Son – b. 1889 Mile End – aged 2
William ISRAEL – Son – b. 1891 Mile End – aged 3 months
Margaret DANBY – General Domestic Servant

1881 Census

Address:

71 Cambridge Road, Bethnal Green

Residents:

Lazarus ISRAEL – Head – b. 1846 London – aged 35 – Clothier
Mary ISRAEL – Wife – b. 1850 London – aged 31 – Clothier
Annie ISRAEL – Daughter – b. 1867 London – aged 14 – Clothier
Maurice ISRAEL – Son – b. 1868 London – aged 13 – Clothier
Hannah ISRAEL – Daughter – b. 1871 London – aged 10 – Scholar
Benjamin ISRAEL – Son – b. 1873 London – aged 8 – Scholar
Elias ISRAEL – Son – b. 1875 London – aged 6 – Scholar
Samuel ISRAEL – Son – b. 1877 Bethnal Green – aged 4 – Scholar
Ellen WHITE – General Domestic Servant

1871 Census

Address:

20 Harrow Alley, Aldgate, London

Residents:

Lazarus ISRAEL – Head – b. 1846 London – aged 25 – General Dealer
Mary ISRAEL – Wife – b. 1849 London – aged 22
Nancy ISRAEL – Daughter – b. 1866 London – aged 5
Moses ISRAEL – Son – b. 1868 London – aged 3
Hannah ISRAEL – Daughter – b. 1870 London – aged 1
[+ three lodgers]

Death:

Lazarus ISRAEL – Q2 1898 [53] BETHNAL GREEN 1c 139.
Buried at Plashet Cemetery – A-13-36 on 13 Jun 1898.

Miriam ISRAEL – Q3 1915 [66] MILE END OLD TOWN 1c 423.
Buried at Plashet Cemetery – L-24-10 on 11 Aug 1915.

JOSEPH, Myer – A-14-21

Died: 15 Nov 1898
Buried: 17 Nov 1898
Partner: Hannah Joseph (d. 1901)
Aged: 81st year

Jewish Chronicle – 18 Nov 1898

JOSEPH – On Tuesday, the 15th of November, Myer Joseph of 15, Ship Alley, Wellclose Square, aged 81, the dearly beloved father of Mrs I. Finberg, of 6, Kilburn Park Road, Maida Vale, W. May his dear soul rest in peace. Amen. Shiva at 15, Ship Alley, Wellclose Square.
JOSEPH – On the 15th November, Myer Joseph, in his 81st year; dearly beloved father of Joseph Joseph – Shiva at 79, Commercial Road, E.

Jewish Chronicle – 30 Jun 1899

The tombstone in loving memory of Mr Myer Joseph, will be set on Sunday next, July 2nd, at Plashet Cemetery, at 4 p.m. Relatives and friends kindly accept this intimation.

Death:

Q4 1898 [80] ST. GEORGE IN THE EAST 1c 235.

1891 Census

Address:

15 Ship Alley, St. George in the East

Residents:

Meyer JOSEPH – Head – b. 1821 Holland – aged 70 – Dealer in Herbs
Hannah JOSEPH – Wife – b. 1829 Holland – aged 62 – Chandler Shopkeeper
Harry JOSEPH – Son – b. 1868 London – aged 23 – Cigar Bundler
Annie DONOVAN – Domestic Servant

1881 Census

Address:

Ships Alley, St. George in the East

JOSEPH, Myer – A-14-21

Residents:

Myer JOSEPH – Head – b. 1818 Amsterdam – aged 63 – Tobacconist
Ann JOSEPH – Wife – b. 1827 Amsterdam – aged 54
Leonard JOSEPH – Son – b. 1861 London – aged 20 – Cigar Maker
Morris JOSEPH – Son – b. 1863 London – aged 18 – Cigar Maker
Henry J. JOSEPH – Son – b. 1868 London – aged 13 – Cigar Maker
Kate McNAMARA – Domestic Servant

1871 Census

Address:

Merton's Court, St. George in the East

Residents:

Myer JOSEPH – Head – b. 1819 Netherlands – aged 52
Kate JOSEPH – Wife – b. 1830 Netherlands – aged 41
Sarah JOSEPH – Daughter – b. 1851 Middlesex – aged 20
Joseph JOSEPH – Son – b. 1853 Middlesex – aged 18
Alice JOSEPH – Daughter – b. 1854 Middlesex – aged 17
Lewis JOSEPH – Son – b. 1857 Middlesex – aged 14
Leonard JOSEPH – Son – b. 1861 Middlesex – aged 10
Morris JOSEPH – Son – b. 1863 Middlesex – aged 8
George JOSEPH – Son – b. 1865 Middlesex – aged 6
Henry JOSEPH – Son – b. 1868 Middlesex – aged 3

Death:

Hannah JOSEPH – Q4 1901 [78] MILE END OLD TOWN 1c 311.
Buried at Plashet Cemetery – B-18-34 on 28 Oct 1901.

KING, Nathaniel – A-10-43

Died: 09 Feb 1898
Buried: 10 Feb 1898
Hebrew Name: Nathan bar Moshe Hacohen
Partner: Maria (Mary) King
Aged: 37th year

Jewish Chronicle – 11 Feb 1898

KING – On the 9th of February, at 3, Eastbury Terrace, Beaumont Square, Mile End, Nathaniel King, in his 37th year. Deeply mourned by his sorrowing wife and children. Shiva as above.

KING – On the 9th of February, at his residence, Beaumont Square, London, Nathaniel King, brother of J. King, 8, Bedford Place, Brighton and S. King, 91, Week Street, Maidstone. Deeply mourned by his sorrowing wife, children, brothers and sisters.

KING, Nathaniel – A-10-43

Jewish Chronicle – 16 Jul 1898

The tombstone in memory of Nathaniel King of 194, Oxford Street, Stepney, will be set at Plashet Cemetery at 4 o'clock on Sunday next, July 17th. Relatives and friends please accept this, the only intimation.

Death:

Q1 1898 [37] MILE END 1c 346.

1891 Census

Address:

55 High Street, Bloomsbury

Residents:

Nathaniel KING – Head – b. 1860 Spitalfields – aged 31 – Tobacconist
Maria KING – Wife – b. 1866 St. Georges – aged 25
Morris KING – Son – b. 1886 Stepney – aged 5 – Scholar
Mildred PLEDGER – Domestic Servant

Marriage:

Nathaniel KING to Mary LORD – Q3 1880 HASLINGDEN 8e 247.

1881 Census

Address:

27 Nassau Road, Tottenham

Residents:

Charles KING – Head – b. 1852 Yelling – aged 29 – Carpenter
Mary Ann KING – Wife – b. 1855 Tottenham – aged 26
Henry John KING – Son – b. 1878 Stoke Newington – aged 3
Frank KING – Son – b. 1881 Tottenham – aged 0
Edgar KING – Brother – b. 1860 Yelling – aged 21 – Carpenter
James KING – Brother – b. 1862 Yelling – aged 19 – Carpenter
Nathaniel KING – Visitor – b. 1859 Yelling – aged 22 – Boot Maker
Eliza STEPPING – Monthly Nurse

1871 Census

Address:

Church End, Colmworth

Residents:

Samuel KING – Head – Widower – b. 1818 Colmworth – aged 53 - Carpenter
Charles KING – Son – b. 1856 Colmworth – aged 15 – Apprentice Carpenter
Richard KING – Son – b. 1857 Colmworth – aged 14 – Apprentice Carpenter
Nathaniel KING – Son – b. 1859 Colmworth – aged 12 – Scholar
Frances E. KING – Daughter – b. 1864 Colmworth – aged 7 – Scholar

LEVY, Harriet – A-12-27

LEVY, Harriet – A-12-27

Died: 14 Apr 1898
Buried: 17 Apr 1898
Partner: Michael Levy
Aged: 34 years

Jewish Chronicle – 22 Apr 1898

LEVY – On the 14th of April, at St. Helen's Terrace, Mile End Road, Harriet, the dearly beloved wife of Michael Levy, aged 34. Deeply mourned by her husband, father, brothers, sisters and relatives. Rest in peace.

Jewish Chronicle – 02 Jul 1898

The tombstone in memory of the late Harriet Levy, of 1, St. Helen's Terrace, will be set on Sunday, July 3rd, at Plashet Cemetery, at 4 p.m. Relatives and friends accept this, the only intimation.

Death:
Q2 1898 [34] MILE END 1c 276.

Marriage:
Michael LEVY to Harriet Reta LEVY – Q4 1894 WHITECHAPEL 1c 575.

1901 Census

Address:
42 Beaumont Square, Mile End Old Town

Residents:
Solomon B. LOTHEIM – Head – b. 1858 Stepney – aged 43 – Fur Skin Merchant
Laura LOTHEIM – Wife – b. 1859 Stepney – aged 42
Alfred LOTHEIM – Son – b. 2883 Stepney – aged 18 – Furrier
Samuel LOTHEIM – Son – b. 1884 Stepney – aged 17 – Warehouse Clerk
Michael LEVY – Brother-in-law – Widower – b. 1861 Stepney – aged 40 – Cigar Maker

Marriage:
Michael LEVY to Hannah HARRIS – Q4 1909 MILE END OLD TOWN 1c 700.

1901 Census

Address:
3 Merchant Street, Bromley, London

Residents:
Hannah HARRIS – Head – b. 1875 Whitechapel – aged 26 – Living on own means

Sophia HARRIS – Daughter – b. 1896 Bow – aged 5
Sarah HARRIS – Daughter – b. 1897 Bow – aged 4
Alfred HARRIS – Son – b. 1899 Bow – aged 2
Sophia HARRIS – Grandmother – b. 1819 London – aged 82 – Living on own means
Minnie WEST – General Domestic Servant
Lizzie SAMUELS – Niece – b. 1887 Aldgate – aged 14 – Cigar Maker

1911 Census
Address:
50a St. Peters Road, Mile End
Residents:
Michael LEVY – Head – b. 1861 London – aged 50 – Publican
Hannah LEVY – Wife (of 1 year) – b. 1875 Whitechapel – aged 36
Sophia HARRIS – Stepdaughter – b. 1896 Bow – aged 15 – Assisting in Business
Sarah HARRIS – Stepdaughter – b.1897 Bow – aged 14 – at School
Alfred Isaac HARRIS – Stepson – b. 1899 Bow – aged 12 – at School
John PIGGIN – Barman

LEVY, Newman – A-14-36

Died: **20 Dec 1898**
Buried: **22 Dec 1898**
Hebrew Name: **Yakutiel bar Hi'am**
Partner: **Hannah Levy (d. 1903)**
Aged: **76 years**

Jewish Chronicle – 23 Dec 1898

LEVY – On the 20th of December, suddenly, at 36, Brushfield Street, E., Newman Levy, father of Hyman Levy, 23, St. George's Road, Kilburn.

Jewish Chronicle – 15 Aug 1899

The tombstone in memory of Newman Levy, late of 36, Brushfield Street, will be set at Plashet Cemetery on Sunday next, September 17th, at 4 o'clock.

Death:
Q4 1898 [76] WHITECHAPEL 1c 170.

1881 Census
Address:
36 Brushfield Street, Old Artillery Ground

LEVY, Newman – A-14-36

Residents:

Newman LEVY – Head – b. 1822 Poland – aged 59 – Piece Broker
Hannah LEVY – Wife – b. 1822 Poland – aged 59
Hyman LEVY – Son – b. 1857 Middlesex – aged 24 – Boot Maker
Kate LEVY – Daughter – b. 1861 Spitalfields – aged 20 – Tailoress
Ada LEVY – Daughter – b. 1867 Whitechapel – aged 14 – Scholar

1871 Census

Address:

Middlesex Street, Whitechapel

Residents:

Newman LEVY – Head – b. 1821 Poland – aged 50
Hannah LEVY – Wife – b. 1823 Poland – aged 48
Hannah LEVY – Daughter – b. 1852 Poland – aged 19
Hyman LEVY – Son – b. 1857 Middlesex – aged 14
Kitty LEVY – Daughter – b. 1861 Middlesex – aged 10
Ada LEVY – Daughter – b. 1869 Middlesex – aged 2

1861 Census

Address:

22 Tilley Street, Spitalfields

Residents:

Newman LEVY – Head – b. 1832 Poland – aged 29 – Tailor
Betsy LEVY – Wife – b. 1836 Poland – aged 25
Sarah LEVY – Daughter – b. 1855 Whitechapel – aged 6
Rebecca LEVY – Daughter – b. 1859 Whitechapel – aged 2
Newman MARKS – Lodger – b. 1844 Poland – aged 17 – Tailor
Margaret RAWLINGS – Domestic Servant

1901 Census

Address:

281/2 Spital Square, Old Artillery Ground

Residents:

Hannah LEVY – Head – Widow – b. 1822 Poland – aged 79
Ada LEVY – Daughter – b. 1872 London – aged 29 – Clerk in Boot Shop

Death:

Chonna LEVY – Q4 1903 [83] BETHNAL GREEN 1c 138.
Buried at Plashet Cemetery – E-13-40 on 06 Dec 1903.

Jewish Chronicle – 11 Dec 1903

LEVY – On the 4th of December, at the residence of her youngest daughter, 9, Mountford House, Victoria Park Square, N.E., Honna Levy, 83, relict of the late

Newman Levy, of Brushfield Street, and beloved mother of Mrs A, Jacoby, 17, Old Ford Road, E., Mrs Hannah Kemp, 21, Newcastle Place, Aldgate, E., Mrs David Levy, 35, Camden Passage, Islington, and Mrs Myer Kemp. God rest her soul. African and New Zealand papers please copy.
LEVY – On the 4th of December, Chona Levy, aged 83, beloved mother of Hyman Levy, 26, Brownswood Park, N.

MAGNUS, Eliza – B-3-46

Died: **01 Sep 1898**
Buried: **04 Sep 1898**
Partner: **Lewis Magnus (d. 1893)**
Aged: 78 years

Jewish Chronicle – 09 Sep 1898

MAGNUS – On the 1st of September, at 357, Cambridge Road, E., Eliza, widow of Lewis Magnus, aged 78. Deeply mourned by her sorrowing children. Beloved by all. Peace be to her soul.

Jewish Chronicle – 28 Jul 1899

The tombstone in memory of the late Mrs Eliza Magnus, of 357, Cambridge Road, N.E., will be set at Plashet Cemetery on Sunday next, at 3.30. Relatives and friends please accept this, the only intimation.

Death:
Q3 1898 [78] BETHNAL GREEN 1c 166.

1891 Census

Address:
357 Cambridge Road, Bethnal Green, London
Residents:
Lewis MAGNUS – Head – b. 1822 Shoreditch – aged 69 - 2nd hand clothier
Eliza MAGNUS – Wife – b. 1819 Westminster – aged 72 – Assistant
Kate MAGNUS – Daughter – b. 1853 Camden Town – aged 38 – Feather Maker
Albert MAGNUS – Son – b. 1862 Birmingham – aged 29 – Clothier
Rose MAGNUS – Daughter – b. 1870 Bethnal Green – aged 21 – Silk Trimming Maker
Clara BOTTING – General Domestic Servant

1881 Census

Address:
357 Cambridge Road, Bethnal Green

Residents:

Lewis MAGNUS – Head – b. 1822 Bethnal Green – aged 59 – Clothier
Eliza MAGNUS – Wife – b. 1817 Bethnal Green – aged 64
Morris MAGNUS – Son – b. 1859 Bethnal Green – aged 22 – Boot Maker
Aaron MAGNUS – Son – b. 1851 Bethnal Green – aged 30 – Boot Maker
Rose MAGNUS – Daughter – b. 1867 Bethnal Green – aged 14

Marriage:

Lewis MAGNUS to Eliza RAPHAEL – Q3 1854 London C 1c 270.

Death:

Lewis MAGNUS – Q2 1893 [72] BETHNAL GREEN 1c 189.
Buried at West Ham Cemetery – E-12-28 on 22 Jan 1893.

Jewish Chronicle – 23 Jun 1893

On the 20th of June, at 357, Cambridge Road, E., Lewis Magnus, aged 72. Deeply mourned by his sorrowing wife, children and sisters. Peace be to his dear soul.

MARKS, Josiah – A-14-5

Died: **29 Jun 1898**
Buried: **01 Jul 1898**
Partner: **Fanny Marks (d. 1908)**
Aged: **70 years**

Jewish Chronicle – 09 Jul 1898

MARKS – On the 29th of June, at 99, Albion Road, N., after two days' illness, Josiah Marks (late of Birmingham), the beloved husband of Fanny Marks, and father of Mrs J. Sasserath and Mrs S. Cohen of Johannesburg, Mrs S. Sasserath of Clissold Park, N., and of Messrs. J and S. Marks of Cape Town. May his soul rest in peace.

Jewish Chronicle – 02 Sep 1898

The tombstone in loving memory of the late Mr Josiah Mark, of 99, Albion Road, N. (formerly of Birmingham), will be set at Plashet Cemetery on Sunday, September 11th, at 3.30 p.m. Relatives and friends kindly accept this, the only intimation.

Death:

Q3 1898 [70] EDMONTON 3a 203.

1891 Census

Address:

90 Princess Road, Edgbaston, Birmingham

Residents:

Josiah MARKS – Head – b. 1829 Poland – aged 62 – Retired Jeweller
Fanny MARKS – Wife – b. 1834 Berlin – aged 57

MARKS, Josiah – A-14-5

Phoebe MARKS – Daughter – b. 1866 Birmingham – aged 25
Jacob SASSERATH – Son-in-law – b. 1871 Mile End – aged 20 – General Dealer
Esther SASSERATH – Daughter – b. 1870 Birmingham – aged 21
Theresa R. SASSERATH – Granddaughter – b. 1888 Porksworth – aged 3
Dorothy P. MARKS – Granddaughter – b. 1891 Birmingham – aged 5 months
Samuel SASSERATH – Visitor – b. 1866 Mile End – aged 25 – Clerk in Patents Office
Elizabeth WILKINSON – General Servant

1881 Census

Address:
70 Hunters Lane, Aston, Warwickshire
Residents:
Josiah MARKS – Head – b. 1828 Poland – aged 53 – Jewellery Factor
Fanny MARKS – Wife – b. 1831 Poland – aged 50
Jacob MARKS – Son – b. 1857 Birmingham – aged 24 – Jewellery Factor
Esther MARKS – Daughter – b. 1860 Birmingham – aged 21
Woolfe MARKS – Son – b. 1864 Birmingham – aged 17 – Solicitor's Clerk
Phoebe MARKS – Daughter – b. 1866 Birmingham – aged 15 – Scholar
Samuel MARKS – Son – b. 1868 Birmingham – aged 13 – Scholar

1871 Census

Address:
The Parade, Birmingham
Residents:
Joshua MARKS – Head – b. 1829 Poland – aged 42 – Jeweller
Fanny MARKS – Wife – b. 1831 Prussia – aged 40
Jacob MARKS – Son – b. 1857 Birmingham – aged 14 – Scholar
Esther MARKS – Daughter – b. 1859 Birmingham – aged 12 - Scholar
Sarah MARKS – Daughter – b. 1861 Birmingham – aged 10 - Scholar
Wolff MARKS – Son – b. 1864 Birmingham – aged 7 - Scholar
Phoebe MARKS – Daughter – b. 1866 Birmingham – aged 5 – Scholar
Samuel MARKS – Son – b. 1868 Birmingham – aged 3
Annie BATES – General Servant

1861 Census

Address:
2 Court, Great Colmore Street, Birmingham
Residents:
Josiah MARKS – Head – b. 1828 Poland – aged 33 – Traveller
Fanny Marks – Wife – b. 1832 Russia – aged 29
Jacob MARKS – Son – b. 1858 Birmingham – aged 3 – Scholar
Esther MARKS – Daughter – b. 1859 Birmingham – aged 2
Mary A. BATES – General Servant

Marriage:
Josiah MARKS to Fanny BERLINER – Q2 1854 BIRMINGHAM 6d 257.

Death:
Fanny MARKS – Q1 1908 [81] HAMPSTEAD 1a 417.
Buried at Plashet Cemetery – A-14-6 on 30 Jan 1908.

Jewish Chronicle – 07 Feb 1908

MARKS – On the 30th of January, after a short illness, Fanny, relict of the late Josiah Marks (of Birmingham), and beloved mother of Mrs S. Sasserath, of 10, Rosslyn Mansions, London, Mrs J. Sasserath and Mrs S. Cohen, of Johannesburg, and Messrs J. and S. Marks of Cape Town. Deeply mourned.

Jewish Chronicle – 18 Sep 1908

MARKS – The tombstone in loving memory of the late Mrs Josiah Marks (mother of Mrs S. Sasserath of 14, Frognal, N.W.), will be set at Plashet on Sunday next, 20th inst., at 11.30 a.m.

MELLER, Abraham – A-11-10

Died: **14 Jan 1898**
Buried: **16 Jan 1898**
Hebrew Name: **Avraham bar Yonatan**
Partner: **Hannah Meller (d. 1916)**
Aged: **75 years**

Jewish Chronicle – 21 Jan 1898

MELLER – On the 14th of January, after much suffering, Abraham Meller, of 1, Wilkes Street, Commercial Street, aged 75. May his soul rest in peace.

Jewish Chronicle – 03 Jun1898

The tombstone to the memory of the late Abraham Meller, will be set on Sunday next, June 5th, at 4 o'clock. Friends will kindly accept this, the only intimation.

Death:
Q1 1898 [75] STRAND 1b 474.

1891 Census

Address:
26 Wood Street, Spitalfields, Tower Hamlets

Residents:
Abraham MELLER – Head – b. 1823 Germany – aged 68 – Leather Seller
Hannah MELLER – Wife – b. 1839 Russia Kurland – aged 52
Jonas MELLER – Son – b. 1865 St. Luke – aged 26 – Fancy Salesman

Sarah MELLER – Daughter – b. 1869 St. Luke – aged 22 – School Teacher
Elliot MELLER – Son – b. 1871 St. Luke – aged 20 – Leather Seller's Assistant

1881 Census

Address:

147 Commercial Street, Spitalfields

Residents:

Abraham MELLER – Head – b. 1822 Germany – aged 59 – Dealer in Nails & Foreign Goods
Hannah MELLER – Wife – b. 1846 Russia – aged 35
Joseph MELLER – Son – b. 1862 Shoreditch – aged 19 – Assistant to Father
Benjamin MELLER – Son – b. 1864 Shoreditch – aged 17 – Assistant to Father
Jonas MELLER – Son – b. 1865 Shoreditch – aged 16 – Apprentice in Fancy Goods
Sarah MELLER – Daughter – b. 1869 Shoreditch – aged 12 – Scholar
Elliott MELLER – Son – b. 1871 Shoreditch – aged 10 – Scholar

1871 Census

Address:

Westmoreland Place, Shoreditch

Residents:

Abraham MELLER (MILLER) – Head – b. 1822 Germany – aged 49
Annie MELLER – Wife – b. 1836 Germany – aged 35
Joseph MELLER – Son – b. 1861 Middlesex – aged 10
Benjamin MELLER – Son – b. 1863 Middlesex – aged 8
Jonas MELLER – Son – b. 1865 Middlesex – aged 6
Sarah MELLER – Daughter – b. 1869 Middlesex – aged 2
Fanny LOWDELL – Lodger – b. 1836 Middlesex – aged 35

Marriage:

Abraham MELLER to Hannah SAKMAN(N) – Q1 1861 LONDON CITY 1c 222.

Death:

Hannah MELLER – Q4 1916 [88] HACKNEY 1b 597.
Buried at Plashet Cemetery – M-22-21 on 18 Oct 1916.

Jewish Chronicle – 20 Oct 1916

MELLER – On the 15th of October at 3, Glaskin Road, Hackney, Hannah, the widow of the late Abraham Meller, and mother of Mrs Ephraim Norden, and Joseph, Benjamin, Jonas and Elliot Meller. Funeral leaves Wednesday at 11 o'clock for Plashet. Prayers each evening at 66, King Edward Road, South Hackney, during week of mourning commencing October 21st, at 7 p.m. Saturday next 5.30.

Jewish Chronicle – 20 Jul 1917

MELLER – The tombstone erected at Plashet Cemetery to the memory of the late Mrs Hannah Meller will be set on Sunday next, July 22nd, at 12 o'clock.

MELLER, Abraham – A-11-10
In Loving Memory of
ABRAHAM MELLER,
WHO DIED 14TH JANUARY 1898,
TEBETH 5658
AGED 76 YEARS.
May his soul rest in Peace

MORRIS, John K. – A-12-15

Died: 09 Apr 1898
Buried: 11 Apr 1898
Partner: Louisa Morris
Aged: 33 years

Jewish Chronicle – 15 Apr 1898

MORRIS – On the 9th of April, at 33, Sillwood Road, Brighton, after a brief illness, John Morris, of 96, Malmesbury Road, Bow, E., aged 33. Deeply mourned by his dear wife, brother and family. Australian papers please copy.

Jewish Chronicle – 09 Sep 1898

The tombstone in memory of the late Mr John Morris of 98, Malmesbury Road, Bow, E., will be set at the Plashet Cemetery on Sunday next, September 11th, at 4 o'clock. Relatives and friends kind accept this intimation.

Death:

Q2 1898 [33] BRIGHTON 2b 124.

1891 Census

Address:

96 Malmesbury Road, Bow or Stratford Le Bow & Bromley, the Tower Hamlets

Residents:

John MORRIS – Head – b. 1865 Bishopsgate – aged 26 - Secretary
Louisa MORRIS – Wife – b. 1867 Brighton – aged 24
Moses H. MORRIS – Son – b. 1891 Mile End – aged 0
Elizabeth ALLERTON – Domestic Servant

Marriage:

John MORRIS to Louisa LEAPMAN – Q2 1889 MILE END OLD TOWN 1c 935.

Marriage:

Louisa MORRIS to Asher LEVY (LEVEY) – Q1 1900 MILE END 1c 582.

1901 Census

Address:

8, Merchant Street, Bromley

Residents:

Asher LEVEY – Head – b. 1864 London – aged 37 – Traveller
Louisa LEVEY – Wife – b. 1867 Brighton – aged 34
Amelia LEVEY – Daughter – b. 1889 Bow – aged 12

Michael LEVEY – Son – b. 1890 Bow – aged 11
Catherine LEVEY – Daughter – b. 1892 Bow – aged 9
Moses H. MORRIS – Stepson – b. 1891 Bow – aged 10
Michael MORRIS – Stepson – b. 1892 Bow – aged 9
Henry MORRIS – Stepson – b. 1898 Bow – aged 3
Michael MORRIS – Brother-in-law – b. 1867 Whitechapel – aged 34 – Traveller
Maria MORRIS – Niece – b. 1890 Bow – aged 11
Sarah MORRIS – Niece – b. 1891 Bow – aged 10
Moses MORRIS – Nephew – b. 1892 Bow – aged 9
Florence KING – General Domestic Servant
Rebecca BACON – General Domestic Servant

MORRIS, Sarah – A-13-18

Died: **12 Jun 1898**
Buried: **14 Jun 1898**
Hebrew Name: **Sarah bat Eliezer**
Partner: **Moses Morris (d. 1895)**
Aged: **44 years**

Jewish Chronicle – 17 Jun 1898

MORRIS – On the 12th of June, at 19, Tredegar Road, Bow, Sarah, relict of the late Moses Morris, daughter of Mr Lawrence Levy, and sister of Mrs Franks, of 1, Coborn Street, Bow, Mr Lewis Levy, of Hawthorn Lodge, 155, Finchley Road, N.W., Mr Moss Levy, of 49, Tredegar Road, Bow, and Mr Asher Levy, of 19, Tredegar Road, Bow, aged 44 years. Shiva at 19, Tredegar Road, Bow. Beloved by all who knew her. May her soul rest in peace. Australian and American papers please copy.

Jewish Chronicle – 09 Sep 1898

The tombstone in memory of the late Mrs Sarah Morris, of 19, Tredegar Road, Bow, E., will be set at the Plashet Cemetery on Sunday next, September 11th, at 4 o'clock. Relatives and friends kindly accept this intimation.

Death:

Q2 1898 [44] POPLAR 1c 311.

1891 Census

Address:

19 Tredegar Road, Bow or Stratford Le Bow, Bow & Bromley, the Tower Hamlets

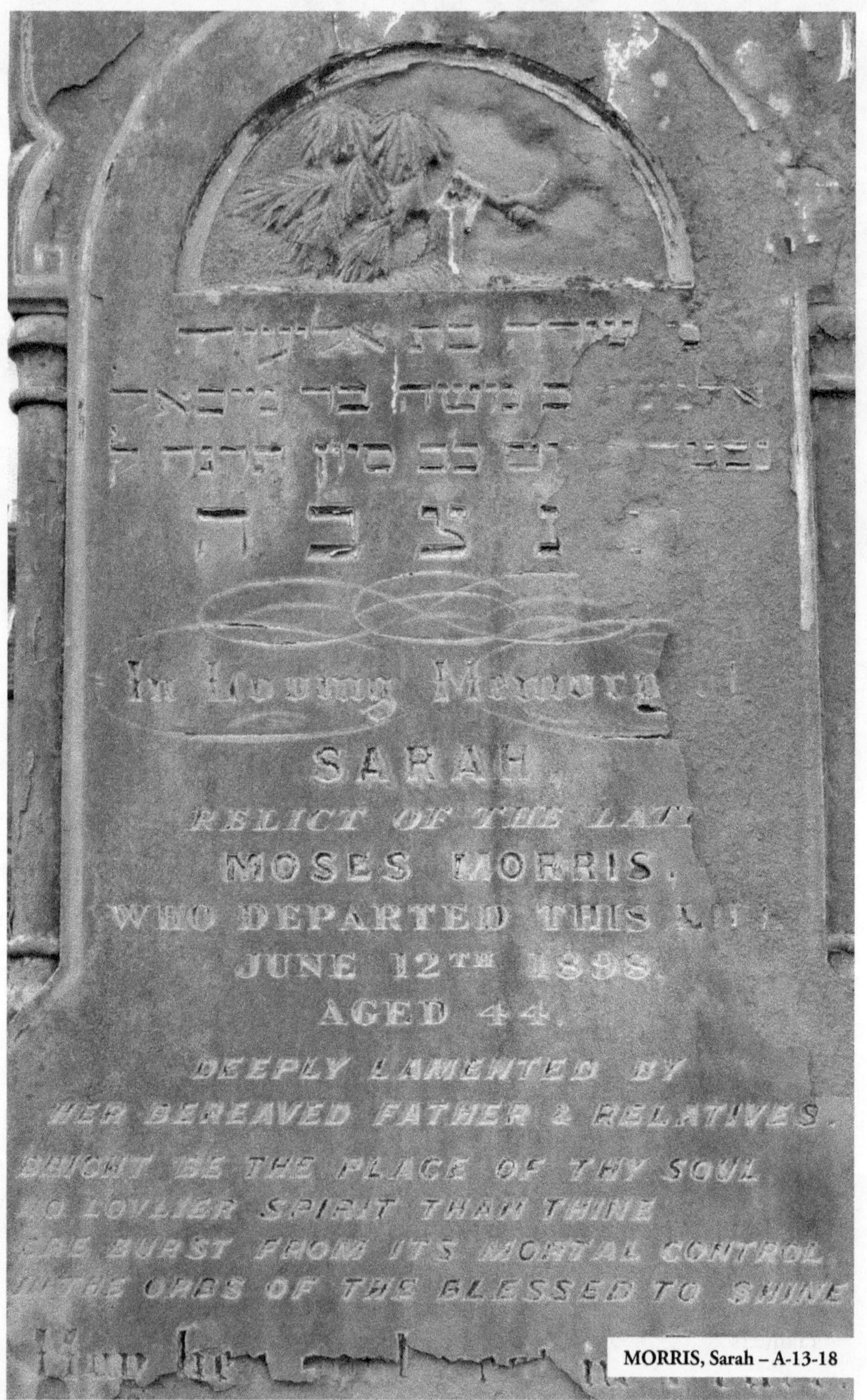

MORRIS, Sarah – A-13-18

Residents:

Moses MORRIS – Head – b. 1841 Spitalfields – aged 50 – Commercial Traveller
Sarah MORRIS – Wife – b. 1855 London – aged 36
Leon MORRIS – Son – b. 1872 London – aged 19 – Warehouseman
Kate LANDER – General Domestic Servant

1881 Census

Address:

21 Leslie Street, Mile End Old Town

Residents:

Moses MORRIS – Head – b. 1841 Spitalfields – aged 40 – Traveller in Sponge Trade
Maria MORRIS – Wife – b. 1843 Aldgate – aged 38
John MORRIS – Son – b. 1865 Bishopsgate – aged 16 – Clerk in Sponge Trade
Michael MORRIS – Son – b. 1867 Aldgate – aged 14 – Warehouseman
Harry MORRIS – Son – b. 1869 Spitalfields – aged 12 – Scholar
Leon MORRIS – Son – b. 1873 Mile End – aged 8 – Scholar
Rachel AROBUS – Niece – b. 1856 Barbican – aged 25 – Tailoress
Mezanne HAWKINS – Domestic Servant

Marriage:

Moses MORRIS to Sarah LEVY – Q3 1889 MILE END OLD TOWN 1c 955.

Death:

Moses MORRIS – Q3 1895 [55] POPLAR 1c 391.
Buried at West Ham Cemetery – A-6-30 buried 07 Aug 1895.

Jewish Chronicle – 19 Aug 1895

MORRIS – On the 5th of August, at 19, Tredegar Road, Bow, Moses Morris, aged 54 years. Deeply mourned by his wife, sons and relatives. Australian papers please copy.

MYERS, Leah – A-11-18

Died: 21 Feb 1898
Buried: 23 Feb 1898
Hebrew Name: Leah bat Yosef Halevi
Partner: Samuel Myers (d. 1918)
Aged: 63 years

Jewish Chronicle – 25 Feb 1898

MYERS – On the 21st of February, at 96, Whitechapel Road, Leah, the dearly

MYERS, Leah – A-11-18

beloved wife of Samuel Myers, and mother of Mrs E. Joseph of 38, Holywell Street, Strand, aged 63. Deeply mourned and missed by her loving husband, sons, daughters, grandchildren and a large circle of friends. Gone, but never to be forgotten. God rest her soul. Amen.
MYERS – On the 21st of February, at 96, Whitechapel Road, Mrs Leah Myers, the beloved sister of Mrs S.A. Green and Mrs Esther Myers. May her dear soul rest in peace. Shiva at 46 Mile End Road.

Jewish Chronicle – 10 Jun 1898

The tombstone in memory of Leah, the dearly beloved wife of Samuel Myers, of 96, Whitechapel Road, will be set on Sunday next, June 12th, at 4.30 at Plashet Cemetery. Relatives and friends please accept this, the only intimation.

Death:

Q1 1898 [63] WHITECHAPEL 1c 250.

1891 Census

Address:

96 Whitechapel Road, Whitechapel, Whitechapel Church

Residents:

Samuel MYERS – Head – b. 1834 Aldgate – aged 57 – Furrier
Leah MYERS – Wife – b. 1836 Spitalfields – aged 55
Maria MYERS – Daughter – b. 1865 Mile End – aged 26 – Fur Liner
Julia MYERS – Daughter – b. 1867 Mile End – aged 24 – Fur Liner
Esther MYERS – Daughter – b. 1873 Mile End – aged 18 – Waistcoat Maker
Abraham MYERS – Son – b. 1877 Mile End – aged 14 – Jeweller
Ellen HAWKINS – General Servant

1881 Census

Address:

21 Finch Street, Whitechapel

Residents:

Samuel MYERS – Head – b. 1833 Middlesex – aged 48 – Boot Rivetter
Leah MYERS – Wife – b. 1837 Middlesex – aged 44 – Dressmaker
Joseph MYERS – Son – b. 1860 Mile End – aged 21 – Boot Rivetter
Sarah MYERS – Daughter – b. 1861 Mile End – aged 20 – Dressmaker
Julia MYERS – Daughter – b. 1867 Mile End – aged 14 – Apprentice
Nathaniel MYERS – Son – b. 1871 Mile End – aged 10 – Scholar
Esther MYERS – Daughter – b. 1874 Mile End – aged 7 – Scholar
Abraham MYERS – Son – b. 1877 Mile End – aged 4 – Scholar
Mary JONES – Domestic Servant

1871 Census

Address:

Finch Street, St. Mary Whitechapel

Residents:

Samuel MYERS – Head – b. 1837 Middlesex – aged 34 – Boot Maker
Leah MYERS – Wife – b. 1837 Middlesex – aged 34
Joseph MYERS – Son – b. 1858 Middlesex – aged 13
Sarah MYERS – Daughter – b. 1860 Middlesex – aged 11
Maria MYERS – Daughter – b. 1864 Middlesex – aged 7
Julia MYERS – Daughter – b. 1866 Middlesex – aged 5
Catherine MYERS - Daughter – b. 1868 Middlesex – aged 3
Judah MYERS – Son – b. 1871 Middlesex – aged 0
Mary CARPENTER – Domestic Servant

Marriage:

Samuel MYERS to Leah LYONS – Q2 1858 LONDON CITY 1c 272.

Death:

Samuel MYERS – Q3 1918 [84] HACKNEY 1b 423.
Buried at Plashet Cemetery – M-12-4 on 27 Sep 1918.

Jewish Chronicle – 04 Oct 1918

MYERS – On the 26th of September, 1918, at 62, Sandringham Road, Dalston, the residence of his daughter Julia, Samuel Myers, the beloved husband of the late Leah Myers, in his 85th year. Dearly beloved father of Joseph Myers, of Fitzroy, Melbourne; Miss Maria Myers and Mrs E. Joseph, of 62, Sandringham Road, Dalston; Mrs E.C. Trinder of "Bonheur", Harrow Road, West Worthing; and Alfred Myers, of 20, Houndsditch, E.C. Deeply mourned by his loving children, grandchildren, nieces, nephews and all who knew him. God rest his soul.

MYERS, Rose – A-12-16

Died: 09 Apr 1898
Buried: 12 Apr 1898
Partner: Solomon Myers (d. 1911)
Aged: 36 years

Jewish Chronicle – 15 Apr 1898

MYERS – On the 9th of April, at Clapton Cottage, Clapton, the dearly beloved wife of Solomon Myers, and daughter of Rachel and the late Jonas Lipman, and beloved sister of Mrs B. Isaacs and Mr I. Belasco, of the "Nag's Head", Houndsditch, aged 36 years. Shiva at "Nag's Head", Houndsditch. May her soul rest in peace.
MYERS – On the 9th of April, Rose, wife of Solomon Myers, of Clapton Cottage, daughter of Mrs Lipman and the late J. Lipman, and sister of Mrs S.A. Romain. Shiva at 17, Ritson Road, Dalston, commenced on Thursday evening.

Jewish Chronicle – 07 Oct 1898

The monument erected to the memory of the lamented Rose Myers, dearly beloved wife of Solomon Myers, Solicitor, of Upper Clapton and Wormwood Street, City, will be set at Plashet Cemetery, Romford Road, (Manor Park Station, GER) on Sunday, the 16th inst., at 1.30 p.m. Relatives and friends kindly accept this, the only intimation.

Death:

Q2 1898 [36] HACKNEY 1b 254.

1891 Census

Address:

59 Amhurst Road, Hackney

Residents:

Solomon MYERS – Head – b. 1861 Mile End – aged 30 – Solicitor
Rose MYERS – Wife – b. 1862 Aldgate – aged 29
Harry M. MYERS – Son – b. 1886 Hackney – aged 5

MYERS, Rose – A-12-16

James L. MYERS – Son – b. 1889 Hackney – aged 2
Esther L. MYERS – Daughter – b. 1890 Hackney – aged 1
Adelaide BLAKE – Nursemaid
Elizabeth SATCHELL – Domestic Servant

Marriage:
Solomon MYERS to Rose LIPMAN – Q3 1885 LONDON CITY 1c 168.

1901 Census

Address:
93, Upper Clapton Road, Hackney

Residents:
Solomon MYERS – Widower – b. 1862 London – aged 39 – Solicitor
Harry Moss MYERS – Son – b. 1887 Hackney – aged 14 – at School
Jonas Louis MYERS – Son – b. 1888 Hackney – aged 13 – at School
Esther Leah MYERS – Daughter – b. 1890 Hackney – aged 11 – at School
Solomon Aaron Michael MYERS – Son – b. 1892 Hackney – aged 9 – at School
Helen IRVIN – Nurse
Mayard WRIGHTMOUR – Domestic Servant

Death:
Solomon MYERS – Q3 1911 [50] HACKNEY 1b 466.
Buried at Plashet Cemetery – E-15-1 on 07 Sep 1911.

Jewish Chronicle – 08 Sep 1911

MYERS – On the 5th of September, at 14, Clapton Common, N.E., Solomon Myers, solicitor, late of 25, Wormwood Street, City, aged 50 years. Shiva at 14, Clapton Common. Deeply mourned by his sorrowing children.

PIZER (PISER), Yetta – A-11-12

Died: **18 Jan 1898**
Buried: **20 Jan 1898**
Partner: **Solomon Pizer (d. 1902)**
Aged: **69 years**

Jewish Chronicle – 21 Jan 1898

PIZER – On the 18th of January, at 39, Fournier Street, Mrs S. Pizer, the beloved sister of Mrs I. Levy. Shiva at 18, Little Alie Street, Commercial Road.
PIZER – On the 18th of January, at 39, Fournier Street, Yetta, the beloved wife of Mr S. Pizer. Shiva at 39, Fournier Street, Spitalfields.

PIZER (PISER), Yetta – A-11-12

Jewish Chronicle – 22 Jul 1898

The tombstone in memory of my dear wife, Yetta Piser, of 39, Fournier Street, Spitalfields, will be set at Plashet Cemetery on Sunday, July 24th 1898, about 3 o'clock.

Death:

Q1 1898 [69] WHITECHAPEL 1c 208.

1891 Census

Address:

15 Church Street, Spitalfields, London, Tower Hamlets

Residents:

Solomon PISER – Head – b.1824 Germany – aged 67 – Tailor
Yetta PISER – Wife – b. 1828 Germany – aged 63

1881 Census

Address:

15 Church Street, Spitalfields

Residents:

Solomon PISER – Head – b. 1826 Germany – aged 55 – Tailor Journeyman
Yetta PISER – Wife – b. 1827 Germany – aged 54
Alfred PISER – Son – b. 1856 Germany – aged 25 – Tailor's Foreman
Rachel PISER – Daughter – b. 1860 Germany – aged 21 – Hairdresser
Rosie PISER – Daughter – b. 1862 Germany – aged 19 – Tailoress
Samuel PISER – Son – b. 1864 St. George E – aged 17 – Tailor's Assistant
Julia PISER – Daughter – b. 1866 St. George E – aged 15
Mary SHEA – General Domestic Servant
Joseph READAJSLE – Boarder – b. 1858 Poland – aged 23 – Tailor's Foreman
Morris SYMONDS – Boarder – b. 1856 Poland – aged 25 – Tailor's Foreman
Elizabeth CHAMBERLINE – Boarder – b. 1855 Palbury – aged 26 – Tailoress
Emily BUTLER – Boarder – b. 1855 St. George E – aged 26 – Tailoress

1871 Census

Address:

Wilkes Street, Christchurch

Residents:

Soloman PISER – Head – b. 1823 Germany – aged 48
Yetta PISER – Wife – b. 1827 Germany – aged 44
Alfred PISER – Son – b. 1854 Germany – aged 17
Janey PISER – Daughter – b. 1855 Germany – aged 16
Rachel PISER – Daughter – b. 1857 Germany – aged 14
Rosa PISER – Daughter – b. 1859 Germany – aged 12
Peter PISER – Son – b. 1861 Middlesex – aged 10
Samuel PISER – Son – b. 1863 Middlesex – aged 8

Fanny PISER – Daughter – b. 1865 London – aged 6
Mrs RHINE – Mother-in-law – b. 1804 Germany – aged 67

1901 Census

Address:
18 Old Kent Road, St. George the Martyr, Southwark

Residents:
Alfred PYSER – Head – b. 1857 Germany – aged 44 – Tailor
Kate PYSER – Wife – b. 1861 Whitechapel – aged 40 – Confectioner & Tobacconist
Nathan PYSER – Son – b. 1883 Bethnal Green – aged 18 – Tailor
Louis PYSER - Son – b. 1884 Spitalfields – aged 17 – Tailor
Solomon PYSER – Father – Widower – b. 1823 Germany – aged 78 – Retired Tailor
Alice PEEL – General Domestic Servant

Death:
Solomon PISER – Q4 1902 [85] SOUTHWARK 1d 34.
Buried at Plashet Cemetery – A-11-13 on 07 Dec 1902.

POZNER, Abraham Louis (Lazarus) – A-11-19

Died: **23 Feb 1898**
Buried: **25 Feb 1898**
Partner: **Julia Pozner (d. 1907)**
Aged: **64 years**

Jewish Chronicle – 25 Feb 1898

POZNER – On the 23rd of February, at 115, Amhurst Road, Abraham Lazarus Pozner, the dearly beloved father of Mrs J. Samuel, 3, Sigdon Road, N.E. May his soul rest in peace. Shiva at 115, Amhurst Road.
POZNER – On the 23rd of February, at 115, Amhurst Road, after a long and painful illness, Abraham Lazarus, the dearly beloved husband of Julia Pozner, aged 64. May his soul rest in peace.

Jewish Chronicle – 13 May 1898

The tombstone to the memory of the late A.L. Pozner, of 27, Aldgate, will be set on Sunday, May 15th, at the Plashet Cemetery, at 4 o'clock. Friends and relatives kindly accept this, the only intimation.

Death:
Q1 1898 [63] HACKNEY 1b 355.

POZNER, Abraham Louis (Lazarus) – A-11-19

1891 Census

Address:

27 Aldgate, St. Katherine Cree, London

Residents:

Abraham L. POZNER – Head – b. 1836 Russia – aged 55 – Tailor
Julia POZNER – Wife – b. 1838 Whitechapel – aged 53
Annie POZNER – Daughter – b. 1865 Whitechapel – aged 26 – Music Teacher
Sarah POZNER – Daughter – b. 1867 Whitechapel – aged 24 – Dressmaker
Ray POZNER – Daughter – b. 1869 Whitechapel – aged 22 – Elocution Teacher
Fred POZNER – Son – b. 1871 Whitechapel – aged 20 – Tailor
Georgina POZNER – Daughter – b. 1872 Whitechapel – aged 19 – Music Teacher
Jennie POZNER – Daughter – b. 1875 Whitechapel – aged 16 – Dressmaker
Harry POZNER – Son – b. 1876 Whitechapel – aged 15 – Scholar
Monty POZNER – Son – b. 1878 Whitechapel – aged 13 – Scholar
Beatie POZNER – Daughter – b. 1880 Whitechapel – aged 11 – Scholar
Lizzy RILEY – General Servant

1881 Census

Address:

27 Aldgate, St. Katherine Cree

Residents:

Abraham Lazarus POZNER – Head – b. 1834 Poland – aged 47 – Tailor
Mrs POZNER – Wife – b. 1839 London – aged 42
Louis POZNER – Son – b. 1864 London – aged 17
Rose POZNER – Daughter – b. 1860 London – aged 21
Annie POZNER – Daughter – b. 1865 London – aged 16
Sarah POZNER – Daughter – b. 1866 London – aged 15
Rachel POZNER – Daughter – b. 1868 London – aged 13
Freddy POZNER – Son – b. 1871 London – aged 10 – Scholar
Georgina POZNER – Daughter – b. 1872 London – aged 9 – Scholar
Jenny POZNER – Daughter – b. 1874 London – aged 7 – Scholar
Harry POZNER – Son – b. 1876 London – aged 5
Monty POZNER – Son – b. 1878 London – aged 3
Rebecca POZNER – Daughter – b. 1879 London – aged 2

Marriage:

Abraham Lazarus POZNER to Julia JACOBS – Q1 1859 LONDON CITY 1c 258.

Death:

Julia POZNER – Q1 1907 [70] HACKNEY 1b 338.
Buried at Plashet Cemetery – G-19-45 on 28 Mar 1907.

Jewish Chronicle – 29 Mar 1907

POZNER – On the 25th of March, at 115, Amhurst Road, N.E., Julia, wife of the late A.L. Pozner, aged 70, and beloved mother of Mrs E. Ansell, 55, Manor Road, N.; Mrs J. Samuel, 70, Burma Road, N.; Mrs A. Liebler, 11, Tufnell Park, N.; Mrs S. Polak, 25, St. Mark's Villas, N.; Mrs G. Whiting, 60, Linthorpe Road, N.; Mrs H. Wasserman, 27, Bethune Road, N.; Fred Pozner, 191, Goldhurst Terrace, N.W.; Harry Pozner, 40, Norcott Road, N.; and Annie, Louis, and Montague Pozner. Deeply mourned by her children, grandchildren, relatives, and by all who knew her. May her dear soul rest in peace.

Jewish Chronicle – 06 Sep 1907

POZNER – The tombstone in loving memory of our dear mother, Mrs Julia Pozner, late of 115, Amhurst Road, Hackney, will be set at Plashet Cemetery on Sunday, September 15th at 4 o'clock. Relatives and friends please accept this, the only intimation.

SAMUEL, Samuel – C-9-1

Died:	**21 Nov 1898**
Buried:	**21 Nov 1898**
Hebrew Name:	**Samuel bar Zvi**
Parents:	**Henry and Rachel Samuel**
Aged:	9 years

Jewish Chronicle – 25 Nov 1898

SAMUEL – On Monday, the 21st of November, at 95, Middlesex Street, Aldgate, Sam, the beloved son of Henry and Rachel Samuel, aged 9 years. God rest his soul in peace.

Jewish Chronicle – 23 Jun 1899

The tombstone in ever loving memory of Sam, beloved son of Rachel and Henry Samuel, of 95, Middlesex Street, will be set at Plashet Cemetery at 4.30., on Sunday, July 2nd. Relatives and friends please accept this, the only intimation.

Death:

Q4 1898 [9] LONDON CITY 1c 2.

Birth:

Samuel SAMUELS – Q3 1889 LONDON CITY 1c 7.

1891 Census

Address:

95 Middlesex Street, Aldgate Without, London

SAMUEL, Samuel – C-9-1

Residents:

Samuel BARNET – Head – b. 1824 Aldgate – aged 67 – Refreshment House Keeper (Imbecile) Henry SAMUEL – Son-in-law – b. 1857 Aldgate – aged 34 – Commission Agent
Rachel SAMUEL – Daughter – b. 1858 Aldgate – aged 33
Rebecca SAMUEL – Granddaughter – b. 1887 Aldgate – aged 4
Samuel SAMUEL – Grandson – b. 1890 Aldgate – aged 1
Benjamin SAMUEL – Grandson – b. 1891 Aldgate – aged 3 weeks
Samuel BARNET – Son – b. 1854 Aldgate – aged 37 – Horse Dealer
Deborah PHILLIPS – Nurse
Fred SADDLER – Boarder – b. 1846 Surrey – aged 45 – Caretaker
Isaac LEVY – Boarder – b. 1866 London – aged 25 – Butcher
David WEITHEMIER – Boarder – b. 1870 London – aged 21 – Butcher
Margaret BALL – General Servant

1901 Census

Address:

95 Middlesex Street, St. Botolph Without Aldgate

Residents:

Henry SAMUEL – Head – b. 1856 London – aged 45 – Clothing Shipper
Rachel SAMUEL – Wife – b. 1858 London – aged 43
Rebecca SAMUEL – Daughter – b. 1887 London – aged 14
Benjamin SAMUEL – Son – b. 1891 London – aged 10
Isaac SAMUEL – Son – b. 1893 London – aged 8
Sarah EMANUEL – Sister – Widow – b. 1848 London – aged 53
Samuel EMANUEL – Nephew – b. 1886 London – aged 15
Samuel BARNETT – Brother-in-law – b. 1854 London – aged 47

1911 Census

Address:

43 Lewiston Place, North Hackney

Residents:

Henry SAMUEL – Head – Widower – b. 1858 London – aged 53 – Secondhand Clothier
Benjamin SAMUEL – Son – b. 1891 London – aged 20 – Secondhand Clothier
Isaac SAMUEL – Son – b. 1893 London – aged 18 – Secondhand Clothier
Samuel EMANUEL – Nephew – b. 1887 London – aged 24 – Secondhand Clothier
Sarah EMANUEL – Sister – Widow – b. 1849 London – aged 62
Benjamin COHEN – Son-in-law – b. 1875 London – aged 36 – General Dealer
Rebecca COHEN – Daughter (wife of above – married 2 years) – b. 1887 London – aged 24
Cecilia PODDINGTON – Domestic Servant

Marriage:
Henry SAMUEL to Rachel BARNETT – Q1 1886 LONDON CITY 1c 98.

Death:
Rachel SAMUEL – Q2 1907 [51] MILE END OLD TOWN 1c 256.
Buried at Plashet Cemetery – G-20-11 on 04 Apr 1907.

Henry SAMUEL – Q3 1914 [59] HACKNEY 1b 429.
Buried at Plashet Cemetery – L-16-42 on 03 Sep 1914.

SEIGENBERG, John – D-8-1

Died: **10 Dec 1898**
Buried: **12 Dec 1898**
Hebrew Name: **Yona bar Yaakov**
Partner: **Julia Seigenberg (d. 1926)**
Age: **53 years**

Jewish Chronicle – 06 Dec 1898

SEIGENBERG – On the 10th of December, 1898, at 56, Romford Road, E., John Seigenberg, the beloved father of Mrs H.I. Freiwald, 127, West 75th Street, New York City, and Braham Seigenberg, 520, East 78th Street, New York City. Gone but not forgotten.

Jewish Chronicle – 21 Apr 1899

The tombstone in memory of the late John Seigenberg, husband of Mrs J. Seigenberg, of 56, Romford Road, E., will be set on Sunday, the 23rd inst., at 4 o'clock at Plashet Cemetery. Relatives and friends please accept this, the only intimation.

Death:
Q4 1898 [63] WEST HAM 4a 15.

1891 Census

Address:
313 Mile End Road, Mile End Old Town

Residents:
John SEIGENBERG – Head – b. 1846 London – aged 45 – Bedding Manufacturer
Julia SEIGENBERG – Wife – b. 1843 Liverpool – aged 48 – Cutter
Louis SEIGENBERG – Son – b. 1874 London – aged 17 – Traveller
Julia SEIGENBERG – Daughter – b. 1872 London – aged 19
Leon SEIGENBERG – Son – b. 1876 London – aged 15 – General Porter
Rosey SEIGENBERG – Daughter – b. 1881 London – aged 10 - Scholar

SEIGENBERG, John – D-8-1

Willie SEIGENBERG – Son – b. 1883 London – aged 8 – Scholar
Leopold SEIGENBERG – Grandson – b. 1889 London – aged 2
Alice FORD – Domestic Servant

1881 Census

Address:
96 Whitechapel Road, Whitechapel

Residents:
John SEIGENBERG – Head – b. 1845 London – aged 36 – Bedding Manufacturer
Julia SEIGENBERG – Wife – b. 1845 Liverpool – aged 36
Jacob SEIGENBERG – Son – b. 1866 Middlesex – aged 15
Abraham SEIGENBERG – Son – b. 1868 Middlesex – aged 13
Sarah SEIGENBERG – Daughter – b. 1870 Middlesex – aged 11
Julia SEIGENBERG – Daughter – b. 1872 Middlesex – aged 9
Lewis SEIGENBERG – Son – b. 1874 Middlesex – aged 7
Lyon SEIGENBERG – Son – b. 1876 Middlesex – aged 5
Michael SEIGENBERG – Son – b. 1877 Middlesex – aged 4
Samuel SEIGENBERG – Son – b. 1879 Middlesex – aged 2
Rosalie SEIGENBERG – Daughter – b. 1881 Middlesex – aged 0
Alice GIBBS – Domestic Servant
Ellen LORDNER – Domestic Servant
George BOHR – Domestic Servant

1871 Census

Address:
12 Commercial Road, East Bedford Place, Mile End Old Town

Residents:
John SEIGENBERG – Head - b. 1846 London – aged 25 – Bedding Manufacturer
Julia SEIGENBERG – Wife – b. 1844 Liverpool – aged 27
Jacob SEIGENBERG – Son – b. 1866 Middlesex – aged 5
Abraham SEIGENBERG – Son – b. 1868 Middlesex – aged 3
Sarah SEIGENBERG – Daughter – b. 1870 Middlesex – aged 1
Jacob SEIGENBERG – Cousin – b. 1850 London – aged 21
James HANCOCK – Servant
Hannah BELCHER – Domestic Servant

Marriage:
Jonas SEIGENBERG to Julia JACOBS – Q1 1865 LONDON CITY 1c 205.

1901 Census

Address:

306 Old Ford Road, Bethnal Green

Residents:

Julia SEIGENBERG – Head – Widow – b. 1844 Liverpool – aged 57 – Bedding Manufacturer
Sarah FRISWALD – Daughter – Widow – b. 1870 Stepney – aged 31
Lyon SEIGENBERG – Son – b. 1875 Whitechapel – aged 26 – Mattress Maker
Rosie SEIGENBERG – Daughter – b. 1881 Whitechapel – aged 20
William SEIGENBERG – Son – b. 1882 Whitechapel – aged 19 – Mattress Maker
Julia SEIGENBERG – Daughter – b. 1890 Whitechapel – aged 11
Alfred LEVY – Visitor –b. 1874 Shoreditch – aged 27 – Tailors Cutter

1911 Census

Address:

16 Pembury Road, Westcliff

Residents:

Samuel SAMUELS – Head – b. 1884 Mile End – aged 27 – Commercial Traveller
Rosalie SAMUELS – Wife (6 years) – b. 1882 Whitechapel – aged 29
Maria Julia SAMUELS – Daughter – b. 1908 W. Ham – aged 3
John SAMUELS – Son – b. 1911 W. Ham – aged 11 months
Julia SEIGENBERG – Mother-in-law – Widow – b. 1845 Liverpool – aged 66
Simeon SAMUELS – Brother – b. 1885 Mile End – aged 26 – Art Traveller
Lily SAYER – Servant
Lydia B. RAVENOR – Boarder – b. 1879 Lymington – aged 32 – Manageress
Evelyn M. RAVENOR – Boarder – b. 1880 Lymington – aged 31 – Manageress

Death:

Julia SEIGENBERG – Q3 1926 [83] ROCHFORD 4a 573.
Buried at Willesden Cemetery – LX-2-37 on 03 Oct 1926.

SIMMONS, Annie – A-13-6

Died: 27 Apr1898
Buried: 29 Apr1898
Hebrew Name: Hannah bat Shlomo
Partner: Joseph Simmons (Yosef Ben Aahron) (d. 1907)
Aged: 48 years

Jewish Chronicle – 29 Apr 1898

SIMMONS – On the 27th of April, at 58, Clissold Road, N., Annie, the beloved wife of Joseph Simmons and sister of H. Joseph, 332, Kingsland Road, aged 48.

SIMMONS, Annie – A-13-6

Jewish Chronicle – 19 Aug 1898

The tombstone in memory of Annie, the beloved wife of Joseph Simmons, of 56, Clissold Road, N., will be set at 1 o'clock on Sunday next, August 21st, at Plashet Cemetery. Relatives and friends kind accept this intimation.

Death:
Q2 1898 [47] ISLINGTON 1b 235.

1891 Census
Address:
129 Boleyn Road, Islington
Residents:
Joseph SIMMONS – Head –b. 1852 London – aged 39 – Commercial Traveller
Annie SIMMONS – Wife – b. 1852 London – aged 39
Elizabeth SIMMONS – Daughter – b. 1891 Islington – 8 months
Ellen FOSTER – General Servant
Laura COLEMAN – Nursemaid

Marriage:
Joseph SIMMONS to Annie JOSEPH – Q3 1887 MARYLEBONE 1a 1263.

1901 Census
Address:
56, Clissold Road, Stoke Newington
Residents:
Joseph SIMMONS – Head – Widower – b. 1852 London – aged 49 – Cigar Dealer
Esther SIMMONS – Sister – b. 1874 London – aged 27
Bessie SIMMONS – Daughter – b. 1891 London – aged 10
Esther SIMMONS – Daughter – b. 1893 London – aged 8
Isabel SIMMONS – Daughter – b. 1895 London – aged 6
Mabel RUSSELL – Nurse/Domestic
Kate SCHAUMCOFPL – General Domestic Servant

Death:
Joseph SIMMONS – Q1 1907 [55] HACKNEY 1b 283.
Buried at Plashet Cemetery – A-13-7 on 13 Jan 1907.

Jewish Chronicle – 18 Jan 1907

SIMMONS – On the 13th of January, at 56, Clissold Road, Clissold Park, N., Joseph Simmons, aged 55.

Jewish Chronicle – 01 Feb1907

The daughters and sisters of the late Joseph Simmons return thanks for kind visits and expressions of sympathy and condolence during their week of mourning – 56, Clissold Road, N.

SOLOMONS, Michael – A-14-25

Died: 29 Oct 1898
Buried: 31 Oct 1898
Hebrew Name: Moshe ben David Halevi
Aged: 68 years

Jewish Chronicle – 04 Nov 1898

SOLOMONS – On the 29th of October, at 43, Bishopsgate Street Without, Michael Solomons (many years with Defries and Sons, Houndsditch), beloved brother of Zalig Solomons, of Leslie Street, Mile End, brother-in-law of Phillip Harris and beloved uncle of Lizzie Harris, of 48, Bishopsgate Street, E.C., and Mrs H. Abrahams, of 168, King's Road, Camden Town. Deeply mourned by his brother, brother-in-law, nieces and nephews and a large circle of friends. Gone, but will not be forgotten. God rest his dear soul.

Jewish Chronicle – 30 Jun 1899

The memorial stone in loving memory of Michael Solomons, late of 43, Bishopsgate Street Without, will be set at Plashet Cemetery, Sunday next, July 2nd, at 3.30. Relatives and friends kindly accept this, the only intimation.

Death:
Q4 1898 [68] LONDON CITY 1c 1.

1881 Census

Address:
St. James Place, St. James, Dukes Place

Residents:
Phillip HARRIS – Head – b. 1829 Middlesex – aged 52 – Commission Agent
Hester HARRIS – Wife – b. 1829 Middlesex – aged 52 – Housekeeper
Lizzie HARRIS – Daughter – b. 1858 Middlesex – aged 23 – Assistant Housekeeper
Michael SOLOMONS – Brother – b. 1830 Middlesex – aged 51 – Warehouseman
Martha DENNISON – Domestic Servant

SOLOMONS, Michael – A-14-25

1871 Census

Address:

21 Rufford's Buildings, Islington

Residents:

Phillip HARRIS – Head – b. 1829 Middlesex – aged 42 – Licensed Victualler
Esther HARRIS – Wife – b. 1829 London – aged 42
Elizabeth HARRIS – Daughter – b. 1857 London – aged 14
Walter HARRIS – Son – b. 1860 London – aged 11
David HARRIS – Son – b. 1862 London – aged 9
Michael SOLOMONS – Brother-in-law – b. 1828 London – aged 43 – Warehouseman

WOOLF, Joel – A-13-11

Died: 25 May 1898
Buried: 26 May 1898
Hebrew Name: Yoel bar Itzak
Partner: Helen/Ellen Woolf (d. 1882)
Aged: 70 years

Jewish Chronicle – 03 Jun 1898

WOOLF – On the 25th of May, at 10, St. Marks Street, Goodman's Fields, London E., Joel Woolf, dearly beloved father of Mrs J. Benjamin and Miss Rose Woolf, of the above address, Godfrey Woolf, 12, Colmar Street, Alderney Road, E., Lawrence Woolf, 257, Balls Pond Road, Essex Road, N., Mrs A. Harris, 81, Commercial Road, E., Mrs A.D. Marks, 28, Highbury New Park, N., Mr Isaac Woolf, 27, Grafton Street, Mile End Road, E. and Mrs Sam. Davis, of Johannesburg. Deeply lamented by his loving children, grandchildren and a large circle of friends. God rest his dear soul.

Jewish Chronicle – 25 Nov 1898

The tombstone in loving memory of Joel Woolf, late of 10, St. Marks Street, Aldgate, will be set at the Plashet Cemetery on Sunday next, November 27th at 3 o'clock. Relatives and friends will please accept this, the only intimation.

Death:

Q2 1898 [71] WHITECHAPEL 1c 199.

1891 Census

Address:

10 St. Marks Street, St. Mary Whitechapel

Residents:

Joel WOOLF – Head – b. 1829 Whitechapel – aged 62 – Baker
Hyman BENJAMIN – Son-in-law – b. 1852 Aldgate – aged 39 – Hotel Manager
Jane BENJAMIN – Daughter – b. 1852 Aldgate – aged 39
Rosetta WOOLF – Daughter – b. 1869 Aldgate – aged 22 – Assistant Baker
Ellen BENJAMIN – Granddaughter – b. 1879 Spitalfields – aged 12 – Scholar
Angels BENJAMIN – Grandson – b. 1882 Whitechapel – aged 9 – Scholar
Susan TAYLOR – Domestic Servant

1881 Census

Address:

10 St. Marks Street, Whitechapel

Residents:

Joel WOOLF – Head – b. 1829 London – aged 52 – Master Baker employing 3 hands
Helen WOOLF – Wife – b. 1829 London – aged 52
Godfrey WOOLF – Son – b. 1856 London – aged 25 – Bakers Assistant
Laurence WOOLF – Son – b. 1859 London – aged 22 – Bakers Assistant
Elizabeth WOOLF – Daughter – b. 1861 London - aged 20 – Bakers Assistant
Susan WOOLF – Daughter – b. 1863 London – aged 18 – Bakers Assistant
Rose WOOLF – Daughter – b. 1867 London – aged 14 – Scholar
Isaac WOOLF – Son – b. 1869 London – aged 12 – Scholar
Charles BRUSHNALL – Bakers Assistant

1871 Census

Address:

4 New Street, Aldgate

Residents:

Joel WOOLF – Head – b. 1829 London – aged 42 – Baker
Ellen WOOLF – Wife – b. 1829 London – aged 42
Jane WOOLF – Daughter – b. 1853 London – aged 18 – Machinist
Godfrey WOOLF – Son – b. 1856 London – aged 15 – Bootmaker
Sarah WOOLF – Daughter – b. 1858 London – aged 13 – Feather Maker
Laurence WOOLF – Son – b. 1860 London – aged 11 – Scholar
Elizabeth WOOLF – Daughter – b. 1861 London – aged 10 – Scholar
Susan WOOLF – Daughter – b. 1863 London – aged 8
Rosetta WOOLF – Daughter – b. 1865 London – aged 6
Isaac WOOLF – Son – b. 1869 London – aged 2
Ann DRISCOL – Domestic Servant

1861 Census

Address:

4 New Street, St. Botolph Aldgate, City of London

Residents:

Joel WOOLF – Head – b. 1828 London – aged 33 – Baker
Ellen WOOLF – Wife – b. 1826 London – aged 35
Jane WOOLF – Daughter – b. 1853 London – aged 8
Godfrey WOOLF – Son – b. 1856 London – aged 5
Sarah WOOLF – Daughter – b. 1858 London – aged 3
Laurence WOOLF – Son – b. 1859 London – aged 2
Elizabeth WOOLF – Daughter – b. 1861 London – aged 9 months
Gabriel PHILLIPS – Servant
Ann MOXLEY – Servant

1851 Census

Address:

13, Butler Street, Christchurch, Tower Hamlets

Residents:

Isaac WOOLF – Head – b. 1793 Amsterdam – aged 58 – General Dealer
Jane WOOLF – Wife – b. 1801 Amsterdam – aged 50
Joel WOOLF – Son – b. 1828 Whitechapel – aged 23 – Baker
Sarah WOOLF – Daughter – b. 1834 Spitalfields – aged 17 – Cap Maker
Fanny WOOLF – Daughter – b. 1836 Spitalfields – aged 15 – Tailoress
Mary JACOBS – Sister-in-law – b. 1811 Amsterdam – aged 40 – House Servant

Marriage:

Joel WOOLF to Helen SOLOMONS – Q4 1851 ST. LUKE 2 455.

Death:

Ellen WOOLF – Q1 1882 [53] WHITECHAPEL 1c 322.
Place of burial unknown.

Jewish Chronicle – 03 Feb 1882

On the 29th of January, at 10, St. Mark Street, Goodman's Fields, Ellen, the beloved wife of Joel Woolf, in her 53rd year. May her soul rest in peace. American papers please copy.

ZEFFERT, Sarah – A-11-9

Died: 11 Jan 1898
Buried: 12 Jan 1898
Partner: Aaron Zeffert (d. 1900)
Aged: 70 years

Jewish Chronicle – 14 Jan 1898

ZEFFERT – On the 11th of January, Sarah, the beloved wife of Aaron Zeffert, of 17, Fort Street, Spital Square, late of Widegate Street, and beloved mother of Mr I.D. Zeffert, N. Zeffert, Mrs Goodman, of Liverpool, Mrs Raymond, Mrs Cohen, Mrs Feldman, and Miss Zeffert, who deeply feel the loss of a true and loving mother. May her soul rest in peace. Shiva at 17, Fort Street.

Jewish Chronicle – 22 Dec 1899

The tombstone in memory of Sarah Zeffert, late of 17, Fort Street, formerly of Widegate Street, will be set at Plashet Cemetery, on Monday next, 25th inst., at 11 o'clock. Relatives and friends kindly accept this, the only intimation. Train leaves Fenchurch Street, 10.28.

Death:

Q1 1898 [70] WHITECHAPEL 1c 207.

1891 Census

Address:

20 Widegate Street, Bishopsgate, London

Residents:

Aaron ZEFFERTT – Head – b. 1826 Poland – aged 65 – Wholesale Cap Maker
Sarah ZEFFERTT – Wife – b. 1829 Poland – aged 62
Joe ZEFFERTT – Son – b. 1859 London – aged 32 – Traveller in Caps
Leah ZEFFERTT – Daughter – b. 1869 London – aged 22 – Cap Maker
Miriam ZEFFERTT – Daughter – b. 1870 London – aged 21 – Cap Maker
Morris GOODMAN – Grandson – b. 1878 Liverpool – aged 13 – Scholar
Bridget – Domestic Servant

1881 Census

Registered as TIFFERT

Address:

20 Widegate Street, St. Botolph Without, Bishopsgate

Residents:

Aaron ZEFFERT – b. 1826 Poland – aged 55 – Cap Maker
Susan ZEFFERT – Wife – b. 1829 Poland – aged 52 – Cap Maker
Joseph ZEFFERT – Son - b. 1857 Middlesex – aged 24 – Cap Maker
Nathan ZEFFERT – Son – b. 1859 Middlesex – aged 22 – Shoemaker
Annie ZEFFERT – Daughter – b. 1860 Middlesex – aged 21 – Cap Maker
Nancy ZEFFERT – Daughter – b. 1864 Middlesex – aged 17 – Feather Maker
Leah ZEFFERT – Daughter – b. 1868 Middlesex – aged 13 – Cap Maker
Miriam ZEFFERT – Daughter – b. 1870 Middlesex – aged 11 - Scholar

1871 Census

Address:

20 Widegate Street, Bishopsgate, City of London

Residents:

Aaron ZEFFERT – Head – b. 1825 Poland – aged 46 – Cap & Hat Manufacturer
Sarah ZEFFERT – Wife – b. 1829 Poland – aged 42
Jane ZEFFERT – Daughter – b. 1854 Middlesex – aged 17
Isaac ZEFFERT – Son – b. 1855 Middlesex – aged 16
Joseph ZEFFERT – Son – b. 1857 Middlesex – aged 14
Nathan ZEFFERT – Son – b. 1859 Middlesex – aged 12
Annie ZEFFERT – Daughter – b. 1861 Middlesex – aged 10
Nancy ZEFFERT – Daughter – b. 1863 Middlesex – aged 8
Leah ZEFFERT – Daughter – b. 1868 Middlesex – aged 3
Miriam ZEFFERT – Daughter – b. 1870 Middlesex – aged 1
Goldy FIELDMAN – Boarder – b. 1848 Poland – aged 23 – unknown
Isaac BLUMMANTHAL – Lodger – b. 1813 Poland – aged 58 – Flat Cleaner
Mary SCANNET – Domestic Servant

1861 Census

Address:

20 Widegate Street, St. Botolph Bishopsgate, London

Residents:

Aaron ZEFFERTT – Head – b. 1829 Poland – aged 32 – Cap Maker
Sarah ZEFFERTT – Wife – b. 1833 Poland – aged 28
Jane ZEFFERTT – Daughter – b. 1854 London – aged 7 – Scholar
Isaac ZEFFERTT – Son – b. 1855 London – aged 6 – Scholar
Joseph ZEFFERTT – Son – b. 1857 London – aged 4 – Scholar
Nathan ZEFFERTT – Son – b. 1859 London – aged 2 – Scholar
Hannah ZEFFERTT – Daughter – b. 1860 London – aged 1
Moses FRIEDLAND – Servant – b. 1842 Austria – aged 19 – Cap Maker
Marie HILL – Domestic Servant

Death:

Aaron ZEFFERT – Q1 1900 [77] WHITECHAPEL 1c 210.
Buried at Plashet Cemetery – B-7-31 on 25 Mar 1900.

Jewish Chronicle – 30 Mar 1900

ZEFFERT – On the 23rd of March, at 17, Fort Street, Spital Square, Aron Zeffert aged 77 years. Deeply mourned. May his soul rest in peace.

Jewish Chronicle – 08 Mar 1901

The tombstone to the memory of the late Aron Zeffert, of Fort Street, will be set, at Plashet Cemetery, on Sunday, March 10th, at 2 p.m. Only intimation. Train from Fenchurch Street, 1.10.

1899

BARNETT, Eva – D-11-31

Died: 20 Mar 1899
Buried: 22 Mar 1899
Parents: Abraham & Fanny Barnett
Aged: 25th year

Jewish Chronicle – 24 Mar 1899

BARNETT – On the 20th of March, 1899, at her residence, 4, Nottingham Place, Commercial Road, E., after a long and painful illness, in her 25th year, Eva, dearly beloved youngest daughter of the late Mr and Mrs Barnett, formerly of 3, Greenfield Street, E. Mourned by her sorrowing sisters and brothers, relatives and a large circle of friends. May her soul rest in peace. Gone from our home, but never from our hearts. South African papers please copy.

Jewish Chronicle – 20 May 1904

The tombstone in loving memory of Eva Barnett will be set at Plashet Cemetery on Sunday, May 29th, 1904, at 4.30 p.m. Relatives and friends please accept this intimation. May her soul rest in peace.

Death:

Q1 1899 [23] HOLBORN 1b 482.

1891 Census

Address:

3 Greenfield Street, Mile End Old Town

Residents:

Joseph LEVY – Head - b. 1866 Poland – aged 25 - Tailor
Dorah LEVY – Wife - b. 1868 Poland – aged 23
Abraham BARNETT - b. 1866 Poland – aged 25 – Waterproofer
Annie BARNETT - b. 1866 Poland – aged 25 – Button Hole Maker
Eva BARNETT - b. 1870 Poland – aged 21 – Button Hole Maker

1881 Census

Address:

18 Nottingham Place, Mile End Old Town

Residents:

Abraham BARNETT – Head – b. 1835 Poland – aged 46 – Rag merchant
Fanny BARNETT – Wife – b. 1831 Poland – aged 50
Isaac BARNETT – Son - b. 1854 Poland – aged 27 – Tailor
Abraham BARNETT – Son - b. 1862 Poland – aged 19 – Waterproofer
Anne BARNETT – Daughter - b. 1863 Poland – aged 18

Dora BARNETT – Daughter - b. 1867 Poland – aged 14
Eve BARNETT – Daughter - b. 1870 Poland - aged 11
Eve DAVIS – Niece - b. 1860 Poland – aged 21

Death:

Abraham BARNETT – Q1 1886 [54] HACKNEY 1b 382.
Buried at West Ham Cemetery – J-3-38 on 22 Jan 1886.

Fanny BARNETT – Q4 1890 [60] MILE END OLD TOWN 1c 360.
Place of burial unknown.

BARNETT, Solomon – B-5-29

Died: **20 Dec 1899**
Buried: **21 Dec 1899**
Hebrew Name: **Solomon ben Baruch**
Partner: **Amelia Leah Barnett (d. 1927)**
Aged: **50 years**

Jewish Chronicle – 22 Dec 1899

BARNETT – On Wednesday, the 20th of December, at 24, Cable Street, E., after a long and painful illness, Solomon Barnett, aged 50. Deeply mourned by his sorrowing wife and children. May his soul rest in peace. American papers please copy.

Jewish Chronicle – 28 Sep 1900

The tombstone in loving memory of the late Solomon Barnett, will be set at 3 p.m. on Sunday, September 30th, at Plashet Cemetery. Relatives and friends please accept this intimation – 24 Cable Street, E.

Death:

Q4 1899 [55] WHITECHAPEL 1c 255.

1891 Census

Address:

24 Cable Street, St. Mary Whitechapel, London

Residents:

Solomon BARNETT – Head – b. 1847 Russia – aged 44 – Clothier
Leah BARNETT – Wife – b. 1853 Russia – aged 38
Samuel BARNETT – Son – b. 1874 Whitechapel – aged 17 – Wood Turner
Harry BARNETT – Son – b. 1875 Whitechapel – aged 16 – Cabinet Maker's Apprentice
Kitty BARNETT – Daughter – b. 1877 Whitechapel – aged 14 – Apprentice Tailoress

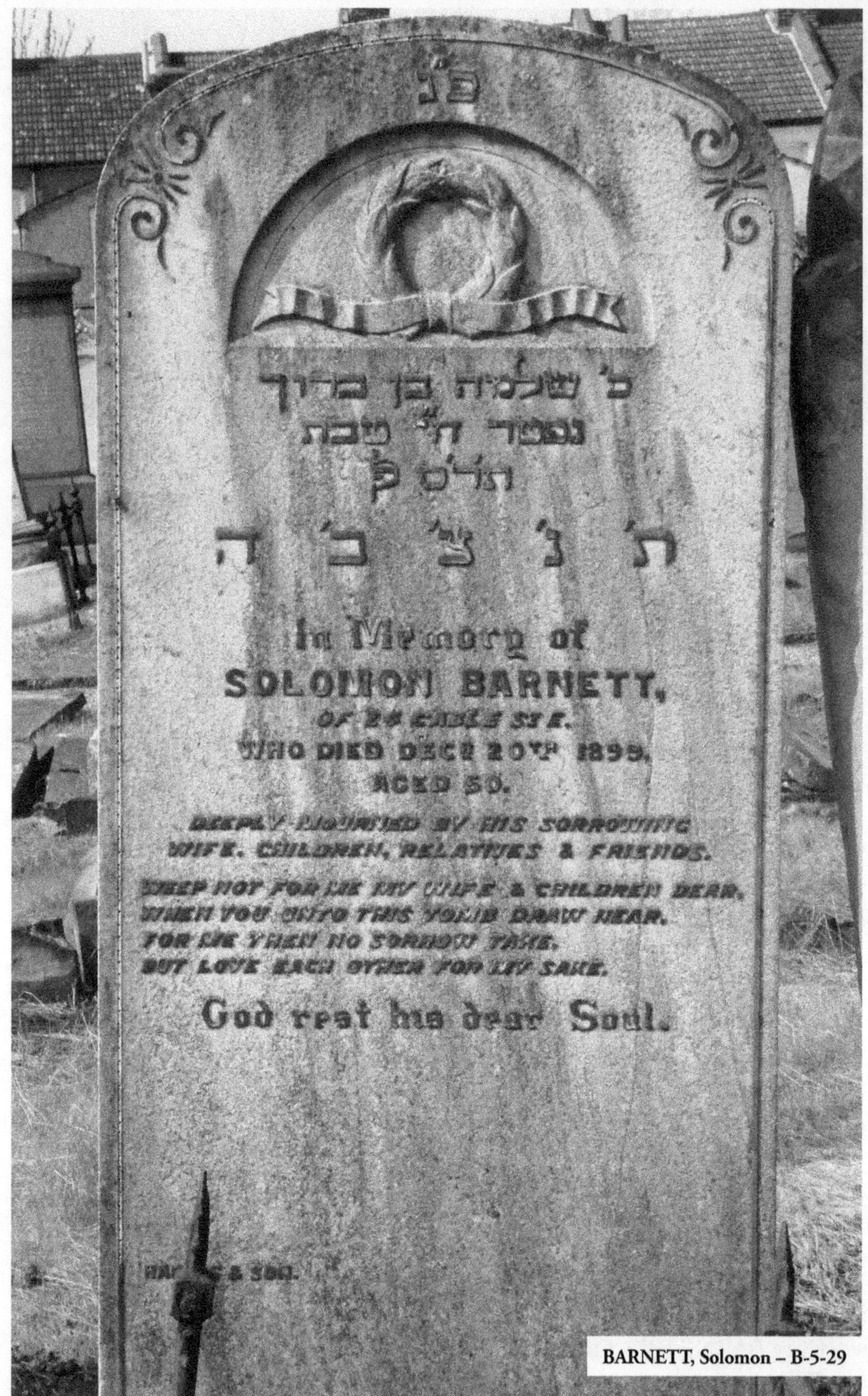

BARNETT, Solomon – B-5-29

Sarah BARNETT – Daughter b. 1879 Whitechapel – aged 12 – Scholar
Louis BARNETT – Son – b. 1880 Whitechapel – aged 11 – Scholar
Israel GOLDBERG – Brother-in-law b. 1865 Russia – aged 26 – Jewellers Assistant
Teresa MOFFAT – Domestic Servant

1881 Census

Address:
54 Cable Street, Whitechapel

Residents:
Solomon BARNETT – Head – b. 1846 Poland – aged 35 – Clothier
Amelia L. BARNETT – Wife – b. 1852 Poland – aged 29
Samuel BARNETT – Son – b. 1874 Whitechapel – aged 7 - Scholar
Harris BARNETT – Son – b. 1875 Whitechapel – aged 6 – Scholar
Kitty BARNETT – Daughter – b. 1877 Whitechapel – aged 4 – Scholar
Sarah BARNETT – Daughter – b. 1879 Whitechapel – aged 2
Lewis BARNETT – Son – b. 1880 Whitechapel – aged 1
Israel GOLDBERG – Boarder – b. 1863 Poland – aged 18 – Traveller (Fancy Goods)
Joseph GOLDBERG – Boarder – b. 1866 Poland – aged 15 – Apprentice Traveller
Agnes WHITE – General Servant

Marriage:
Solomon BARNETT to Amelia Leah GOLDBERG – Q4 1871 LONDON CITY 1c 212.

1871 Census

Address:
Hackney Road, Bethnal Green, London

Residents:
Solomon BARNETT – Head – b. 1845 Russia – aged 26
Abraham BARNETT – Brother – b. 1847 Russia – aged 24
Henry BARNETT – Brother – b. 1850 Russia – aged 21
Ephraim BARNETT – Brother – b. 1853 Russia – aged 18
Sophia BARNETT – Mother – b. 1814 Russia – aged 57
Fanny BARNETT – Sister – b. 1843 Russia – aged 28

Death:
Amelia L. BARNETT – Q1 1927 [75] BRENTFORD 3a 268.
Buried at Willesden Cemetery – LX-5-4 on 08 Feb 1927.

Jewish Chronicle – 11 Feb 1927

BARNETT – On Sunday, the 6th of February, 1927, at the residence of her son, Louis B. Barnett, "The Chestnuts", Hamilton Road, Ealing Common, W.5, Amelia Leah, relict of the late Solomon Barnett, aged 75. Sorrowfully mourned by her sons and daughters, Samuel, Kitty, Sadie (Mrs Sol. Fredman, Bulawayo), and Louis, daughter-in-law and grandchildren, brother and sister-in-law, Harry and Jules Goldberg. Shiva at the above address.

BLOM, Lewis Reginald - C-13-27

Died: **04 Oct 1899**
Buried: **05 Oct 1899**
Parents: **Nathan & Jane Blom**
Aged: **6 months**

Jewish Chronicle – 06 Oct 1899

BLOM – On the 4th of October, at 462, Hackney Road, N.E., Lewis Reginald, beloved son of Nathan and Jane Blom, aged 6 months. May his soul rest in peace.

Jewish Chronicle – 08 Jun 1900

The tombstone to the loving memory of Reggie, the infant son of Nathan and Jane Blom, 462, Hackney Road, will be set on Sunday, June 10th, at Plashet Cemetery, at 4 o'clock. Relatives and friends accept this, the only intimation.

Death:

Louis Reginald BLOM – Q4 1899 [0] BETHNAL GREEN 1c 116.

Birth:

Louis Reginald BLOM – Q2 1899 BETHNAL GREEN 1c 145.

1891 Census

Address:

10 Carlton Square, Mile End Old Town

Residents:

Nathan BLOM – Head – b. 1861 Spitalfields – aged 30 – Foreman Cigar Maker
Jane BLOM – Wife – b. 1867 London – aged 24
Elizabeth BLOM – Daughter – b. 1890 Mile End – aged 1
Harry BLOM – Son – b. 1891 Mile End – aged 3 months
Elizabeth BLOM – Sister – b. 1886 Whitechapel – aged 5
John BLOM – Visitor – b. 1889 St. Annes – aged 2
Harriett GRIMES – General Servant
Bella CLASH – General Servant

1901 Census

Address:

462 Hackney Road, Bethnal Green

Residents:

Nathan BLOM (BLOOME) – Head – b. 1861 Spitalfields – aged 40 – Cigar Manufacturer
Jane BLOM – Wife – b. 1864 Spitalfields – aged 37
Elizabeth BLOM – Daughter – b. 1890 Mile End – aged 11
Harold BLOM – Son – b. 1891 Mile End – aged 10
Alfred BLOM – Son – b. 1893 Mile End – aged 8
Mary JONES – Domestic Servant

Marriage:

Nathan BLOM to Jane VAN SLUIS – Q4 1888 LONDON CITY 1c 163.

Death:

Nathan BLOM – Q3 1911 [50] BETHNAL GREEN 1c 176.
Buried at Plashet Cemetery – K-24-13 on 14 Jul 1911.

Jewish Chronicle – 21 Jul 1911

BLOM – On the 12th of July, at 462, Hackney Road, Nathan Blom, beloved husband of Jane Blom. Deeply mourned by his sorrowing wife, sons and daughter. God rest his dear soul.

Jewish Chronicle – 19 Apr 1912

BLOM – The tombstone in loving memory of the late Nathan Blom will be consecrated at Plashet Cemetery on Sunday, April 28th, at 3 p.m. - 462, Hackney Road, NE.

Death:

Jane BLOM – Q4 1930 [66] HAMPSTEAD 1a 644.
Buried at Plashet Cemetery – K-24-14 on 28 Oct 1930.

Jewish Chronicle – 31 Oct 1930

BLOM – On Saturday, the 25th of October, Jane Blom, widow of Nathan Blom, beloved mother of Bessie (Mrs Sydney Solomon), Harold and Alfred. Sadly missed by her children, brothers, sister and grandchildren. God rest her dear soul. 51, Greencroft Gardens, Hampstead, N.W.6.
BLOM – On the 25th of October, at 51, Greencroft Gardens, Jane Blom, beloved sister of Jack Solomons, 23, Norfolk Square, Brighton.
BLOM – On the 25th of October, at 51, Greencroft Gardens, Jane Blom, beloved sister of Mrs Hannah Blom. Shiva at 60, Carlton Mansions, Stamford Hill, N.

BUCKS, Michael – A-14-53

Died: 19 Feb 1899
Buried: 21 Feb 1899
Partner: Hannah Bucks (d. 1911)
Aged: 68th year

Jewish Chronicle – 24 Feb 1899

BUCKS – On the 19th of February, at 12, Cannon Street Road, St. George's E., in his 68th year, Michael, the dearly beloved husband of Hannah Bucks, father of Mrs J. Levy, of 91, Bishop's Road, N.E. and Mrs S. Pyzer, of 300, Hackney-road, and brother of Charles Bucks of Birmingham. Shiva at 12, Cannon Street-road, E.

Jewish Chronicle – 08 Sep 1899

The tombstone in memory of Michael Bucks, beloved husband of Hannah Bucks, of 12, Cannon Street Road, E., will be set on Sunday next, September 10th, at Plashet Cemetery, at 3.30 p.m. Friends please accept this, the only intimation.

Death:

Q1 1899 [69] ST. GEORGE IN THE EAST 1c 260.

1891 Census

Address:

12 Cannon Street Road, St. George in the East

Residents:

Michael BUCKS – Head – b. 1831 Poland – aged 60 – Tailor
Hannah BUCKS – Wife – b. 1837 Poland – aged 54 – Tailoress
Eva BUCKS – Daughter – b. 1863 Whitechapel – aged 28 – Tailoress
Morris BUCKS – Son – b. 1873 Spitalfields – aged 18 – School Master
Hyman BUCKS – Son – b. 1875 Spitalfields – aged 16 – Tailors cutter
Charles BUCKS – Brother – b. 1854 Poland – aged 37 - Tailor
Joseph LEVY – Grandson – b. 1882 London – aged 9 – Scholar

1881 Census

Address:

12 (Tailor Shop) Cannon Street, St. George in the East

Residents:

Michael BUCKS – Head – b. 1833 Poland – aged 48 – Tailor employing 2 hands
Hannah BUCKS – Wife – b. 1839 Poland – aged 42
Eve BUCKS – Daughter – b. 1862 Whitechapel – aged 19
Mark BUCKS – Son – b. 1864 Spitalfields – aged 17 – Woollen Draper

Abraham BUCKS – Son – b. 1868 Spitalfields – aged 13 – Scholar
Wolf BUCKS – Son – b. 1870 Spitalfields – aged 11 – Scholar
Morris BUCKS – Son – b. 1872 Spitalfields – aged 9 – Scholar
Hyman BUCKS – Son – b. 1874 Spitalfields – aged 7 – Scholar

1871 Census

Address:
Pelham Street, Spitalfields

Residents:
Michael BUCKS – Head – b. 1837 Poland – aged 34
Anna BUCKS – Wife – b. 1841 Poland – aged 30
Janba BUCKS – Daughter – b. 1859 Middlesex – aged 12
Louisa BUCKS – Daughter – b. 1862 Middlesex – aged 9
Marks BUCKS – Son – b. 1864 Middlesex – aged 7
Abraham BUCKS – Son – b. 1867 Middlesex – aged 4
Wolf BUCKS – Son – b. 1870 Middlesex – aged 1

Marriage:
Michael BUCK to Hannah RAILTON – Q1 1856 EAST WARD WESTMORLAND, 10b 579.

Death:
Hannah BUCKS – Q4 1911 [74] BETHNAL GREEN 1c 222.
Buried at Plashet Cemetery – I-25-45 on 24 Dec 1911.

Jewish Chronicle – 29 Dec 1911

BUCKS – On the 22nd of December, at 97, Bishop's Road, N.E., Hannah, widow of the late Michael Bucks, in her 75th year. Mother of Mrs J. Levy, 97, Bishop's Road, N.W.; Mrs S. Pyzer, 300, Hackney Road; Morris Bucks, 36, Bergholt Crescent, Stamford Hill; and Mark, Alfred, Walter and Harry Bucks of Philadelphia. Shiva at 97, Bishop's Road, N.E.

CASSELL, Bennett – D-16-2

Died:	**30 Aug 1899**
Buried:	**01 Aug 1899**
Hebrew Name:	**Baruch bar Asher Halevi**
Partner:	**Dinah Cassell (d. 1901)**
Age:	**61 years**

Jewish Chronicle – 02 Sep 1899

CASSELL – On Wednesday, the 30th of August, at 63, Victoria Dock Road,

CASSELL, Bennett – D-16-2

Canning Town, Barnett Cassell, the dearly beloved husband of Dinah Cassell and father of Sol Cassell, aged 61, for ten years president of the Poplar Synagogue. God rest his dear soul.

Jewish Chronicle – 19 Jan 1900

The tombstone to the memory of the late Bennett Cassell, of Victoria Dock Road, Canning Town, late President of Poplar Synagogue, will be set at Plashet Cemetery, Sunday, January 28th, at 3 o'clock. Friends and relatives please accept this, the only intimation.

Death:

Q3 1899 [61] WEST HAM 4a 111.

1891 Census

Address:

187a East India Road, Poplar

Residents:

Bennett CASSELL – Head – b. 1838 Prussia – aged 53 – Sewing & Domestic Machine Dealer
Dinah CASSELL – Wife – b. 1842 Houndsditch – aged 49
Soloman CASSELL – Son – b. 1863 Aldgate – aged 28

Marriage:

Bennet CASSEL to Dinah NATHAN – Q2 1862 LONDON CITY 1c 237.

Death:

Dinah CASSELL – Q4 1901 [58] W. HAM 4a 79. [Dina bat Shlomo]
Buried at Plashet Cemetery – B-19-1 on 18 Nov 1901.

Jewish Chronicle – 15 Nov 1901

CASSELL – On the 7th of November, corresponding with the 25th of Heshvan, suddenly, at 63, Victoria Dock Road, Canning Town, Dinah, widow of the late Bennett Cassell, beloved mother of Solomon Cassell, in her 59th year. May her dear soul rest in peace.

Jewish Chronicle – 22 Aug 1902

The tombstone in memory of the late Dinah Cassell, widow of the late Bennett Cassell, will be set at Plashet Cemetery, Sunday 24th, 4 o'clock. Relatives and friends please accept this, the only intimation.

COHEN, George – D-9-12

Died: 27 Jan 1899
Buried: 29 Jan 1899
Partner: Mr & Mrs Morris Cohen
Aged: 16 years

Jewish Chronicle – 03 Feb 1899

COHEN – On the 27th of January, George, youngest son of Mr and Mrs M. Cohen, of 88, and 90, Burdett Road, aged 16. Deeply mourned by his sorrowing parents, sisters, brother, relatives and a large circle of friends. Loved by all who knew him. May God rest his dear soul in peace.

COHEN – On the 27th of January, 1899, after a short illness, George, youngest brother of Mrs J. Cohen, of 38, Burdett Road, Mile End, E. Deeply mourned by his loving sister, Harriett. May his dear soul rest in peace. Gone but never to be forgotten.

Jewish Chronicle – 26 Jan 1900

The tombstone in loving memory of the late George Cohen, dearly beloved son of Mr and Mrs Cohen of 88 and 90 Burdett Road, E., will be set at Plashet Cemetery, on Sunday, January 28th, at 3.30 p.m. Relatives and friends kindly accept this, the only intimation.

Death:
Q1 1899 [16] MILE END OLD TOWN 1c 344.

Birth:
Q2 1882 MILE END OLD TOWN 1c 549.

1891 Census

Address:
90 Burdett Road, Mile End Old Town

Residents:
Morris COHEN – Head - b. 1851 Russia – aged 40 – Glass Cutter Shop
Harriett COHEN – Daughter - b. 1876 – aged 15
Lewis COHEN – Son - b. 1878 – aged 13 – Scholar
Fanny COHEN – Daughter - b. 1879 – aged 12
Rebecca COHEN – Daughter b. 1882 – aged 9
George COHEN – Son - b. 1883 – aged 8

1881 Census

Address:
90, Burdett Road, Mile End Old Town

Residents:

Morris COHEN – Head - b. 1851 – aged 30 – Glazier
Sarah COHEN – Wife - b. 1855 Poland – aged 26
Harriet COHEN – Daughter - b. 1876 – aged 5
Lewis COHEN – Son - b. 1878 – aged 3
Lina COHEN – Daughter - b. 1879 – aged 2

Marriage:

Morris COHEN to Sarah Rachael BARNETT – Q4 1874 LONDON CITY 1c 193.

Death:

Sarah COHEN – Q4 1889 [31] MILE END OLD TOWN 1c 372.
Buried at West Ham Jewish Cemetery – K-19-15 on 15 Dec 1889.

1901 Census

Address:

90 Burdett Road, Mile End Old Town (Lead Merchants)

Residents:

Morris COHEN – Head - b. 1851 Russia - aged 50 – Builder's materials dealer
Lewis COHEN – Son - b. 1878 London – aged 23
Jane COHEN – Daughter - b. 1879 London – aged 22
Rebecca COHEN – Daughter - b. 1882 London – aged 19

1911 Census

Address:

34 Burdett Road, E.

Residents:

Morris COHEN – Head – (Married 36 yrs) – b. 1852 Russia – aged 59
Builders Merchant
Rebecca COHEN – Daughter – b. 1885 London – aged 26 – Housekeeper
Florries HARRISON – Domestic Servant

Death:

Morris COHEN – Q1 1915 [65] MILE END 1c 577.
Buried at Plashet Cemetery – K-48-9 on 28 Apr 1915.

COHEN, John – A-14-57

Died: 27 Feb 1899
Buried: 28 Feb 1899
Partner: Jane Cohen (d. 1902)
Aged: 63rd year

COHEN, John – A-14-57

Jewish Chronicle – 03 Mar 1899

COHEN – On the 27th of February, at 448, Commercial Road, E., John Cohen, in his 63rd year. African and Australian papers please copy.

Jewish Chronicle – 28 Jul 1899

The tombstone in memory of the lamented Mr John Cohen, of 448, Commercial-road, E., will be set on Sunday next, July 30th, at Plashet Cemetery at 4.30 p.m. Relatives and friends please accept this, the only intimation.

Death:

Q1 1899 [63] STEPNEY 1c 806.

1891 Census

Address:

345 Commercial Yard, Mile End Old Town

Residents:

John COHEN – Head – b. 1835 London – aged 56 – Cigar Maker
Jane COHEN – Wife – b. 1836 London – aged 55
Mary A. PATTEN – Visitor – b. 1876 London – aged 15 - Housemaid
Rebecca COHEN – Niece – b. 1873 London – aged 18

1881 Census

Address:

345 Commercial Road, Mile End Old Town

Residents:

John COHEN – Head – b. 1836 London – aged 45 – Cigar Manufacturer
Jane COHEN – Wife – b. 1837 London – aged 44
Rachel MARTIN – Niece – b. 1860 London – aged 21 – Tobacco Shop Assistant
Annie BURNS – General Servant

1871 Census

Address:

Steward Street, Old Artillery Ground

Residents:

John COHEN – Head – b. 1836 Middlesex – aged 35
Jane COHEN – Wife – b. 1836 Middlesex – aged 35
Rachel MARTIN – Niece – b. 1860 Middlesex – aged 11
Mary LANE – Servant

Death:

Jane COHEN – Q3 1902 [67] MILE END OLD TOWN 1c 286.
Buried at Plashet Cemetery – E-4-13 on 02 Sep 1902.

Jewish Chronicle – 05 Sep 1902

COHEN – On the 1st of September, at 6, Tollett Street, Globe Road, Jane, widow of the late John Cohen, formerly of 448, Commercial Road, aged 67. Deeply mourned by her relatives and friends. May her soul rest in peace.

Jewish Chronicle – 27 Nov 1903

The tombstone in memory of Jane, widow of the late John Cohen, of Commercial Road, E., will be set on Sunday next, November 29th, at 3.30 at Plashet Cemetery. Relatives and friends please accept this, the only intimation.

COHEN, Joseph – D-15-1

Died: **10 Jul 1899**
Buried: **12 Jul 1899**
Partner: **Rachel Cohen**
Aged: **40 years**

Jewish Chronicle – 14 Jul 1899

COHEN – On Monday, the 10th of July, Joseph Cohen, of 51, North Block, Stoney Lane, loving husband of Rachel Davis, son of Isaac Cohen, 64, Vallance Road (late of Baker's Row). Deeply lamented by his family and all who knew him. May his soul rest in peace. Shiva at 64, Vallance Road.

Jewish Chronicle – 23 Mar 1900

The tombstone in memory of the late Joseph Cohen, lamented husband of Ray Cohen (nee Davis), of 170, Whitechapel Road, E., will be set on Sunday next, March 25th, 3 p.m., at Plashet Cemetery.

Death:

Q3 1899 [40] HOLBORN 1b 525.

Birth:

Q4 1854 SHEFFIELD, YORKS. 9c 283.

1891 Census

Address:

3 Mount Place, Whitechapel

Residents:

Woolf DAVIS – Head – b. 1831 Russian Poland – aged 60 – Boot Manufacturer
Dora DAVIS – Wife – b. 1844 Russian Poland – aged 47
Phoebe DAVIS – Daughter – b. 1872 Aldgate – aged 19 – Dressmaker
Leah DAVIS – Daughter – b. 1874 Aldgate – aged 17 – Dressmaker

Michael DAVIS – Son – b. 1876 Aldgate – aged 15
Kate DAVIS – Daughter – b. 1878 Aldgate – aged 13 – Scholar
Joseph DAVIS – Son – b. 1880 Aldgate – aged 11 – Scholar
Rebecca DAVIS – Daughter – b. 1882 Aldgate – aged 9 – Scholar
Amelia DAVIS – Daughter – b. 1885 Aldgate – aged 6 – Scholar
Rachel COHEN – Daughter – Married – b. 1868 Aldgate – aged 23
David COHEN – Grandson – b. 1890 London – aged 1
Hetty BUCKNER – Niece – b. 1871 Whitechapel – aged 20

1881 Census

Address:

64 Bakers Row, Mile End New Town

Residents:

Isaac COHEN – Head – b. 1832 Poland – aged 49 – Woolen Draper
Rebecca COHEN – Wife – b. 1844 Poland – aged 37
Joseph COHEN – Son – b. 1858 Sheffield – aged 22 – Legging & Bag Maker
Myer COHEN – Son – b. 1861 Mile End – aged 20 – Boot Trade
Louis COHEN – Son – b. 1864 Mile End – aged 17 – Boot Trade
Jane COHEN – Daughter – b. 1858 Sheffield – aged 23 – General Servant
Sarah COHEN – Daughter – b. 1862 Mile End – aged 19 – Tailoress
Rosa COHEN – Daughter – b. 1865 Mile End – aged 16 – General Servant

Marriage:

Joseph COHEN to Rachel DAVIS – Q2 1889 LONDON CITY 1c 103.

1901 Census

Address:

170 Whitechapel Road, Whitechapel

Residents:

Woolf DAVIS – Head - b. 1827 Russian Poland – aged 74 – Boot Manufacturer
Dora DAVIS – Wife - b. 1841 Russian Poland – aged 60
Kate DAVIS – Daughter - b. 1880 London – aged 21 – Tailoress
Rebecca DAVIS – Daughter - b. 1883 London – aged 18 – Dressmaker
Rachel COHEN-DAVIS – Daughter –Widow - b. 1869 London – aged 32 – Dressmaker
Eva COHEN – Granddaughter - b. 1898 London – aged 3
Joseph COHEN – Grandson - b. 1900 London – aged 1
Jane HOLLOWAY – Domestic Servant
Amelia DAVIS – Daughter - b. 1885 London – aged 16 – Scholar

1901 Census

Address:

64 Vallance Road, Mile End New Town

Residents:

Isaac COHEN – Head – b. 1833 Russia – aged 68 – Piece Baker Shopkeeper
Rebecca COHEN – Wife – b. 1843 Russia – aged 58
Louis COHEN – Son – b. 1862 Mile End – aged 39 – Mantle Makers Assistant
Philip MAMLOCK – Grandson – b. 1887 Holborn – aged 14

1911 Census

Address:

54 Sandringham Road, Dalston

Residents:

Dora DAVIS – Head – Widow – b. 1842 Russia – aged 69
Amelia DAVIS – Daughter – b. 1885 Bishopsgate – aged 26 – Shorthand Typist
Evelyn COHEN – Granddaughter – b. 1898 London – aged 13 – at School
Joseph COHEN – Grandson – b. 1900 Whitechapel – aged 11 – at School
Henry I. KERNER – Son-in-law – b. 1880 Austria – aged 31 – Furrier
Rebecca KERNER – Daughter (married 9 years) – b. 1882 London – aged 29
Walter KERNER – Grandson – b. 1904 Whitechapel – aged 7 – at School
Ray KERNER – Granddaughter – b. 1906 Shoreditch – aged 5
Sophia FLOWERS – General domestic servant

COHEN, Michael – D-10-33

Died: **10 Mar 1899**
Buried: **14 Mar 1899**
Partner: **Bloomah Cohen (d. 1901)**
Age: **74 years**

Jewish Chronicle – 17 Mar 1899

COHEN – On Friday, the 10th of February, Michael Cohen, aged 74 years, of 204, Mile End Road, the dearly beloved husband of Bloomah Cohen, father of Esther Cohen, Mrs A. Rosenthall, 86, Commercial Street, Spitalfields, Mrs M. Myers, St. Katherine Dock Hotel, Mark Cohen, 3, Stoney Lane, E., Angel Cohen, Johannesburg, and Joseph M. Cohen, Baltimore. Deeply mourned by his sorrowing children, grandchildren, great-grandchildren, and a large circle of relatives and friends. African and American papers please copy.

COHEN – On Friday, the 10th of February, Michael Cohen, of 204, Mile End Road, the dearly beloved grandfather of Mrs M. Moses, 141, Victoria Dock Road, E., Mrs A. Canter, 5, Agate Road, Hammersmith and Mark A. Rosenthall, of Johannesburg.

Jewish Chronicle – 01 Sep 1899

The tombstone in loving memory of the late Michael Cohen, beloved husband of Bloomer Cohen, 204, Mile End Road, E., will be set on Sunday next, 3 September, at Plashet Cemetery, at 4 o'clock. Relatives and friends will please accept this intimation.

Death:

Q1 1899 [73] WHITECHAPEL 1c 250

1881 Census

Address:

3 Short Street, Spitalfields

Residents:

Michael COHEN – Head – b. 1828 Mile End – aged 53 – Furniture Broker
Bloomah COHEN – Wife – b. 1830 St. Lukes – aged 51
Aaron COHEN – Son – b. 1859 Mile End – aged 22 – Furniture Broker
Angel COHEN – Son – b. 1861 Mile End – aged 20 – Furniture Broker
Joseph COHEN – Son – b. 1864 London City – aged 17 – Cabinet Maker
Esther COHEN – Daughter – b. 1851 London City – aged 30 – Tailoress
Josephine COHEN – Daughter – b. 1861 Mile End – aged 20 – Tailoress
Louisa WOOD – Domestic Servant

1871 Census

Address:

3 Short Street, Christ Church

Residents:

Michael COHEN – Head – b. 1826 Spitalfields – aged 45 – Furniture Broker
Blanch COHEN – Wife – b. 1829 St. Lukes – aged 42
Esther COHEN – Daughter – b. 1848 Bishopsgate – aged 23 – Tailoress
Sarah COHEN – Daughter – b. 1853 Spitalfields – aged 18 – Tailoress
Mark COHEN – Son – b. 1855 Spitalfields – aged 16 – Tailor
Aaron COHEN – Son – b. 1859 Spitalfields – aged 12
Angel COHEN – Son – b. 1861 Spitalfields – aged 10 – Scholar
Joseph COHEN – Son – b. 1865 Spitalfields – aged 6 – Scholar
Emma SNABLE – Domestic Servant

1861 Census

Address:

9 Coxs Square, Christchurch, Spitalfields

Residents:

Michael COHEN – Head – b. 1837 Spitalfields – aged 24 – Furniture Broker
Bloomah COHEN – Wife – b. 1829 Cripplegate – aged 32

Sarah COHEN – Daughter – b. 1852 Aldgate – aged 9
Mark COHEN – Son – b. 1855 Spitalfields – aged 6
Aaron COHEN – Son – b. 1859 Spitalfields – aged 2
Angel COHEN – Son – b. 1861 Spitalfields – aged 9 months
Mary DONOVAN – Domestic Servant

1851 Census

Address:
3 Short Street, Christchurch, Tower Hamlets

Residents:
Michael COHEN – Head – b. 1828 Spitalfields – aged 23 – Furniture Broker
Bloomah COHEN – Wife – b. 1828 Cripplegate – aged 23
Esther COHEN – Daughter – b. 1848 Bishopsgate – aged 3
Rachael COHEN – Daughter – b. 1851 Houndsditch – aged 5 months

Marriage:
Michael COHEN to Bloomah SOLOMONS – Q3 1847 LONDON CITY 2 192.

1901 Census

Address:
204 Mile End Road, Mile End Old Town

Residents:
Bloomah COHEN – Head – Widow – b. 1828 Whitechapel – aged 73 – Living on Independent Means
Esther COHEN – Daughter – b. 1849 Whitechapel – aged 52
Clara EVESHAM – Domestic Servant

Death:
Bloomah COHEN – Q2 1901 [73] MILE END OLD TOWN 1c 260
Buried at Plashet Cemetery – B-15-7 on 09 Apr 1901.

Jewish Chronicle – 12 Apr 1901

COHEN – On Sunday, the 7th day of April, Bloomah, relict of the late Michael Cohen, of 204, Mile End Road, mother of Esther Cohen, Mrs A. Rosenthall, 17, Station Road, Manor Park, Mrs M.J. Myers, of St. Katherine Dock Hotel, Mark Cohen, 40, Stoney Lane, Angel Cohen, of Johannesburg, Joseph Cohen, Clarksburg, USA. Deeply mourned by her children, grandchildren and great-grandchildren, and a large circle of friends. Shiva at 204, Mile End Road.

DAVIDS, Rachel – D-13-25

Died: 17 Jun 1899
Buried: 19 Jun 1899
Hebrew Name: Mirat Rachel bat Alexander
Partner: Louis Edward Davids (d. 1916)
Age: 73 years

Jewish Chronicle – 23 Jun 1899

DAVIDS – On the 17th of June, at 19, British Street, Bow, the beloved wife of L. Davids, aged 73. Deeply mourned by her husband, sons and daughters. Shiva at above address.

Jewish Chronicle – 04 May 1900

The tombstone in memory of the late Mrs L. Davids will be set at Plashet Cemetery on Sunday next, May 6th, at 4 o'clock.

Death:

Q2 1899 [73] POPLAR 1c 368.

1891 Census

Registered as DAVIS

Address:

435 Mile End Road, Mile End Old Town

Residents:

Louis DAVIS – Head – b. 1831 Holland – aged 60 – Commission Agent
Rachel DAVIS – Wife – b. 1827 Holland – aged 64
Hannah DAVIS – Daughter – b. 1857 Holland – aged 34
Nanette DAVIS – Daughter – b. 1867 Spitalfields – aged 24
Julias DAVIS – Son – b. 1868 Spitalfields – aged 23 – Agent
Rachel DAVIS – Granddaughter – b. 1882 Bow – aged 9 - Scholar
Polly LOCK – Domestic Servant
Cassintre POER – Dometic Servant

1881 Census

Address:

435 Mile End Road, Mile End Old Town

Residents:

Lewis DAVIDS – Head – b. 1831 Holland – aged 50 – Diamond Merchant
Rachel DAVIDS – Wife – b. 1828 Holland – aged 53
Hannah DAVIDS – Daughter – b. 1856 Holland – aged 25

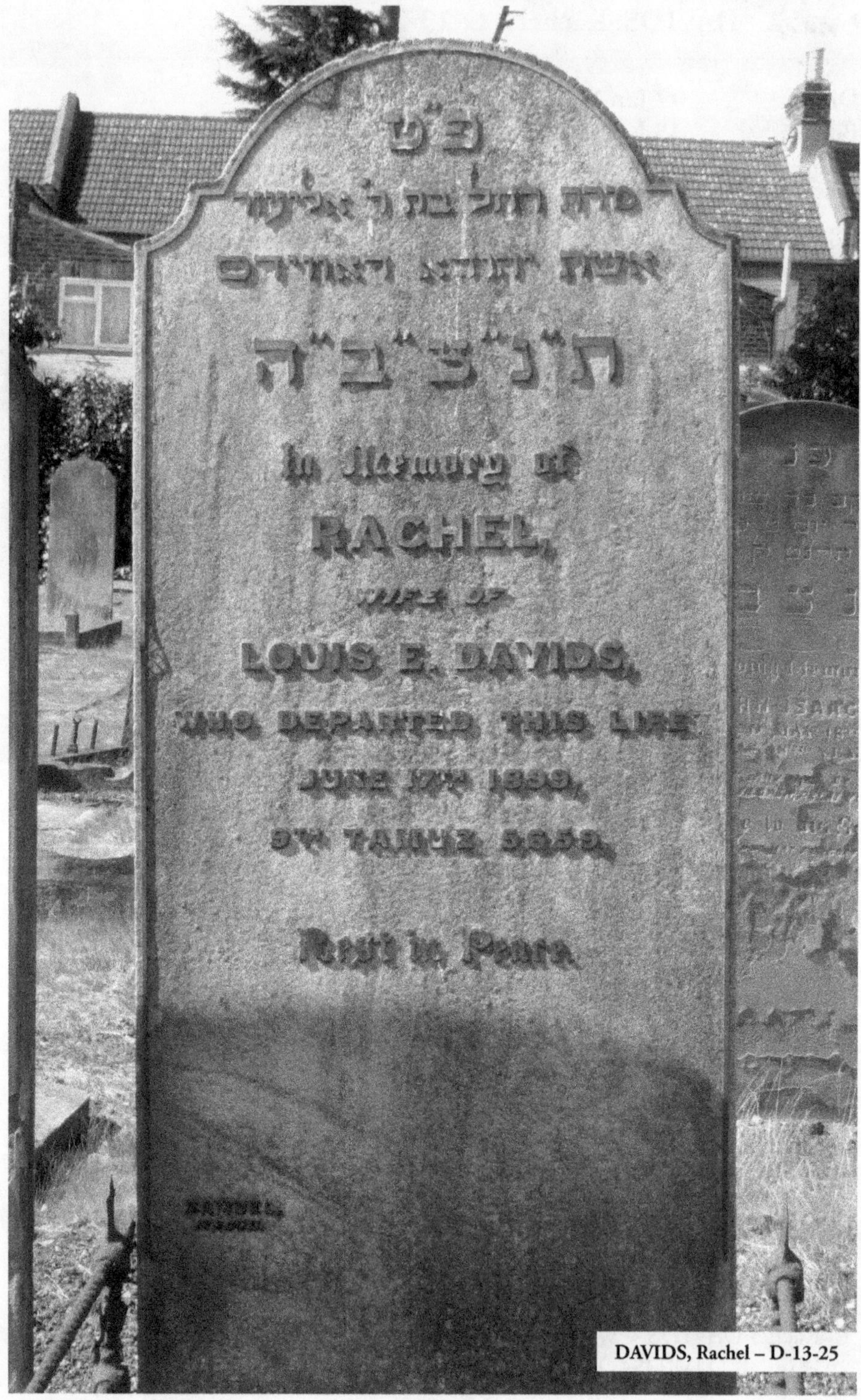

DAVIDS, Rachel – D-13-25

Nancy DAVIDS – Daughter – b. 1867 Mile End – aged 14
Julius DAVIDS – Son – b. 1868 Mile End – aged 13
Julius VLEIT – Servant – Married
Bertha VLEIT – Servant – Married
Sarah HILLIARD – General Domestic Servant

1871 Census

Address:
70 New Road, St. Mary Whitechapel

Residents:
Louis DAVIDS – Head – b. 1831 Holland – aged 40 – Commission Agent – Diamonds
Rachel DAVIDS – Wife – b. 1827 Holland – aged 44
Samuel DAVIDS – Brother – b. 1834 Holland – aged 37 – Diamond Cutter
Elizabeth DAVIDS – Sister-in-law – b. 1836 Holland – aged 35
Edward DAVIDS – Son – b. 1854 Holland – aged 17 - Commission Agent – Diamonds
Alexander DAVIDS – Son – b. 1855 Holland – aged 16 – Cigar Bundler
Hannah DAVIDS – Daughter – b. 1856 Holland – aged 15 – Tailoress
Barnard DAVIDS – Son – b. 1858 Holland – aged 13 – Scholar
Morris DAVIDS – Son – b. 1859 Holland – aged 12 – Scholar
Nancy DAVIDS – Daughter – b. 1867 London – aged 4
Julius DAVIDS – Son – b. 1868 London – aged 3
Nanette DAVIDS – Niece – b. 1867 Holland – aged 4
Rachel DAVIDS – Niece – b. 1870 London – aged 1

1911 Census

Address:
86 Lordship Road, Stoke Newington

Residents:
Julius DAVIDS – Head – b. 1868 London E – aged 43 – Diamond Broker
Jeanette DAVIDS – Wife (14 years) – b. 1869 Amsterdam – aged 42
Henrietta DAVIDS – Daughter – b. 1898 Bow – aged 13 – at School
Louis DAVIDS – Son – b. 1899 Bow – aged 12 – at School
Rachel DAVIDS – Daughter – b. 1901 Bow – aged 10 – at School
Bertha DAVIDS – Daughter – b. 1902 Stoke Newington – aged 9 – at School
Arthur DAVIDS – Son – b. 1906 Stoke Newington – aged 5
Annette DAVIDS – Daughter – b. 1910 Stoke Newington – aged 1
Louis DAVIDS – Father – Widower – b. 1830 Amsterdam – aged 81
Annie SKOENS – Domestic Servant

Death:
Louis Edward DAVIDS – Q1 1916 [85] HACKNEY 1b 453.
Buried at Plashet Cemetery – M-16-29 on 12 Jan 1916.

DE SMITH, Dinah – D-13-8

DE SMITH, Dinah – D-13-8

Died: 21 May 1899
Buried: 23 May 1899
Hebrew Name: Bra'ha bat Baruch Hacohen
Partner: Daniel B. De Smith (d. 1903)
Age: 73 years

Jewish Chronicle – 26 May 1899

DE SMITH – On the 21st of May, at 62 Myrdle Street, Commercial Road, E., Dinah, beloved wife of D.B. De Smith, aged 73, fond mother of B. de Smith, Boston, USA, Bernard de Smith and Mrs H. Hamburg, 58, Bedford Street, Stepney, Simon de Smith, 48, Bromshead Street, Stepney, Mrs L. Vorst, 125, Stepney Green Dwellings, and of Phoebe, Louis and Ray de Smith. Deeply mourned. Shiva at 62, Myrdle Street.

Death:
Q2 1899 [73] MILE END 1c 275 (Registered as DE SMITT).

1891 Census

Address:
62 Myrdle Street, Mile End Old Town

Residents:
Daniel DE SMITH (SMITH) – Head – b. 1829 Amsterdam – aged 62 – Cigar Maker
Dinah DE SMITH – Wife – b. 1826 Amsterdam – aged 65
Hannah BOOT – b. 1852 Amsterdam – aged 39 – Cigar Maker
Phoebe DE SMITH – Daughter – b. 1856 Amsterdam – aged 35 – Cigar Maker
Louis DE SMITH – Son – b. 1865 Stepney – aged 26 – Diamond Polisher
Rachel DE SMITH – Daughter – b. 1868 Stepney – aged 23 – Machinist
Ellen HALEY – General Domestic Servant

1881 Census

Address:
62 Myrdle Street, Mile End Old Town

Residents:
Daniel DE SMITH – Head – b. 1829 Amsterdam – aged 52 – Cigar Maker
Dinah DE SMITH – Wife – b. 1826 Germany – aged 55
Merlina DE SMITH – Daughter – b. 1853 Amsterdam – aged 28 – Cigar Marker
Phoebe DE SMITH – Daughter – b. 1856 Amsterdam – aged 25 – Cigar Maker

Benjamin DE SMITH – Son – b. 1858 Amsterdam – aged 23 – Cigar Maker
Bernard DE SMITH – Son – b. 1860 Amsterdam – aged 21 – Clothier
Simon DE SMITH – Son – b. 1864 Amsterdam – aged 17 – Diamond Polisher
Lewis DE SMITH – Son – b. 1866 Spitalfields – aged 15 – Diamond Polisher
Rachel DE SMITH – Daughter – b. 1868 Spitalfields – aged 13 – Seamstress

1871 Census

Address:

29 Fashion Street, Christchurch Spitalfields

Residents:

Daniel DE SMITH – Head – b. 1829 Amsterdam – aged 42 – Cigar Maker
Dinah DE SMITH – Wife – b. 1826 Germany – aged 45
Leah DE SMITH – Daughter – b. 1852 Amsterdam – aged 19 – Dressmaker
Hannah DE SMITH – Daughter – b. 1854 Amsterdam – aged 17 – Cap Maker
Phoebe DE SMITH – Daughter – b. 1856 Amsterdam – aged 15 – Tailoress
Benjamin DE SMITH – Son – b. 1858 Amsterdam – aged 13 – Scholar
Barnett DE SMITH – Son – b. 1860 Amsterdam – aged 11 – Scholar
Simon DE SMITH – Son – b. 1864 Amsterdam – aged 7 – Scholar
Lewis DE SMITH – Son – b. 1866 London – aged 5 – Scholar
Rachael DE SMITH – Daughter – b. 1868 London – aged 3

Death:

Daniel DE SMITH – Q3 1903 [75] LONDON CITY 1c 2.
Buried at Plashet Cemetery – D-46-8 on 13 Sep 1903.

Jewish Chronicle – 18 Sep 1903

DE SMITH – On the 9th of September, suddenly, Daniel B. De Smith, of 62, Myrdle Street, Commercial Road, E., aged 75, beloved father of Benj. de Smith, of Boston, USA; Bernard de Smith, 45, Bancroft Road, E.; Mrs Hamburg, 23, Ford Square, E.; Mrs L. Vorst and Simon de Smith, 93, St Thomas's Road, N.E.; Louis, Phoebe and Ray de Smith. Deeply mourned. Shiva terminates this day (Friday).

FREIWALD, Fanny – D-9-26

Died:	**13 Feb 1899**
Buried:	**15 Feb 1899**
Hebrew Name:	**Fromit bat Samuel**
Partner:	**Isaac Freiwald (d. 1880)**
Age:	**56 years**

FREIWALD, Fanny – D-9-26

Jewish Chronicle – 17 Feb 1899

FREIWALD – On the 13th of February, at 31, Leman Street, Fanny, widow of the late Isaac Freiwald, aged 56, mother of Mrs Maurice Charik, of 255, Commercial Road, Mr H.I. Freiwald, of New York, and Mrs H. Weiss, of Western Australia. Deeply mourned by her sorrowing children, grandchildren and a large circle of friends. God rest her soul. Shiva at above address.

FREIWALD – On Monday, the 13th of February, at 31, Leman Street, Aldgate, Fanny Freiwald, mother of Mrs Jacob Seigenberg, of 44, Cedars Road, Stratford, E.

Jewish Chronicle – 21 Jul 1899

The tombstone in loving memory of the late Mrs Fanny Freiwald, will be set at Plashet Cemetery on Sunday, July 23rd, at 3 p.m. Relatives and friends will kindly accept this, the only intimation.

Death:

Q1 1899 [56] WHITECHAPEL 1c 248.

1891 Census

Registered as FRAIWALD

Address:

31 Leman Street, St. Mary Whitechapel

Residents:

Fanny FRAIWALD – Head – Widow – b. 1842 Germany – aged 49
Samuel FRAIWALD – Son – b. 1869 Whitechapel - aged 22
Henry FRAIWALD – Son – b. 1871 Whitechapel – aged 20 – Furniture Salesman
Miriam FRAIWALD – Daughter – b. 1873 Whitechapel – aged 18
Esther FRAIWALD – Daughter – b. 1875 Whitechapel – aged 16 – Tailoress
Frederick CRAIG – Lodger – b. 1869 Whitechapel – aged 22 – Professional Singer
Henry MACHENBAUM – Lodger – b. 1846 Russia – aged 45 – Dealer in Fancy Goods

1881 Census

Address:

31 Leman Street, Whitechapel

Residents:

Fanny FREIWALD – Head – Widow – b. 1841 Germany – aged 40 – Plumber & Gas Fitter
Annie FREIWALD – Daughter – b. 1864 Whitechapel – aged 17
Hyam FREIWALD – Son – b. 1865 Whitechapel – aged 16 – Plumber
Leah FREIWALD – Daughter – b. 1867 Whitechapel – aged 14 – Tailoress

Samuel FREIWALD – Son – b. 1869 Whitechapel – aged 12 – Scholar
Miriam FREIWALD – Daughter – b. 1873 Whitechapel – aged 8 – Scholar
Esther FREIWALD – Daughter – b. 1875 Whitechapel – aged 6 – Scholar
Isidore FREIWALD – Son – b. 1877 Whitechapel – aged 4 – Scholar
Kate BLACK – General Domestic Servant

Death:

Isaac FREIWALD – Q1 1880 [52] WHITECHAPEL 1c 304.
Place of burial unknown.

Jewish Chronicle – 13 Feb 1880

WIDOW FRIEWALD RELIEF FUND

An earnest appeal is made on behalf of the widow and eight children of the late Isaac Freiwald, who recently died leaving them entirely destitute and totally unprovided for. The deceased was well known for his readiness to contribute to public and private charities, and it is hoped the Appeal in this deserving case will be responded to by the Benevolent public, and that a sum may be got together sufficient to place the Widow in some way of business, and enable her to maintain her young family.

GOLDSMID, Kate – B-4-5

Died: **15 Oct 1899**
Buried: **17 Oct 1899**
Parents: **Jacob (1862) & Rachel Goldsmid (1893)**
Aged: **62 years**

Jewish Chronicle – 20 Oct 1899

GOLDSMID – On the 15th of October, at 16, St. Peter's Road, E., at the residence of her sister, Mrs Raphael Hart, Kate Goldsmid, for many years teacher at the Jews' Free School, Spitalfields. Deeply mourned.

GOLDSMID – On the 15th of October, at 16, St. Peter's Road, E., Kate Goldsmid, sister of Mrs Joseph Cohen, 30, New Road, Commercial Road. Deeply mourned. Shiva at 16, St. Peter's Road, E.

GOLDSMID – On the 15th of October, at 16, St. Peter's Road, E., Kate Goldsmid, sister of Mr Henry Goldsmid, of the above address, and Mr Abraham Goldsmid, of 13, Trafalgar Square, White Horse Lane. Deeply mourned. Shiva at 16, St. Peter's Road, E.

Jewish Chronicle – 06 Jul 1900

The relatives and friends of the late Miss Kate Goldsmid, (late senior Teacher at the Jews' Free School), are respectfully informed that the memorial stone to her affectionate memory will be set at Plashet, on Sunday next, July 8th, at 4.30 p.m. The Rev. A.A. Green, of Hampstead Synagogue, will officiate – 16, St. Peter's Road, E.

Jewish Chronicle – 13 Jul 1900 – p. 16

The late Miss Kate Goldsmid – On Sunday last, the tombstone to the memory of Miss Kate Goldsmid, for 47 years teacher at the Jews' Free School, was set at Plashet Cemetery. The Rev. A.A. Green, an old Sabbath School pupil of Miss Goldsmid, and an attached friend of the deceased lady, officiated. After the ceremony, Mr Green addressed a few words to those assembled. He said that the best monument to the memory of their departed friend was not the stone before which they stood, but her influence upon their lives. Her sweet disposition, her high idea of life and duty, her constant courage and her unassuming piety had left traces, as an example, in the recollection of those privileged to come under her influence. The opportunity of the teacher was very great. Facts and figures informed the mind but character was the real education. It was noble work when done by such teachers as Miss Goldsmid, and it behoved all who wished to do her honour to remember that they could best reverence her by trying to live up to her ideals. The monument is a handsome red granite stone and the work has been executed by Mr A. Van Praagh.

Death:

Q4 1899 [62] MILE END OLD TOWN 1c 329.

1891 Census

Address:

32 Varden Street, Mile End Old Town

Residents:

Rachel GOLDSMID – Head – Widow – b. 1815 London – aged 76
Kate GOLDSMID – Daughter – b. 1845 London – aged 46 – Teacher in Elementary School
Henry GOLDSMID – Son – b. 1847 London – aged 44 – Fruiterer
Stella FINGESKI – Granddaughter – b. 1882 London – aged 9 – Scholar
Mary PEASLE – Domestic Servant

1881 Census

Address:

32 Varden Street, Mile End Old Town

Residents:

Rachel GOLDSMID – Head – Widow – b. 1817 Bishopsgate – aged 64 – Retired
Kate GOLDSMID – Daughter – b. 1845 Bishopsgate – aged 36 – Teacher in Public Free School
Henry GOLDSMID – Son – b. 1847 Bishopsgate – aged 34 – Fruiterer
Esther GOLDSMID – Daughter – b. 1862 Bishopsgate – aged 19 – Milliner
Emma MAYES – Domestic Servant

1871 Census

Address:

4 New Norfolk Street, Mile End Old Town

Residents:

Rachel GOLDSMID – Head – Widow – b. 1815 Middlesex – aged 56
Kate GOLDSMID – Daughter – b. 1841 Middlesex – aged 30
Rebecca GOLDSMID – Daughter – b. 1843 Middlesex – aged 28
Henry GOLDSMID – Son – b. 1845 Middlesex – aged 26
Elizabeth GOLDSMID – Daughter – b. 1847 Middlesex – aged 24
Martha GOLDSMID – Daughter – b. 1849 Middlesex – aged 22
Samuel GOLDSMID – Son – b. 1851 Middlesex – aged 20
Abraham GOLDSMID – Son – b. 1853 Middlesex – aged 18
Lewis GOLDSMID – Son – b. 1855 Middlesex – aged 16
Joseph GOLDSMID – Son – b. 1857 Middlesex – aged 14
Esther GOLDSMID – Daughter – b. 1862 Middlesex – aged 9

1861 Census

Address:

10 Artillery Lane, St. Botolph Bishopsgate, London

Residents:

Jacob GOLDSMID – Head – b. 1810 Middlesex – aged 51
Rachael GOLDSMID – Wife – b. 1815 Middlesex – aged 46
Kate GOLDSMID – Daughter – b. 1838 Middlesex – aged 23 – Teacher in Public School
Rebecca GOLDSMID – Daughter – b. 1841 Middlesex – aged 20 – Tailoress
Harry GOLDSMID – Son – b. 1842 Middlesex – aged 19
Elias GOLDSMID – Son – b. 1844 Middlesex – aged 17 – Upholsterer
Elizabeth GOLDSMID – Daughter – b. 1846 Middlesex – aged 15 – Tailoress
Martha GOLDSMID – Daughter – b. 1848 Middlesex – aged 13 – Scholar
Samuel GOLDSMID – Son – b. 1850 Middlesex – aged 11 – Scholar
Abraham GOLDSMID – Son – b. 1852 Middlesex – aged 9 – Scholar
Lewis GOLDSMID – Son – b. 1855 Middlesex – aged 6 – Scholar
Joseph GOLDSMID – Son – b. 1857 Middlesex – aged 4 – Scholar

Death:

Rachel GOLDSMID – Q1 1893 [77] MILE END OLD TOWN 1c 345.
Buried at West Ham Jewish Cemetery – E-10-16 on 03 Feb 1893.
[Note death registered under the name of GOLDSMITH.]

Jacob GOLDSMID – Q2 1862 LEWES 2b 91.
Place of burial unknown.

GREEN, Rose – D-18-1

Died: 29 Dec 1899
Buried: 01 Jan 1900
Partner: Samuel Green (d. 1908)
Aged: 61 years

Jewish Chronicle – 05 Jan 1900

GREEN – On Friday, 29th December, after a long and painful illness, Rose Green, sister of Mrs A. Phillips, 108, Great Russell Street, Bedford Square. May her dear soul rest in peace.
GREEN – On the 29th of December, at Margate, after a long and painful illness, Rose, the beloved wife of Simon Green, of 73, Mansell Street, Aldgate, aged 61. Deeply mourned by her sorrowing husband, sons, daughters, and grandchildren, and a large circle of friends. May her soul rest in peace.

Jewish Chronicle – 14 Sep 1900

The tombstone in memory of the late Mrs Rose Green, of 73, Mansell Street, Aldgate, will be set on Sunday next, September 16th, at Plashet Cemetery, at 3 o'clock. Relatives and friends accept this, the only intimation.

Death:
Q4 1899 [60] THANET 2a 655.

1891 Census
Address:
73, Mansell Street, Whitechapel, Tower Hamlets, London
Residents:
Samuel M. GREEN – Head – b. 1836 Russia Poland – aged 55 – Tailor
Rosa GREEN – Wife – b. 1841 London – aged 50
Joseph GREEN – Son – b. 1867 London – aged 24 – Tailors Cutter
George GREEN – Son – b. 1875 London – aged 16 – Clerk
Phillip GREEN – Son – b. 1876 London – aged 15 – Tailors Assistant
Eleazor GREEN – Son – b. 1879 London – aged 12 – Scholar
Maud R. GREEN – Daughter – b. 1881 London – aged 10 – Scholar
Isaac GREEN – Son – b. 1883 London – aged 8 – Scholar
Phoebe MANEWELL – Domestic Servant

Marriage:
Samuel GREEN to Rose Anna MORTON – Q1 1865 NEWINGTON 1d 190.

1901 Census

Address:

73, Mansell Street, Whitechapel

Residents:

Samuel GREEN – Head – Widower – b. 1834 Germany – aged 67 – Tailor
Phillip GREEN – Son – b. 1876 London – aged 25 – Boot Makers Clerk
Eleazer GREEN – Son – b. 1879 London – aged 22 – Tailor
Maud GREEN – Daughter – b. 1881 London – aged 20 – Tailoress
Isaac GREEN – Son – b. 1883 London – aged 18 – Furrier

Death:

Samuel GREEN – Q2 1908 WHITECHAPEL 1c 173.
Buried at Plashet Cemetery – I-8-28 buried 15 May 1908.

Jewish Chronicle – 15 May 1908

GREEN – On Wednesday, the 13th of May, at 73, Mansell Street, Aldgate, Samuel Marks Green, aged 75, after a long and painful illness; beloved father of Mrs J. Gleitzman, Mrs H. Joseph, Henry, Joe, Woolf, Phillip, Eleazer, Maud and Isaac Green. May his dear soul rest in peace. Deeply mourned by his grandchildren. Shiva at above address. Funeral on Friday at 2 o'clock.

GUTTENBERG, Henry – D-16-15

Died: 20 Sep 1899
Buried: 22 Sep 1899
Hebrew Name: Zvi ben Aahron
Partner: Rachel Guttenberg (d. 1925)
Age: 43 years

Jewish Chronicle – 23 Sep 1899

GUTTENBERG – On the 20th of September, at 39, Ferntower Road, Canonbury, N., Henry Guttenberg, aged 43. Deeply mourned by his sorrowing wife, children and relatives.

Jewish Chronicle – 28 Sep 1900

The tombstone in loving memory of the late Henry Guttenberg, will be set at 3 p.m. on Sunday, September 30th, at Plashet Cemetery. Relatives and friends please accept this only intimation – 39, Ferntower Road, Canonbury, N.

Death:

Q3 1899 [43] ISLINGTON 1b 290.

GUTTENBERG, Henry – D-16-15

1891 Census

Address:

21 Princes Street, Spitalfields, London, Tower Hamlets

Residents:

Henry GUTTENBERG – Head – b. 1857 Austria – aged 34 – Jeweller
Rachel GUTTENBERG – Wife – b. 1861 London – aged 30
Gertrude GUTTENBERG – Daughter – b. 1880 Spitalfields – aged 11 Scholar
Samuel GUTTENBERG – Son – b. 1881 Spitalfields – aged 10 – Scholar
Leopold GUTTENBERG – Son – b. 1883 Spitalfields – aged 8 – Scholar
Arthur GUTTENBERG – Son – b. 1885 Spitalfields – aged 6 – Scholar
Sydney GUTTENBERG – Son – b. 1888 Spitalfields – aged 3 – Scholar
Beatrice GUTTENBERG – Daughter – b. 1889 Spitalfields – aged 2
Ellen KISKETT – Domestic Servant
Rosa SPENCER – Domestic Servant

Marriage:

Henry GUTTENBERG to Rachel POSNER – Q1 1879 LONDON CITY 1c 114.

1901 Census

Address:

39 Ferntower Road, Islington

Residents:

Raie GUTTENBERG – Head – Widow – b. 1861 London – aged 40
Samuel GUTTENBERG – Son – b. 1881 London – aged 20 – Jeweller
Gertrude GUTTENBERG – Daughter – b. 1880 London – aged 21 – Dressmaker
Leopold GUTTENBERG – Son – b. 1883 London – aged 18 – Stationery Business
Arthur GUTTENBERG – Son – b. 1885 London – aged 16 – Stationery Business
Sidney GUTTENBERG – Son – b. 1888 London – aged 13 – Scholar
Beatrice GUTTENBERG – Daughter – b. 1890 London – aged 11 – Scholar
Hannah GUTTENBERG –Daughter – b. 1892 London – aged 9 – Scholar
Louis GUTTENBERG – Son – b. 1894 Islington – aged 7 – Scholar
Maud GUTTENBERG – Daughter – b. 1896 Islington – aged 5
Miriam GUTTENBERG – Daughter – b. 1899 Islington – aged 2
Eleanor CLARK – Domestic Servant

1911 Census

Address:

60 Grosvenor Road, London N.

Residents:

Rachel GUTTENBERG – Head – Widow – b. 1860 London – aged 51
Samuel GUTTENBERG – Son – b. 1881 Spitalfields – aged 30 – General Dealer
Leopold GUTTENBERG – Son – b. 1883 Spitalfields – aged 28 – Traveller
Arthur GUTTENBERG – Son – b. 1885 Spitalfields – aged 26 – Tailor's Assistant
Louis GUTTENBERG – Son – b. 1894 Islington – aged 17 – Post Office Stores HMG
Beatrice GUTTENBERG – Daughter – b. 1889 Spitalfields – aged 22
Hannah GUTTENBERG – Daughter – b. 1892 Islington – aged 19 – Milliner
Maud GUTTENBERG – Daughter – b. 1897 Islington – aged14
Charles POSNER – Father – b. 1840 Poland – aged 71 – Tailor
Augusta POSNER – Mother (52 years) – b. 1842 Poland – aged 69

Death:

Augusta POSNER – Q4 1913 [73] ISLINGTON 1b 420
Buried at Plashet Cemetery – L-14-19 on 23 Dec 1913.

Charles POSNER – Q4 1918 [81] ISLINGTON 1b 750
Buried at Plashet Cemetery – L-14-18 on 21 Oct 1918

Death:

Rachel GUTTENBERG – Q2 1925 [65] ISLINGTON 1b 305.
Place of burial unknown.

Jewish Chronicle – 22 May 1925

GUTTENBERG – On the 15th of May, at her residence, 60, Grosvenor Road, Canonbury, N.5, Raie Guttenberg, in her 60th year. Deeply mourned by her children and relatives

GUTTENBERG – On the 15th of May, Raie Guttenberg, dearly beloved sister of Mrs Moss Smith, of 23, Harley Street, Bow. Deeply mourned by her heart-broken sister, nieces and nephews. May her dear soul rest in everlasting peace.

GUTTENBERG – On the 15th of May, Rachel (Raie) Guttenberg. Deeply mourned by her affectionate sister, Mathilda Koski, 76, Grovenor Road, N.5. Rest in peace.

HARRIS, Augustus Henry – D-13-22

Died: 11 Jun 1899
Buried: 14 Jun 1899
Hebrew Name: Aahron bar Avraham
Partner: Hetty (Florence) Harris (d. 1913)
Age: 43 years

HARRIS, Augustus Henry – D-13-22

Jewish Chronicle – 16 Jun 1899

HARRIS – On the 11th of June, after a long illness, Augustus H. Harris, aged 43 years, beloved husband of Hetty Harris. May his soul rest in peace.
HARRIS – On the 11th of June, to the inexpressible grief of his sorrowing parents and sisters, after a long illness, Augustus H. Harris, aged 43 years, beloved and only son of Abraham and Annie Harris, of 6, White Horse Lane, Stepney. May his soul rest in peace. Gone, never to be forgotten.

Jewish Chronicle – 18 Aug 1899

The tombstone in loving memory of the late lamented Augustus H. Harris, only son of Abraham and Annie Harris, will be set at Plashet Cemetery on Sunday, the 20th, at 4 p.m. – 6, White Horse Lane, Stepney, E.

Death:
Q2 1899 [43] MILE END 1c 306.

1891 Census

Address:
The Elms, Avenue Road, St. Marylebone, East Marylebone

Residents:
Augustus H.G. HARRIS – Head – b. 1852 France – aged 39 – Sheriff of the City of London
Florence E.G. HARRIS – Wife – b. 1860 Plymouth – aged 31
Florence A.G. HARRIS – Daughter – b. 1884 London – aged 7 – Scholar
Sarah WALLEN – Cook / Domestic Servant
Mary HANDLEY – Parlour Maid
Mary PARISH – House Maid
Emilie NORRIS – Nurse Maid

Marriage:
Augustus Henry H. HARRIS to Florence Edgcumbe RENDLE – Q4 1881 KENSINGTON 1a 87.

1881 Census

Address:
47 Smith Street, Mile End Old Town

Residents:
Abraham A. HARRIS – Head – b. 1830 London – aged 51 – Agent
Annie HARRIS – Wife – b. 1826 London – aged 55
Augustus HARRIS – Son – b. 1856 London – aged 25 – Shirt Maker
Florence HARRIS – Daughter – b. 1858 London – aged 23 – Tailoress
Dinah HARRIS – Daughter – b. 1864 London – aged 17

1871 Census

Address:

35 Rutland Street, Stepney

Residents:

Abraham HARRIS – Head – b. 1830 Middlesex – aged 41 – General Merchant
Anne HARRIS – Wife – b. 1824 Middlesex – aged 47
Augustus HARRIS – Son – b. 1855 Middlesex – aged 16 – Walking Stick Maker
Florence HARRIS – Daughter – b. 1858 Middlesex – aged 13 – Tailoress
Dina HARRIS – Daughter – b. 1863 Middlesex – aged 8 - Scholar

1901 Census

Address:

22 The Elms, Avenue Road, Hampstead

Residents:

Florence E. HARRIS – Head – Widow – b. 1860 Plymouth – aged 41 – Living on own means
Florence N. HARRIS – Daughter – b. 1884 London – aged 17
Sarah WALLEN – Cook / Domestic
Lena OECHSLE – Parlour Maid / Domestic
Clara LANSDELL – Housemaid / Domestic

Death:

Florence HARRIS – Q1 1913 [55] MARYLEBONE 1a 799.
Buried at Plashet Cemetery – L-6-40 on 19 Mar 1913.

HARRIS, Lewis – D-10-4

Died: 11 Feb 1899
Buried: 14 Feb 1899
Hebrew Name: Le'ev bar Zvi
Partner: Jane Harris (d. 1929)
Age: 56 years

Jewish Chronicle – 17 Feb 1899

HARRIS – On the 11th of February, at 53, Commercial Road, E., Lewis Harris, aged 56, the dearly beloved husband of Jane Harris, and father of Mrs L. Symelman, of 56, York Road, King's Cross. Deeply mourned by his loving wife, sons, daughters and a large circle of friends. May his soul rest in peace.

Jewish Chronicle – 29 Dec 1899

The tombstone in loving memory of the late Lewis Harris, of 53, Commercial Road, E., will be set at Plashet Cemetery on Sunday next, Dec. 31st, at 2.30 p.m. Relatives and friends kindly accept this, the only intimation.

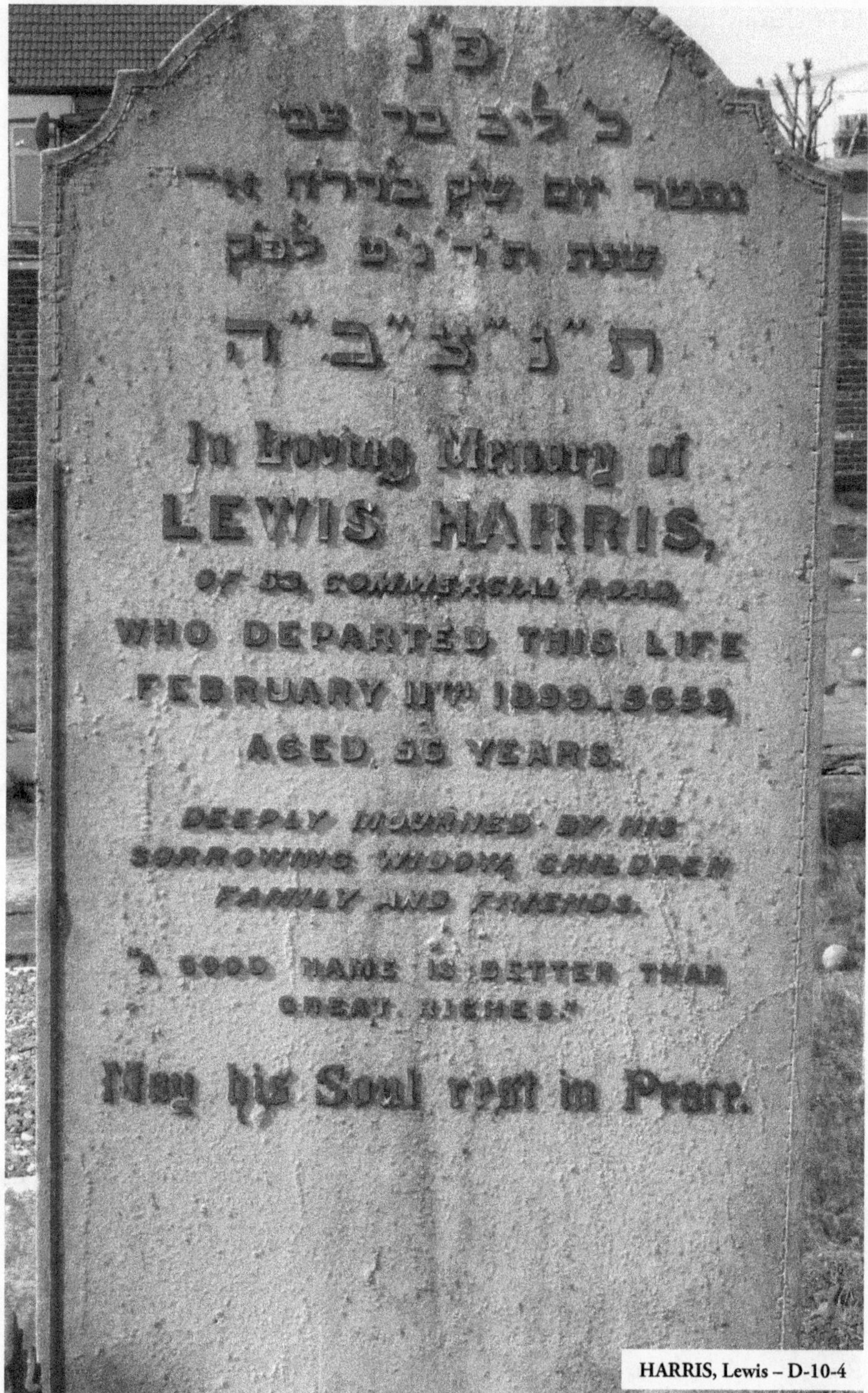

HARRIS, Lewis – D-10-4

Death:

Q1 1899 [56] WEST HAM 4a 197.

1881 Census

Address:

2 Little Alie Street, Whitechapel

Residents:

Louis HARRIS – Head – b. 1842 Poland – aged 39 – Jeweller
Jane HARRIS – Wife – b. 1842 Germany – aged 39
Amelia HARRIS – Daughter – b. 1868 Cambridge – aged 13 – Scholar
Rachel HARRIS – Daughter – b. 1869 Cambridge – aged 12 – Scholar
Hirsch HARRIS – Son – b. 1871 Mile End – aged 10 – Scholar
Henry HARRIS – Son – b. 1873 Mile End – aged 8 – Scholar
Joseph HARRIS – Son – b. 1875 Mile End – aged 6 – Scholar
Leah HARRIS – Daughter – b. 1877 Mile End – aged 4 – Scholar
Ephraim HARRIS – Son – b. 1881 Mile End – aged 0

1871 Census

Address:

7 Langley Place, Commercial Road, Mile End Old Town

Residents:

Lewis HARRIS – Head – b. 1843 Poland – aged 28 – Jeweller & Tobacconist
Jane HARRIS – Wife – b. 1843 Germany – aged 28
Amelia HARRIS – Daughter – b. 1868 Cambridge – aged 3
Rachel HARRIS – Daughter – b. 1869 Cambridge – aged 2
Hirsch Myer HARRIS – Son – b. 1871 Mile End – aged 8 months
Ellen EDWARDS – Domestic Servant

Marriage:

Lewis HARRIS to Jane HART – Q4 1866 LONDON CITY 1c 242.

1901 Census

Address:

53 Commercial Road, Mile End Old Town

Residents:

Jane HARRIS – Head – Widow – b. 1845 Germany – aged 56 – Jeweller
Ray HARRIS – Daughter – b. 1874 Cambridge – aged 27 – Shop Assistant
Henry HARRIS – Son – b. 1875 Mile End – aged 26 – Shop Assistant
Leah HARRIS – Daughter – b. 1879 Mile End – aged 22 – Shop Assistant
Moss HARRIS – Son – b. 1885 Mile End – aged 16 – Zinc Worker
Sarah HARRIS – Daughter – b. 1882 Mile End – aged 19 – Shop Assistant
Gertrude HARRIS – Daughter – b. 1887 Whitechapel – aged 14

1911 Census

Address:

37 Goldhawk Road, Fulham

Residents:

William HYMAN – Head – b. 1876 Austria – aged 35 – Ladies Tailor
Lily HYMAN – Wife (7 years) – b. 1879 Whitechapel – aged 32
Lennie HYMAN – Son – b. 1906 Shepherds Bush – aged 5
Jane HARRIS – Mother-in-law – b. 1843 Germany – aged 68
Mary BATES – Domestic Servant

Death:

Jane HARRIS – Q1 1929 [85] HACKNEY 1b 756.
Buried at Plashet Cemetery – F-15-B on 10 Mar 1929.

Jewish Chronicle – 15 Mar 1929

HARRIS – On the 7th of March, Jane Harris, aged 85, relict of the late Lewis Harris, dearly beloved mother of Millie Simpson, Marlborough House, Green Lanes, N.4; Ray Radges, 76, Duckett Road, Harringay; Lily Hyman, 37, Goldhawk Road, Shepherd's Bush; Montague M. Harris, 359, Romford Road, Forest Gate; Harry Harris, New York; Ephraim Harris, Cape Town; and Sarah Allen, Sydney, Australia. May her sweet soul rest in peace. She has joined her life's partner after thirty years.

Jewish Chronicle – 08 Nov 1929

HARRIS – The tombstone in loving memory of Mrs Jane Harris, late of 37, Goldhawk Road, Shepherd's Bush, will be consecrated on Sunday next, November 10th, at 2.30 prompt, at Plashet East Ham Cemetery. Will relatives and friends kindly accept this, the only intimation.

HARRIS, Moss – D-16-14

Died: **17 Sep 1899**
Buried: **21 Sep 1899**
Partner: **Clara Harris**
Aged: **43rd year**

Jewish Chronicle – 23 Sep 1899

HARRIS – On the 17th of September, in his 43rd year, after a long and painful illness, Moss Harris, of 23, Rockmead Road, Victoria Park, late proprietor of Height's Hotel, Johannesburg, the dearly beloved husband of Clara Harris. Deeply mourned by his sorrowing wife. Peace be to his dear soul. African papers please copy.

Death:

Q3 1899 [42] WINDSOR 2c 299

1901 Census

Address:

23 Rockmead Road, Hackney

Residents:

Clara HARRIS – Widow – b. 1875 London – aged 26 - No occupation
Sarah WILKS – Mother – b. 1852 London – aged 49
Lewis MIGERS – Uncle – b. 1846 Essex – aged 55 – Builder Marker
Moris JACOBS – Uncle – b. 1839 Clapton – aged 62 – Commercial Traveller
Mellie JACOBS – Cousin – b. 1861 Clapton – aged 40 – General Domestic
Julia ROSENTHAL – Visitor – b. 1869 London – aged 32
Harry ROSENTHAL – Visitor - b. 1893 London – aged 8
Bessie ROSENTHAL – Visitor – b. 1901 London – aged 0

Marriage:

Moss HARRIS to Clara WILKS – Q2 1896 LONDON CITY 1c 111.

Marriage:

Clara HARRIS to Joseph Gomes DA COSTA – Q2 1908 LONDON CITY 1c 74.

1911 Census

Address:

37 Cawley Road, South Hackney

Residents:

Joseph DA COSTER – Head – b. 1866 Mile End – aged 45 – Tailor
Clara DA COSTER – Wife (2 years) – b. 1877 Spitalfields – aged 34
Sarah WILKS – Mother-in-law – b. 1853 Spitalfields – aged 58
Emily COAST – General Domestic Servant

HART, Sarah – D-17-35

Died: 24 Dec 1899
Buried: 26 Dec 1899
Hebrew Name: Sarah bat Eliezer
Partner: Moses Hart (d. 1900) (Moshe ben David)
Age: 84 years

Jewish Chronicle – 29 Dec 1899

HART – On the 24th of December, at 26, Casson Street, Chicksand Street, E., Sarah, beloved wife of Moses Hart, aged 84. Mother of Mr D. Hart, 11, Nicholas

HART, Sarah – D-17-35

Street, E., Mr J. Hart, 117, New Road, E., Mrs Wolfsbergen, 23, Green Street, N.E., Mrs S. Harris, 66, Commercial Road, E., Mrs H. Harris, 101, Hoxton Street, N. Shiva at 26, Casson Street, E.

Jewish Chronicle – 6 July 1900

The tombstone to the memory of the late Mr and Mrs Moses Hart, of 26, Casson Street, Chicksand Street, E., will be set on Sunday, July 15th, 1900 at 5 p.m. at Plashet Cemetery.

Death:

Q4 1899 [84] WHITECHAPEL 1c 246.

1891 Census

Address:

26 Casson Street, Mile End New Town

Residents:

Moses HART – Head- b. 1815 Aldgate – aged 76 – Black Lead Pencil Maker
Sarah HART – Wife – b. 1816 Whitechapel – aged 75 – Dressmaker
Mary HART – Daughter – b. 1845 Mile End – aged 46 – Tailoress
Esther HART – Daughter – b. 1847 Mile End – aged 44 – Dressmaker

1881 Census

Address:

8 George Street, Mile End New Town

Residents:

Moses HART – Head – b. 1815 Aldgate – aged 66 – Black Lead Pencil Maker
Sarah HART – Wife – b. 1816 Whitechapel – aged 65 – Dressmaker
Mary HART – Daughter – b. 1845 Mile End – aged 36 – Tailoress
Esther HART – Daughter – b. 1847 Mile End – aged 34 – Dressmaker
Elizabeth HART – Daughter – b. 1859 Mile End – aged 22 – Tailoress
Clara GORDON – Granddaughter – b. 1868 Mile End – aged 13 – Tailoress
Mary DAY – General Servant

1871 Census

Address:

8 George Street, Mile End New Town

Residents:

Moses HART – Head – b. 1815 Aldgate – aged 56 – Black Lead Pencil Maker
Sarah HART – Wife – b. 1816 Whitechapel – aged 55 – Dressmaker
David HART – Son – b. 1843 Mile End – aged 28 – Shop Assistant (Glass & China)
Mary HART – Daughter – b. 1845 Mile End – aged 26 – Dressmaker
Esther HART – Daughter – b. 1847 Mile End – aged 24 – Dressmaker
Julia HART – Daughter – b. 1849 Mile End – aged 22 – Boot maker
Lewis HART – Son – b. 1852 Mile End – aged 19 – Warehouseman
Joel HART – Son – b. 1854 Mile End – aged 17 – Boot Sole Cutter
Jane HART – Daughter – b. 1856 Mile End – aged 15 – Tailoress
Elizabeth HART – Daughter – b. 1859 Mile End – aged 12 – Scholar
Abraham GORDON – Grandson – b. 1869 Spitalfields – aged 2

1861 Census

Address:

4 Old Montague Street, Stepney

Residents:

Moses HART – Head – b. 1815 Aldgate – aged 46 – Black Lead Pencil Maker
Sarah HART – Wife – b. 1816 Whitechapel – aged 45 – Dressmaker
Rachel HART – Daughter – b. 1842 Mile End – aged 19 – Glass Dealer
David HART – Son – b. 1843 Mile End – aged 18 – Shoe Maker
Esther HART – Daughter – b. 1847 Mile End – aged 14 – Dressmaker
Lazarus HART – Son – b. 1852 Mile End – aged 9 – Scholar
Joel HART – Son – b. 1853 Mile End – aged 8 – Scholar
Jane HART – Daughter – b. 1856 Mile End – aged 5 – Scholar
Elizabeth HART – Daughter – b. 1859 Mile End – aged 2

1851 Census

Address:

5 Montague Street, Saint Dunstan Stepney, Tower Hamlets

Residents:

Moses HART – Head – b. 1815 Aldgate – aged 36 – Black Lead Pencil Maker
Sarah HART – Wife – b. 1816 Whitechapel – aged 35 – Dressmaker
Rachel HART – Daughter – b. 1842 Mile End – aged 9 – Scholar
David HART – Son – b. 1843 Mile End – aged 8 – Scholar
Mary HART – Daughter – b. 1845 Mile End – aged 6 – Scholar
Esther HART – Daughter – b. 1847 Mile End – aged 4
Julia HART – Daughter – b. 1849 Mile End – aged 2
Caroline LEVY – Visitor

1841 Census

Address:

Montague Street, Stepney, Mile End New Town, Tower Hamlets

Residents:

Moses HART – Head – b. 1816 Aldgate – aged 25
Sarah HART – Wife – b. 1816 Whitechapel – aged 25

Marriage:

Moses HART to Sarah MOSES – Q1 1841 LONDON CITY 2 130B.

Death:

Moses HART – Q1 1900 [85] WHITECHAPEL 1c 215.
Buried at Plashet Cemetery – D-17-36 on 04 Jan 1900.

Jewish Chronicle – 05 Jan 1900

HART –On the 3rd of January, at 26, Casson Street, Chicksand Street, E., Moses Hart , aged 85, beloved father of Mr D. Hart, 11, Nicholas Street, Mile End, E., Mr J. Hart, 117, New Road, E., Mrs Wolfsbergen, 23, Green Street, N.E., Mrs S. Harris, 66, Commercial Road, E., Mrs H. Harris, 101, Hoxton Street, N. Shiva at 26, Casson Street, E.

Obituary – p. 18

MR MOSES HART – The late Mr Moses Hart, who died on Wednesday last, at the advanced age of 85 years, was the last surviving founder of the Marriage Portion Society, of which he was also a Life Trustee. The esteem in which he was regarded was shown as recently as the Wednesday before his death, when he was the recipient of an illuminated address in recognition of his having been connected with the Society for a period of forty-nine years. Mr Hart was President of the "Daughters of Israel", Confined Mourning and Sick Benefit Society, and was also one of the founders of the Metropolitan Promoters of Charity. Mr Hart was present at the opening of the New Synagogue in Great St. Helen's in 1838, was one of its oldest members, and regularly attended synagogue until July last, when he met with an accident, from which he never completely recovered. His wife predeceased him by nine days, and this aged couple, who performed unostentatious deeds of charity, will be sorely missed by many of the poor in the district of Spitalfields, where Mr and Mrs Hart lived.

Jewish Chronicle – 6 July 1900

The tombstone to the memory of the late Mr and Mrs Moses Hart, of 26, Casson Street, Chicksand Street, E., will be set on Sunday, July 15th, 1900 at 5 p.m. at Plashet Cemetery.

HENDRICKS, Jane – D-11-3

Died: **03 Apr 1899**
Buried: **05 Apr 1899**
Parents: **Aaron & Ann Hendricks**
Aged: **70 years**

Jewish Chronicle – 07 Apr 1899

HENDRICKS – On the 3rd of April, Jane Hendricks, the dearly beloved sister of Mrs Alfred Emanuel, of 33, Church Lane and sister of Mrs Alfred Jacobson, of 145, High Street, Aldgate, E.

Jewish Chronicle – 30 Sep 1899

The tombstone in loving memory of Jane Hendricks, late of 33, Church Lane, Commercial Road, will be set at the Plashet Cemetery, on Sunday, October 8th, at 3 o'clock. Relatives and friends will please accept this, the only intimation.

Death:

Q2 1899 [70] CAMBERWELL 1c 417.

1891 Census

Address:

4 Effra Parade, East Brixton

Resident:

Jane HENDRIK – Head – Single – b. 1833 Pimlico – aged 58 – Living on own means

1881 Census

Address:

33 Church Lane, Whitechapel

Residents:

Alfred EMANUEL – Head – b. 1827 Whitechapel – aged 54 – Tobacconist
Emma EMANUEL – Wife – b. 1827 Whitechapel – aged 54
Jane HENDRICKS – Sister – Single – b. 1836 Whitechapel – aged 45

1871 Census

Address:

45 Wellington Street, St. Paul Covent Garden, Westminster

Resident:

Jane HENDRICK – Lodger – b. 1828 Middlesex – aged 43

1861 Census

Address:

24 High Street, Whitechapel

Residents:

Jane HENDRICK – Head – Unmarried – b. 1835 Whitechapel – aged 26 – Independent
Louisa HENDRICK – Sister – b. 1841 Bethnal Green – aged 20 – School Teacher
Jane JONES – House Servant

1851 Census

Address:

32 Castle Street, Whitechapel, Tower Hamlets

Residents:

Aaron HENDRICKS – Head - b. 1783 Aldgate – aged 68 – Undertaker
Ann HENDRICKS – Wife - b. 1798 Whitechapel – aged 53
Charles HENDRICKS – Son - b. 1827 Whitechapel – aged 24 – Shop Man
Jane HENDRICKS – Daughter - b. 1830 Whitechapel – aged 21
Priscilla HENDRICKS – Daughter - b. 1833 Whitechapel – aged 18 – Dressmaker
Ellen HENDRICKS – Daughter - b. 1835 Whitechapel – aged 16 – Dressmaker
Louisa HENDRICKS – Daughter - b. 1839 Whitechapel – aged 12 – Scholar

Deaths:

Aaron HENDRICKS – Q3 1853 WHITECHAPEL 1c 235.
Ann HENDRICKS – Q3 1859 WHITECHAPEL 1c 266.

HESS, Alice – D-10-1

Died: 21 Jan 1899
Buried: 23 Jan 1899
Hebrew Name: Alkla bat Avraham
Partner: Samuel Hess (d. 1905) (Samuel bar Shlomo)
Aged: 69 years

Jewish Chronicle – 27 Jan 1899

HESS – On the 21st of January, at 57, Grosvenor Road, Highbury New Park, N., Alice, the beloved wife of Samuel Hess, aged 69.

Jewish Chronicle – 10 Mar 1899

The tombstone in memory of the late Mrs Samuel Hess, will be set on Sunday next, March 12th, at Plashet Cemetery, at 3.30 o'clock. Relatives and friends will kindly accept this intimation.

Death:

Q1 1899 [69] ISLINGTON 1b 292.

1891 Census

Address:

57 Grosvenor Road, Islington

Residents:

Samuel HESS – Head – b. 1824 Merzy Germany – aged 67 – Cap Peak Manufacturer
Alice HESS – Wife – b. 1830 Aldgate – aged 61
Kate HESS – Daughter – b. 1859 Bishopsgate – aged 32
Minnie HESS – Daughter – b. 1862 Bishopsgate – aged 29
Esther HESS – Daughter – b. 1865 Whitechapel – aged 26
Louie HESS – Daughter – b. 1866 Whitechapel – aged 25 – Teacher
Abraham HESS – Son – b. 1868 Whitechapel – aged 23 – Assistant in Peak Factory
Sarah PARROTT – General Domestic Servant
Rose WILSON – Housemaid / Servant

1881 Census

Address:

57 Grosvenor Road, Islington

Residents:

Samuel HESS – Head – b. 1824 Prussia – aged 57 – Cap Manufacturer (employing 40 people)
Alice HESS – Wife – b. 1830 Aldgate – aged 51

HESS, Alice – D-10-1

Solomon HESS – Son – b. 1856 London – aged 25 – Cap Manufacturer
Julia HESS – Daughter – b. 1858 London – aged 23
Kate HESS – Daughter – b. 1859 London – aged 22
Jacob HESS – Son – b. 1860 London – aged 21 – Warehouseman
Miriam HESS – Daughter – b. 1862 London – aged 19 – Scholar
Esther HESS – Daughter – b. 1865 London – aged 16 – Scholar
Louisa HESS – Daughter – b. 1866 London – aged 15 – Scholar
Abraham HESS – Son – b. 1868 London – aged 13 – Scholar
Susan NEWCOMBE – Domestic Servant
Elizabeth SHAILER – Domestic Servant

1871 Census

Address:
57 Grosvenor Road, Islington

Residents:
Samuel HESS – Head – b. 1824 Germany – aged 47 – Wholesale Cap Peak Manufacturer
Alice HESS – Wife – b. 1830 London – aged 41
Solomon HESS – Son – b. 1856 London – aged 15
Julia HESS – Daughter – b. 1858 London – aged 13 – Scholar
Kate HESS – Daughter – b. 1859 London – aged 12 – Scholar
Jacob HESS – Son – b. 1860 London – aged 11 – Scholar
Miriam HESS – Daughter – b. 1862 London – aged 9 – Scholar
Esther HESS – Daughter – b. 1865 Whitechapel – aged 6 – Scholar
Louisa HESS – Daughter – b. 1866 Whitechapel – aged 5 – Scholar
Abraham HESS – Son – b. 1868 Whitechapel – aged 3
Margaret DRISCOLL – Domestic Servant

Marriage:
Samuel HESS to Alice CANTOR – Q4 1854 ST LUKE 1b 801.

1901 Census

Address:
57 Grosvenor Road, Islington

Residents:
Samuel HESS – Head – Widower – b. 1825 Germany – aged 76 – Retired Cap Manufacturer
Minnie HESS – Daughter – b. 1861 London – aged 40
Louie HESS – Daughter – b. 1866 London – aged 35 – School Secretary
Albert HESS – Son – b. 1868 London – aged 33 – Printer's Engineer
Emily GREEN – Housemaid / Servant
Annie FLINN – Cook

Death:

Samuel HESS – Q2 1905 [81] ISLINGTON 1b 196.
Buried at Plashet Cemetery – D-10-2 on 23 Apr 1905.

Jewish Chronicle – 28 Apr 1905

HESS – On the 20th of April, 1st day of Passover, at 57, Grosvenor Road, N., Samuel Hess, in his 82nd year. Deeply mourned.

Jewish Chronicle – 07 Jul 1905

The tombstone in memory of the late Mr Samuel Hess will be set on Sunday next, 9th inst., at Plashet Cemetery, at 4 o'clock. Relatives and friends kindly accept this intimation.

HYAMS, Joseph Mitchell – B-5-7

Died: **06 Dec 1899**
Buried: **07 Dec 1899**
Partner: **Annette Sarah Hyams (d. 1938)**
Aged: **42 years**

Jewish Chronicle – 08 Dec 1899

HYAMS – On Wednesday, the 6th of December, 1899, Joseph Mitchell Hyams, dearly beloved husband of Annette Sarah Hyams, of 14, Artillery Passage, and 44, Artillery Lane, E.C. Deeply mourned by his sorrowing wife and children. Respected by all who knew him. African and American papers please copy.
HYAMS – On Wednesday, the 6th of December, Joseph Hyams, of 14, Artillery Passage, Spitalfields, E., brother of Mrs M. Hyams, of 25, Wilkes Street, E., and Emanuel Hyams, of 22, Forster Street. Shiva at 25, Wilkes Street, Spitalfields, E.

Jewish Chronicle – 22 Jun 1900

The tombstone in memory of the late Joseph Mitchell Hyams, of 44, Artillery Lane, and 14, Artillery Passage, Bishopsgate, E.C., will be set on Sunday, 1st July, 1900, at 4 p.m., at Plashet Cemetery. Friends and relatives accept this, the only intimation

Death:

Q4 1899 [42] WHITECHAPEL 1c 196.

1891 Census

Address:

14 Artillery Passage, Spitalfields, London, Whitechapel

Residents:

Joseph Mitchell HYAMS – Head – b. 1858 London – aged 33 – Fish Merchant

Annette HYAMS – Wife – b. 1861 London – aged 30
Edward S. HYAMS – Son – b. 1880 London – aged 11
Leah S. HYAMS – Daughter – b. 1881 London – aged 10
Morris S. HYAMS – Son – b. 1883 London – aged 8
Esther S. HYAMS – Daughter – b. 1886 London – aged 5
Michel S. HYAMS – Son – b. 1888 London – aged 3
Louisa S. HYAMS – Daughter – b. 1891 London – aged 3 weeks
Sarah PERCY – General Servant

1881 Census

Address:
14 Artillery Passage, Old Artillery Ground

Residents:
Joseph HYAMS – Head – b. 1859 City – aged 22 – Fishmonger
Annette S. HYAMS – Wife – b. 1861 Bethnal Green – aged 20
Edward S. HYAMS – Son – b. 1880 Old Artillery Ground – aged 1
Elizabeth HILLIAM – Domestic Servant

Marriage:
Joseph HYAMS to Jeanette DE YOUNG – Q3 1879 LONDON CITY 1c 168.

1901 Census

Addreess:
44 Artillery Lane, Old Artillery Ground

Residents:
Annette S. HYAMS – Head – Widow – b. 1862 London – aged 39 – Fishmonger
Edward S. HYAMS – Son – b. 1880 London – aged 21 – Fish Curer
Morris HYAMS – Son – b. 1883 London – aged 18 - Fish Curer
Esther HYAMS – Daughter – b. 1886 London – aged 15 – Dancer
Michael HYAMS – Son – b. 1889 London – aged 12 – at School
Louisa HYAMS – Daughter – b. 1891 London – aged 10 – at School
Charles Solomon HYAMS – b. 1895 London – aged 6 – at School

1911 Census

Address:
47b Hanbury Street, Spitalfields

Residents:
Annette S. HYAMS – Head – Widow – b. 1861 Holborn – aged 50
Michael HYAMS – Son – b. 1889 Stepney – aged 22 – China Packer
Charles HYAMS – Son – b. 1896 Stepney – aged 15 – Tailor's Apprentice
Myer LEVY – Son-in-law – b. 1888 London – aged 23 – Fish Fryer
Esther LEVY – Daughter - Wife (2½ years) – b. 1887 Stepney – aged 24

Frederick LEVY – Son – b. 1909 Finsbury – aged 2
Cesira LEVY – Daughter – b. 1910 Finsbury – aged 10 months

Death:
Annette S. HYAMS – Q4 1938 [78] STEPNEY 1c 284.
Buried at East Ham Jewish Cemetery – K-5-312 on 22 Dec 1938.

HYAMS, Kate – D-15-9

Died: 02 Aug 1899
Buried: 06 Aug 1899
Parents: Solomon & Rachel Hyams
Aged: 67 years

Jewish Chronicle – 04 Aug 1899
HYAMS – On the 2nd of August, at 304, Grays Inn Road, Kate Hyams, aged 67, formerly of Leman Street.

Jewish Chronicle – 08 Dec 1899
The tombstone in loving memory of the late Kate Hyams, of 304, Grays Inn Road, will be set at Plashet Cemetery on Sunday, December 10th, at 2.30 o'clock. Relatives and friends will accept this, the only intimation.

Death:
Q3 1899 [67] PANCRAS 1b 40.

1881 Census
Address:
15, Commercial Street, Whitechapel
Residents:
Moses V. ROSS – Head – b. 1841 Alphen, Holland – aged 40 – Cattle dealer
Leah ROSS – Wife - b. 1843 Middlesex – aged 38
Abraham ROSS – Son - b. 1879 Whitechapel – aged 2
Lewis ROSS – Son - b. 1881 Whitechapel – aged 0
Kate HYAMS – Visitor - b. 1837 Whitechapel – aged 44 – General Dealer
Julia NELSON – Domestic
Newende ENOCH – Boarder – b. 1855 Poland – Aged 26 - Bootmaker

1871 Census
Address:
123 Leman Street, Whitechapel
Residents:
Rachel HART – Head – b. 1795 London – aged 76

Kate HYAMS – Daughter - b. 1833 London – aged 38
Leah RAPHAEL – Boarder - b. 1845 London – aged 26
Mary O'BRIEN – Domestic servant

1861 Census

Address:
112, Middlesex Street East Side, Whitechapel N., London

Residents:
Michael C. HART – Head – b. 1792 Ickenham – aged 69 – Fishmonger
Rachael HART – Wife – b. 1796 Whitechapel – aged 65
Catherine HYAMS – Wife's daughter – b. 1834 Whitechapel – aged 27 – Dressmaker
Susana WATERLOW – General servant

1851 Census

Address:
112, Petticoat Lane, Saint Mary Whitechapel, Tower Hamlets

Residents:
Michael HART – Head – b. 1795 Tottenham – aged 56 – Fishmonger
Rachel HART – Wife - b. 1806 Spitalfields – aged 45
Catherine HYAMS – Daughter of Wife – b. 1832 Whitechapel – aged 19
Elizabeth HYAMS – Daughter of Wife – b. 1835 Whitechapel – aged 16
Julia LEVI – Lodger - b. 1827 Whitechapel – aged 24 – General Dealer
Mary HART – Daughter – b. 1839 Aldgate – aged 12

Marriage:
Michael HART to Rachel HYAMS – Q3 1850 LONDON, 2, 208a.

Death:
Solomon HYAMS – Q3 1845 LONDON CITY, 2, 139
Place of burial unknown.

1841 Census

Address:
Petticoat Lane, St. Mary Whitechapel, Tower Hamlets

Residents:
Solomon HYAMS – Head – b. 1796 Middlesex – aged 45
Rachel HYAMS – Wife - b. 1806 Middlesex – aged 35
David HYAMS – Son – b. 1827 Middlesex – aged 14
Joshua HYAMS – Son - b. 1829 Middlesex aged 12
Samuel HYAMS – Son – b. 1835 Middlesex – aged 6
Catherine HYAMS – Daughter – b. 1831 Middlesex – aged 10
Leah HYAMS – Daughter – b. 1825 Middlesex – aged 16

Betsey HYAMS – Daughter – b. 1833 Middlesex – aged 8
Isaac SOLOMONS – Boarder b. 1811 Middlesex – aged 30

Jewish Victorian – p. 217

RACHAEL HART

Death 31 Aug 1878 at her residence, 123 Leman Street, Whitechapel, relict of the late Michael Hart, aged 77 years, dearly beloved mother of Kate Hyams of 123 Leman Street and David Hyams of 182 Drury Lane, sister of Mrs E Levy, 25 Newcastle Street, Whitechapel and Mrs L. Isaacs, 39 Duke Street, Aldgate. May her soul rest in peace. American papers please copy (taken from the Jewish Chronicle).

Jewish Victorian – p. 216

MICHAEL HART

Death 25 Mar 1871 at 123 Leman Street, Whitechapel, aged 79. May his soul rest in peace. American papers please copy (taken from the Jewish Record).

ISAACS, Alexander – D-15-4

Died: **20 Jul 1899**
Buried: **23 Jul 1899**
Hebrew Name: **Alexander ben Shlomo**
Partner: **Henrietta Sarah Isaacs**
Age: **25 years**

Jewish Chronicle – 21 Jul 1899

ISAACS – On Thursday, the 20th of July, at 4, Cowley Road, South Hackney, Alexander Isaacs, aged 25 years, son of the late Solomon Isaacs, of 4, Gravel Lane, Houndsditch, and Mrs Esther Isaacs, of 73, Lauriston Road, South Hackney. Deeply mourned by his sorrowing wife, children, mother, brothers, sisters and a large circle of friends. Shiva at 73, Lauriston Road. Funeral will leave No. 4, Cowley Road, on Sunday next, the 23rd inst., at 3 o'clock, for Plashet Cemetery. Relatives and friends please accept this, the only intimation. God rest his soul in peace.

Jewish Chronicle – 06 Apr 1900

The tombstone in loving memory of my late lamented husband, Alexander Isaacs, late of 4, Cawley Road, South Hackney, will be set on Sunday next, April 8th, at 3 o'clock, at Plashet Cemetery. Relatives and friends please accept this, the only intimation.

Death:

Q3 1899 [25] HACKNEY 1b 384.

Marriage:

Alexander ISAACS to Henrietta Sarah BARNETT – Q3 1896 LONDON CITY 1c 102.

ISAACS, Alexander – D-15-4

1901 Census

Address:

64 Kenninghall Road, Hackney

Residents:

Lewis BARNETT – Head – Widower – b. 1841 Wandsworth – aged 60 – Tobacco Manufacturer
Samuel BARNETT – Son – b. 1871 St. Lukes – aged 30 – Tobacco Manufacturer
Buirs BARNETT – Daughter-in-law – b. 1870 Bethnal Green – aged 31
Lillie BARNETT – Daughter – b. 1874 St. Lukes – aged 27
Henrietta ISAACS – Daughter – Widow – b. 1876 St. Lukes – aged 25
Madeline BARNETT – Daughter – b. 1880 St. Lukes – aged 21
Ester ISAACS – Granddaughter – b. 1897 Hackney – aged 4
Lewis ISAACS – Grandson – b. 1899 Hackney – aged 2
Edith CLARK – Domestic Servant
Lily POWIS – Domestic Servant

Marriage:

Henrietta Sarah ISAACS to Alexander JACOBS – Q2 1902 LONDON CITY 1c 81.
[according to the Jewish Chronicle the marriage took place on 17 June 1902 at 64 Kenninghall Road, Hackney.]

1911 Census

Address:

29 Tollington Park, Islington

Residents:

Alexander JACOBS – Head – b. 1875 Bethnal Green – aged 36 – Company Director
Henrietta Sarah JACOBS – Wife (8 years) – b. 1878 Shoreditch – aged 33
Lewis Isleman ISAACS – Stepson – b. 1899 Hackney – aged 12 – at School
Esther ISAACS – Stepdaughter – b. 1898 Hackney – aged 13 – at School
Hettie MARTIN – Visitor – b. 1904 Hackney – aged 7

ISAACS, Amelia – B-5-16

Died: 16 Dec 1899
Buried: 18 Dec 1899
Partner: Simeon Isaacs (d. 1855)
Aged: 95 years

Jewish Chronicle – 22 Dec 1899

ISAACS – On the 16th of December, Amelia Isaacs, the beloved mother of Mrs

Henry Solomons, aged 95 years. Deeply mourned by her sorrowing daughter, son, grandchildren and a large circle of friends. God rest her dear soul in peace. Shiva at 3, Clarence Mansions, Hackney.

Jewish Chronicle – 16 Mar 1900

The tombstone in memory of the late Amelia Isaacs (Aunt Milly), wife of Simeon Isaacs, late of Hoxton, and aunt of Woo Davis of Shacklewell Lane, will be set on Sunday next, at 4 o'clock, at Plashet Cemetery.

Death:
Q4 1899 [96] HACKNEY 1b 375.

1891 Census

Address:
104a Bridge Street, Mile End Old Town

Residents:
Amelia ISAACS – Widow – b. 1813 Amsterdam – aged 78 – Living on her own means

1881 Census

Address:
8 Ewing Street, Mile End Old Town

Residents:
Thomas ABBOTT – Head – b. 1830 Middlesex – aged 51 – Poulterer
Mary ABBOTT – Wife – b. 1832 Middlesex – aged 49
Alice ABBOTT – Daughter – b. 1861 Middlesex – aged 20 – Seamstress
William ABBOTT – Son – b. 1863 Middlesex – aged 18 – Hosier
Arthur ABBOTT – Son – b. 1865 Middlesex – aged 16 – Page Boy in Service
Clara ABBOTT – Daughter – b. 1869 Middlesex – aged 12 – Scholar
Emma ABBOTT – Daughter – b. 1872 Middlesex – aged 9 – Scholar
Amelia ISAACS – Boarder – Widow – b. 1811 Netherlands – aged 70 – Annuitant

1871 Census

Address:
Gloucester Street

Residents:
Amelia ISAACS – b. 1812 Netherlands – aged 59

1861 Census

Address:
75 Goulston Street, Whitechapel, Middlesex

Residents:

Amelia ISAACS – Head – Widow – b. 1812 Amsterdam – aged 49 – Cap Maker
Elizabeth ISAACS – Daughter – b. 1841 Spitalfields – aged 20 – Tailoress
Jean ISAACS – Son – b. 1846 Spitalfields – aged 15 -Shoemaker
Aaron ISAACS – Son – b. 1847 Spitalfields – aged 14 – Shoemaker
Henry SALOMONS – Boarder – b. 1841 Manchester – aged 20 – Shoemaker

Death:

Simeon Isaacs – Q2 1855 WHITECHAPEL 1c 251.
Place of burial unknown.

ISAACS, Asher – A-14-43

Died: **31 Jan 1899**
Buried: **02 Feb 1899**
Partner: **Esther Isaacs (d. 1904)**
Aged: **74th year**

Jewish Chronicle – 03 Feb 1899

ISAACS – On the 30th of January, at 10, St. Thomas Road, South Hackney, in his 74th year, Asher Isaacs, formerly of 48, Great Alie Street, E. Father of I.A. Isaacs and E.A. Isaacs, of Manchester, Mrs Isaac Jacobs, of 7, White Street, E.C., Mrs W. Rutkowski, of 10, St. Thomas Road, and Mrs C. Boss, of 86, Colvestone Crescent, Dalston. Deeply mourned by his sorrowing widow and family. Shiva at 10, St. Thomas Road.

Jewish Chronicle – 10 Feb 1899

Mrs Asher Isaacs, Mr I.A. Isaacs (Manchester), Mr E.A. Isaacs (Manchester), Mrs Isaac Jacobs (7, White Street, E.C)., Mrs Woolf A. Rutkowski (10, St. Thomas Road, South Hackney), and Mrs C. Boss (86, Colvestone Crescent, Dalton), return sincere thanks for the numerous expressions of sympathy received during the week of mourning for their late lamented husband and father, Asher Isaacs – 10, St. Thomas Road, South Hackney.

Jewish Chronicle – 09 Feb 1900

The tombstone in loving memory of the late Asher Isaacs, of 48, Great Alie Street, E., will be set at Plashet Cemetery, on Sunday, February 11th, at 12 o'clock. Relatives and friends please accept this, the only intimation – 10, St. Thomas Road, N.E.

Death:

Q1 1899 [74] HACKNEY 1b 398.

1891 Census

Address:

48, Great Alie Street, Whitechapel

Residents:

Asha ISAACS – Head – b. 1825 Russia – aged 66 – Tailor's Trimming Seller
Esther ISAACS – Wife – b. 1824 Russia – aged 67

1881 Census

Address:

48, Great Alie Street, Whitechapel

Residents:

Asher ISAACS – Head – b. 1826 Russia – aged 55 – Tailors Trimming Seller
Esther ISAACS – Wife – b. 1825 London – aged 56
Elisha ISAACS – Son – b. 1861 London – aged 20 – Traveller in Shirts
Fanny ISAACS – Daughter – b. 1863 London – aged 18 – General Shop-woman
Leah ISAACS – Daughter – b. 1865 London – aged 16 – Pupil Teacher
David JACOBS – Grandson – b. 1877 London – aged 4 – Scholar

1871 Census

Address:

48, Great Alie Street, St. Mary Whitechapel

Residents:

Asher ISAACS – Head – b. 1825 The Netherlands – aged 46 – Rag Merchant
Esther ISAACS – Wife – b. 1825 Spitalfields – aged 46
David ISAACS – Son – b. 1850 Aldgate – aged 21 – Teacher
Isaac ISAACS – Son – b. 1852 Whitechapel – aged 19 – Assistant to Rag Merchant
Jane ISAACS – Daughter – b. 1853 Whitechapel – aged 18 – Parasol Maker
Susan ISAACS – Daughter – b. 1855 Whitechapel – aged 16 – Parasol Maker
Hyman ISAACS – Son – b. 1858 Whitechapel – aged 13 – Scholar
Elisha ISAACS – Son – b. 1862 Whitechapel – aged 9 – Scholar
Fanny ISAACS – Daughter – b. 1864 Whitechapel – aged 7 – Scholar
Leah ISAACS – Daughter – b. 1866 Whitechapel – aged 5 – Scholar

1861 Census

Registered as ISAAC

Address:

48, Great Alie Street, Whitechapel

Residents:

Asher ISAACS – Head – b. 1825 Russia – aged 36 – Rag Merchant
Esther ISAACS – Wife – b. 1824 Spitalfields – aged 37
David ISAACS – Son – b. 1850 London – aged 11 – Scholar

Isaac ISAACS – Son – b. 1852 London – aged 9 – Scholar
Jane ISAACS – Daughter – b. 1853 London – aged 8 – Scholar
Susan ISAACS – Daughter – b. 1855 London – aged 6 – Scholar
Hyman ISAACS – Son – b. 1858 London – aged 3 – Scholar
Elisha ISAACS – Son – b. 1861 – aged 6 months
Hannah BURKE – House Servant

1851 Census

Address:
48, Great Alie Street, Whitechapel, Tower Hamlets

Residents:
Asher ISAACS – Head – b. 1826 Russia – aged 25 – Tailor & Trimming Seller
Esther ISAACS – Wife – b. 1824 Spitalfields – aged 27
David ISAACS – Son – b. 1850 London – aged 1
Betsey SULLIVAN – House Servant

Marriage:
Asher ISAACS to Esther DAVIS – Q4 1847 ST. LUKE 2 314.

1901 Census

Address:
10, St. Thomas Road, Hackney

Residents:
Woolf RUSKOWSKI – Head – b. 1865 Russia – aged 36 – Rag Merchant
Fanny RUSKOWSKI – Wife – b. 1863 Whitechapel – aged 38
Esther ISAACS – Mother-in-law – b. 1823 Spitalfields – aged 78
Isidore RUSKOWSKI – Son – b. 1888 Whitechapel – aged 13 – Scholar
Celia RUSKOWSKI – Daughter – b. 1890 Whitechapel – aged 11 – Scholar
Annie RUSKOWSKI – Daughter – b. 1891 Whitechapel – aged 10 – Scholar
Leopold RUSKOWSKI – Son – b. 1895 Hackney – aged 6 – Scholar
Estella RUSKOWSKI – Daughter – b. 1897 Hackney – aged 4
Alfred RUSKOWSKI – Son – b. 1900 Hackney – aged 1
Rose MULVIHILL – Domestic Servant

Death:
Esther ISAACS – Q3 1904 [81] HACKNEY 1b 321.
Buried at Plashet Cemetery – E-19-38 on 12 Jul 1904.

Jewish Chronicle – 15 Jul 1904

ISAACS – On the 11th of July, at 82, Victoria Park Road, South Hackney (the residence of her son-in-law), Esther, relict of the late Asher Isaacs, formerly of 48, Great Alie Street, E., in her 82nd year. The dearly loved mother of I.A. Isaacs and E.A. Isaacs, of Manchester, Mrs Isaac Jacobs, of 11, Spital Square, Mrs W.A.

Rutkowski, of 82, Victoria Park Road, N.E., Mrs C. Boss, of 86, Colvestone Crescent, Dalston, and sister of Myer Davis, 106, Brondesbury Villas, Kilburn. Deeply mourned by her children, grandchildren, relatives and a large circle of friends. Shiva terminates on Monday.

ISAACS, Sarah – D-8-1A

Died: 25 Feb 1899
Buried: 28 Feb 1899
Hebrew Name: Sarah bat Mizraki
Partner: Angel Isaacs (d. 1917)
Age: 66 years

Jewish Chronicle – 03 Mar 1899

ISAACS – On the 25th of February, at 15, Bancroft Road, Mile End, Sarah, the beloved wife of Angel Isaacs, after a long illness borne with great fortitude. May her dear soul rest in peace. American and Australian papers please copy.

Death:

Q1 1899 [66] MILE END 1c 355.

1891 Census

Address:

15 Bancroft Road, Mile End Old Town

Residents:

Angel ISAACS – Head – b. 1829 Aldgate – aged 62 – Living on Own Means
Sarah ISAACS – Wife – b. 1831 Spitalfields – aged 60
Sarah SOLOMONS – Niece – b. 1885 Mile End – aged 6
Ellen COCKLIN – Domestic Servant

1881 Census

Address:

15 Bancroft Road, Mile End Old Town

Residents:

Angel ISAACS – Head – b. 1830 London – aged 51 – Retired Traveller
Sarah ISAACS – Wife – b. 1831 London – aged 50
Rebecca DEFRIES – Niece – b. 1859 Tower Hamlets – aged 22
Elizabeth ISAACS – Mother – Widow – b. 1809 London – aged 72
Eliza NOOKE – Domestic Servant

ISAACS, Sarah – D-8-1A

1871 Census

Address:

31 New Castle Street, Whitechapel

Residents:

Angel ISAACS – Head – b. 1828 Aldgate – aged 43 – Commission Agent
Sarah ISAACS – Wife – b. 1831 Spitalfields – aged 40
Rebecca DEFRIES – Niece – b. 1858 Spitalfields – aged 13 – Scholar
Rose DOVE – Domestic Servant

1861 Census

Address:

14 Tenter Street, Spitalfields

Residents:

Mark ISAACS – Head – b. 1787 Aldgate – aged 74 – Traveller
Elizabeth ISAACS – Wife – b. 1811 Aldgate – aged 50
Angel ISAACS – Son – b. 1830 Aldgate – aged 31 – Traveller
Sarah ISAACS – Daughter – b. 1837 Spitalfields – aged 24 – Dressmaker
Lewis ISAACS – Son – b. 1839 Spitalfields – aged 22 – Cigar Maker
Henry ISAACS – Son – b. 1841 Spitalfields – aged 20 – Cigar Maker
Isaac ISAACS – Son – b. 1843 Spitalfields – aged 18 – Engraver
Catherine ISAACS – Daughter – b. 1845 Spitalfields – aged 16 – Tailoress

Marriage:

Angel ISAACS to Sarah MOSES – Q1 1862 LONDON CITY 1c 198.

1901 Census

Address:

15 Bancroft Road, Mile End Old Town

Residents:

Angel ISAACS – Head – Widower – b. 1830 London – aged 71 – Living on Own Means
Rebecca SOLOMONS – Niece – Widow – b. 1861 Stepney – aged 40 – Housekeeper
Sarah SOLOMONS – Niece – b. 1885 Mile End – aged 16
Henry SOLOMONS – Nephew – b. 1887 Mile End – aged 14
David SOLOMONS – Nephew – b. 1890 Mile End – aged 11
Phillip SOLOMONS – Nephew – b. 1892 Mile End – aged 9
Angel SOLOMONS – Nephew – b. 1897 Mile End – aged 4
Annie HARBORN – General Domestic Servant
Hetty CLARK – General Domestic Servant

1911 Census

Address:

15 Bancroft Road, Mile End Old Town

Residents:

Angel ISAACS – Head – b. 1831 London – aged 80 – no occupation
Rebecca SOLOMONS – Niece – Widow – b. 1859 Stepney – Housekeeper
Sarah SOLOMONS – Niece – b. 1885 Stepney – aged 26
Thomas SOLOMONS – Nephew – b. 1888 Mile End – aged 23 – Dealer
Phillip SOLOMONS – Nephew – b. 1893 Mile End – aged 18 – Lithographer
Angel SOLOMONS – Nephew – b. 1897 Mile End – aged 14 – at School
Kellie BAPET – Domestic Servant / Boarder

Death:

Angel ISAACS - Q1 1917 [86] MILE END 1c 478
Buried at Plashet Cemetery – D-8-1B – 17 Jan 1917.

Jewish Chronicle – 19 Jan 1917

ISAACS – On the 14th of January, at his residence, 15, Bancroft Road, Mile End, Angel Isaacs, in his 87th year. Beloved uncle of Rebecca Solomons, and devoted foster-father to her children, Henry (on active service in France), Sarah, Philip and Angel. Beloved by all who knew him.

ISAACS – On the 14th of January, at his residence, 15, Bancroft Road, Mile End, Angel Isaacs, in his 87th year. Deeply mourned by his nephews and nieces, Mr and Mrs Ross Joel and Mr Mark Angel Hart, of 141, Bancroft Road, E.; Mr and Mrs Daniel Rogers, 41, Diggon Street, E.; and Mr and Mrs Lewis Hart, 596, High Road, Leytonstone. God rest his dear soul.

ISAACS – On the 14th of January, Angel Isaacs, in his 87th year. Deeply mourned by his nephew and niece, Mr and Mrs Alec Cohen, 80, Belgrade Road, Stoke Newington.

ISAACS – On the 14th of January, at 15, Bancroft Road, Mile End, Angel Isaacs, beloved uncle of Angel and Sophie Aarons. God rest his soul.

ISAACS – On the 14th of January, at his residence, 15, Bancroft Road, Mile End, Angel Isaacs, in his 87th year. Deeply mourned by his sister-in-law, Betsy Isaacs, and family, of 24, Bancroft Road, Mile End. May his dear soul rest in peace.

Jewish Chronicle – 12 Oct 1917

ISAACS – The tombstone in memory of the late Angel Isaacs, of 15, Bancroft Road, Mile End, and the tablet to the memory of his late nephew, Henry Solomon, killed in action in France, will be consecrated at the Plashet Cemetery on Sunday, October 21st, at 3 o'clock. Relatives and friends will accept this, the only intimation.

ISRAEL, Rachel – A-14-23

Died: 22 Jan 1899
Buried: 24 Jan 1899
Hebrew Name: Rachel bat Alexander
Partner: Joseph Israel (d. 1912)
Aged: 54 years

Jewish Chronicle – 27 Jan 1899

ISRAEL – On the 22nd of January, at her residence, 11, Wentworth Street, Spitalfields, Rachel, the beloved wife of Joseph Israel, aged 54. Deeply mourned by her loving husband, children, sisters and brother and by everyone who knew her. New York papers please copy.

Jewish Chronicle – 07 Apr 1899

The tombstone of the late Rachel Israel of 11, Wentworth Street, Spitalfields and also of the late Caroline Israel (A-11-43) of 5, Arthur Street, Oxford Street, will be set at Plashet Cemetery, on Sunday, April 9th, at 4 o'clock. The only intimation.

Death:

Q1 1899 [54] WHITECHAPEL 1c 187.

1891 Census

Address:

7 Wentworth Street, Spitalfields, London, Whitechapel

Residents:

Joseph ISRAEL – Head – b. 1845 Spitalfields – aged 46 – Greengrocer
Rachel ISRAEL – Wife – b. 1845 Spitalfields – aged 46
Israel ISRAEL – Son – b. 1872 Spitalfields – aged 19 – Tailor
Esther ISRAEL – Daughter – b. 1875 Spitalfields – aged 16 – Greengrocer's Assistant
Alexander ISRAEL – Son – b. 1877 Spitalfields – aged 14 – Greengrocer's Assistant
Simon ISRAEL – Son – b. 1878 Spitalfields – aged 13 – Greengrocer's Assistant
Leah ISRAEL – Daughter – b. 1881 Spitalfields – aged 10 – Scholar
Barnet ISRAEL – Son – b. 1884 Spitalfields – aged 7 – Scholar
Sarah ISRAEL – Daughter – b. 1890 - aged 1

1881 Census

Address:

6 Short Street, Spitalfields

ISRAEL, Rachel – A-14-23

Residents:

Joseph ISRAEL – Head – b. 1845 Whitechapel – aged 36 – Cigar Maker
Rachel ISRAEL – Wife – b. 1846 London – aged 35 – Cigar Maker
Israel ISRAEL – Son – b. 1872 Spitalfields – aged 9 – Scholar
Esther ISRAEL – Daughter – b. 1874 Spitalfields – aged 7 – Scholar
Alexander ISRAEL – Son – b.1876 Spitalfields – aged 5 – Scholar
Simon ISRAEL – Son – b. 1878 Spitalfields – aged 3 – Scholar
Leah ISRAEL – Daughter – b. 1881 Spitalfields – aged 0

1871 Census

Address:

Short Street, Christ Church

Residents:

Joseph ISRAEL – Head – b. 1845 Middlesex – aged 26
Rachel ISRAEL – Wife – b. 1846 Middlesex – aged 25

Marriage:

Joseph ISRAEL to Catherine (Rachel) HYAMS – Q4 1870 LONDON CITY 1c 215.

1901 Census

Address:

52 Middlesex Street, Whitechapel

Residents:

Joseph ISRAEL – Head – Widower – b. 1842 Whitechapel – aged 59 – Greengrocer
Israel ISRAEL – Son – b. 1872 Whitechapel – aged 29 – Tailor's Cutter
Esther ISRAEL – Daughter – b. 1874 Whitechapel – aged 27 – Domestic Housekeeper
Alexander ISRAEL – Son – b. 1876 Whitechapel – aged 25 – Greengrocer
Simon ISRAEL – Son – b. 1878 Whitechapel – aged 23 – Greengrocer
Barnet ISRAEL – Son – b. 1883 Whitechapel – aged 18 – Tailor's Cutter
Leah ISRAEL – Daughter – b. 1881 Whitechapel – aged 20 – Cigar Maker

1911 Census

Address:

9 Wentworth Street, Spitalfields

Residents:

Joseph ISRAEL – Head – Widower – b. 1843 Whitechapel – aged 68 – Greengrocer
Israel ISRAEL – Son – b. 1872 Whitechapel – aged 39 – Tailor's Cutter
Esther ISRAEL – Daughter – b. 1874 Whitechapel – aged 37 – Housekeeper
Alex. ISRAEL – Son – b. 1876 Whitechapel – aged 35 – Assisting in Business

Simon ISRAEL – Son – b. 1878 Whitechapel – aged 33 – Carman
Leah ISRAEL – Daughter – b. 1881 Whitechapel – aged 30 – Cigar Maker
Barnett ISRAEL – Son – b. 1883 Whitechapel – aged 28 – Tailor's Cutter
Jack SHAW – Lodger – b. 1879 Bradford – aged 32 – Greengrocer's Assistant

Death:

Joseph ISRAEL – Q3 1912 [67] ST OLAVE SOUTHWARK 1d 133.
Buried at Plashet Cemetery – N-6-12 on 20 Aug 1912.

Jewish Chronicle – 23 Aug 1912

ISRAEL – On the 17th of August (Ellul 4th), 1912, at 9, Wentworth Street, Spitalfields, Joseph Israel, the dearly beloved father of Issey, Esther, Alec, Leah, Simon and Barnett. Deeply mourned by his sorrowing children, daughters-in-law, granddaughter, relatives and a large circle of friends. Aged 67. Gone but not forgotten. Shiva at above address.

Jewish Chronicle – 14 Mar 1913

ISRAEL – The tombstone in loving memory of our dear father, Joseph Israel, 9, Wentworth Street, Spitalfields, will be consecrated at Plashet Cemetery on Sunday, 16th March, at 4 o'clock.

ISRAEL, Samuel – A-14-39

Died: **24 Oct 1899**
Buried: **25 Oct 1899**
Parents: **Lazarus & Miriam Israel**
Aged: **23rd year**

Jewish Chronicle – 27 Jan 1899

ISRAEL – On the 24th of January at 31, Cambridge Heath Road, Mile End, Samuel, the fourth son of Miriam (Polly) and the late Lazarus Israel, in his 23rd year. Deeply mourned by his sorrowing mother, sisters, brothers, relatives and a large circle of friends. God rest his dear soul in peace.

Jewish Chronicle – 02 Sep 1899

The tombstones in loving memory of Nancy (A-14-16) and Samuel Isaac, son and daughter of Polly and the late Lazarus Israel of 31, Cambridge Road, E., will be set at Plashet Cemetery on Sunday next, September 3rd, at 4 o'clock.

Death:

Q1 1899 [22] BETHNAL GREEN 1c 162.

Birth:

Q3 1876 BETHNAL GREEN 1c 237.

1891 Census

Address:

59 Cambridge Road, Bethnal Green, London

Residents:

Lazarus ISRAEL – Head – b. 1845 Aldgate – aged 46 – Fishmonger
Miriam ISRAEL – Wife – b. 1850 Aldgate – aged 41 – Clothier
Nancy ISRAEL – Daughter – b. 1867 Aldgate – aged 24 – Domestic Servant
Hannah ISRAEL – Daughter – b. 1871 Aldgate – aged 20 – Feather Curler
Benjamin ISRAEL – Son – b. 1873 Whitechapel – aged 18 – Fishmonger
Elias ISRAEL – Son – b. 1875 Whitechapel – aged 16 – Clothiers Assistant
Samuel ISRAEL – Son – b. 1877 Mile End – aged 14 – Pupil Teacher
Joseph ISRAEL – Son – b. 1882 Mile End – aged 9 – Scholar
Esther ISRAEL – Daughter – b. 1885 Mile End – aged 6 – Scholar
Betsy ISRAEL – Daughter – b. 1887 Mile End – aged 4 – Scholar
Bernhard ISRAEL – Son – b. 1889 Mile End – aged 2
William ISRAEL – Son – b. 1891 Mile End – aged 3 months
Margaret DANBY – General Servant

1881 Census

Address:

71 Cambridge Road, Bethnal Green

Residents:

Lazarus ISRAEL – Head – b. 1846 London – aged 35 – Clothier
Mary ISRAEL – Wife – b. 1850 Fishmongers Alley – aged 31 – Clothier
Annie ISRAEL – Daughter – b. 1867 Middlesex Street – aged 14 – Clothier
Maurice ISRAEL – Son – b. 1868 Harrow Alley – aged 13 – Clothier
Hannah ISRAEL – Daughter – b. 1871 Swan Street – aged 10 – Scholar
Benjamin ISRAEL – Son – b. 1873 George Yard – aged 8 – Scholar
Elias ISRAEL – Son – b. 1875 George Yard – aged 6 – Scholar
Samuel ISRAEL – Son – b. 1877 Bethnal Green – aged 4 – Scholar
Ellen WHITE – General Servant

1871 Census

Address:

20 Harrow Alley, Aldgate, London

Residents:

Lazarus ISRAEL – Head – b. 1846 London – aged 25 – General Dealer
Mary ISRAEL – Wife – b. 1849 London – aged 22
Nancy ISRAEL – Daughter – b. 1866 London – aged 5

Moses ISRAEL – Son – b. 1868 London – aged 3
Hannah ISRAEL – Daughter – b. 1870 London – aged 1

Marriage:
Lazarus ISRAEL to Mary Ann JOSEPH – Q1 1867 EAST LONDON 1c 47.

Death:
Lazarus ISRAEL – Q2 1898 [53] BETHNAL GREEN 1c 139.
Buried at Plashet Cemetery – A-13-36 on 13 Jun 1898.

Miriam ISRAEL – Q3 1915 [66] MILE END OLD TOWN 1c 423.
Buried at Plashet Cemetery – L-24-10 on 11 Aug 1915.

JACOBS, Abigail – B-5-1

Died: **29 Nov 1899**
Buried: **01 Dec 1899**
Hebrew Name: **Abigail bat Shlomo**
Partner: **Abraham Lewis (Lew) Jacobs (d. 1912)**
Aged: **51 years**

Jewish Chronicle – 01 Dec 1899

JACOBS – On the 29th of November, suddenly, at 80, Grosvenor Road, Canonbury, N., Abigail, the dearly beloved wife of Abraham Lewis Jacobs, and dearly beloved mother of Mrs Joseph E. Blank, of 119, Farleigh Road, Stoke Newington, N., of Lewis Jacobs, 3, Lidfield Road, Green Lanes, and of Alexander Jacobs, Cape Town, aged 51. Deeply mourned by her bereaved husband, sons, daughters, and relatives and a wide circle of friends. May her honoured soul find eternal rest. Shiva at 80, Grosvenor Road.

JACOBS – On the 29th of November, suddenly, at 80, Grosvenor Road, Canonbury, N., Abigail Jacobs, the ever-beloved and fondly to be remembered sister of Mrs Cassell, 63, Victoria Dock Road, Mrs Morris, 16, Statham Grove, N., Mrs Henry Davis, 16, Leconfield Road, Canonbury, Mrs Hillier, of 10, New Street, Houndsditch, and Miss S. Nathan, of 80, Grosvenor Road.

Jewish Chronicle – 29 Dec 1899

The tombstone to the memory of the late lamented Abigail Jacobs, beloved wife of A.L. Jacobs, of 80, Grosvenor Road, Highbury New Park, will be set on Sunday, January 7th, at Plashet Cemetery at 2.30 p.m. Relatives and friends will please accept this intimation.

Death:
Q4 1899 [51] ISLINGTON 1b 319.

JACOBS, Abigail – B-5-1

1891 Census

Address:

80 Grosvenor Road, Islington

Residents:

Abraham JACOBS – Head – b. 1848 Aldgate – aged 43 – Commission Agent
Abigail JACOBS – Wife – b. 1849 Aldgate – aged 42
Solomon JACOBS – Son – b. 1872 London – aged 19 – Traveller
Lewis JACOBS – Son – b. 1873 Mile End – aged 18 – Traveller
Alexander JACOBS – Son – b. 1875 Mile End – aged 16 – Apprentice Printer
David JACOBS – Son – b. 1877 Mile End – aged 14 – Apprentice
Samuel JACOBS – Son – b. 1879 Mile End – aged 12 – at School
Bertie JACOBS – Son – b. 1880 Mile End – aged 11 – at School
Hannah JACOBS – Daughter – b. 1881 Mile End – aged 10 – at School
Ada JACOBS – Daughter – b. 1883 Bow – aged 8 – at School
John JACOBS – Son – b. 1885 Bow – aged 6 – at School
Ethel JACOBS – Daughter – b. 1887 Bow – aged 4
Elizabeth JACOBS – Daughter – b. 1891 Islington – aged 1 month
Sara NATHAN – Wife's sister – b. 1866 Aldgate – aged 25
Mary DRISCOLL – Domestic Housemaid
Alice WOOD – Domestic Nurse

1881 Census

Address:

64 St. Peters Road, Mile End Old Town

Residents:

Abraham JACOBS – Head – b. 1849 Aldgate – aged 32 – General Dealer
Abigail JACOBS – Wife – b. 1849 St. Georges – aged 32
Matilda JACOBS – Daughter – b. 1870 St Georges – aged 11 – Scholar
Solomon JACOBS – Son – b. 1872 Bethnal Green – aged 9 – Scholar
Lewis JACOBS – Son – b. 1874 Bethnal Green – aged 7 – Scholar
Alexander JACOBS – Son – b. 1875 Bethnal Green – aged 6 – Scholar
David JACOBS – Son – b. 1876 Bethnal Green – aged 5 – Scholar
Samuel JACOBS – Son – b. 1878 Mile End – aged 3 – Scholar
Barnett JACOBS – Son – b. 1880 Mile End – aged 1
Eliza DAY – Domestic Servant
Mary A. WHITE – Domestic Servant

1871 Census

Address:

Grace's Alley, St. Mary Whitechapel

Residents:

Abraham JACOBS – Head – b. 1848 Middlesex – aged 23 – Commercial agent

Abigail JACOBS – Wife – b. 1849 Middlesex – aged 22
Matilda JACOBS – Daughter – b. 1870 Middlesex – aged 1

Marriage:
Abraham JACOBS to Abigail NATHAN – Q4 1868 EAST LONDON 1c 60.

1901 Census

Address:
80 Grosvenor Road, Islington

Residents:
Abraham L. JACOBS – Head – Widower – b. 1851 London – aged 50 – Sports Correspondent
David JACOBS – Son – b. 1877 London – aged 24 – Licensed Victualler & Glass Importer
Samuel JACOBS – Son – b. 1879 London – aged 22 – Clerk to above
Bertie JACOBS – Son – b. 1880 London – aged 21 – Tailors (Womens) Merchant
Hannah JACOBS – Daughter – b. 1883 London – aged 18
Ada JACOBS – Daughter – b. 1884 London – aged 17
John JACOBS – Son – b. 1885 London – aged 16 – Watchmakers Clerk
Ethel JACOBS – Daughter – b. 1887 London – aged 14
Lizzie JACOBS – Daughter – b. 1891 Islington – aged 10
Sarah NATHAN – Sister-in-law – b. 1868 London – aged 33 – Lady's Help
Selina SMITH – General Servant
Jessie TUBB – Housemaid

1911 Census

Address:
8 Brondesbury Road, Kilburn, N.W.

Residents:
Abraham Lewis JACOBS – Head – Widower – b. 1851 London – aged 60 – Press Agent
Solomon JACOBS – Son – b. 1872 London – aged 39 – Press Agent Manager
Hannah JACOBS – Daughter – b. 1883 London – aged 28
Ethel JACOBS – Daughter – b. 1888 London – aged 23
Elizabeth JACOBS – Daughter – b. 1891 London – aged 20
Sarah NATHAN – Sister-in-law – b. 1866 London – aged 45
Mary PIPER – Domestic Servant
Jessie WARTON – Domestic Servant

Death:
Abraham Lewis JACOBS - Q1 1912 [60] WILLESDEN 3a 304.
Buried at Plashet Cemetery – B-5-2 on 27 Feb 1912. [Avraham ben Yehuda]

Jewish Chronicle – 01 Mar 1912

JACOBS – On Shabbath, February 24th – Adar 6th, at his residence, 8, Brondesbury Road, Kilburn, N.W., Abraham (Lew) Jacobs, aged 61. Deeply mourned by his sorrowing children; Mrs Joseph E. Blank, 119, Farleigh Road, Stoke Newington; Lewis Jacobs, 65, Bethnal Road, Stoke Newington; Alec Jacobs (of San Francisco); Samuel Jacobs, 96, Kyverdale Road, Stamford Hill; Mrs M. Solomon, 55, Rostrevor Avenue, Stamford Hill; also Solomon (Chubbs), Bertie (of Los Angeles), Jack, Hannah, Ethel, Lisbeth, and by his brothers, sisters, grandchildren and other relatives. God rest his dear soul in peace.

JACOBS – On the 24th of February, at 8, Brondesbury Road, Kilburn, in his 61st year, Abraham (Lew), dearly beloved brother of Jack Jacobs, 30, Colberg Place, Stamford Hill. Deeply mourned. Shiva at Colberg Place.

JACOBS – On the 24th of February, at 8, Brondesbury Road, Kilburn, Abraham (Lew), aged 61, the dearly beloved brother of Barney, 5, Manor Place, Amhurst Road, Hackney. Deeply mourned.

JACOBS – On the 24th of February, at 8, Brondesbury Road, Kilburn, Abraham Lewis (Lew), the dearly beloved brother of Mrs H. Abrahams, of 71, Pembroke Crescent, Hove, aged 61. May his dear soul rest in peace. Shiva at "The White Hart", 55, Walworth Road, London S.E.

JACOBS – On the 24th of February, at 8, Brondesbury Road, Kilburn, Abraham, the dearly beloved brother of Mrs A. Isaacs. Shiva at the "Box Tree", Gravel Lane, Houndsditch. God rest his dear soul.

Jewish Chronicle – 30 Aug 1912

JACOBS – The tombstone in loving remembrance of the late lamented Abraham Lewis Jacobs, of 8, Brondesbury Road, N.W., will be consecrated at Plashet Cemetery on Sunday, September 1st, at 4 p.m. Relatives and friends kindly accept this, the only intimation.

KAUFMAN, Elias – A-14-49

Died: **07 Feb 1899**
Buried: **09 Feb 1899**
Partner: **Esther Kaufman (d. 1911)**
Aged: **65 years**

Jewish Chronicle – 10 Feb 1899

KAUFMAN – On the 7th of February, at 40, Coborn Road, Bow, Elias Kaufman, aged 65. Deeply mourned by his sorrowing wife and children. Foreign papers please copy.

KAUFMAN – On the 7th of February, after 2 days' illness, Elias Kaufman, husband of Esther Kaufman (nee Esther Hyman); and father of Mrs Baines, 15,

Lichfield Road, Bow, and Mr Jacob Kaufman, 134, Old Ford Road, E., aged 65. Deeply mourned by his sorrowing wife and family. May his soul rest in peace. American and Australian papers please copy.

Jewish Chronicle – 27 Dec 1912

KAUFMAN – The tombstone in memory of our dear father and mother, Elias and Esther, will be consecrated at Plashet Cemetery on Sunday next, December 29th at 12 o'clock. Relatives and friends accept this, the only intimation.

Death:

Q1 1900 [65] POPLAR 1c 378.

1891 Census

Address:

165, Grove Road, Bethnal Green

Residents:

Chas. KAUFMAN – Head – b. 1838 City – aged 53 – Cutter
Esther KAUFMAN – Wife – b. 1838 Spitalfields – aged 53
Jane KAUFMAN – Daughter – b. 1863 Spitalfields – aged 28 – Umbrella Maker
Judah KAUFMAN – Son – b. 1868 Spitalfields – aged 23 – Laster
Hannah KAUFMAN – Daughter – b. 1869 Spitalfields – aged 22 – Umbrella Maker
Lizzy KAUFMAN – Daughter – b. 1872 Spitalfields – aged 19 – Umbrella Maker
Abraham KAUFMAN – Son – b. 1873 Spitalfields – aged 18 – Laster
Katherine KAUFMAN – Daughter – b. 1876 Spitalfields – aged 15
Rebecca KAUFMAN – Daughter – b. 1879 Old Ford – aged 12
Sarah ISAACS – Sister-in-law – Widow – b. 1831 Spitalfields – aged 60

1881 Census

Address:

66 Ellesmer Road, Bethnal Green

Residents:

Chas KAUFMAN – Head – b. 1837 City – aged 44 – Cutter
Esther KAUFMAN – Wife – b. 1837 Spitalfields – aged 44
Jacob KAUFMAN – Son – b. 1859 Whitechapel – aged 22 – Trimmer
Rosetta KAUFMAN – Daughter – b. 1861 Whitechapel – aged 20
John KAUFMAN – Son – b. 1863 St. Georges – aged 18
Hannah KAUFMAN – Daughter – b. 1865 St. Georges – aged 16 – Scholar
Judah KAUFMAN – Son – b. 1867 St. Georges – aged 14 – Scholar
Elizabeth KAUFMAN – Daughter – b. 1869 St. Georges – aged 12 – Scholar
Katharine KAUFMAN – Daughter – b. 1874 St. Georges – aged 7 – Scholar
Rebecca KAUFMAN – Daughter – b. 1878 Bethnal Green – aged 3 – Scholar

1871 Census

Address:

Chapman Street, Lower, St. George East

Residents:

Elias KAUFMAN – Head – b. 1837 Middlesex – aged 34
Esther KAUFMAN – Wife – b. 1841 Middlesex – aged 30
Jacob KAUFMAN – Son – b. 1859 Middlesex – aged 12
Rosetta KAUFMAN – Daughter – b. 1859 Middlesex – aged 12
Jane KAUFMAN – Daughter – b. 1861 Middlesex – aged 10
Hannah KAUFMAN – Daughter – b. 1862 Middlesex – aged 9
Judah KAUFMAN – Son – b. 1866 Middlesex – aged 5
Elizabeth KAUFMAN – Daughter – b. 1868 Middlesex – aged 3
Fanny HYMAN – Sister-in-law – b. 1836 Middlesex – aged 35
Molean HYMAN – Visitor – b. 1836 Netherlands – aged 35
Margaretta DIX – Domestic Servant

Marriage:

Elias KAUFMAN to Esther HYMAN – Q4 1856 LONDON CITY 1c 294.

Death:

Esther KAUFMAN – Q2 1911 [74] MILE END OLD TOWN 1c 233.
Buried at Plashet Cemetery – A-14-50 on 25 May 1911.

Jewish Chronicle – 26 May 1911

KAUFMAN – On Monday, the 22nd of May, 1911, Esther, widow of the late Elias Kaufman. Deeply mourned by her sorrowing children, Jack, Jane, Hannah, Juda, Lizzie, Kate, Abraham and Rebecca. Shiva, 108, Grove Road, Bow.
KAUFMAN – On Monday, the 22nd of May, 1911, Esther, widow of the late Elias Kaufman. Deeply mourned by her sorrowing sisters, Fanny and Norma Hyman. Shiva at 108, Grove Road, Bow.

Jewish Chronicle – 27 Dec 1912

KAUFMAN – The tombstone in memory of our dear father and mother, Elias and Esther, will be consecrated at Plashet Cemetery on Sunday next, December 29th at 12 o'clock. Relatives and friends accept this, the only intimation.

KLEIN, Moses – D-11-2

Died: 25 Apr 1899
Buried: 28 Apr 1899
Partner: Sophia Klein (d. 1885)
Aged: 77 years

Jewish Chronicle – 28 Apr 1899

KLEIN – On the 25th of April, at the Hand in Hand Home, Hackney, Moses Klein, father of Joseph Klein, of "Hartfield", 119, Colworth Road, Leytonstowe. Deeply mourned by his sorrowing son. Shiva at above address.

Jewish Chronicle – 25 Aug 1899

The tombstone in loving memory of our late father, Moses Klein, will be set at Plashet Cemetery, at 3 o'clock on Sunday, August 27th. Relatives and friends please accept this, the only intimation.

Death:

Q2 1899 [77] HACKNEY 1b 337 [Moses KLIEN]

1891 Census

Address:

23-25 Widows Home or Hand-in-Hand Asylum, Wells Street, Hackney

Residents:

41 Inmates including
Moses KLEIN – Inmate – Widower b. 1822 Poland – aged 69

1881 Census

Address:

13 Stewart Street, Old Artillery Ground

Residents:

Moses KLEIN – Head b. 1824 Germany – aged 57 – Tailor employing 3 men
Sophia KLEIN – Wife b. 1835 Germany – aged 46 – Tailor
Israel KLEIN – Son b. 1863 London – aged 18 – Tailor
Lipman KLEIN – Son b. 1863 London – aged 16 – Tailor
Abraham KLEIN – Son b. 1869 London – aged 12 – Tailor
Jessie KLEIN – Daughter b. 1871 London – aged 10 – Scholar
Fanny KLEIN – Daughter b. 1873 London – aged 8 – Scholar
Mary MURRAY – Domestic Servant

1871 Census

Address:

Goulston Street, St. Mary Whitechapel

Residents:

Moses KLEIN – Head b.1824 Russia – aged 47
Sophia KLEIN – Wife b. 1832 Germany – aged 39
John KLEIN – Son b. 1853 London – aged 18
Rebecca KLEIN – Daughter b. 1854 London – aged 17
Joseph KLEIN – Son b. 1856 London – aged 15
Samuel KLEIN – Son b. 1859 London – aged 12

Jacob KLEIN – Son (b. 1861 London) – aged 10
Israel KLEIN – Son (b. 1863 London) – aged 8
Lipman KLEIN – Son (b. 1865 London) – aged 6
Abraham KLEIN – Son (b. 1867 London) – aged 4
Jesse KLEIN – Daughter (b. 1871 London) – aged 0
Elizabeth PARSONE – Servant

Death:
Sophia KLEIN - Q1 1885 [52] WHITECHAPEL 1c 203.
Place of burial unknown.

LANCASTER, Polly – D-13-7

Died: **15 May 1899**
Buried: **18 May 1899**
Partner: **Simeon Lancaster (d. 1934)**
Aged: **47th year**

Jewish Chronicle – 19 May 1899

LANCASTER – On the 16th of May, at 39, Lewis Grove, Lewisham, Pollie Lancaster, in her 47th year, dearly beloved wife of Sim Lancaster, beloved sister of G. Marks, Curtain Road, H. Marks, Urswich Road, N.E., B. Marks, Canning Town, and Julia Jones, Gt. Yarmouth.

Jewish Chronicle – 18 May 1900

The tombstone in loving memory of the late Mrs Polly Lancaster, of 39, Lewis Grove, Lewisham, S.E., will be set at Plashet Cemetery, on Sunday next, May 20th, at 4 p.m.

Death:
Q2 1899 [47] LEWISHAM 1d 615.

1891 Census

Address:
39 Lewis Grove, Lewisham

Residents:
Simeon LANCASTER – Head - b. 1855 Hull – aged 36 - Tailor
Mary LANCASTER – Wife - b. 1853 London – aged 38
Amelia LANCASTER – Daughter - b. 1880 London – aged 11 – Scholar
Adolph LANCASTER – Son - b. 1883 London – aged 8 – Scholar
Maurice LANCASTER – Son - b. 1886 London – aged 5 – Scholar
Catherine LANCASTER – Daughter - b. 1890 London – aged 1
Elizabeth NULING – Domestic servant

1901 Census

Address:

39 Lewis Grove, Lewisham

Residents:

Simon LANCASTER – Head – Widower - b. 1856 Hull – aged 45 - Tailor Shop Keeper
Amelia LANCASTER – Daughter - b. 1880 London – aged 21
Adolph LANCASTER – Son - b. 1883 London – aged 18 – Tailor
Maurice LANCASTER – Son - b. 1886 London – aged 15 – Clerk
Catherine LANCASTER – Daughter - b. 1890 London – aged 11
Hannah DAVIS – Domestic Servant

1911 Census

Address:

11 Vartry Road, Stamford Hill, N.

Residents:

Simeon LANCASTER – Head – Widower – b. 1855 Hull - Commercial Traveller
Catherine LANCASTER – Daughter – Spinster - b. 1890 – aged 21 – House Keeper
Maurice LANCASTER – Son – Single - b. 1886 London – aged 25 – Commercial Traveller

Marriage:

Simeon LANCASTER to Marie PHILLIPS – Q3 1911 HACKNEY 1b 1207.

Death:

Simeon LANCASTER – Q1 1934 [79] HACKNEY 1b 626.
Buried at East Ham Cemetery – XB-14-952 buried on 02 Mar 1934.

Jewish Chronicle – 02 Mar 1934

LANCASTER – On the 28th of February – Adar 13th, Simeon Lancaster, of 4, Park Lane, N.16, beloved husband of Miral, father of Adolph, of Victoria, B.C., Maurice, of Scunthorpe, Mrs B. Luwisch, of 97, Lordship Road, N.16, and Mrs J. Jacobus, of 313, Finchley Road, N.W. Shiva at 97, Lordship Road.

LEAPMAN, Lewis – A-14-35

LEAPMAN, Lewis – A-14-35

Died: 04 Feb 1899
Buried: 04 Feb 1899
Hebrew Name: Yehuda ben Yitzhak Halevi
Partner: Miriam Leapman (d. 1899) (Miriam bat Yaakov)
Aged: 66 years

Jewish Chronicle – 10 Feb 1899

LEAPMAN – On the 4th of February, at 165, Kennington Park Road, Louis Leapman, aged 66 years. Deeply regretted by his sorrowing wife, sons, daughters and grandchildren. May his dear soul rest in peace.

Jewish Chronicle – 17 Feb 1899

Mr Moss Leapman, 69, Petherton Road, Highbury New Park, N., returns thanks for kind expressions of sympathy received during the week of mourning for his dear brother, Lewis Leapman, aged 65 years.

Jewish Chronicle – 09 Feb 1900

The tombstones in memory of the late Mr and Mrs Lewis Leapman, late of 165, Kennington Park Road, will be set at Plashet Cemetery on Sunday next, 11th February, at 1.30. Please accept this, the only intimation.

Death:

Q1 1899 [65] ST. SAVIOUR 1d 98.

1891 Census

Address:

145 Kennington Park Road, Newington

Residents:

Lewis LEAPMAN – Head – b. 1836 Bristol – aged 55 – Gold Jeweller
Miriam LEAPMAN – Wife – b. 1837 Newport – aged 54
Alfred LEAPMAN – Son – b. 1865 London – aged 26 – Gold Jeweller
Isadore LEAPMAN – Son – b. 1867 Walworth – aged 24 – Merchant
Moss C. LEAPMAN – Son – b. 1870 Camberwell – aged 21 – Gold Jeweller
Leopold LEAPMAN – Son – b. 1872 Walworth – aged 19 – Gold Jeweller
Charlotte LEAPMAN – Daughter – b. 1873 Camberwell – aged 18
Berge LEAPMAN – Son – b. 1875 Walworth – aged 16 – Gold Jeweller
Fanny LEAPMAN – Daughter – b. 1876 Camberwell – aged 15
Elizabeth HILL – Domestic Cook
Harriett TIVOYE – Domestic Servant

1881 Census

Address:

155 Camberwell Road, Camberwell

Residents:

Lewis LEAPMAN – Head – b. 1835 Bristol – aged 46 – Jeweller
Miriam LEAPMAN – Wife – b. 1835 Newport – aged 46
Henry LEAPMAN – Son – b. 1862 Bristol – aged 19
Alfred LEAPMAN – Son – b. 1864 London – aged 17
Kate LEAPMAN – Daughter – b. 1866 London – aged 15
Isadore LEAPMAN – Son – b. 1868 London – aged 13 – Scholar
Mossy LEAPMAN – Son – b. 1870 London – aged 11 – Scholar
Leopold LEAPMAN – Son – b. 1872 London – aged 9 – Scholar
Charlotte LEAPMAN – Daughter – b. 1874 London – aged 7
Sidney LEAPMAN – Son – b. 1875 London – aged 6
Fanny LEAPMAN – Daughter – b. 1877 London – aged 4
John ADELSTONE – Nephew – b. 1858 London – aged 23 – Jeweller's Assistant
Mary MANN – Nursemaid
Mary ALDRIDGE – Housemaid

1871 Census

Address:

Wansey Street, Newington

Residents:

Lewis LEAPMAN – Head – b. 1834 Gloucestershire – aged 37
Miriam LEAPMAN – Wife – b. 1838 Shropshire – aged 33
Clara LEAPMAN – Daughter – b. 1860 Somerset – aged 11
Gertrude LEAPMAN – Daughter – b. 1861 Somerset – aged 10
Henry LEAPMAN – Son – b. 1863 Somerset – aged 8
Alfred LEAPMAN – Son – b. 1864 Middlesex – aged 7
Kate LEAPMAN – Daughter – b. 1866 Middlesex – aged 5
H.A. LEAPMAN – Son – b. 1868 Surrey – aged 3
Moss LEAPMAN – Son – b. 1870 Surrey – aged 1
Christina PAGE – Domestic Servant
Ann BARRY – Domestic Servant

1861 Census

Address:

34 High Street, St. Nicholas, Bristol

Residents:

Lewis LEAPMAN – Head – b. 1834 Bristol – aged 27 – Auctioneer
Miriam LEAPMAN – Wife – b. 1836 Newport – aged 25

Clara LEAPMAN – Daughter – b. 1860 Bristol – aged 1
Gertrude LEAPMAN – Daughter – b. 1861 Bristol – aged 3 months
Matilda SESSOM – Domestic Servant

Marriage:
Lewis LEAPMAN to Miriam JOEL – Q4 1858 BRISTOL 6a 214.

Death:
Miriam LEAPMAN – Q1 1899 [65] ST. SAVIOUR 1d 103.
Buried at Plashet Cemetery – A-14-59 on 05 Mar 1899.

Jewish Chronicle – 03 Mar 1899

LEAPMAN – On the 1st of March, at 165, Kennington Park Road, Miriam, the widow of the late Lewis Leapman, in her 66th year. God rest her dear soul.

Jewish Chronicle – 09 Feb 1900

The tombstones in memory of the late Mr and Mrs Lewis Leapman, late of 165, Kennington Park Road, will be set at Plashet Cemetery on Sunday next, 11th February, at 1.30. Please accept this, the only intimation.

LEVY, Dinah – D-13-6

Died: **09 May 1899**
Buried: **12 May 1899**
Aged: 77 years

Jewish Chronicle – 12 May 1899

LEVY – On the 9th of May, at 307, Mile End Road, E., Dinah Levy, aged 77. Deeply lamented by her beloved cousins, Michael and Leah Isaacs and children.

Jewish Chronicle – 21 Jul 1899

The tombstones to the memory of the late Dinah Levy, of 307, Mile End Road, E. (erected by her cousins, the children of Michael and Leah Isaacs, as a token of love), and that of the late Lewis Lee (A-12-17), of Newcastle-on-Tyne, (erected by his nephews, Asher and Michael Isaacs), will be set on Sunday next, (23/7/1899), at Plashet Cemetery at 5.40 p.m.

Death:
Q2 1899 [77] MILE END OLD TOWN 1c 298.

1891 Census

Address:
307 Mile End Road, Mile End Old Town

Residents:

Michael ISAACS – Head - b. 1838 London – aged 53 – Furniture Broker
Leho (Leah) ISAACS – Wife - b. 1839 London – aged 52
Levy ISAACS – Son - b. 1869 London – aged 22 – General Dealer
Kate ISAACS – Daughter - b. 1870 London – aged 21 – Milliner
Elias ISAACS – Son - b. 1872 London – aged 19 – General Dealer
Fanny ISAACS – Daughter - b. 1874 London – aged 17 – Dress Maker
Esther ISAACS – Daughter - b. 1876 London – aged 15 – Tailoress
Asher ISAACS – Son - b. 1877 London - aged 14
Lizzie ISAACS – Daughter - b. 1879 London – aged 12
Rachel ISAACS – Daughter - b. 1881 London – aged 10
Dinah ISAACS – Daughter - b. 1884 London – aged 7
Dinah LEVY – Boarder - b. 1823 London – aged 68
Susan SALOMAN – General Servant

1881 Census

Address:

418, Mile End Road, Mile End Old Town

Residents:

Michael ISAACS – Head – b. 1836 Spitalfields – aged 45 – Commission Agent
Leah ISAACS – Wife – b. 1836 London – aged 45
Isaac ISAACS – Son – b. 1867 Spitalfields – aged 14 – Scholar
Levy ISAACS – Son – b. 1868 Spitalfields – aged 13 – Scholar
Kate ISAACS – Daughter – b. 1870 Spitalfields – aged 11 – Scholar
Elias ISAACS – Son – b. 1872 Spitalfields – aged 9 – Scholar
Fanny ISAACS – Daughter – b. 1874 Whitechapel – aged 7 – Scholar
Ester ISAACS – Daughter – b. 1876 Whitechapel – aged 5 – Scholar
Asher ISAACS – Son – b. 1877 Whitechapel – aged 4 – Scholar
Lizzie ISAACS – Daughter – b. 1879 Whitechapel – aged 2
Rachel ISAACS – Daughter – b. 1881 Tower Hamlets – aged 0
Levy COHEN – Father-in-law – b. 1810 Leicester – aged 71 – Collector
Dinah LEVY – Boarder – b. 1823 Spitalfields – aged 58
Mary CANNOLL – Domestic Servant
Ester LEVY – Visitor – b. 1861 St. George E., - aged 20 - Tailoress

1871 Census

Address:

Hutchison's Street, Aldgate, London

Residents:

Levy COHEN – Head - b. 1809 – aged 62
Esther COHEN – Wife - b. 1807 – aged 64
Isaac COHEN – Son - b. 1847 – aged 24
Moss COHEN – Son - b. 1850 – aged 21
Dinah LEVY – Niece - b. 1824 – aged 47

LEVY, John – D-13-21

Died: **07 Jun 1899**
Buried: **09 Jun 1899**
Partner: Mary Levy (d. 1873)
Aged: **90th year**

Jewish Chronicle – 09 Jun 1899

LEVY – On the 7th of June, at 100, Mildmay Road, Mildmay Park, John Levy, in his 90th year. Shiva at 100, Mildmay Road.

MR JOHN LEVY – A well-known figure passed away on Wednesday morning last, by the death in his 90th year of Mr John Levy, who was in the employ of Messrs. Defries, of Houndsditch, for the remarkably long period of 64 years. In his early days he was a schoolmaster, but he never filled any official position of the community. For many years he acted as Baal Tokeh at the Hall of the Great Synagogue on New Year. He was highly respected among a large circle.

Death:

Q2 1899 [89] ISLINGTON 1b 250.

1891 Census

Address:

100 Mildmay Road, Islington

Residents:

John LEVY – Head – Widower – b. 1808 Bristol – aged 83 – Clerk Pensioner
Katie LEVY – Daughter – b. 1866 London – aged 25 – Vocalist Teacher of Piano and Singing
Mary JUSTICE – General domestic servant

1881 Census

Address:

55 Mildmay Grove, Islington

Residents:

John LEVY – Head – Widower – b. 1810 Bristol – aged 71 – Clerk
Kate LEVY – Daughter – b. 1857 Goodman's Fields – aged 24
Annie LEVY – Daughter – b. 1859 Goodman's Fields – aged 22
Maria BRIGHT – Domestic Servant

1871 Census

Address:

10 North Grove, Islington

Residents:

John LEVY – Head – b. 1810 Bristol – aged 61 – Clerk for Messrs Defries of Houndsditch
Mary LEVY – Wife – b. 1811 Southwark – aged 60
Dinah LAZARUS – Sister-in-law – b. 1814 Middlesex – aged 57
Leon LEVY – Son – b. 1845 Middlesex – aged 26 – General Clerk in Solicitors Office
Kate LEVY – Daughter – b. 1854 Middlesex – aged 17
Annie LEVY – Daughter – b. 1856 Middlesex – aged 15

1861 Census

Address:

4 Circus, St. Botolph Aldgate, London

Residents:

John LEVY – Head – b. 1810 Bristol – aged 51 – Clerk
Mary LEVY – Wife – b. 1812 London – aged 49
Sarah LEVY – Daughter – b. 1839 London – aged 22
Leon LEVY – Son – b. 1845 London – aged 16 – Junior Clerk
Moss LEVY – Son – b. 1850 London – aged 11 – Scholar
Kate LEVY – Daughter – b. 1853 London – aged 8 – Scholar
Anne LEVY – Daughter – b. 1855 London – aged 6 – Scholar
Julia LEVY – Aunt – b. 1811 Bristol – aged 50
Ann – Domestic Servant

1851 Census

Address:

60 Mansell Street, Saint Mary Whitechapel, Tower Hamlets

Residents:

John LEVY – Head – b. 1811 Bristol – aged 40 – Grocer
Mary LEVY – Wife – b. 1812 London – aged 39
Sarah LEVY – Daughter – b. 1839 Aldgate – aged 12
Leon LEVY – Son – b. 1845 Aldgate – aged 6
Alfred LEVY – Son – b. 1848 Whitechapel – aged 3
Moss LEVY – Son – b. 1850 Whitechapel – aged 18 months
Julia LEVY – Sister – b. 1795 Bristol – aged 56
Cath GANTEY – Domestic Servant

1841 Census

Address:

St. James Place, St. James Dukes Place, London

Residents:

John LEVY – Head – b. 1811 – aged 30 – School Master

Mary LEVY – Wife – b. 1811 Middlesex – aged 30
Sun McFARLIN – b. 1825 Middlesex – aged 16

Marriage:
John L. LEVY to Mary MAGNAY – Q4 1840 KENSINGTON 3 259.

Death:
Mary LEVY – Q4 1873 [63] ISLINGTON 1b 241.
Buried at West Ham Cemetery – ORCHM-1-98 buried 24 Oct 1873.

Jewish Chronicle – 31 Oct 1873

On the 22nd inst., at 10, North Grove, Mildmay Park, N. after a short but painful illness, Mary, the beloved wife of John Levy, in her 63rd year. Deeply lamented by her sorrowing family. May her soul rest in peace! – Melbourne papers please copy.

LEWIS, Bernard – C-9-25

Died:	**22 Sep 1899**
Buried:	**24 Sep 1899**
Parents:	**Abraham & Lucy Lewis**
Aged:	**8 years**

Jewish Chronicle – 30 Sep 1899

LEWIS – On the 22nd of September, at 78, Grosvenor Road, Canonbury, Bernard, the beloved son of Abraham and Lucy Lewis, aged 8 years. God rest his dear soul. Shiva commenced Wednesday evening, September 27th. American papers please copy.

Jewish Chronicle – 22 Jun 1900

The tombstone in loving memory of the late Bernhard, son of Mr and Mrs A. Lewis, of 78, Grosvenor Road, Highbury, will be set at Plashet Cemetery on Sunday next, June 24th, at 4.30. Relatives and friends please accept this, the only intimation.

Death:
Q3 1899 [8] ISLINGTON 1b 289.

Birth:
Q4 1891 GREENWICH 1d 1050 [Bernard LEWIS]

1891 Census

Address:
334 New Cross Road, St. Paul Deptford

LEWIS, Bernard – C-9-25

Residents:

Abraham LEWIS – Head – b. 1868 London – aged 23 – Tailor
Lucy LEWIS – Wife – b. 1868 London – aged 23
Minnie LEWIS – Daughter – b. 1889 London – aged 2
Annie LUCAS – Domestic Servant

1901 Census

Address:

78 Grosvenor Road, Islington

Residents:

Abraham LEWIS – Head – b. 1867 London – aged 34 – Merchant Tailor
Ada LEWIS – Wife – b. 1867 London – aged 34
Minnie LEWIS – Daughter – b. 1889 London – aged 12
Joseph LEWIS – Son – b. 1891 London – aged 10
Hannah LEWIS – Daughter – b. 1893 London – aged 8
Charles LEWIS – Son – b. 1895 London – aged 6
Walter LEWIS – Son – b. 1896 London – aged 5
Harold LEWIS – Son – b. 1899 London – aged 2
Mary COSTELL – Domestic Servant

1911 Census

Address:

7 Highbury Quadrant, London N.

Residents:

Abraham LEWIS – Head – b. 1867 London – aged 44 – Tailoring Manufacturer
Lucie LEWIS – Wife (of 24 years) – b. 1868 London – aged 43
Minnie LEWIS – Daughter – b. 1889 Greenwich – aged 22
Joseph LEWIS – Son – b. 1892 Greenwich – aged 19 – Tailoring business
Hannah LEWIS – Daughter – b. 1894 Greenwich – aged 17
Charles LEWIS – Son – b. 1895 Greenwich – aged 16
Walter LEWIS – Son – b. 1896 Greenwich – aged 15
Harold LEWIS – Son – b. 1899 Islington – aged 12
Rita LEWIS – Daughter – b. 1904 Islington – aged 7
Maud WADDINGTON – Domestic Servant
Esther KEYWORTH – Domestic Servant
John MASSANO – Visitor – b. 1890 Italy – aged 21

Marriage:

Abraham LEWIS to Lucy SMITH – Q3 1888 LONDON CITY 1c 177.

MARKS, Solomon – D-15-20

Died: 29 Aug 1899
Buried: 30 Aug 1899
Partner: Hannah Marks (d. 1921)
Aged: 62 years

Jewish Chronicle – 01 Sep 1899

MARKS – On the 29th of August, at 10, Hutchinson Street, Aldgate, Solomon Marks, aged 62. Deeply mourned by his sorrowing wife, children and a large circle of friends. May his dear soul rest in peace. African and American papers please.
MARKS – On the 29th of August, at 10, Hutchinson Street, Aldgate, Solomon Marks, aged 62, dearly beloved father of Mr Moss Marks, of 47, St. Peter's Road, Mile End, and Mrs Joseph Isaacs, of 10, Lesbia Road, Lower Clapton. Shiva at 10, Hutchison Street. Deeply mourned.

Jewish Chronicle – 07 Jun 1900

The tombstone in memory of the late Solomon Marks, of 10, Hutchinson Street, Aldgate, will be set on Sunday, June 10th a Plashet Cemetery, at 4 o'clock.

Death:

Q3 1899 [62] LONDON CITY 1c 31.

1891 Census

Registered as MARK

Address:

10 Hutchinson Street, Aldgate, London

Residents:

Solomon MARK – Head – b. 1837 Aldgate – aged 54 – General Dealer
Anna MARK – Wife – b. 1841 Aldgate – aged 50
Rosie MARK – Daughter – b. 1872 Aldgate – aged 19 – Tailoress
Moss MARK – Son – b. 1873 Aldgate – aged 18 – Dealer
Joseph MARK – Son – b. 1878 Aldgate – aged 13 – Printer
Lizzie MARK – Daughter – b. 1880 Aldgate – aged 11 – Scholar
Samuel MARK – Son – b. 1883 Aldgate – aged 8 – Scholar

1881 Census

Address:

1 Sadlers Hall Court, St. Botolph Without Aldgate

Residents:

Solomon MARKS – Head – b. 1837 Aldgate – aged 44 – General Dealer
Hannah MARKS – Wife – b. 1841 Aldgate – aged 40

Rose MARKS – Daughter – b. 1872 Aldgate – aged 9 – Scholar
Moss MARKS – Son – b. 1874 Aldgate – aged 7 – Scholar
Matilda MARKS – Daughter – b. 1875 Aldgate – aged 6 – Scholar
Joseph MARKS – Son – b. 1878 Aldgate – aged 3
Elizabeth MARKS – b. 1880 Aldgate – aged 1
Kate CONNOR – General servant

Marriage:
Solomon MARKS to Hannah COLE – Q1 1867 EXETER 5b 142.

1901 Census

Address:
10 Hutchinson Street, St. Botolph Without Aldgate

Residents:
Hannah MARKS – Head – Widow – b. 1840 London – aged 61
Rose RUSHLANDER – Daughter – b. 1871 London – aged 30
Lizzie MARKS – Daughter – b. 1880 London – aged 21 – Feather Hand
Samuel MARKS – Son – b. 1883 London – aged 18 – Traveller in Leather
Nannie RUSHLANDER – Granddaughter – b. 1894 Whitechapel – aged 7
Lillie RUSHLANDER – Granddaughter – b. 1897 Johannesburg – aged 4
Harry RUSHLANDER – Grandson – b. 1900 Johannesburg – aged 1

1911 Census

Address:
10 Hutchinson Street, E.C.

Residents:
Hannah MARKS – Head – Widow – b. 1841 London – aged 70
Rose RUSHLANDER – Daughter – Widow – b. 1874 London – aged 37
Annie RUSHLANDER – Granddaughter – b. 1895 London – aged 16 – Cap Machinist
Harry RUSHLANDER – Grandson – b. 1899 Johannesburg – aged 12 – at School
Eyres OAKES – Lodger – Widow – b. 1861 London – aged 50
Jenny OAKES – Lodger – b. 1893 London – aged 18 – Waitress
Mary OAKES – Lodger – b. 1895 London – aged 16 – Cigarette Hand

Death:
Hannah MARKS – Q4 1921 [80] HOLBORN 1b 683.
Place of burial unknown.

MORDECAI, Mark – D-13-1

MORDECAI, Mark – D-13-1

Died: 30 Apr 1899
Buried: 02 May 1899
Partner: Hannah Mordecai (d. 1912)
Age: 68th year

Jewish Chronicle – 05 May 1899

MORDECAI – On the 30th of April, at 2, Bancroft Road, Mile End, E., Mark Mordecai, in his 68th year. Dearly loved and deeply mourned by his bereaved wife and family. Father of Lewis Mordecai, 30, Grafton Street, Abraham Mordecai, 4, Bancroft Road, Mrs Henry Harris, 1, Bancroft Road, Mrs J. Emanuel, Chapel Street, W.C., Mrs B. Isaacs, Kentish Town Road, Mrs D. Israel, Grafton Street, and brother of Mr Joseph Mordecai, of 119, Haggerston Road, N. Shiva at 2, Bancroft Road.

Jewish Chronicle – 18 May 1900

The tombstone in memory of the lamented Mark Mordecai, of 2, Bancroft Road, Mile End, E., will be set on Sunday next, May 20th, at Plashet at 4 p.m. Relatives and friends please accept this, the only intimation.

Death:

Q2 1899 [67] MILE END 1c 295.

1891 Census

Address:

2 Bancroft Road, Mile End Old Town

Residents:

Mark MORDECAI – Head – b. 1835 Mile End – aged 56 – Cigar Manufacturer
Hannah MORDECAI – Wife – b. 1837 Mile End – aged 54
Abraham MORDECAI – Son – b. 1871 Mile End – aged 20 – Assistant Manufacturer
Julia MORDECAI – Daughter – b. 1873 Mile End – aged 18 – Assistant Manufacturer
Rebecca MORDECAI – Daughter – b. 1875 Mile End – aged 16 – Scholar
Jane MORDECAI – Daughter – b. 1877 Mile End – aged 14 – Scholar
Harriet BESTOW – General Domestic Servant
Emma JONES – General Domestic Servant

1881 Census

Address:

6 Bancroft Road, Mile End Old Town

Residents:

Mark MORDECAI – Head – b. 1835 Mile End – aged 46 – Cigar Manufacturer
Hannah MORDECAI – Wife – b. 1838 Mile End – aged 43
Louis MORDECAI – Son – b. 1861 Mile End – aged 20 – Cigar Manufacturer
Sarah MORDECAI – Daughter – b. 1862 Mile End – aged 19 – Dressmaker
Joseph MORDECAI – Son – b. 1865 Mile End – aged 16 – Cigar Maker
Esther MORDECAI – Daughter – b. 1866 Mile End – aged 15 – Cigar Maker
Deborah MORDECAI – Daughter – b. 1868 Mile End – aged 13 – Scholar
Abraham MORDECAI – Son – b. 1870 Mile End – aged 11 – Scholar
Julia MORDECAI – Daughter – b. 1874 Mile End – aged 7 – Scholar
Rebecca MORDECAI – Daughter – b. 1876 Mile End – aged 5 – Scholar
Jane MORDECAI – Daughter – b. 1878 Mile End – aged 3
Elizabeth FOWLER – General Domestic Servant

1871 Census

Address:

Raven Terrace, Mile End Old Town

Residents:

Mark MORDECAI – Head – b. 1835 Middlesex – aged 36
Hannah MORDECAI – Wife – b. 1838 London – aged 33
Lazarus MORDECAI – Son – b. 1857 Yorkshire – aged 14
Lewis MORDECAI – Son – b. 1860 Middlesex – aged 11
Sarah MORDECAI – Daughter – b. 1862 Middlesex – aged 9
Joseph MORDECAI – Son – b. 1865 Middlesex – aged 6
Esther MORDECAI – Daughter – b. 1867 Middlesex – aged 4
Deborah MORDECAI – Daughter – b. 1869 Middlesex – aged 2
Tilley ALLERS – Domestic Servant

1861 Census

Address:

3 Horse Shoe Alley, Whitechapel

Residents:

Mark MORDECAI – Head – b. 1835 Spitalfields – aged 26 – Cigar Maker
Hannah MORDECAI – Wife – b. 1837 Aldgate – aged 24
James MORDECAI – Son – b. 1858 Spitalfields – aged 3
Louis MORDECAI – Son – b. 1857 Spitalfields – aged 4
Esther MORDECAI - Mother – b. 1788 Spitalfields – aged 73

1851 Census

Address:

3 Horse Shoe Alley, Whitechapel

Residents:

Eleazor MORDECAI – Head – b. 1793 Spitalfields – aged 58 – Clothes Dealer
Esther MORDECAI – Wife – b. 1791 Spitalfields – aged 60 – Clothes Dealer
Sarah MORDECAI – Daughter – b. 1829 Spitalfields – aged 22 – Tailoress
Rebecca MORDECAI – Daughter – b. 1831 Spitalfields – aged 20 – Domestic
Mark MORDECAI – Son – b. 1835 Spitalfields – aged 16 – Cigar Maker
Abraham MORDECAI – Son – b. 1837 Spitalfields – aged 14 – Cigar Maker

1901 Census

Address:

2 Bancroft Road, Mile End Old Town

Residents:

Hannah MORDECAI – Head – Widow – b. 1836 London – aged 65 – Cigar Manufacturer
Rebecca MORDECAI – Daughter – b. 1876 Mile End – aged 25
Henry HARRIS – Son-in-law – b. 1860 Stepney – aged 41 – Stone Mason
Sarah HARRIS – Daughter – b. 1863 London – aged 38
Emanuel HARRIS – Grandson – b. 1884 Mile End – aged 17 – Stone Mason
Mark HARRIS – Grandson – b. 1887 Mile End – aged 14 – Stone Mason
Hannah HARRIS – Granddaughter – b. 1889 Mile End – aged 12
Sarah HARRIS – Granddaughter – b. 1893 Mile End – aged 8
Louise BINWELL – Domestic Servant
Annie LISK – Domestic Servant

1911 Census

Address:

2 Bancroft Road, Mile End, London E.

Residents:

Hannah MORDECAI – Head – Widow – b. 1835 Whitechapel – aged 76
Henry HARRIS – Son-in-law – b. 1860 Stepney – aged 51 – Monumental Mason
Sarah HARRIS – Daughter (married 28 years) – b. 1864 Whitechapel – aged 47
Hannah HARRIS – Granddaughter – b. 1889 Stepney – aged 22 – Dressmaker
Sarah HARRIS – Granddaughter – b. 1892 Stepney – aged 19
Lily HAWKINS – Domestic Servant
Caroline BIFIELD – Domestic Servant
187118

Death:

Hannah MORDECAI - Q3 1912 [79] MILE END 1c 425.
Buried at Plashet Cemetery – D-13-2 on 17 Sep 1912.

Jewish Chronicle – 20 Sep 1912

MORDECAI – On Sunday, the 15th of September, at 2, Bancroft Road, Mile End,

E., Hannah, relict of the late Mark Mordecai, in her 79th year. Beloved mother of Lazarus Mordecai, of Kinnoull Mansions, Clapton; Lewis Mordecai, of 59, Bancroft Road; Mrs Henry Harris, 216, Mile End Road, E.; Mrs Joseph Emanuel, 4, Pentonville Road, N.; Mrs Barney Barney, 154, Kentish Town Road, N.W.; Mrs David Israel, 9, Tilford Gardens, Brixton; Mrs Richmond, 2, Bancroft Road, E.; and Mrs Sol. Samuel, 34, Hawthorn Road, Croydon. Deeply and sincerely mourned by her sorrowing children, grandchildren, great-grandchildren, relatives and all who knew her. Shiva at 2, Bancroft Road, E. American papers please copy.

MORRIS, Rachel – D-9-1B

Died: 25 Mar 1899
Buried: 28 Mar 1899
Partner: Harris/Henry Morris (d. 1893)
Age: 71st year

Jewish Chronicle – 31 Mar 1899

MORRIS – On the 25th of March, corresponding with the 13th day of Nisan, at the residence of her daughter, Mrs Morris Cohen, of 11, Spital Square, Rachel Morris, widow of the late Harris Morris, in her 71st year. Deeply mourned by her sorrowing children, Hyman Morris, Johannesburg, Moss Morris, Oudtshoorn, Mrs Jacob Rosenberg, Commercial Street, Mrs Solomon Myers, Wilkes Street, Mrs Morris Cohen, Spital Square, Mrs John Hart, Johannesburg, grandchildren and great grandchildren. Shiva commences Sunday, April 2nd, at 11, Spital Square.

Jewish Chronicle – 23 Mar 1900

The tombstone in loving memory of the late Mrs R. Morris, late of 11, Spital Square, Bishopsgate, will be set on Sunday, 25th inst., at Plashet Cemetery, at 3.30 p.m.

Death:

Q1 1899 [70] WHITECHAPEL 1c 192.

1891 Census

Address:

67 Ernest Street, Mile End Old Town

Residents:

Henry MORRIS – Head – b. 1831 Bishopsgate – aged 60 – Clothes Dealer
Rachel MORRIS – Wife – b. 1829 Bishopsgate – aged 62

1881 Census

Address:

48 Old Montague Street, Whitechapel

MORRIS, Rachel – D-9-1B

Residents:

Henry MORRIS – Head – b. 1833 London – aged 48 – General Dealer
Rachel MORRIS – Wife – b. 1827 London – aged 54
Betty MORRIS – Daughter – b. 1864 London – aged 17 – Cigar Maker
Esther MORRIS – Daughter – b. 1866 London – aged 15 – Cigar Maker
Rosa MORRIS – Daughter – b. 1868 London – aged 13

1871 Census

Address:

Nelson Court, Christ Church Spitalfields

Residents:

Henry MORRIS – Head – b. 1832 London – aged 39
Rachel MORRIS – Wife – b. 1829 London – aged 42
Isabel MORRIS – Daughter – b. 1861 London – aged 10
Esther MORRIS – Daughter – b. 1863 London – aged 8
Rose MORRIS – Daughter – b. 1867 London – aged 4

1861 Census

Address:

2 Three Tun Alley, Whitechapel, Middlesex

Residents:

Henry MORRIS – Head – b. 1833 Aldgate – aged 28 – General Dealer
Rachel MORRIS – Wife – b. 1829 Spitalfields – aged 32
Hannah MORRIS – Daughter – b. 1847 Aldgate – aged 4
Isabella MORRIS – Daughter – b. 1861 Aldgate – aged 7 months

Marriage:

Henry MORRIS to Rachel BARNETT – Q3 1859 LONDON CITY 1c 311.

Death:

Henry MORRIS – Q1 1893 [56] MILE END OLD TOWN 1c 378.
Place of burial unknown.

NATHAN, Sarah – B-4-47

Died: 17 Nov 1899
Buried: 20 Nov 1899
Partner: Nathan Nathan (d. 1908)
Aged: 58 years

Jewish Chronicle – 24 Nov 1899

NATHAN – On the 17th of November, at her residence, 431, Mile End Road, E., Sarah, the dearly beloved wife of Nathan Nathan, aged 58 years. Deeply mourned

by her sorrowing husband and children. Gone but not forgotten.
NATHAN – On the 17th of November, at 431, Mile End Road, Sarah, the dearly beloved mother of Mrs Sam Hyams, of 188, Camden Road, N.W. Shiva at Mile End.

Jewish Chronicle – 04 May 1900

The tombstone to the memory of the late Mrs Sarah Nathan, will be set on Sunday next, 6th inst., at Plashet Cemetery, at 3.30 p.m. Relatives and friends please accept this, the only intimation.

Death:
Q4 1899 [58] MILE END OLD TOWN 1c 368.

1891 Census

Address:
431 Mile End Road, Mile End Old Town

Residents:
Nathan NATHAN – Head – b. 1838 Spitalfields – aged 53 – Traveller
Sarah NATHAN – Wife – b. 1844 Spitalfields – aged 47
Hannah NATHAN – Daughter – b. 1869 Aldgate – aged 22 – Machinist
Milly NATHAN – Daughter – b. 1869 Aldgate – aged 22 – Cap Maker
Rebecca NATHAN – Daughter – b. 1870 Aldgate – aged 21
David NATHAN – Son – b. 1870 Aldgate – aged 21
Louisa NATHAN – Daughter – b. 1872 Aldgate – aged 19 – Shoe Trimmer
Kate NATHAN – Daughter – b. 1874 Aldgate – aged 17 – Dressmaker
Esther NATHAN – Daughter – b. 1877 Aldgate – aged 14 – Dressmaker
Lewis NATHAN – Son – b. 1878 Aldgate – aged 13 – Clickers Apprentice
Nathan NATHAN – Son – b. 1879 Bow – aged 12 – Scholar
Rose NATHAN – Daughter – b. 1881 Bow – aged 10 – Scholar
Harry NATHAN – Son – b. 1883 Bow – aged 8 – Scholar
Hannah NATHAN – Mother – Widow – b. 1813 Bow – aged 78 – Living on Own Means
Bessy LEVY – Aunt – Widow – b. 1811 Spitalfields – aged 80 – Deaf & Dumb
Clara MAIDDLE – Domestic Servant

1881 Census

Address:
69 Lincoln Street, Mile End Old Town

Residents:
Nathan NATHAN – Head – b. 1839 Spitalfields – aged 42 – Sportsman
Sarah NATHAN – Wife – b. 1843 Aldgate – aged 38
Rebecca NATHAN – Daughter – b. 1870 Whitechapel – aged 11 – Scholar
David NATHAN – Son – b. 1870 Whitechapel – aged 11 – Scholar
Amelia NATHAN – Daughter – b. 1871 Whitechapel – aged 10 – Scholar

Louisa NATHAN – Daughter – b. 1873 Whitechapel – aged 8 – Scholar
Kate NATHAN – Daughter – b. 1874 Whitechapel – aged 7 – Scholar
Esther NATHAN – Daughter – b. 1876 Whitechapel – aged 5 – Scholar
Louis NATHAN – Son – b. 1878 Whitechapel – aged 3
Nathan NATHAN – Son – b. 1879 Whitechapel – aged 2
Rose NATHAN – Daughter – b. 1871 Mile End – aged 10
David MOSES – Nephew – b. 1857 Middlesex – aged 24 – Elementary Teacher
Elizabeth LEVY – Aunt – Widow – b. 1813 Whitechapel – aged 68 – Deaf & Dumb
Elizabeth COLLISON – Domestic Servant
Rose ABBOT – Nursemaid

1871 Census

Address:
96a Middlesex Street, Whitechapel

Residents:
Nathan NATHAN – Head – b. 1839 Middlesex – aged 32 – Cigar Maker
Sarah NATHAN – Wife – b. 1844 Middlesex – aged 27
Rebecca NATHAN – Daughter – b. 1870 Middlesex – aged 1
Elizabeth JACKSON – Domestic Servant

Marriage:
Nathan NATHAN to Sarah ISAACS – Q2 1866 LONDON CITY 1c 225.

Death:
Nathan NATHAN – Q2 1908 [69] WEST HAM 4a 19.
Buried at Plashet Cemetery – J-3-27 on 19 Apr 1908.

Jewish Chronicle – 24 Apr 1908

NATHAN – On the 16th of April, at 17, Norwich Road, Romford Road, E., Nathan Nathan, in his 70th year, beloved brother of Mrs Kate Lyons, 6, Poet's Road, Canonbury, N., and Mr Cushman Nathan, 43, Middlesex Road, Aldgate. Shiva at above addresses. God rest his soul.

NATHAN – On the 16th of April, at 17, Norwich Road, Forest Gate, Nathan Nathan, the dearly beloved father of Mrs Sam Hyams, Mrs J.P. Alymer, of 5, Trinity Street, Norwich; also Louisa, Milly, Rose and Nat Nathan; in his 70th year. May his dear soul rest in everlasting peace. Shiva at Forest Gate.

NATHAN – On the 16th of April, at 17, Norwich Road, Forest Gate, Nathan Nathan, the dearly beloved father of Mrs John Crabb and Lew Nathan, of 77, Coldharbour Lane, Camberwell, in his 70th year. May his dear soul rest in everlasting peace. Shiva at Forest Gate.

RAPHAEL, James – D-16-18

Died: 23 Sep 1899
Buried: 25 Sep 1899
Hebrew Name: Itzhak bar Hi'iam
Partner: Caroline Raphael (d. 1900)
Age: 72 years

Jewish Chronicle – 30 Sep 1899

RAPHAEL – On the 23rd of September, at his residence, 3, Morgan Street, Bow, after a long and painful illness, James, much beloved and devoted husband of Caroline Raphael, and father of Mrs G. Rosen, of 34, Frederick Place, Bow, aged 72. Deeply mourned by his sorrowing grandchildren, relatives and friends. Highly respected by all who knew him. Peace to his dear soul. Shiva at 3, Morgan Street.

Jewish Chronicle – 18 May 1900

The tombstone in affectionate memory of my late lamented husband, James Raphael, will be set at Plashet Cemetery, on Sunday, 27th inst., 4 p.m. Relatives and friends kindly note this intimation – 3, Morgan Street, Bow.

Death:

Q3 1899 [72] MILE END 1c 392.

1891 Census

Address:

2 Morgan Street, Mile End Old Town

Residents:

James RAPHAEL – Head – b. 1830 Beard – aged 61 – Trimming Maker
Caroline RAPHAEL – Wife – b. 1836 Whitechapel – aged 55
Henrietta GODBOLD – General Servant

1881 Census

Address:

1, Raymond Road, Mile End Old Town

Residents:

James RAPHAEL – Head – b. 1829 Warsaw – aged 52 – Fancy Trimming Manufacturer
Caroline RAPHAEL – Wife – b. 1833 Whitechapel – aged 48
Esther RAPHAEL – Daughter – b. 1859 Middlesex – aged 22

1871 Census

Address:

Regent Street, North West Side

RAPHAEL, James – D-16-18

Residents:

James RAPHAEL – Head – b. 1828 Poland – aged 43
Caroline RAPHAEL – Wife – b. 1835 Middlesex – aged 36
Esther RAPHAEL – Daughter – b. 1859 Middlesex – aged 12

1861 Census

Address:

4, Upper Fountain Place, St. Luke

Residents:

James RAPHAEL – Head – b. 1828 Warsaw – aged 33 – Stick Manufacturer
Caroline RAPHAEL – Wife – b. 1833 Whitechapel – aged 28
Esther RAPHAEL – Daughter – b. 1859 St. Lukes – aged 2
Matilda BENJAMIN – Sister in Law – b. 1832 Whitechapel – aged 29
Joel GOLDBERG – Workman – b. 1843 Prague – aged 18 – Stick Scraper

Marriage:

James RAFHAEL to Caroline BENJAMIN – Q1 1858 LONDON CITY 1c 219.

Death:

Caroline RAPHAEL - Q4 1900 [68] MILE END OLD TOWN 1c 289.
Buried at Plashet Cemetery – D-23-3 on 23 Oct 1900.

Jewish Chronicle – 05 Jul 1901

The tombstone in loving memory of my dear mother, Mrs James Raphael, late of 3, Morgan Street, Bow, will be set on Sunday, the 7th, at 4 p.m. at Plashet Cemetery. Relatives and friends accept this intimation – 34, Frederick Place, Bow.

SACKSHIVER, Betsy – A-14-51

Died: **12 Feb 1899**
Buried: **13 Feb 1899**
Partner: **Solomon Sackshiver (d. 1922)**
Aged: **56th year**

Jewish Chronicle – 24 Feb 1899

SACKSHIVER – On Sunday, the 12th of February, at 13, Fashion Street, Spitalfields, Betsy (Bayla), the beloved wife of Solomon Sackshiver, and the dear mother of Mrs Solomons, of 20, St. Mark's Street, E., of Morris Freeman, of 47, Cleveland Street, E., and of D. Myers, 44, Brick Lane, E., and sister of Mrs Bernstein, in her 56th year. Deeply mourned by her sorrowing children, relatives and a large circle of friends. Gone by never forgotten. May her dear soul rest in peace.

SACKSHIVER, Betsy – A-14-51

Jewish Chronicle – 28 Apr 1899

The tombstone in memory of the late lamented wife of Solomon Sackshiver of 13, Fashion Street, will be set on Sunday, April 30th, at the Plashet Cemetery, at 4 o'clock. Friends and relatives kindly accept this, the only intimation.

Death:

Q1 1899 [54] WHITECHAPEL 1c 189.

1891 Census

Address:

13 Fashion Street, Spitalfields, London, Tower Hamlets

Residents:

Solomon SACKSHIVER – Head – b. 1853 Poland – aged 38 – Tailor
Betsy SACKSHIVER – Wife – b. 1843 Poland – aged 48
Fanny SACKSHIVER – Daughter – b. 1870 Poland – aged 21 – Tailoress
Morris SACKSHIVER – Son – b. 1872 Whitechapel – aged 19 – Tailor's Cutter
Galig SACKSHIVER – Son – b. 1872 Whitechapel – aged 19 – Tailor
Perger SACKSHIVER – Son – b. 1874 Whitechapel – aged 17 – Tailor's Machinist
Marchel SACKSHIVER – Daughter – b. 1878 Whitechapel – aged 13
Mark SACKSHIVER – Son – b. 1880 Whitechapel – aged 11 – Scholar
Joseph SACKSHIVER – Son – b. 1882 Whitechapel – aged 9 – Scholar

1881 Census

Registered as JACKSHERE

Address:

13 Fashion Street, Spitalfields

Residents:

Solomon SACKSHIVER – Head – b. 1845 Poland – aged 36 – Tailor
Betsey SACKSHIVER – Wife – b. 1843 Poland – aged 38 – Tailor
David M. SACKSHIVER – Son – b. 1863 Poland – aged 18 – Tailor
Jane SACKSHIVER – Daughter – b. 1870 Poland – aged 11 – Scholar
Morris SACKSHIVER – Grandfather – b. 1821 Poland – aged 60 – Tailor
Moses SACKSHIVER – Son – b. 1872 Whitechapel – aged 9 – Scholar
Zalick SACKSHIVER – Son – b. 1873 Whitechapel – aged 8 – Scholar
Pizer SACKSHIVER – Son – b. 1874 Whitechapel – aged 7 – Scholar
Rachel SACKSHIVER – Daughter – b. 1878 Whitechapel – aged 3 – Scholar
Mark SACKSHIVER – Son – b. 1880 Whitechapel – aged 1
Harris SACKSHIVER – Uncle – b. 1863 Poland – aged 18 – Tailor

1901 Census

Address:

13 Fashion Street, Spitalfields

Residents:

Solomon SACKSHIVER – Head – b. 1853 Russia – aged 48 – Master Tailor
Rachael SACKSHIVER – Daughter – b. 1878 Whitechapel – aged 23 – Attending House Domestic
Marks SACKSHIVER – Son – b. 1880 Spitalfields – aged 21 – Tailor's Assistant
Joseph SACKSHIVER – Son – b. 1882 Spitalfields – aged 19 – Tailor's Assistant

Marriage:

Solomon SACKSHIVER to Annie ARDBETSKY – Q4 1902 MILE END 1c 926.

Death:

Solomon SACKSHIVER – Q1 1922 [69] ST. GEORGE EAST 1c 424.
Buried at East Ham Cemetery – G-10-18 on 08 Jan 1922.

Jewish Chronicle – 13 Jan 1922

SACKSHIVER – On Thursday, the 5th of January, at 19, Lower Chapman Street, Cannon Street Road, E., Solomon Sackshiver, the beloved husband of Fanny Sackshiver, and devoted father of Hal Goldstein, 176, Coltman Streeet, Hull (late of London). Deeply mourned by his heart-stricken wife, broken-hearted daughter, and son, Mark Sackshiver, 154, Jamaica Street, Stepney; beloved brother, Harris Sackshiver, 78, Brady Street Mansions; sister, Rachel Barnett, 159, Mile End Road; stepson, Maurice Freeman, 33, Tollett Street, Mile End; his daughter-in-law, son-in-law, and grandchildren. Loved and respected by all who knew him. God rest his dear soul in everlasting peace. Amen.

SAMUEL, Henry – D-7-1A

Died: **03 Mar 1899**
Buried: **06 Mar 1899**
Partner: **Sarah Deborah Samuel (d. 1904)**
Aged: **65 years**

Jewish Chronicle – 10 Mar 1899

SAMUEL – On the 3rd of March, 1899, at 42, Barlborough Street, New Cross, after a long and painful illness, Henry, the dearly beloved husband of Sarah Samuel, aged 65 years. Deeply mourned by his sorrowing wife, sons, daughters, sister and brothers. May his dear soul rest in peace. Australian papers please copy.

Jewish Chronicle – 01 Dec 1899

The tombstone in loving memory of the late Mr Henry Samuel, of 42, Barlborough Street, New Cross, will be set at Plashet Cemetery on Sunday, December 10th, at 2 o'clock. Relatives and friends will kindly accept this, the only intimation.

Death:

Q1 1899 [65] GREENWICH 1d 674.

1891 Census

Address:

42, Barlborough Street, St. Paul Deptford

Residents:

Henry SAMUEL – Head of family - b. 1831 Mile End – aged 59 - Salesman
Sarah D. SAMUEL – Wife - b.1835 Spitalfields – aged 56
Clara SAMUEL – Daughter - b. 1867 Poplar – aged 24 - Dressmaker
Ellen SAMUEL – Daughter - b. 1871 Poplar – aged 20 - Dressmaker
Bluma SAMUEL – Daughter - b. 1873 Poplar – aged 18 – Feather worker
Moss B. SAMUEL – Son - b. 1875 Poplar – aged 16 – Apprentice Upholsterer
Julia SAMUEL – Daughter - b. 1879 Poplar – aged 12 - Scholar

1881 Census

Address:

261, India Road, Bromley

Residents:

Henry SAMUEL – Head - b. 1832 Mile End – aged 49 - Pawnbroker
Sarah SAMUEL – Wife - b. 1836 Spitalfields – aged 45
Elizabeth SAMUEL – Daughter - b. 1862 Stepney – aged 19
Barnett SAMUEL – Son - b. 1865 Bromley – aged 16 – Shop Boy
James SAMUEL – Son - b. 1866 Bromley – aged 15 – Stonemason
Clara SAMUEL – Daughter - b. 1869 Bromley – aged 12 – Scholar
Ellen SAMUEL – Daughter - b. 1870 Bromley – aged 11 – Scholar
Morris SAMUEL – Son - b. 1872 Bromley - aged 9 – Scholar
Blunea SAMUEL – Daughter - b. 1873 Bromley – aged 8 – Scholar
Moss SAMUEL – Son - b. 1875 Bromley – aged 6 – Scholar
Julia SAMUEL – Daughter - b. 1878 Bromley – aged 3 – Scholar
Emma SULLIVAN – Servant

1871 Census

Address:

East India Road, Bromley

Residents:

Henry SAMUEL – Head - b. 1834 – aged 37
Sarah Deborah SAMUEL – Wife - b. 1837 – aged 34
Elizabeth SAMUEL – Daughter - b. 1862 – aged 9
Barnett SAMUEL – Son - b. 1865 – aged 6
James SAMUEL – Son - b. 1866 – aged 5
Clara SAMUEL – Daughter - b. 1869 – aged 2

Ellen SAMUEL – Daughter - b. 1871 – aged 0
Bloomer LEVY – Mother-in-law - b. 1794 – aged 77
Rose EMMIS – Servant
Edward C. CANING – Boy

1861 Census

Address:

12, Corner of Eastfield Street and Henry Street, Limehouse

Residents:

Henry SAMUEL – Head - b. 1832 – aged 29 – Pawnbroker
Sarah D. SAMUEL – Wife - b. 1838 – aged 23
Flora LEVY – Visitor – Widow - b. 1794 – aged 67
Ellen LEVY – Visitor - b. 1848 – aged 13
John DUNN – Servant & Errand Boy

Marriage:

Henry SAMUEL to Sarah Deborah LEVY – Q3 1860 LONDON CITY 1C 263.

1901 Census

Address:

42, Barlborough Street, St. Paul Deptford

Residents:

Deborah S. SAMUEL – Head – Widow - b. 1832 Spitalfields – aged 69
Clara SAMUEL – Daughter - b. 1870 Bromley – aged 31 – Dressmaker
Nellie SAMUEL – Daughter - b. 1872 Bromley – aged 29 – Dressmaker
Shunn SAMUEL – Daughter - b. 1874 Bromley – aged 27 – Dressmaker
Moss SAMUEL – Son - b. 1876 Bromley – aged 25 – Upholsterer
Julia SAMUEL – Daughter - b. 1879 Bromley – aged 22 – Dressmaker
Florrie CROUCHER – General Services Domestic

Death:

Sarah Deborah SAMUEL – Q4 1903 [74] GREENWICH 1d 584.
Buried at Plashet Cemetery – D-49-4 on 01 Jan 1904.

Jewish Chronicle – 01 Jan 1904

SAMUEL – On the 30th of December, at 42, Barlborough Street, New Cross, Deborah Sarah, widow of Henry Samuel, aged 74 years. Deeply mourned by her children. Funeral leaves for Plashet, Friday, 11 a.m.

SHINBERG, Rebecca – D-15-2

Died: 28 Sep 1899
Buried: 29 Sep 1899
Parents: Julius & Gietel Shinberg
Age: 36 years

Jewish Chronicle – 06 Oct 1899

SHINBERG – On the 28th of September, at 37, Mecklenburgh Square, Rebecca, the dearly beloved daughter of Julius Shinberg, and the late Geitel Shinberg, aged 36. Deeply mourned by her sorrowing father, stepmother, sisters and brothers. Rest in peace.
SHINBERG – On the 28th of September, at the residence of her sister, 37, Mecklenburgh Square, Rebecca Shinberg, the fondly loved and loving sister of Mrs H. Friedlander. Deeply and sincerely mourned by sorrowing relatives. Peace perfect peace.
SHINBERG – On the 28th of September, at 37, Mecklenburgh Square, Rebecca Shinberg, the dearly beloved sister of Mrs M. Bloomberg, of 283, New Cross Road, aged 36. God rest her dear soul.
SHINBERG – On the 28th of September, at 37, Mecklenburgh Square, Rebecca Shinberg, the devoted sister of Mrs J. Forest, 43, Great Prescot Street, also of Abraham Shinberg, of 71, Great Prescot Street. May her soul rest in peace.

Jewish Chronicle – 30 Sep 1904

In loving memory of Rebecca Shinberg, who died September 27th, 1899. Sincerely mourned by her sorrowing sisters Mrs H. Friedlander, Mrs J. Forest, Mrs M. Bloomberg. May her dear soul rest in peace.

Death:
Q3 1899 [35] PANCRAS 1b 50.

1891 Census

Address:
68 Great Prescot Street, Whitechapel

Residents:
Hyman BLOOMBERG – Head – b. 1849 Poland – aged 42 – Tailor
Eva BLOOMBERG – Wife – b. 1850 Poland – aged 41
Mark BLOOMBERG – Son – b. 1870 London – aged 21 – Tailor
Morris BLOOMBERG – Son – b. 1872 London – aged 19 – Tailor
Solomon BLOOMBERG – Son – b. 1876 London – aged 15 – Tailor
Barnett BLOOMBERG – Son – b. 1882 London – aged 9
Alfred BLOOMBERG – Son – b. 1888 London – aged 3

SHINBERG, Rebecca – D-15-2

Emily BROWN – Domestic General Servant
Rebecca SHINBERG – Lodger – b. 1864 London – aged 27 – Bow Maker
Jenny SHINBERG – Lodger – b. 1859 London – aged 32 – Bow Maker

1871 Census

Address:

Leman Street, Whitechapel

Residents:

Julius SHINBERG – Head – b. 1831 Poland – aged 40 – Tie Maker
Catherine SHINBERG – Wife – b. 1832 Poland – aged 39
Sarah SHINBERG – Daughter – b. 1858 Middlesex – aged 13
Matilda SHINBERG – Daughter – b. 1860 Middlesex – aged 11
Rebecca SHINBERG – Daughter – b. 1862 Middlesex – aged 9
Abraham SHINBERG – Son – b. 1863 Middlesex – aged 8
Jenny SHINBERG – Daughter – b. 1867 Middlesex – aged 4
Samuel SHINBERG – Son – b. 1869 Middlesex – aged 2
Jacob SHINBERG – Nephew – b. 1851 Middlesex – aged 20 - Mechinist
Mary ROBERTS – Daughter – b. 1853 Middlesex – aged 18

SHOCK, Solomon – B-4-2

Died: **11 Oct 1899**
Buried: **12 Oct 1899**
Hebrew Name: **Shlomo Salmon ben Mordecai**
Partner: **Flora Shock (d. 1941)**
Aged: **46 years**

Jewish Chronicle – 13 Oct 1899

SHOCK – On the 11th of October, at 11, Second Avenue, Walthamstow, to the inexpressible grief of his wife and family, Solomon Shock (late of Liverpool), aged 46.

Jewish Chronicle – 31 Aug 1900

The tombstone in loving memory of our dear husband and father, Solomon Shock (late of Liverpool), will be set at Plashet Cemetery on Sunday next, September (02/09/1900), at 4 o'clock. Relatives and friends kindly accept this, the only intimation.

Death:

Q4 1899 [46] HACKNEY 1b 384.

1891 Census

Address:

104 Pembroke Place, Liverpool

SHOCK, Solomon – B-4-2

Residents:

Solomon SHOCK – Head – b. 1853 Russia – aged 38 – House Furnisher
Flora SHOCK – Wife – b. 1857 Liverpool – aged 34
Miriam SHOCK – Daughter – b. 1879 – aged 12
Bertha SHOCK – Daughter – b. 1881 – aged 10
Aaron SHOCK – Son – b. 1883 – aged 8
Sarah SHOCK – Daughter – b. 1885 – aged 6
Emanuel SHOCK – Son – b. 1887 – aged 4
Isadore SHOCK – Son – b. 1889 – aged 2
Rose RABINOWITZ – Domestic Servant

1881 Census

Address:

46 Pleasant Street, Liverpool

Residents:

Solomon SHOCK – Head – b. 1853 Russia – aged 28 – Cap Manufacturer (Hatter)
Flora SHOCK – Wife – b. 1857 Liverpool – aged 24
Miriam SHOCK – Daughter – b. 1879 Liverpool – aged 2
Bertha SHOCK – Daughter – b. 1881 Liverpool – aged 0
Marcus SHOCK – Father – Widower – b. 1823 Russia – Capmaker (Hatter)
Annie SHOCK – Sister – b. 1862 Liverpool – aged 19 – Seamstress
Marks GOLDSTONE – Boarder – b. 1862 Russia – aged 19 – Butcher
Sarah ORTON – General Domestic Servant

Marriage:

Solomon SHOCK to Flora LEWIS – Q1 1877 LANCASHIRE 8b 765.

1871 Census

Address:

Boundary Place, West Derby, Liverpool

Residents:

Michael MYERS – Head – b. 1839 Germany – aged 32 – Cap Maker
J. MYERS – Wife – b. 1847 Germany – aged 24
Betsy MYERS – Daughter – b. 1867 Lancashire – aged 4
Myer MYERS – Son – b. 1868 Lancashire – aged 3
Lester MYERS – Son – b. 1871 Lancashire – aged 0
Marcus SHOCK – Father-in-law – b. 1822 Germany – aged 49 – Glazier
Rebecca SHOCK – Mother-in-law – b. 1822 Germany – aged 49
Solomon SHOCK – Son-in-law – b. 1852 Germany – aged 19 – Shop man
Lazarus SHOCK – Son-in-law – b. 1856 Germany – aged 15
Annie SHOCK – Daughter-in-law – b. 1863 Lancashire – aged 8

1901 Census

Address:

372 Hoe Street, Walthamstow

Residents:

Blooma SHOCK – Head – Widow – b. 1859 Liverpool – aged 42 – Clothier
Miriam SHOCK – Daughter – b. 1879 Liverpool – aged 22
Bertha SHOCK – Daughter – b. 1881 Liverpool – aged 20 – Embroiderer
Ernest SHOCK – Son – b. 1883 Liverpool – aged 18 – Clerk in Brass Foundry
Sarah SHOCK – Daughter – b. 1885 Liverpool – aged 16 – Embroiderer
Emanuel SHOCK – Son – b. 1887 Liverpool – aged 14 – Clerk for Tobacconist
Isadore SHOCK – Son – b. 1889 Liverpool – aged 12
Rosetta SHOCK – Daughter – b. 1892 Liverpool – aged 9
Dora SHOCK – Daughter – b. 1895 Liverpool – aged 6

1911 Census

Address:

99 Graham Road, Dalston, London N.E.

Residents:

Ernest SHOCK – Head – b. 1883 Liverpool – aged 28 – Chartered Accountant
Flora SHOCK – Mother – Widow – b. 1857 Liverpool – aged 54
Minnie SHOCK – Sister – b. 1884 Liverpool – aged 27 – Shop Assistant
Bertha SHOCK – Sister – b. 1886 Liverpool – aged 25 – Cashier
Stella SHOCK – Sister – b. 1887 Liverpool – aged 24
Charles SHOCK – Brother – b. 1891 Liverpool – aged 20 – Shop Assistant
Rosetta SHOCK – Sister – b. 1894 Liverpool – aged 17 – Clerk
Doris SHOCK – Sister – b. 1896 Liverpool – aged 15
Lizzie DANBY – General Domestic Servant

Death:

Bloomah SHOCK – Q3 1941 [84] HENDON 3a 720.
Buried at Willesden Jewish Cemetery – FX-9-384 on 30 Sep 1941.

SHUTER, Esther – D-13-31

Died: **26 Jun 1899**
Buried: **29 Jun 1899**
Hebrew Name: **Esther bat Ze'ev**
Partner: **Samuel Shuter (d. 1903)**
Aged: **81 years**

Jewish Chronicle – 30 Jun 1899

SHUTER – On Monday, the 26th of June, at 37, Stepney Green, Esther, the beloved wife of Samuel Shuter, aged 81 years. For 25 years matron of the Home for Aged Jews. Deeply mourned by her sorrowing husband, children, and a large circle of friends. Australian and Johannesburg papers please copy.

Jewish Chronicle – 16 Mar 1900

The tombstone in memory of Mrs S. Shuter, late Matron of the Jewish Home will be set at Plashet Cemetery, on Sunday, March 18th, at 4.30 o'clock. Relatives and friends will please accept this intimation.

Death:
Q2 1899 [81] MILE END OLD TOWN 1c 281.

1891 Census

Address:
37 & 39 Stepney Green (Jewish Home), Mile End Old Town

Residents:
Samuel SHUTER – Head – Married – b. 1826 Germany – aged 65 – Master of the Home
Esther SHUTER – Wife – Married – b. 1821 – aged 70 - Matron

1881 Census

Address:
37 & 39 Stepney Green (Jewish Home), Mile End Old Town

Residents:
Samuel SHUTER – Head – b. 1827 Prussia – aged 54 – Master of Jewish Home
Esther SHUTER – Wife – b. 1821 London – aged 60 – Matron of Jewish Home
Matilda SHUTER – Daughter – b. 1861 London – aged 20
[2 staff]
[37 inmates]

1871 Census

Address:
13 Brushfield Street, North, Liberty of the Old Artillery Ground

Residents:
Samuel SHUTER – Head – b. 1826 Germany – aged 45 – Cloth Manufacturer
Esther SHUTER – Wife – b. 1821 London – aged 50
Amelia SHUTER – Daughter – b. 1851 London – aged 20
Elizabeth SHUTER – Daughter – b. 1853 London – aged 18
Michael SHUTER – Son – b. 1855 London – aged 16
Adolph SHUTER – Son – b. 1856 London – aged 15 – Scholar
Charles SHUTER – Son – b. 1859 London – aged 12 – Scholar
Matilda SHUTER – Daughter – b. 1861 London – aged 10 – Scholar

Mary CAUNERL – Domestic Servant

1851 Census

Address:

39 Union Street, Liberty of the Old Artillery Ground, Tower Hamlets

Residents:

Samuel SHUTER – Head – b. 1825 Lissa, Germany – aged 26 – Hat & Cap Maker
Annala SHUTER – Wife – b. 1824 Whitechapel – aged 27
Amelia SHUTER – Daughter – b. 1851 Old Artillery Ground – aged 1 month

Marriage:

Samuel SHUTER to Hannah WOOLF – Q2 1850 ST LUKES 2 348.

Death:

Samuel SHUTER – Q1 1903 [79] ISLINGTON 1b 244.
Buried at Plashet Cemetery – D-13-32 on 20 Jan 1903.

Jewish Chronicle – 23 Jan 1903

SHUTER – On the 17th of January, at 103, Grosvenor Road, Highbury, N., Samuel Shuter, the dearly beloved father of Mrs H.M. Pollock, late master of the Home for Aged Jews, in his 80th year. May his dear soul rest in peace.
SHUTER – On the 17th of January, Samuel Shuter, the dearly beloved father of Mrs H. Charig, of the "Red Lion", Bevis Marks, E.C., in his 80th year. May his dear soul rest in peace – Shiva at 103, Grosvenor Road, Highbury, N.
SHUTER – On the 17th of January, at the residence of his daughter, Mrs H.M. Pollock, Samuel Shuter, the dearly beloved parent of Alfred Shuter, of Johannesburg, S.A.; Charles Shuter, of Fitzroy, Melbourne, and Mrs J. Woolf, of Chelsea, Mass, USA, in his 80th year. May his dear soul rest in peace. Cape, American and Australian papers please copy.

Jewish Chronicle – 16 Oct 1903

The tombstone in memory of the late Mr Samuel Shuter, of 103, Grosvenor Road, Highbury, will be set at Plashet of Sunday next, October 18th, at 1 o'clock. Relatives and friends kindly accept this intimation.

SILVER, Solomon – D-13-3

Died: 30 Apr 1899
Buried: 04 May 1899
Partner: Simelia Silver (d. 1908)
Age: 68 years

Jewish Chronicle – 05 May 1899

SILVER – On the 30th of April, at 20, St. Peter's Road, Mile End, after a serious accident, Solomon Silver, aged 68, the dearly beloved husband of Simelia Silver. Deeply mourned by his sorrowing widow, sons, daughter, sisters, grandchildren, relatives and a numerous circle of friends. Beloved by all who knew him. Gone, but never to be forgotten. May his dear soul rest in peace.

SILVER – On the 30th of April, at 20, St. Peter's Road, Mile End, Solomon Silver, the dearly beloved father of Mrs Hannah Rosen, of 39, Grafton Street, E. Deeply mourned and sadly missed. Shiva at 20, St. Peter's Road.

SILVER – On the 30th of April, at 20, St. Peter's Road, Mile End, Solomon Silver, the dearly beloved brother of Mrs Jane Woolf, of 43, Pyrland Road, Canonbury. God rest his dear soul.

Jewish Chronicle – 18 May 1900

The tombstone in memory of the late Solomon Silver, of 20, St. Peter's Road, will be set at Plashet Cemetery, on Sunday, May 20th, at 4 p.m. Relatives and friends will kindly accept this, the only intimation.

Death:

Q2 1899 [68] MILE END 1c 273.

1891 Census

Address:

20 St. Peters Road, Mile End Old Town

Residents:

Solomon SILVER – Head – b. 1831 Amsterdam – aged 60 – Metal Merchant
Simmey SILVER – Wife – b. 1832 London – aged 59
Henry SILVER – Son – b. 1861 Spitalfields – aged 30 – Metal Refiner
David SILVER – Son – b. 1865 Spitalfields – aged 26 – Jeweller
Abraham SILVER – Son – b. 1869 Spitalfields – aged 22 – Jeweller
Daniel SILVER – Son – b. 1870 Spitalfields – aged 21 – Metal Refiner
Florence CALLION – General Servant

1881 Census

Address:

20 St. Peters Road, Mile End Old Town

Residents:

Solomon SILVER – Head – b. 1831 Holland – aged 50 – Metal Merchant
Simmey SILVER – Wife – b. 1837 Mile End – aged 44
Henry SILVER – Son – b. 1860 Aldgate – aged 21 – Metal Merchant
David SILVER – Son – b. 1865 Aldgate – aged 16 – Apprentice Jeweller
Abraham SILVER – Son – b. 1869 Aldgate – aged 12 – Scholar
Samuel SILVER – Son – b. 1870 Aldgate – aged 11 – Scholar

SILVER, Solomon – D-13-3

Sarah ZEALANDER – Niece – b. 1857 Mile End – aged 24
Esther DANS – Visitor – b. 1860 Mile End – aged 21 – Cigar Maker
Ann EMERSON – Domestic Servant

1871 Census

Address:
7 Fashion Street, Christ Church, Spitalfields

Residents:
Solomon SILVER – Head – b. 1831 Amsterdam – aged 40 – Metal Merchant
Simmey SILVER – Wife – b. 1834 Spitalfields – aged 37
Henry SILVER – Son – b. 1860 Spitalfields – aged 11 – Scholar
Hannah SILVER – Daughter – b. 1863 Spitalfields – aged 8 – Scholar
David SILVER – Son – b. 1864 Spitalfields – aged 7 – Scholar
Abraham SILVER – Son – b. 1869 Spitalfields – aged 2
Samuel SILVER – Son – b. 1870 Spitalfields – aged 1
Sarah ZEALANDER – Niece – b. 1855 Mile End – aged 16
Ellen PRICE – Domestic Servant

1861 Census

Address:
6 South side of Fashion Street, Spitalfields

Residents:
Solomon SELVER/SILVER – Head – b. 1831 Amsterdam – aged 30 – Metal Merchant
Simmey SILVER – Wife – b. 1833 Whitechapel – aged 28
Henry SILVER – Son – b. 1860 Spitalfields – aged 1
Ellen MIDDLETON – Domestic Servant

1851 Census

Address:
4 Whites Row, Christchurch, Tower Hamlets

Residents:
Henry SILVER – Head – b. 1792 Amsterdam – aged 59 – Dealer in Spectacles
Hannah SILVER – Wife – b. 1795 Amsterdam – aged 56
Solomon SILVER – Son – b. 1831 Amsterdam – aged 20 – Cigar Maker
Clari ZEALANDER – Daughter – b. 1825 London – aged 26 – Cigar Maker
Jacob ZEALANER – Son-in-law – b. 1827 Amsterdam – aged 24 – Cigar Maker
Mayer ZEALANDER – Grandson – b. 1851 Christchurch – aged 7 months

Marriage:
Solomon SILVER to Simney ABRAHAMS – Q3 1857 LONDON CITY 1c 281.

1901 Census

Address:

20 St. Peters Road, Mile End Old Town

Residents:

Simelia SILVER – Head – Widow – b. 1838 Stepney – aged 63
Henry SILVER – Son – b. 1860 Spitalfields – aged 41 – Metal Dealer
Abraham SILVER – Son – b. 1868 Spitalfields – aged 33 – Jeweller
Samuel SILVER – Son – b. 1871 Spitalfields – aged 30 – Metal Dealer
Florrie CALLIEN – General Domestic Servant
Lily CLULOW – General Domestic Servant

Death:

Simelia SILVER – Q4 1908 [70] MILE END 1c 268.
Buried at Plashet Cemetery – D-13-4 on 28 Oct 1908.

Jewish Chronicle – 30 Oct 1908

SILVER – On Saturday, the 24th of October, at 20, St. Peter's Road, Mile End, after a short illness, Simelia Silver, widow of the late Solomon Silver, aged 70 years. Deeply mourned by her sorrowing children, grandchildren, son-in-law, daughter-in-law, brothers and Florrie, also a large circle of relations and friends. God rest her dear soul in everlasting peace. American papers please copy.

SILVER – On the 24th of October, at 20, St. Peter's Road, the dearly beloved mother of David Silver, of 4, Grafton Street, Mile End. God rest her dear soul. Shiva at 20, St. Peter's Road.

SILVER – On Saturday, the 24th of October, after a short illness, at 20, St. Peter's Road, Simelia Silver, the dearly beloved mother of Mrs Louis Rosen, Haslemere, 2, Kitchener Road, Forest Gate. God rest her dear soul. Shiva, 20, St. Peter's Road, E.

SILVER – On Saturday, the 24th of October, after a short illness, Simelia Silver, beloved sister of Abraham Abrahams, 107, Globe Road, E., Dan Braham, of Chicago; and Mannie Braham, of Brooklyn. Deeply mourned by her sorrowing brothers, nieces and nephews. Peace be to her soul. Shiva at 20, St. Peter's Road, Mile End.

SOMERS, John Isaac – D-16-4

Died: 07 Sep 1899
Buried: 08 Sep 1899
Partner: Emily Somers
Age: 44 years

Jewish Chronicle – 16 Sep 1899

SOMERS – On the 7th of September, at 241, Brixton Road, John Isaac, the dearly loved husband of Emily Somers, aged 44. May his soul rest in peace.

Jewish Chronicle – 02 Feb 1900

The tombstone in loving memory of the late John Somers, of 241, Brixton Road, will be set at Plashet Cemetery on Sunday next, February 4th. Friends kindly accept this, the only intimation.

Death:
Q3 1899 [44] LAMBETH 1d 834.

1891 Census

Address:
29 Nutford Place, St. Marylebone

Residents:
John SOMERS – Head – b. 1832 Kilkanny, Ireland – aged 59 – Tailor
Emily SOMERS – Wife – b. 1845 London – aged 46 – Tailoress

Marriage:
John Isaac SOMERS to Emily GRANT – Q3 1889 TOXTETH PARK 8b 499.
Emily SOMERS to Simon LIPKIE – Q4 1901 ORMSKIRK 8b 1329.

SYMONDS/SYMONS, Elizabeth – D-14-12

Died: 2 Jul 1899
Buried: 14 Jul 1899
Partner: Isaac Symons (d. 1917)
Age: 44th year

Jewish Chronicle – 14 Jul 1899

SYMONS – On the 12th of July, after a severe illness, Lizzie, the dearly beloved wife of Isaac Symonds, of 49, Hare Street, Bethnal Green, daughter of Henry Lee and sister of Mrs S. Levy, in her 44th year. Deeply mourned by her sorrowing husband, children and a large circle of friends. May her dear soul rest in peace.

Jewish Chronicle – 22 Jun 1900

The tombstone in loving memory of the late Elizabeth Symons, late of 49, Hare Street, E., will be set at Plashet Cemetery, on Sunday, June 24th, at 4.30 p.m.

Death:
Q3 1899 [44] BETHNAL GREEN 1c 144.

1891 Census

Address:
107 Bishops Road, Bethnal Green, London, North East Bethnal Green

Residents:
Isaac SYMONDS – Head – b. 1856 Bishopsgate – aged 35 – General Dealer

SYMONDS/SYMONS, Elizabeth – D-14-12

Elizabeth SYMONDS – Wife – b. 1857 Chatham, Kent – aged 34
Julia SYMONDS – Daughter – b. 1879 Shoreditch – aged 12
Henry SYMONDS – Son – b. 1881 Shoreditch – aged 10
Phoebe SYMONDS – Daughter – b. 1883 Shoreditch – aged 8
Sarah SYMONDS – Daughter – b. 1885 Bethnal Green – aged 6
Rachel SYMONDS – Daughter – b. 1887 Bethnal Green – aged 4
Rose SYMONDS – Daughter – b. 1890 Bethnal Green – aged 1
Maria GODDARD – General Domestic Servant

1881 Census

Address:
43 Goldsmith Row, Shoreditch

Residents:
Isaac SYMONS – Head – b. 1856 Bishopsgate – aged 25 – Tailors Cutter
Elizabeth SYMONS – Wife – b. 1857 Chatham – aged 24
Julia SYMONS – Daughter – b. 1879 Hackney – aged 2
Harry SYMONS – Son – b. 1881 Hackney – aged 0
Mary A. THOMAS – Domestic Servant

Marriage:
Isaac SYMONS to Elizabeth LEE – Q4 1876 BETHNAL GREEN 1c 761 – OR
Isaac SYMONS to Elizabeth LEE – Q2 1877 LONDON CITY 1c 162.

1901 Census

Address:
49 Hare Street, Bethnal Green

Residents:
Isaac SYMONS – Head – Widower – b. 1856 London – aged 45 - Pawnbroker's Manager
Julia SYMONS – Daughter – b. 1879 Shoreditch – aged 22 – Housekeeper
Phoebe SYMONS – Daughter – b. 1883 Shoreditch – aged 18 – Music Teacher
Sarah SYMONS – Daughter – b. 1885 Shoreditch – aged 16 – Milliner
Rachel SYMONS – Daughter – b. 1886 Bethnal Green – aged 15
Rose SYMONS – Daughter – b. 1890 Mile End – aged 11
Barnett B.V. SYMONS – Son – b. 1898 Bethnal Green – aged 3
Phoebe CAPOD – Domestic Servant

Marriage:
Isaac SYMONS to Sarah WOOLF – Q1 1910 LONDON CITY 1c 98.

1911 Census

Address:
72 Cricketfield Road, Clapton, London N.E.

Residents:

Isaac SYMONS – Head – b. 1856 London – aged 55 – General Dealer
Sarah SYMONS – 2nd Wife – b. 1868 – aged 43
Rachel SYMONS – Daughter – b. 1886 Bethnal Green – aged 25 – Dressmaker
Rose SYMONS – Daughter – b. 1890 Bethnal Green – aged 21
Myer WOOLF –Wife's father – b. 1836 Chatham – aged 75
Margaret HENOEQ – Domestic Servant

Death:

Isaac SYMONS – Q1 1917 [61] HACKNEY 1b 765
Buried at Plashet Cemetery – D-14-13 on 27 Mar 1917.

Jewish Chronicle – 30 Mar 1917

SYMONS – On the 24th of March, at 33, Shore Road, Hackney, Isaac Symons, relict of the late Elizabeth Symons, dearly beloved father of Mrs Sidney Drage, Mrs Cant of Colchester, and Mrs Felber, of Kilburn. Deeply mourned. Shiva at "Rosendale", 17, West Heath Drive, Golders Green, N.W.

SYMONS – On the 24th of March, Isaac, the beloved husband of Sarah Symons, of 33, Shore Road, South Hackney, aged 61. God rest his dear soul in peace. Shiva at "Rosendale", 17, West Heath Drive, Golder's Green. American papers please copy.

SYMONS – On Saturday, the 24th of March, at 33, Shore Road, Hackney, Isaac Symons, beloved father of Mrs Phil Greenberg and Mrs Arthur Bailey. God rest his dear soul. Shiva at 242, New Kent Road, S.E. and 19, Brookfield Avenue, Walthamstow.

SYMONS – On the 24th of March, 1917, at 33, Shore Road, Hackney, E., Isaac, the dearly beloved brother of Mrs Lewis Harris, 38, Vernon Gardens, Seven Kings, and 7, Wilson Street, E.C. Deeply mourned. May his dear soul rest in peace.

SYMONS – On Saturday, the 24th of March, at 33, Shore Road, Hackney, Isaac Symons, beloved brother of Barnett Symons, of 15, Rylett Road, Ravenscourt Park, W. Deeply mourned.

SYMONS – On the 24th of March, at 33, Shore Road, Hackney, Isaac Symons, 61, relict of the late Elizabeth Symons, father of Harry Symons, of London and New York; and Barnett Symons, prisoner of war. Deeply mourned. May his dear soul rest in peace.

VAN BOOLEN, Flora – D-11-1

Died: **31 Mar 1899**
Buried: **03 Apr 1899**
Partner: **Reuben Van Boolen (d. 1916)**
Age: **37 years**

Jewish Chronicle – 07 Apr 1899

VAN BOOLEN – On the 31st of March, at 13, Bancroft Road, Mile End, after a few days' illness, Flora, the beloved wife of Reuben van Boolen, youngest daughter

of Cosman Citroen, aged 37. Deeply regretted by her husband, father, sister, Mrs R. Goldman, of Nottingham, brothers, Messrs J., L., M., B., and S. Citroen, and her sorrowing relatives and a large circle of friends. May her soul rest in peace. Amen. Dutch papers please copy – Shiva at 13, Bancroft Road.
VAN BOOLEN – On the 31st of March, at 13, Bancroft Road, Mile End, Flora van Boolen, dearly beloved sister of Jack Citroen, of 26, Newnham Street, Aldgate, Louis Citroen, of St. Ermin's Mansions, Westminister, Michael Citroen, of 7, Bancroft Road, Mile End, S. Citroen, of 1, Margaret Street, Cavendish Square, S. Citroen, of Amsterdam. Shiva at 13, Bancroft Road.
VAN BOOLEN – On the 31st of March, at 13, Bancroft Road, Flora van Boolen, dearly beloved sister of Mrs R. Goldman, of Nottingham. God rest her dear soul in peace.

Jewish Chronicle – 06 Oct 1899

The monument in memory of Flora, the beloved wife of Reuben van Boolen, of 13, Bancroft Road, will be set at Plashet Cemetery, on Sunday next, the 8th inst., at 3 o'clock. Relatives and friends will please accept this intimation.

Death:
Q2 1899 [37] MILE END 1c 286.

1881 Census

Address:
12 Chisenhale Road, Bethnal Green

Residents:
Esther VAN BOOLEN – Head – b. 1819 Spitalfields – aged 62 – Wife of Diamond Merchant
Reuben VAN BOOLEN – Son – b. 1860 Spitalfields – aged 21 – Diamond Merchant
Manas SCHOP – Boarder – b. 1858 Netherlands – aged 23 – Professional Violinist
Mary HARDING – Domestic Servant

Marriage:
Reuben VAN BOOLEN to Flora CITROEN – Q2 1884 LONDON CITY 1c 155.

1901 Census

Address:
112 Grosvenor Road, Islington

Residents:
Reuben VAN BOOLEN – Head – b. 1862 Hoxton – aged 39 – Diamond Polisher

VAN BOOLEN, Flora – D-11-1

Sarah VAN BOOLEN – Wife (1 year) – b. 1878 London – aged 23
Julia COHEN – Visitor – b. 1881 London – aged 20
Esther ROCO – Domestic Servant

1911 Census

Address:
82a Uxbridge Road, Shepherd's Bush, London W.

Residents:
Reuben VAN BOOLEN – Head – b. 1860 Hoxton – aged 51 – Dealer in Precious Stones
Sadie VAN BOOLEN – Wife (11 years) – b. 1878 Aldgate – aged 33
Annie CATCHPOLE – General Domestic Servant

Death:
Reuben VAN BOOLEN – Q3 1916 [56] MARYLEBONE 1a 518.
Buried at Willesden Cemetery – CX-19-5 on 03 Sep 1916.

Jewish Chronicle – 08 Sep 1916

VAN BOOLEN – On the 1st of September, at the Middlesex Hospital, Reuben Van Boolen, darling loved husband of Sadie Van Boolen, of 82A, Uxbridge Road, Shepherd's Bush. Deeply mourned and sadly missed. May his dear soul rest in peace. A silent sufferer, but brave to the last.

VAN GELDER, Lydia – A-12-1

Died: **08 Sep 1899**
Buried: **11 Sep 1899**
Parents: **Isaac & Annie Van Gelder**
Aged: **5 years**

Jewish Chronicle – 16 Sep 1899

VAN GELDER – On Friday, the 8th of September, Lydia, the dearly beloved daughter of Mr and Mrs I.L. Van Gelder, of 'Rosedale', 2, Brushwood, Leytonstone, aged 5 years. God rest her dear soul.

Jewish Chronicle – 06 Apr 1900

The tombstone erected in loving memory of Lydia, the darling child of Mr and Mrs I.L. Van Gelder, will be set at Plashet Cemetery on Sunday next, April 8th, at 4 pm. Relatives and friends kindly accept this, the only intimation – "Rosedale", Brushwood, Leytonstone.

Death:
Q3 1899 [5] WEST HAM 4a 235.

VAN GELDER, Lydia – A-12-1

Birth:

Lydia VAN GELDER – Q2 1894 WHITECHAPEL 1c 314.

1891 Census

Address:

10 Sidney Square, Mile End Old Town

Residents:

Isaac L. VAN GELDER – Head – b. 1862 London – aged 29 – Cigar Manufacturer
Annie VAN GELDER – Wife – b. 1864 London – aged 27
Louis VAN GELDER – Son – b. 1884 London – aged 7 – Scholar
Alex VAN GELDER – Son – b. 1886 London – aged 5 – Scholar
Sophia VAN GELDER – Daughter – b. 1888 London – aged 3
Sidney VAN GELDER – Son – b. 1890 London – aged 1
Esther VAN GELDER – General Domestic Servant

Marriage:

Isaac Louis VAN GELDER to Hannah DE HAAS – Q1 1882 LONDON CITY 1c 149.

1901 Census

Address:

Rosedale, Brushwood (or Avenue Road), Lower Leyton

Residents:

Isaac L. VAN GELDER – Head – b. 1862 Spitalfields – aged 39 – Cigar Manufacturer
Annie VAN GELDER – Wife – b. 1864 Whitechapel – aged 37
Louis VAN GELDER – Son – b. 1884 St. Geo. E – aged 17 – Assistant Mariner
Alex VAN GELDER – Son – b. 1886 St. Geo.E – aged 15
Sophia VAN GELDER – Daughter – b. 1888 Stepney – aged 13
Sidney VAN GELDER – Son – b. 1890 Stepney – aged 11
Elizabeth HARVEY – Domestic Cook
Kate CLAYTON – Domestic Servant

VAN LEER, Elias – D-10-31

Died: 11 Mar 1899
Buried: 13 Mar 1899
Hebrew Name: Alexander bar Me'ir
Parents: Marks & Sarah Van Leer
Age: 22 years

Jewish Chronicle – 17 Mar 1899

VANLEER – On the 11th of February, 1899, at 5, Beaumont Square, E., after a very long and painful illness, Elias, youngest son of the late Marks and Sarah Vanleer, formerly of 10, Middlesex Street, Aldgate, E. Beloved and deeply mourned by his sorrowing sisters, brother, relatives and a very large circle of friends. Peace to his soul. Amen. South African papers please copy.

Jewish Chronicle – 13 Oct 1899

The tombstone in loving memory of the late Elias Van Leer, of 5, Beaumont Square, E., will be set on Sunday, October 15th, at 2.30 p.m., at Plashet Cemetery. Relatives and friends please accept this intimation.

Death:

Q1 1899 [22] MILE END 1c 328.

1891 Census

Address:

11 Beaumont Square, Mile End Old Town

Residents:

Moss VAN LEER – Head – b. 1861 Spitalfields – aged 30 – Diamond Polisher
Isaac VAN LEER – Brother – b. 1868 Spitalfields – aged 23 – Diamond Cutter
Elizabeth VAN LEER – Sister – b. 1869 Spitalfields – aged 22
Philip VAN LEER – Brother – b. 1873 Spitalfields – aged 18 – Hawker
Kate VAN LEER – Sister – b. 1874 Spitalfields – aged 17 – Tailoress
Elias VAN LEER – Brother – b. 1877 Spitalfields – aged 14

1881 Census

Address:

10 Middlesex Street, St. Botolph Without Aldgate

Residents:

Marks VAN LEER – Head – b. 1825 Utrecht – aged 56 – Picture Frame Maker
Sarah VAN LEER – Wife – b. 1837 Utrecht – aged 44
Moss VAN LEER – Son – b. 1852 Whitechapel – aged 29 – Diamond Polisher
Isaac VAN LEER – Son – b. 1863 Whitechapel – aged 18 – Apprentice
Elizabeth VAN LEER – Daughter – b. 1869 Whitechapel – aged 12 – Scholar
Philip VAN LEER – Son – b. 1873 Whitechapel – aged 8 – Scholar
Kate VAN LEER – Daughter – b. 1874 Whitechapel – aged 7 – Scholar
Elias VAN LEER – Son – b. 1877 Whitechapel – aged 4 – Scholar
Leah VAN LEER – Daughter – b. 1878 Whitechapel – aged 3
Henrietta VAN LEER – Daughter – b. 1880 Whitechapel – aged 1

VAN LEER, Elias – D-10-31

VANDERSLUIS, Julia – D-12-18

Died: 11 May 1899
Buried: 14 May 1899
Partner: Isaac Vandersluis (d. 1910)
Aged: 72 years

Jewish Chronicle – 19 May 1899

VANDERSLUIS – On the 11th of May, 1899, at 48, New Kent Road, the dearly beloved wife of Isaac Vandersluis, aged 72. Deeply lamented by her beloved children. May her dear soul rest in peace.

Jewish Chronicle – 04 Aug 1899

The tombstone in loving memory of Julia Vandersluis, of 48, New Kent Road, S.E., will be set at Plashet Cemetery on Sunday, August 13th, at 4.30. Relatives and friends kindly accept this intimation.

Death:

Julia VANDERSLIUS – Q2 1899 [72] ST. SAVOUR 1d 78.

1891 Census

Address:

48 New Kent Road, Newington

Residents:

Isaac VANDERSLUIS – Head – b.1831 Holland – aged 60 – Fishmonger
Julia VANDERSLUIS – Wife – b. 1832 Clerkenwell – aged 59
Lauther E. VANDERSLUIS – b. 1863 London – aged 28 – Stationery Assistant
Samuel VANDERSLUIS – b. 1864 London – aged 27 – Salesman
Barnett VANDERSLUIS – b. 1868 London – aged 23 – Book Binder
Benjamin VANDERSLUIS – b. 1870 London – aged 21 – Packer
Solomon VANDERSLUIS – b. 1872 London – aged 19 – Potman
Arthur SHAW – Lodger – Lapidary
Abraham VANDERSLUIS – (b. 1866 London) – aged 25 – Jobbing Man

1881 Census

Registered as VANDERSLINS

Address:

27 Valentine Place, St. George The Martyr, Southwark

Residents:

Isaac VANDERSLINS – Head – b. 1830 The Netherlands – aged 51 – Cigar Maker
Julia VANDERSLINS – Wife – b. 1831 Middx – aged 50

Elizabeth VANDERSLINS – Daughter - b. 1864 Middx – aged 17 – Strap Maker
Samuel VANDERSLINS – Son - b. 1865 Surrey – aged 16 – Hatter
Abraham VANDERSLINS – Son - b. 1867 Surrey – aged 14 – Printer
Barnett VANDERSLINS – Son - b. 1868 Surrey – aged 13 – Scholar
Benjamin VANDERSLINS – Son - b. 1870 Surrey – aged 11 – Scholar
Solomon VANDERSLINS – Son - b. 1872 Surrey – aged 9 – Scholar

1871 Census

Address:
Waterloo Road, Lambeth, Surrey

Residents:
Isaac VANDERSLUIS – Head - b. 1830 Netherlands – aged 41
Julia VANDERSLUIS – Wife - b. 1831 England – aged 40
Elizabeth VANDERSLUIS – Daughter - b. 1863 England – aged 8
Samuel VANDERSLUIS – Son - b. 1865 England – aged 6
Abraham VANDERSLUIS – Son - b. 1866 England - aged 5
Barnett VANDERSLUIS – Son - b. 1868 England – aged 3
Benjamin VANDERSLUIS – Son - b. 1870 England – aged 1

Marriage:
Isaac VANDERSLUIS to Julia KASNER – Q3 1862 ST JAMES WESTMINSTER 1a 789.

1901 Census

Address:
48 New Kent Road, Newington, Southwark

Residents:
Isaac VANDERSLUIS – Head – Widower – b. 1831 Holland – aged 70 – Shell Fish Dealer
Samuel VANDERSLUIS – Son – b. 1866 London – aged 35 – Shell Fish Dealer
Abraham VANDERSLUIS – Son – b. 1868 London – aged 33 – Shell Fish Dealer
Benjamin VANDERSLUIS – Son – b. 1871 London – aged 30 – Shell Fish Dealer
Solomon VANDERSLUIS – Son – b. 1875 London – aged 26 – Shell Fish Dealer

Death:
Isaac VANDERSLUIS – Q1 1910 [82] SOUTHWARK 1d 45.
Buried at Plashet Cemetery – I-15-33 on 24 Jan 1910.

Jewish Chronicle – 28 Jan 1910

VANDERSLUIS – Isaac, the beloved father of Mrs Elizabeth Shaw, of 88, Mildmay Road, N. Deeply mourned by his sons, daughter and sons-in-law. Shiva at 48, New Kent Road.

WESTHEIMER, Ivan Isaac – C-9-4

Died: 24 Jan 1899
Buried: 26 Jan 1899
Parents: Meta & Baruch Westheimer
Aged: 7 years

Jewish Chronicle – 27 Jan 1899

WESTHEIMER – On (Hebrew) the 24th of January, at 61, Victoria Park Road, Ivan, dearly beloved only son of Mr and Mrs B. Westheimer, aged 7 years and three months. May his soul rest in eternal peace.

Jewish Chronicle – 28 Feb 1902

The tombstones in memory of my late lamented wife and son, Meta and Ivan Westheimer, late of 61, Victoria Park Road, will be set at Plashet Cemetery, Sunday March the 2nd, at 3 o'clock. Friends and relatives will please accept this, the only intimation.

Death:

Q1 1899 [7] HACKNEY 1b 395.

Birth:

Ivan Chagim I. WESTHEIMER – Q4 1891 HACKNEY 1b 590.

1901 Census

Address:

61 Victoria Park Road, Hackney

Residents:

Baruch H. WESTHEIMER – Head – b. 1859 Germany – aged 42 – Commercial Traveller
Meta WESTHEIMER – Wife – b. 1868 Germany – aged 33
Beatrice WESTHEIMER – Daughter – b. 1895 Hackney – aged 6
Henry B. MYLVAGANAM – Boarder – b. 1870 Ceylon – aged 31 – Medical profession
Louise TESSEN – Domestic Servant

WHITE, Jacob – D-16-34

Died: 06 Oct 1899
Buried: 09 Oct 1899
Partner: Rachael White (d. 1904)
Aged: 69th year

WESTHEIMER, Ivan Isaac – C-9-4

Jewish Chronicle – 13 Oct 1899

WHITE – On the 6th of October, at 49, Wentworth Street, E., Jacob, beloved husband of Rachael White, in his 69th year. Brother of Mr L.A. White, of 127, Portsdown Road, Maida Vale. Deeply mourned by his sorrowing wife and children.

Jewish Chronicle – 18 May 1900

The tombstone in memory of the late lamented Jacob White, of 49, Wentworth Street, E., will be set at Plashet Cemetery on Sunday, the 20th inst., at 4 p.m. Relatives and friends please accept this intimation.

Death:

Q4 1899 [69] WHITECHAPEL 1c 189.

1891 Census

Address:

24 Wentworth Street, Spitalfields, London

Residents:

Jacob WHITE – Head – b. 1832 London – aged 59 – Butcher
Rachel WHITE – Wife – b. 1841 London – aged 50
Leah WHITE – Daughter – b. 1863 London – aged 28 – Tailors Machinist
David WHITE – Son – b. 1865 London – aged 26 – Butchers Assistant
Lizzie WHITE – Daughter – b. 1867 London – aged 24
Michael WHITE – Son – b. 1868 London – aged 23 – Boot Maker
Sarah WHITE – Daughter – b. 1871 London – aged 20 – Cigar Maker
Lewis WHITE – Son - b. 1874 London – aged 17 – Boot Maker
Annie WHITE – Daughter – b. 1876 London – aged 15

1881 Census

Address:

116 Middlesex Street, Whitechapel

Residents:

Jacob WHITE – Head – b. 1831 London – aged 50 – Master Butcher
Rachel WHITE – Wife – b. 1831 London – aged 50
Abraham WHITE – Son – b. 1862 Surrey – aged 19 – Fur Cutter
Leah WHITE – Daughter – b. 1863 Surrey – aged 18 – Tailoress
David WHITE – Son – b. 1865 Surrey – aged 16 – Butcher Assistant
Louisa WHITE – Daughter - b. 1866 London – aged 15
Michael WHITE – Son – b. 1867 London – aged 14 – Clothing Renovator (Tailor)
George WHITE – Son – b. 1871 London – aged 10 - Scholar
Sarah WHITE – Daughter – b. 1872 London – aged 9 – Scholar
Louis WHITE – Son – b. 1873 London – aged 8 – Scholar
Annie WHITE – Daughter – b. 1876 London – aged 5 – Scholar

1871 Census

Address:

Middlesex Street, Whitechapel

Residents:

Jacob WHITE – Head – b. 1830 Middlesex – aged 41
Rachel WHITE – Wife – b. 1831 Middlesex – aged 40
Abraham WHITE – Son – b. 1862 Surrey – aged 9
Leah WHITE – Daughter – b. 1863 Surrey – aged 8
David WHITE – Son - b. 1864 Surrey – aged 7
Elizabeth WHITE – Daughter – b. 1865 Middlesex – aged 6
Michael WHITE – Son – b. 1866 Middlesex – aged 5
George WHITE – Son – b. 1870 Middlesex – aged 1

Marriage:

Jacob WHITE to Rachel MYERS – Q2 1861 LONDON CITY 1c 253.

1861 Census

Address:

13 Great Suffolk Street, St. George The Martyr

Residents:

Jacob WHITE – Head – b. 1832 Spitalfields – aged 29 – Butcher
Mark MARKS – Servant – b. 1842 Aldgate – aged 19 – Butcher

1861 Census

Address:

116 Middlesex Street, Whitechapel N., London

Residents:

David MYERS – Head – b. 1804 Whitechapel – aged 57 – Butcher
Leah MYERS – Wife – b. 1805 Bishopsgate – aged 56 – Butcher
Rachael MYERS – Daughter b. 1834 Whitechapel – aged 27 – Dressmaker
Margaret CALLIHAM – House servant

1901 Census

Address:

49 Wentworth Street, Spitalfields

Residents:

Rachel WHITE – Head – b. 1841 London – aged 60 – Butcher
David WHITE – Son – b. 1865 Southwark – aged 36 – Butcher's Assistant
Elizabeth WHITE – Daughter – b. 1866 Southwark - aged 35 – Butcher's Assistant
Michael WHITE – Son – b. 1867 London – aged 34 – Provision Merchant
Sarah WHITE – Daughter – b. 1871 Whitechapel – aged 30 – Butcher's Assistant

Annie WHITE – Daughter – b. 1879 Whitechapel – aged 22 – Butcher's Assistant

Death:

Rachael WHITE – Q4 1904 [71] WHITECHAPEL 1c 164.
Buried at Plashet Cemetery – F-2-20 on 27 Dec 1904.

Jewish Chronicle – 30 Dec 1904

WHITE – On the 25th of December, at 49, Wentworth Street, Spitalfields, Rachel, relict of the late Jacob White. Deeply mourned by her sorrowing children, and respected by all who knew her. May her soul rest in peace. Amen.
WHITE – On the 25th of December, at 49, Wentworth Street, Spitalfields, Rachel White, the dearly beloved mother-in-law of Rebecca White – 70, Sandringham Road, Dalston.

1900

ABRAHAMS, Emanuel – B-6-16

ABRAHAMS, Emanuel – B-6-16

Died: 24 Jan 1900
Buried: 26 Jan 1900
Partner: Paulina Abrahams (d. 1900)
Aged: 67 years

Jewish Chronicle – 21 Jan 1900

ABRAHAMS – On the 24th of January, at 116, Cable Street, E., Emanuel Abrahams, aged 67. Deeply mourned by his sorrowing wife, son and daughters. May his dear soul rest in peace.

Jewish Chronicle – 08 Feb 1901

The tombstone in loving memory of the late Emanuel and Paulina Abrahams (of 116, Cable Street), will be set at Plashet Cemetery on Sunday next, February 10th, at 3.30.

Death:

Q1 1900 [67] ST. GEORGE IN THE EAST 1c 280.

1891 Census

Address:

116 Cable Street, St. George in the East

Residents:

Emanuel ABRAHAMS – Head – B. 1836 Russia – aged 55 – Outfitter
Paulina ABRAHAMS – Wife – b. 1857 Germany – aged 34
Isaac ABRAHAMS – Son – b. 1866 London – aged 25 – Clerk
Laura ABRAHAMS – Daughter – b. 1868 London – aged 23
Esther GROUSE – Granddaughter – b. 1889 Paddington – aged 2
Phoebe PUGH – Domestic Servant

1881 Census

Address:

116 Cable Street, St. George in the East

Residents:

Emanuel ABRAHAMS – Head – b. 1835 Russia – Clothier & Outfitter
Selina ABRAHAMS – Wife – b. 1836 Germany – aged 45
Fanny ABRAHAMS – Daughter – b. 1862 Middlesex – aged 19
Sarah ABRAHAMS – Daughter – b. 1865 Middlesex – aged 16
Isaac ABRAHAMS – Son – b. 1866 Middlesex – aged 15 – Clerk in Wool Business
Laura ABRAHAMS – Daughter – b. 1868 Middlesex – aged 13 – Scholar
Clara HILL – Domestic Servant

1871 Census

Address:

72 Cable Street, St. George, East

Residents:

Edmund ABRAMS – Head – b. 1831 Russia – aged 40 - Tailor
Helena ABRAMS – Wife – b. 1831 Germany – aged 40
Fanny ABRAMS – Daughter – b. 1861 Middlesex – aged 10
Sarah ABRAMS – Daughter – b. 1863 Middlesex – aged 8
Jessie ABRAMS – Daughter – b. 1865 Middlesex – aged 6
Laura ABRAMS - Daughter – b. 1867 Middlesex – aged 4
Fanny KARSING – Visitor – b. 1846 Russia – aged 25

1861 Census

Address:

2 Commercial Street, Spitalfields

Residents:

Emanuel ABRAHAMS – Head – b. 1836 Poland – aged 25 – Glazier
Selina ABRAHAMS – Wife – b. 1831 Germany – aged 30

Death:

Pauline ABRAHAMS – Q1 1900 [76] ST. GEORGE IN THE EAST 1c 285.
Buried at Plashet Cemetery – B-6-17 on 01 Mar 1900.

Jewish Chronicle – 02 Mar 1900

ABRAHAMS – On the 27th of February, at 116, Cable Street, E., Pauline, widow of the late Emanuel Abrahams, aged 76. Deeply mourned by her sorrowing son and daughters. May her dear soul rest in peace.

BARNETT, Aaron – B-7-46

Died: 18 Apr 1900
Buried: 19 Apr 1900
Hebrew Name: Aahron bar Issaka
Partner: Priscilla Barnett (d. 1899)
Aged: 82 years

Jewish Chronicle – 27 Apr 1900

BARNETT – On the 18th of April, at the residence of his son, 63, Cephas Street, Mile End, Aaron Barnett, aged 82, late of Grafton Street, the beloved father of Bearon Barnett and Mina Woolf, 180, Bow Road. Deeply mourned. God rest his soul.

BARNETT, Aaron – B-7-46

Jewish Chronicle – 14 Sep 1900

The tombstone in loving memory of our lamented parents, Aaron and Priscilla Barnett, will be set on Sunday, 16th September, at Plashet Cemetery, at 4 o'clock. Relatives and friends will please accept this, the only intimation.

Death:

Q2 1900 [82] MILE END 1c 289.

1881 Census

Address:

65 Beaumont Square, Mile End Old Town

Residents:

Aaron BARNETT – Head – b. 1821 London – aged 60 – Hebrew Teacher
Priscilla BARNETT – Wife – b. 1831 London – aged 50
Bearon BARNETT – Son – b. 1854 Australia – aged 27 – Leather Dealer (Currier)
Agnes BARNETT – Daughter-in-law – b. 1851 London – aged 30
Aaron BARNETT – Grandson – b. 1878 Hackney – aged 3
Elizabeth BARNETT – Granddaughter – b. 1880 London – aged 1
Moss GOODMAN – Nephew – b. 1860 Goodmans Fields – aged 21 – Cigar Maker
Isaac LEVY – Boarder – b. 1820 Poland – aged 61 – Gilder & Carver
Elizabeth WARNER – General Domestic Servant

1871 Census

Address:

Prince's Street, Spitalfields

Residents:

Aaron BARNETT – Head – b. 1821 London – aged 50
Priscilla BARNETT – Wife – b. 1832 London – aged 39
Bearon BARNETT – Son – b. 1853 Australia – aged 18
Volumina* BARNETT – Daughter – b. 1855 Australia – aged 16
Roda LYNES – Servant
Moss GOODMAN – Nephew – b. 1859 Middlesex – aged 12
Sarah VALLENTINE – Lodger – b. 1800 Middlesex – aged 71

* According to Jewish Victorian (p. 40) the spelling of her name is VALLIMENA.

Death:

Priscilla BARNETT - Q4 1899 [69] WHITECHAPEL 1c 233.
Buried at Plashet Cemetery – B-5-3 on 04 Dec 1899.

Jewish Chronicle – 8 Dec 1899

BARNETT – On Saturday, the 2nd of December, after a short and severe illness,

Priscilla, the dearly beloved wife of Aaron Barnett, 16, Grafton Street, aged 69, beloved mother of Bearon Barnett, 63, Cephas Street, Mile End and Mina Woolf, 180, Bow Road; sister of Hannah Barnard, 33, Bancroft Road, and Julia Woolf, 29, Grafton Street. God rest her dear soul. Shiva, 16, Grafton Street, Mile End.

Jewish Chronicle – 14 Sep 1900

The tombstone in loving memory of our lamented parents, Aaron and Priscilla Barnett, will be set on Sunday, 16th September, at Plashet Cemetery, at 4 o'clock. Relatives and friends will please accept this, the only intimation.

BARNETT, Simon John – B-9-34

Died: **13 Jul 1900**
Buried: **16 Jul 1900**
Hebrew Name: **Shimon ben Yehuda**
Partner: **Julia Barnett (d. 1895)**
Mary Barnett (d. 1892)
Aged: **72 years**

Jewish Chronicle – 20 July 1900

BARNETT – On the 13th of July, 1900, at 103, Whitechapel Road, late of 187, Hornsey Road, Holloway, S.J. Barnett, pawnbroker, husband of the late Julia Barnett, also brother of Mrs M. Lyons, of 103, Whitechapel Road. May his dear soul rest in peace. Shiva at 103, Whitechapel Road.

Jewish Chronicle – 28 Sep 1900

The tombstone in loving memory of Simon John Barnett, late of 103, Whitechapel Road, will be set at Plashet Cemetery on Sunday next, September 30th, at 4 o'clock. Relatives and friends please accept this intimation.

Death:

Q3 1900 [72] WHITECHAPEL 1c 174.

1891 Census

Address:

137 Hornsey Road, Islington

Residents:

Simon John BARNETT – Head – b. 1828 Amsterdam – aged 63 – Pawnbroker
Mary BARNETT – Wife – b. 1816 Hertfordshire – aged 75
Helen DEAL – Niece – b. 1877 St. John's Wood – aged 14 – Scholar
Elizabeth GREGORY – General Servant

BARNETT, Simon John – B-9-34

1881 Census

Address:

137 Hornsey Road, Islington

Residents:

Simon J. BARNETT – Head – b. 1829 Amsterdam – aged 52 – Pawnbroker
Mary A. BARNETT – Wife – b. 1815 Ware – aged 66
Florence GREENSLADE – Visitor – b. 1868 Holloway Rd – aged 13

1871 Census

Address:

Hornsey Road, St. Mary Islington

Residents:

Simon J. BARNETT – Head – b. 1829 Netherlands – aged 42
Mary A. BARNETT – Wife – b. 1821 Hertfordshire – aged 50
Edward J. PETERS – Servant
Thomas G. CLARKE – Servant
Alexander MOSES – Servant
Sarah Ann VEALE – Servant

Marriage:

Simon John BARNETT to Mary Ann HUMPHREYS – Q4 1848 ST. PANCRAS 1 340.
Simon John BARNETT to Julia LAZARUS – Q2 1893 ISLINGTON 1b 626.

Death:

Mary BARNETT – Q3 1892 [80] LAMBETH 1d 205.
Place of burial unknown.

Julia BARNETT – Q2 1895 [42] ISLINGTON 1b 217.
Buried at West Ham Jewish Cemetery – A-5-23 on 28 May 1895.

Jewish Chronicle – 31 May 1895

BARNETT – On the 26th of May, at 137, Hornsey Road, Holloway, after a painful illness, Julia Barnett, wife of S.J. Barnett (late widow of Barnett Lazarus), aged 42 years. Deeply lamented by her sorrowing husband, son, mother, brothers and sisters, and a large circle of friends. May her soul rest in peace. No flowers, by request.

BENJAMIN, Maria – B-8-38

BENJAMIN, Maria – B-8-38

Died: 12 May 1900
Buried: 15 May 1900
Hebrew Name: Miriam bat Itzhak Halevi
Partner: Joseph Benjamin (d. 1951)
Aged: 33 years

Jewish Chronicle – 18 May 1900

BENJAMIN – On the 12th of May, at 295, Upper Street, Islington, Maria, beloved wife of Joseph Benjamin, and daughter of Mr and Mrs J. Levy. Deeply mourned by her sorrowing husband, parents, brothers and sisters, and relatives. Shiva at the above address.

Jewish Chronicle – 28 Sep 1900

The tombstone in loving memory of the late Maria, wife of J. Benjamin, and daughter of Mr and Mrs J. Levy, of 295, Upper Street, N., will be set at Plashet Cemetery on Sunday, September 30th, 1900. Relatives and friends please accept this, the only intimation.

Death:

Q2 1900 [33] ISLINGTON 1b 231.

Marriage:

Joseph BENJAMIN to Maria LEVY – Q1 1897 LONDON CITY 1c 75.

1901 Census

Address:

295 Upper Street, Islington

Residents:

Jacob LEVY – Head – b. 1835 Limehouse – aged 66 – Porcelain Flower Seller
Leah LEVY – Wife – b. 1836 London – aged 65
Esther LEVY – Daughter – b. 1863 France – aged 38
Jane LEVY – Daughter – b. 1865 France – aged 36
Raphael LEVY – Brother – b. 1839 Limehouse – aged 62
Joseph BENJAMIN – Son-in-law – Widower – b. 1872 London – aged 29 – Cigar Maker

1891 Census

Address:

13 Bath Street, Bethnal Green

Residents:

Jacob LEVY – Head – b. 1835 London – aged 56 – General Dealer
Leah LEVY – Wife – b. 1836 London – aged 55
Rebecca LEVY – Daughter – b. 1858 France – aged 33
Esther LEVY – Daughter – b. 1863 France – aged 28
Jane LEVY – Daughter – b. 1865 France – aged 26
Marie LEVY – Daughter – b. 1867 France – aged 24
Raphael LEVY – Brother – b. 1839 London – aged 52

1911 Census
Address:

1 Colmar Street, Mild End, E.

Residents:

Elias ISAACS – Head – b. 1877 Whitechapel – aged 34 – Tailors Cutter
Fanny ISAACS – Wife (of 8 years) – b. 1877 Whitechapel – aged 34
Fanny ISAACS – Daughter – b. 1904 Mile End – aged 7 – at School
Alfred ISAACS – Son – b. 1906 Mile End – aged 5 – at School
Joseph BENJAMIN – Boarder – b. 1871 Hackney – aged 40 – Tailors Cutter
Rose COGGINS – General Domestic Servant

Death:

Joseph BENJAMIN – Q1 1951 [79] HENDON 5e 732.
Buried at East Ham Cemetery – U-18-1161 on 15 Mar 1951.

BRESLAR, Raphael – B-6-1

Died: 12 Jan 1900
Buried: 14 Jan 1900
Hebrew Name: Rafael bar Me'ir
Partner: Rebecca Breslar (d. 1901)
Aged: 65th year

Jewish Chronicle – 18 Jan 1900

BRESLAR – On the 12th of January, at Percy House, South Hackney, suddenly, Raphael Breslar, in his 65th year. Requiescat.

Jewish Chronicle – 16 Nov 1900

The memorial stone in loving memory of the late Raphael Breslar, will be set at 3 o'clock on Sunday, 25th inst., at Plashet Cemetery. Friends and relations please note – "Percy House", South Hackney.

BRESLAR, Raphael – B-6-1

Death:

Q1 1900 [65] HACKNEY 1b 453.

1891 Census

Address:

42 Wells Street, Hackney

Residents:

Raphael BRESLAR – Head – b. 1841 Poland – aged 50 – Shoe Manufacturer
Rebecca BRESLAR – Wife – b. 1845 Melksham – aged 46
Meyer L. BRESLAR – Son – b. 1864 London – aged 27 – Shoe Manufacturer
Deborah BRESLAR – Daughter – b. 1868 Spitalfields – aged 23 – Housekeeper
David BRESLAR – Son – b. 1870 Spitalfields – aged 21 – Manager of Rough Dept
Judah BRESLAR – Son – b. 1872 Spitalfields – aged 19 – Warehouse Manager
Leah BRESLAR – Daughter – b. 1874 Spitalfields – aged 17 – School Board Teacher
Rose A. BRESLAR – Daughter – b. 1876 Spitalfields – aged 15 – Trimmings Assistant
Moses BRESLAR – Son – b. 1878 Spitalfields – aged 13 – Warehouse Assistant
Minnie BRESLAR – Daughter – b. 1880 Spitalfields – aged 11 – Scholar
Flora BRESLAR – Daughter – b. 1882 Spitalfields – aged 9 – Scholar
Rhoda BRESLAR – Daughter – b. 1884 Limehouse – aged 7 – Scholar
Fanny SAINTMERE – Domestic Servant

1881 Census

Address:

17 Sandy's Row, Spitalfields

Residents:

Raphael BRESLAR – Head – b. 1833 Poland – aged 48 – Watchmaker
Rebecca BRESLAR – Wife – b. 1843 Melksham Wiltshire – aged 38
Meyer BRESLAR – Son – b. 1863 Middlesex – aged 18 – Teacher
Deborah BRESLAR – Daughter – b. 1867 Spitalfields – aged 14
David BRESLAR – Son – b. 1868 Spitalfields – aged 13 - Scholar
Judah BRESLAR – Son – b. 1871 Spitalfields – aged 10 - Scholar
Leah BRESLAR – Daughter – b. 1872 Spitalfields – aged 9 – Scholar
Ada BRESLAR – Daughter – b. 1874 Spitalfields – aged 7 – Scholar
Moses BRESLAR – Son – b. 1867 Spitalfields – aged 14 – Scholar
Minnie BRESLAR – Daughter – b. 1879 Spitalfields – aged 2
(Flora) BRESLAR – Daughter – b. 1881 Spitalfields – aged 0

1871 Census

Address:

Sandy's Row, Christ Church Spitalfields

Residents:

Raphael BRESLAR – Head – b. 1835 Poland – aged 36
Rebecca BRESLAR – Wife – b. 1843 Wiltshire – aged 28
Myer BRESLAR – Son – b. 1862 Middlesex – aged 9
Isabella BRESLAR – Daughter – b. 1864 Middlesex – aged 7
Deborah BRESLAR – Daughter – b. 1866 Middlesex – aged 5
David BRESLAR – Son – b. 2869 Middlesex – aged 2
Judah BRESLAR – Son – b. 1870 Middlesex – aged 1
Mary TUCKFIELD – Servant

Marriage:

Raphael BRESLAR to Rebecca LYONS – Q1 1861 LONDON CITY 1c 226.

1901 Census

Address:

42 Well Street, Hackney

Residents:

Rebecca BRESLAR – Head – Widow – b. 1845 Melksham – aged 56
Major L.R. BRESLAR – Son – b. 1867 London – aged 34 – Shoe Manufacturer
David BRESLAR – Son – b. 1871 Mile End – aged 30 – Commercial Traveller
Judah BRESLAR – Son – b. 1873 London – aged 28 – Forman Clicker
Rose Ada BRESLAR – Daughter – b. 1877 London – aged 24 – Bow Maker
Moses BRESLAR – Son – b. 1879 London – aged 22 – Mechanical Engineer
Minnie BRESLAR – Daughter – b. 1881 London – aged 20
Flora BRESLAR – Daughter – b. 1883 London – aged 18
Rhoda BRESLAR – Daughter – b. 1885 Stepney – aged 16
Jennie M. THOMPSON – Domestic Servant

Death:

Rebecca BRESLAR - Q3 1901 [60] HACKNEY 1b 340
Buried at Plashet Cemetery – B-6-2 on 20 Aug 1901.

Jewish Chronicle – 23 Aug 1901

BRESLAR – On the 17th of August, at Percy House, South Hackney, Rebecca, the beloved wife of the late Raphael Breslar. Deeply mourned.

Jewish Chronicle – 22 Nov 1901

The memorial stone in affectionate memory of Mrs Rebecca Breslar, late of Percy House, South Hackney, will be set at Plashet Cemetery on Sunday next, November 24th, at 3 p.m.

CITROEN, Cosman – D-20-1

Died: 26 Feb 1900
Buried: 28 Feb 1900
Partner: Rosa Citroen (d. 1895)
Age: 74 years

Jewish Chronicle – 02 Mar 1900

CITROEN – On the 26th of February, after a prolonged illness, at 13, Bancroft Road, Mile End, Cosman Citroen, aged 74 years, formerly of Prescot Street and Kirby Street, Hatton Gardens; dearly beloved father of Jack Citroen, 13, Bancroft Road, L. Citroen, St. Ermins Hotel, S.W., M. Citroen, 7, Bancroft Road, B. Citroen, 1, Margaret Street, Cavendish Square, W., S. Citroen, Amsterdam and Mrs R. Goldman, Nottingham. Deeply mourned by his children, grandchildren, relatives and a large circle of friends. May his dear soul rest in peace. Dutch papers please copy. Shiva at 13, Bancroft Road.

Jewish Chronicle – 19 Oct 1900

The tombstone in loving memory of the late Cosman Citroen, of 13, Bancroft Road, Mile End, will be set at 4 o'clock on Sunday next, the 21st inst., at Plashet Cemetery.

Death:

Q1 1900 [74] MILE END 1c 393.

1881 Census

Registered as CITRON

Address:

66 Great Prescot Street, Whitechapel

Residents:

Cosman CITRON – Head – b. 1826 Netherlands – aged 55 – Diamond Polisher & Diamond Cutter
Rosa CITRON – Wife – b. 1826 Netherlands – aged 55
Rachel CITRON – Daughter – b. 1858 Netherlands – aged 23
Lance CITRON – Son – b. 1860 London – aged 21 – Diamond Polisher
Flora CITRON – Daughter – b. 1862 London – aged 19
Woolf CITRON – Son – b. 1864 London – aged 17 – Printer
Barnet CITRON – Son – b. 1866 London – aged 15 – at School
Michael CITRON – Son – b. 1867 London – aged 14 - Printer
Solomon CITRON – Son – b. 1868 London – aged 13 – at School
Henry CITRON – Son – b. 1872 London – aged 9 – at School
Frank CITRON – Brother – b. 1828 Amsterdam – aged 53 – Blind
Ellen COLLINS – General Servant
Annie ATONY – General Servant

1871 Census

Registered as CITRON

Address:

Butler Street, Christ Church, Spitalfields

Residents:

Cosman CITRON – Head - b. 1826 Netherlands – aged 45
Rosa CITRON – Wife – b. 1826 Netherlands – aged 45
Jacob CITRON – Son – b. 1856 Middlesex – aged 15
Louis CITRON – Son – b. 1860 Middlesex – aged 11
Barnard CITRON – Son – b. 1868 Middlesex – aged 3
Michael CITRON – Son – b. 1866 Middlesex – aged 5
Rachel CITRON – Daughter – b. 1858 Middlesex – aged 13
Flora CITRON – Daughter – b. 1862 Middlesex – aged 9
Wolff CITRON – Son – b. 1864 Middlesex – aged 7

Marriage:

Cosman Jacob CITROEN to Rosa Levie VOORZANGER – Q4 1855 LONDON CITY 1c 285.

Parents:

Cosman Jacob's parents were Jacob Cosman Citroen & Vogeltje Isaac Park.

Death:

Rosa CITROEN died 1895 in Amsterdam.

COHEN, Saul – B-7-5

Died: 25 Feb 1900
Buried: 27 Feb 1900
Partner: Leah Cohen
Aged: 47 years

Jewish Chronicle – 02 Mar 1900

COHEN – On Sunday, the 25th of February, Saul Cohen, of 6, Dock Street, E., aged 47 years. God rest his soul.

Jewish Chronicle – 14 Sep 1900

The memorial stone in loving memory of Saul Cohen, late of 6, Dock Street, E., will be set at Plashet Cemetery on Sunday next, September 16th, at 3 o'clock. Relatives and friends kindly accept this intimation.

Death:

Q1 1900 [47] WHITECHAPEL 1c 272.

1891 Census

Address:

6 Dock Street, St. Mary Whitechapel, London

Residents:

Saul COHEN – Head – b. 1856 Whitechapel – aged 35 – Builder
Abraham COHEN – Brother – Widower – b. 1848 Whitechapel – aged 43 – Living on Own Means
Leah COHEN – Wife – b. 1863 Whitechapel – aged 28
Joseph COHEN – Son – b. 1886 Whitechapel – aged 5
Lewis COHEN – Son – b. 1887 Whitechapel – aged 4
Catherine COHEN – Daughter – b. 1889 Whitechapel – aged 2
Mary HANLEY – General Domestic Servant
Margaret HOWELL – Nurse/Domestic Servant

Marriage:

Saul COHEN to Leah LEVY – Q3 1885 LONDON CITY 1c 142.

1901 Census

Address:

6 Dock Street, Whitechapel

Residents:

Abraham COHEN – Head – b. 1847 Whitechapel – aged 54 – Builder
Leah COHEN – Wife – b. 1861 Whitechapel – aged 40
Joseph COHEN – Nephew – b. 1886 Whitechapel – aged 15
Lewis COHEN – Nephew – b. 1887 Whitechapel – aged 14
Catherine COHEN – Niece – b. 1891 Whitechapel – aged 10
Esther COHEN – Niece – b. 1892 Whitechapel – aged 9
Rose COHEN – Niece – b. 1893 Whitechapel – aged 8
George COHEN – Nephew – b. 1896 Whitechapel – aged 5
Mark COHEN – Nephew – b. 1897 Whitechapel – aged 4
Rosetta MORLY – Domestic Cook

1911 Census

Address:

6 Dock Street, London E.

Residents:

Abraham COHEN – Head – b. 1846 Whitechapel – aged 65 – Private Means
Leah COHEN – Wife (of 10 years) – b. 1866 Whitechapel – aged 45
Miriam COHEN – Daughter – b. 1903 Whitechapel – aged 8 – at School
Elizabeth COHEN – Daughter – b. 1906 Whitechapel – aged 5 – at School

Joseph COHEN – Nephew – b. 1886 Whitechapel – aged 25
Lewis COHEN – Nephew – b. 1888 Whitechapel – aged 23
Catherine COHEN – Niece – b. 1890 Whitechapel – aged 21
Esther COHEN – Niece – b. 1892 Whitechapel – aged 19
Rose COHEN – Niece – b. 1894 Whitechapel – aged 17
George COHEN – Nephew – b. 1895 Whitechapel – aged 16
Mark COHEN – Nephew – b. 1896 Whitechapel – aged 15

COWEN, Rose – D-22-2

Died: 27 Aug 1900
Buried: 28 Aug 1900
Parents: Annie & Samuel Cowen
Aged: 24 years

Jewish Chronicle – 31 Aug 1900

COWEN – On the 27th of August, at 69, Greenwood Road, Dalston, N.E., Rose, second daughter of Mrs and the late Samuel Cowen, sister of Mrs Charles Phillips, aged 24. May her dear soul rest in peace.

Jewish Chronicle – 16 Aug 1901

The tombstone in loving memory of Rose Cowen, who died 2nd Ellul, 5660, corresponding with 27th August 1900, will be set at Plashet Cemetery, on Sunday, 18th inst., at 4 o'clock – 15, Alvington Crescent, N.E.

Death:
Q3 1900 [24] HACKNEY 1b 303.

1891 Census

Address:
39, Fitzroy Street, St. Pancras, London

Residents:
Samuel COWEN – Head – b. 1839 Poland – aged 52 – Tailor
Annie COWEN – Wife – b. 1843 Poland – aged 48
Bessie COWEN – Daughter – b. 1871 Poland – aged 20
Rose COWEN – Daughter – b. 1874 Whitechapel – aged 17
Ray COWEN – Daughter – b. 1876 Whitechapel – aged 15 – Scholar
Benjamin COWEN – Son – b. 1877 Whitechapel – aged 14 – Scholar
Harriet SCHMITT – General Servant
Jane CLIFFORD – Visitor

Death:
Samuel COWEN – Q2 1898 [63] BETHNAL GREEN 1c 84.
Buried at Plashet Cemetery – A-11-62 on 04 Apr 1898.

Jewish Chronicle – 08 Apr 1898

COWEN – On the 1st of April, at 120, Hackney Road, N.E., Samuel Cowen, aged 63, many years resident in W.C. district. May his soul rest in peace.

Jewish Chronicle – 21 Oct 1898

The tombstone in loving memory of the late Samuel Cowen will be set at Plashet Cemetery on Sunday next, the 23rd inst., at 3.30 p.m. Please accept this, the only intimation. – 120, Hackney Road.

DE FRIEND, Clara – D-19-17

Died: **15 Feb 1900**
Buried: **18 Feb 1900**
Hebrew Name: **Gila bat Me'ir Halevi**
Partner: **Louis De Friend (d. 1931)**
Age: **53 years**

Jewish Chronicle – 16 Feb 1900

DE FRIEND – On the 15th of February, at 31, St. Peter's Road, E., Mrs De Friend, sister of Mrs S. Cohen. Shiva at 122, Amhurst Road, Hackney Downs.
DE FRIEND – On the 15th of February, 1900, at 31, St. Peter's Road, Mile End, Clara, the dearly beloved wife of Louis De Friend, deeply mourned by her sorrowing husband, children, grandchildren, sister and brothers, relatives and a large circle of friends. Gone, but never to be forgotten. God rest her dear soul. Funeral on Sunday next at two o'clock.

Jewish Chronicle – 14 Sep 1900

The tombstone in loving memory of our dear wife and mother, Clara De Friend, of 31, St. Peter's Road, Mile End will be set at Plashet Cemetery on Sunday next, September 16th at 4 o'clock. Relatives and friends please accept this, the only intimation.

Death:

Q1 1900 [53] MILE END 1c 353.

1891 Census

Address:

31 St. Peters Road, Mile End Old Town

Residents:

Louis DE FRIEND – Head – b. 1844 Holland – aged 47 – Cigar Maker
Clara DE FRIEND – Wife – b. 1847 Whitechapel – aged 44
Rachel DE FRIEND – Daughter – b. 1872 Whitechapel – aged 19
Solomon DE FRIEND – Son – b. 1876 Whitechapel – aged 15 - Cigar Maker

DE FRIEND, Clara – D-19-17

Rebecca DE FRIEND – Daughter – b. 1878 Whitechapel – aged 13 – Cigar Maker
Isaac DE FRIEND – Son – b. 1881 Mile End – aged 10
Phoebe DE FRIEND – Daughter – b. 1883 Mile End – aged 8
Hannah DE FRIEND – Daughter – b. 1886 Mile End – aged 5
Amelia DE FRIEND – Daughter – b. 1889 Mile End – aged 2
Frances DRUSE – Domestic Servant

1881 Census

Address:
10 Shepherd Street, Spitalfield
Residents:
Louis DE FRIEND – Head – b. 1844 Amsterdam – aged 37 – Cigar Maker
Clara DE FRIEND – Wife – b. 1846 Spitalfields – aged 35 – Cigar Maker
Makel DE FRIEND – Son – b. 1864 Spitalfields – aged 17 – Clicker
Myer DE FRIEND – Son – b. 1866 Spitalfields – aged 15 – Boot Maker
Henry DE FRIEND – Son – b. 1869 Spitalfields – aged 12 – Scholar
Rachel DE FRIEND – Daughter – b. 1872 Spitalfields – aged 9 – Scholar
Solomon DE FRIEND – Son – b. 1876 Spitalfields – aged 5 – Scholar
Rebecca DE FRIEND – Daughter – b. 1878 Spitalfields – aged 3 – Scholar
Isaac DE FRIEND – Son – b. 1881 Spitalfields – aged 0

1871 Census

Address:
10 Shepherd Street, Christ Church, Spitalfields
Residents:
Louis DE FRIEND – Head – b. 1844 Amsterdam – aged 27 – Cigar Maker
Clara DE FRIEND – Wife – b. 1846 Amsterdam – aged 25
Michael DE FRIEND – Son – b. 1865 Amsterdam – aged 6 – Scholar
Meyer DE FRIEND – Son – b. 1867 London – aged 4
Henry DE FRIEND – Son – b. 1870 London – aged 1
Mary MURPHY – Domestic Servant

Marriage:
Lewis DE FRIEND to Clara SILVER – Q2 1864 LONDON CITY 1c 227

1901 Census

Address:
31 St. Peters Road, Mile End Old Town
Residents:
Louis DE FRIEND – Head – Widower – b. 1844 Holland – aged 57 – Cigar Maker
Rachel DE FRIEND – Daughter – b. 1874 Whitechapel – aged 27
Phoebe DE FRIEND – Daughter – b. 1883 Mile End – aged 18 – Cigar Bundler

Hannah DE FRIEND – Daughter – b. 1886 Mile End – aged 15 – Cigar Bundler
Amelia DE FRIEND – Daughter – b. 1890 Mile End – aged 11
Sarah GROVE – Domestic Servant

Marriage:
Louis DE FRIEND to Caroline FURBY – Q1 1910 WHITECHAPEL 1c 355.

1911 Census

Address:
189 Hanbury Street, London E.

Residents:
Louis DE FRIEND – Head – b. 1844 (American) – aged 67
Caroline DE FRIEND – Wife – b. 1855 London – aged 56
Emma BRYANT – Domestic Servant

Death:
Louis DE FRIEND – Q1 1931 [87] HACKNEY 1b 580.
Buried at Plashet Cemetery – D-19-18 on 04 Jan 193

Caroline DE FRIEND – Q1 1945 [89] SHOREDITCH 1c 32.
Place of burial not found.

DE HAAS, Bertha – B-6-36

Died: **04 Feb 1900**
Buried: **07 Feb 1900**
Born: **03 Oct 1831**
Partner: **Emanuel De Haas (d. 1922)**
Aged: **68 years**

Jewish Chronicle – 09 Feb 1900

DE HAAS – On the 4th of February, 1900, at 37, Sandringham Road, West Hackney, N.E., suddenly, Bertha, dearly beloved wife of Emanuel De Haas, of 10, Crescent, Minories, E.C., and beloved mother of Mrs D. Goldsmith, of 31, Colvestone Crescent, N.E., aged 68 years. Deeply mourned by her sorrowing husband and children.

Jewish Chronicle – 20 Jul 1900

The memorial stone in loving memory of Bertha, wife of Emanuel De Haas will be set at Plashet Cemetery on Sunday next, July 22nd, at 4.30 o'clock. Friends will kindly accept this, the only intimation – 87, Sandringham Road, West Hackney.

DE HAAS, Bertha – B-6-36

Death:

Q1 1900 [68] HACKNEY 1b 427.

1891 Census

Address:

37 Sandringham Road, Hackney

Residents:

Emanuel DE HAAS – Head – b. 1831 Holland – aged 60 – Bookbinder
Bertha DE HAAS – Wife – b. 1832 Prussia – aged 59
Sydney E. DE HAAS – Son – b. 1863 Whitechapel – aged 28 – Bookbinder's Foreman
Caroline DE HAAS – Daughter – b. 1867 Whitechapel – aged 24
Ray DE HAAS – Daughter – b. 1870 Aldgate – aged 21 – Book Sewer
Harriett DE HAAS – Daughter – b. 1872 Aldgate – aged 19 – Pupil Teacher

1881 Census

Address:

7 Mitre Square, St. James Dukes Place

Residents:

Emanuel DE HAAS – Head – b. 1831 The Netherlands – aged 50 – Bookbinder – employing 3 Men and 1 Boy
Bertha DE HAAS – Wife – b. 1832 Westphalia – aged 49
Simon DE HAAS – Son – b. 1863 London – aged 18 – Bookbinder
Betsy DE HAAS – Daughter – b. 1865 London – aged 16 – Teacher
Caroline DE HAAS – Daughter – b. 1867 London – aged 14 – Teacher
Rachael DE HAAS – Daughter – b. 1870 London – aged 11 – Scholar
Harriet DE HAAS – Daughter – b. 1872 London – aged 9 – Scholar
Phoebe FRANKS – Boarder – Widow – b. 1836 London – aged 45 – Annuitant
Sophia VAN GELDER – General Servant

1871 Census

Address:

Mitre Square, St. James Dukes Place, London

Residents:

Emanuel DE HAAS – Head – b. 1831 Netherlands – aged 40
Bertha DE HAAS – Wife – b. 1831 Germany – aged 40
Simon DE HAAS – Son – b. 1863 London – aged 8
Betsey DE HAAS – Daughter – b. 1865 London – aged 6
Caroline DE HAAS – Daughter – b. 1867 London – aged 4
Rachael DE HAAS – Daughter – b. 1870 London – aged 1

1861 Census

Address:

53 Mansell Street, Whitechapel

Residents:

Emanuel DE HAAS – Head – b. 1831 Holland – aged 30 – Bookbinder
Bertha DE HAAS – Wife – b. 1831 Prussia – aged 30

1901 Census

Address:

37 Sandringham Road, Hackney

Residents:

Emanuel DE HAAS – Head – b. 1831 Holland – aged 70 – Bookbinder
Sydney E. DE HAAS – Son – b. 1863 Mile End – aged 38 – Bookbinder
Carrie DE HAAS – Daughter – b. 1867 Mile End – aged 34
Ray DE HAAS – Daughter – b. 1869 Aldgate – aged 32 – Bookbinder
Henriette DE HAAS – Daughter – b. 1872 Aldgate – aged 29 – School Teacher

Death:

Emanuel DE HASS – Q3 1922 [91] WILLESDEN 3a 242.
Buried at Plashet Cemetery – P-10-13 on 13 Aug 1922.

Jewish Chronicle – 18 Aug 1922

DE HAAS – On the 10th of August (Ab 16th), at 61, Blenheim Gardens, Cricklewood, N.W.2, Emanuel De Haas, aged 91 years, the dearly loved father of Mrs D. Goldsmith, 4, Ackland Road, Willesden Green, N.W.2., Sydney, Carrie, Ray and Harriet.

FRANKEL, Joseph Archer (Asher) – B-11-29

Died: 23 Oct 1900
Buried: 24 Oct 1900
Partner: Rose Frankel (d. 1926)
Aged: 41 years

Jewish Chronicle – 02 Nov 1900

FRANKEL – On the 23rd of October, at 36, Mildmay Park, Joseph Archer Frankel, aged 41. Deeply mourned by his sorrowing wife, children, relatives and friends. May God rest his soul.

Jewish Chronicle – 31 Nov 1900

The tombstone in loving memory of the late Joseph Archer Frankel will be set at Plashet Cemetery on Sunday, December 2nd, at 2.30 p.m. – 36, Mildmay Park, N.

FRANKEL, Joseph Archer (Asher) – B-11-29

Death:

Q4 1900 [41] ISLINGTON 1b 232.

1891 Census

Address:

1 James Street, St. Luke, London

Residents:

Joseph A. FRANKEL – Head – b. 1859 Austria – aged 32 – Furrier
Rose FRANKEL – Wife – b. 1858 Austria – aged 33
Harry FRANKEL – Son – b. 1883 Paris – aged 8 – Scholar
Aaron FRANKEL – Son – b. 1885 St Luke – aged 6 – Scholar
Annie FRANKEL – Daughter – b. 1889 St. Luke – aged 2
Simche GELBERG – Nephew – b. 1871 Austria – aged 20 – Furrier

1901 Census

Address:

36 Mildmay Park, Islington

Residents:

Rose FRANKEL – Head – Widow – b. 1859 Austria – aged 42
Harry FRANKEL – Son – b. 1883 France – aged 18 – Furrier
Aaron FRANKEL – Son – b. 1885 St. Lukes – aged 16 – Warehouseman (Furrier)
Annie FRANKEL – Daughter – b. 1888 St. Lukes – aged 13
Walter FRANKEL – Son – b. 1892 St. Lukes – aged 9
Queenie FRANKEL – Daughter – b. 1894 St. Lukes – aged 7
Isy FRANKEL – Son – b. 1896 St. Lukes – aged 5
Minnie FRANKEL – Daughter – b. 1899 St. Lukes – aged 2
Gertrude FRANKEL – Daughter – b. 1900 St. Lukes – aged 1
Josephine FRANKEL – Daughter – b. 1901 Islington – aged 2 months

1911 Census

Address:

19 Beresford Road, London N.

Residents:

Rose FRANKEL – Head – Widow – b. 1861 Austria – aged 50
Harry FRANKEL – Son – b. 1883 France – aged 28 – Furrier
Aaron FRANKEL – Son – b. 1885 Finsbury – aged 26 – Furrier Assistant
Annie FRANKEL – Daughter – b. 1888 Finsbury – aged 23
Walter FRANKEL – Son – b. 1892 Finsbury – aged 19
Fanny Molly FRANKEL – Daughter – b. 1894 Finsbury – aged 17
Isidore FRANKEL – Son - b. 1896 Finsbury – aged 15 – Furrier Assistant
Minnie FRANKEL – Daughter – b. 1898 Finsbury – aged 13 – at School
Gertrude FRANKEL – Daughter – b. 1900 Finsbury – aged 11 – at School
Josephine FRANKEL – Daughter – b. 1901 Islington – aged 10 – at School

Death:

Rose FRANKEL – Q1 1926 [65] ISLINGTON 1b 379.
Buried at Plashet Cemetery – G-16-E on 11 Jan 1926.

Jewish Chronicle – 15 Jan 1932

FRANKEL – On Saturday, the 9th of January, at 16, Clephane Road, Canonbury, N., Rose Frankel, relict of the late Joseph Asher Frankel, and devoted mother of Harry Aarons, Wally (Walter), Isy (Isadore), Annie, Queenie (Mrs V.A. Lyons), Gertie, and Josie. Deeply mourned by her heartbroken children, daughters-in-law, son-in-law, intended son-in-law, grandchildren, sister (Mrs Kunstler), and brother (Morris Springer). Shiva at above address.

FRANKELL, Sophie – D-23-4

Died: **30 Oct 1900**
Buried: **02 Nov 1900**
Partner: **Michael Frankell (d. 1921)**
Aged: **52 years**

Jewish Chronicle – 02 Nov 1900

FRANKELL – On Tuesday, the 30th of October, 1900, at 21, Church Crescent, South Hackney, Sophie, the beloved wife of Michael Frankell, aged 52. Deeply mourned by her sorrowing husband, children, relatives and friends. May her dear soul rest in peace. Amen.

Jewish Chronicle – 18 Oct 1901

The tombstone in memory of Sophie, the well beloved wife of Michael Frankell, will be set on Sunday, the 20th instant, at Plashet, at 3.30 o'clock. Relatives and friends please accept this, the only intimation.

Death:

Q4 1900 [52] HACKNEY 1b 332.

1891 Census

Address:

243 Victoria Park Road, Hackney

Residents:

Michael FRANKELL – Head – b. 1849 Swansea – aged 42 – Pawnbroker
Sophie FRANKELL – Wife – b. 1853 London – aged 38
Ida E FRANKELL – Daughter – b. 1884 S. Hackney – aged 7
Mabel D FRANKELL – Daughter – b. 1885 S. Hackney – aged 6
Florence R FRANKELL – Daughter – b. 1890 S. Hackney – aged 1

David KYAN – Boarder – b. 1866 – aged 25 – Pawnbroker's Assistant
Emma STEPHENSON – General Servant Domestic
Lettice COLLINS – General Servant Domestic

1881 Census

Address:
243 Victoria Park Road, Hackney
Residents:
Michael FRANKELL – Head – Single – b. 1849 Swansea – aged 32 – Pawnbroker
Ellen SPELLER – General Domestic Servant

Marriage:
Michael FRANKELL to Sophia JACOBS – Q1 1882 LONDON CITY 1c 155.

1901 Census

Address:
21 Church Crescent, Hackney
Residents:
Michael FRANKELL – Head – b. 1849 Swansea – aged 52 – Pawnbroker
Ida FRANKELL – Daughter – b. 1884 Hackney – aged 17 – Clerk
Mabel FRANKELL – Daughter – b. 1885 Hackney – aged 16
Florence FRANKELL – Daughter – b. 1890 Hackney – aged 11
Kate KEMP – General Domestic
Emily CRUTCHEY – Domestic Cook
Reginald CULLEY – Servant – Pawnbroker's Assistant
Thomas KEMPSTER – Servant – Pawnbroker's Assistant
Henry DE SPOLLA – Visitor – Professor of Music
Hannah DE SOLLA – Visitor
Jacob DE SOLLA – Visitor – Traveller in Tapestry
Jane DE SOLLA – Visitor – Dressmaker
Rachel DE SOLLA – Visitor
Lillian COHEN – Visitor
Hannah BUTTON – Visitor
Bernard KAHN – Visitor

1911 Census

Address:
27 Cassland Road, Homerton
Residents:
Michael FRANKELL – Head – b. 1849 Swansea – aged 62 – Pawnbroker & Salesman
Ida Esther FRANKELL – Daughter – b. 1884 S. Hackney – aged 27 – Shop Assistant

Florrie Rachel FRANKELL – Daughter – b. 1890 S. Hackney – aged 21 – Shop Assistant
Mabel Deborah MARKS – Daughter – b. 1885 S. Hackney – aged 26
Moss Albert MARKS – Son-in-Law – b. 1883 S. Hackney – aged 28 – Shop Assistant
Solomon Sidney MARKS – Grandson – b. 1907 S. Hackney – aged 4
Walter Edgar CLARK – Assistant – b. 1893 Battersea – Shop Assistant
George William PEREIRA – Assistant – b. 1891 Tottenham – Shop Assistant
Alfred ADAMS – Assistant – b. 1895 Bethnal Green – Shop Assistant
Charlotte REUSCH – Domestic
Beatrice Marion PERKINS – Domestic

Death:

Michael FRANKELL – Q3 1921 [73] HACKNEY 1b 350.
Buried at East Ham Cemetery – E-5-17 buried on 28 Jul 1921.

Jewish Chronicle – 29 Jul 1921

FRANKELL – On Monday, the 25th of July, Michael Frankell, of 27, Cassland Crescent, E.9, in his 74th year. Beloved father of Ida Frankell, Mrs Moss Marks, and Mrs Harry Welby. Deeply mourned. Shiva at above address.

Jewish Chronicle – 16 Jun 1922

FRANKELL – The tombstone in loving memory of Michael Frankell will be consecrated on Sunday, June 18th, 1922, at 5 o'clock at East Ham Cemetery.

FRIEDBERG, Hyam Solomon – C-17-5

Died: **17 Feb 1900**
Buried: **19 Feb 1900**
Hebrew Name: **Hyam Shlomo ben Moshe Yehoshua**
Parents: **Morris & Deborah Friedberg**
Aged: **14 months**

Jewish Chronicle – 23 Feb 1900

FRIEDBERG – On the 17th of February, at "Albany House", 79, Victoria Park Road, N.E., Hyam Solomon, the dearly beloved son of Morris Friedberg, aged 14 months. Shiva up on Sunday morning. God rest his soul in peace.

Jewish Chronicle – 07 Sep 1900

The tombstone in memory of the late Master Hyam Friedberg, will be set at Plashet on Sunday, September 16th, at 3.30 p.m. Relatives and friends will please accept this, the only intimation.

FRIEDBERG, Hyam Solomon – C-17-5

Death:

Q1 1900 [1] HACKNEY 1b 473.

Birth:

Hame Solomon FRIEDBERG – Q1 1899 HACKNEY 1b 587.

1901 Census

Address:

79 Victoria Park Road, Hackney

Residents:

Morris FRIEDBERG – Head – b. 1865 Russia – aged 36 – Wholesale Furrier
Deborah FRIEDBERG – Wife – b. 1869 Russia – aged 32 – Deaf
Netty FRIEDBERG – Daughter – b. 1893 Hackney – aged 8
Barney FRIEDBERG – Son – b. 1895 Stepney – aged 6
Markie FRIEDBERG – Son – b. 1897 Stepney – aged 4
Millie FRIEDBERG – Daughter – b. 1901 Hackney – aged 4 months
Jessie REEVES – Domestic Housemaid
Minnie LEPLEY – Domestic Cook
Edith POOLE – Domestic Nursemaid

1911 Census

Address:

79 Victoria Park Road, South Hackney, London N.E.

Residents:

Morris FRIEDBERG – Head – b. 1864 Russia – aged 47 – Manufacturing Furrier
Debora FRIEDBERG – Wife (of 23 years) – b. 1869 Russia – aged 42
Lewis FRIEDBERG – Son – b. 1891 Mile End – aged 20 – Manufacturing Furrier
Barney FRIEDBERG – Son – b. 1895 Mile End – aged 16 – Furrier
Markie FRIEDBERG – Son – b. 1897 Mile End – aged 14
Millie FRIEDBERG – Daughter – b. 1901 Hackney – aged 10
Jacky FRIEDBERG – Son – b. 1903 Hackney – aged 8
Bertha FRIEDBERG – Daughter – b. 1905 Hackney – aged 6
Samury FRIEDBERG – Son – b. 1908 Hackney – aged 3
Rosalie BARNETT – General Domestic Servant

Marriage:

Morris FRIEDBERG to Matilda BARNETT – Q1 1892 HACKNEY 1b 660A.

FUNK, Nicholas – B-9-23

FUNK, Nicholas – B-9-23

Died: **10 Jul 1900**
Buried: **11 Jul 1900**
Partner: **Lizzy Funk (d. 1871)**
Rosalie Funk (d. 1918)
Aged: 74 years

Jewish Chronicle – 13 Jul 1900

FUNK – On the 10th of July, at 28, Tredegar Square, Bow, Nicholas Funk, aged 74. Deeply mourned by his beloved wife, sons and daughters. May his soul rest in peace. Cape papers please copy.

Jewish Chronicle – 28 Jun 1901

The tombstone in loving memory of the late Nicholas Funk, of 28, Tredegar Square, Bow, will be set on Sunday next, at Plashet Cemetery, at 4.30. Relatives and friends please accept this intimation.

Death:

Not found in the registers

1891 Census

Address:

28 Tredegar Square, Mile End Old Town

Residents:

Nicholas FUNK – Head – b. 1832 – aged 59 – Gentleman
Rosa FUNK – Wife – b. 1847 – aged 44
Amelia FUNK – Daughter – b. 1868 London – aged 23
Rebecca FUNK – Daughter – b. 1870 London – aged 21
Miriam FUNK – Daughter – b. 1872 London – aged 19
Alfred FUNK – Son – b. 1874 London – aged 17 – Fine Art Publisher

1881 Census

Address:

28 Tredegar Square, Mile End Old Town

Residents:

Nicholas FUNK – Head – b. 1830 Russia – aged 51 – Furrier
Rosa FUNK – Wife – b. 1839 Germany – aged 42
Fanny FUNK – Daughter – b. 1861 Whitechapel – aged 20
Minsy FUNK – Daughter – b. 1863 Whitechapel – aged 18
Leah FUNK – Daughter – b. 1865 Whitechapel – aged 16
Rachael FUNK – Daughter – b. 1868 Whitechapel – aged 13 – Scholar

Rebecca FUNK – Daughter – b. 1870 Whitechapel – aged 11 – Scholar
Miriam FUNK – Daughter – b. 1872 Whitechapel – aged 9 – Scholar
Alfred FUNK – Son – b. 1874 Whitechapel – aged 7 – Scholar
Raphael FUNK – Son – b. 1876 Whitechapel – aged 5
Sarah PERKINS – Domestic Servant

Marriage:

Nicholas FUNK to Rosalie ALEXANDER – Q2 1871 LONDON CITY 1c 205.

Jewish Victorian – p. 168

Marriage between Nicholas Funk and Rosalie Alexander, eldest daughter of Rev. W. Alexander of Freinwalde, Prussia – date of marriage – 23 May 1871 at the residence of Rev. S.M. Gollancz, 15 Bury Street, St. Mary Axe.

Death:

Lizzy FUNK [39] Q1 1871 WHITECHAPEL 1c 300.
Buried at West Ham Cemetery – MiscGraves-56-29 on 25 Jan 1871.

1871 Census

Address:

40 New Castle Street, Whitechapel

Residents:

Nicholas FUNK – Head – b. 1832 Poland – aged 39 – Grocer
George FUNK – Son – b. 1856 Middlesex – aged 15
Henry FUNK – Son – b. 1858 Surrey – aged 13
Fanny FUNK – Daughter – b. 1860 Whitechapel – aged 11
Deborah FUNK – Daughter – b. 1862 Middlesex – aged 9
Milly FUNK – Daughter – b. 1864 Middlesex – aged 7
Leah FUNK – Daughter – b. 1866 Middlesex – aged 5
Rachel FUNK – Daughter – b. 1868 Middlesex – aged 3
Rebecca FUNK – Daughter – b. 1871 Middlesex – aged 0

1901 Census

Address:

28 Tredegar Square, Mile End Old Town

Residents:

Rose FUNK – Head – Widow – b. 1841 Germany – aged 60
George FUNK – Son – b. 1854 London – aged 47 – Merchant
Minnie FUNK – Daughter-in-law – b. 1861 Bristol – aged 40
Moss P. FUNK – Grandson – b. 1895 Johannesburg – aged 6
Elizabeth FUNK – Granddaughter – b. 1898 London – aged 3
Barbara H. DANIELS – Domestic Servant

Naturalisation:

Registration - HO 45/9341/22653
Nicholas Funk from Poland
Certificate A775 issued 2 July 1872.

Death:

Rosa FUNK-ALEXANDER – Q4 1918 [86] ISLINGTON 1b 756.
Buried at Plashet Cemetery – N-49-8 on 27 Oct 1918.

Jewish Chronicle – 01 Nov 1918

FUNK (ALEXANDER) – On the 27th of October, at 86, Petherton Road, Highbury, Rose Funk (Alexander), aged 86. Deeply mourned by her sorrowing children, grandchildren and relatives. Shiva at "Lord Napier", 86, Victoria Dock Road. African and American papers please copy.

GLANTZ, Rosetta/Rose – B-11-36

Died: **28 Oct 1900**
Buried: **30 Oct 1900**
Partner: **Benjamin Glantz (d. 1917)**
Aged: **62 years**

Jewish Chronicle – 02 Nov 1900

GLANTZ – On the 28th of October, at 21, New Road, Whitechapel, Rosette, the beloved wife of Benjamin Glantz, aged 62. Deeply mourned by her sorrowing husband, children, sisters and friends. May her dear soul rest in peace.

Jewish Chronicle – 15 Mar 1901

The tombstone in memory of Rosetta, the beloved wife of Benjamin Glantz, of 21, New Road, Commercial Road, will be set on Sunday next, 17th March, at 3.30 at Plashet Cemetery.

Death:

Q4 1900 [59] MILE END 1c 272.

1881 Census

Address:

13 Ellison Street, St. Botolph Without Aldgate

Residents:

Benjamin GLANTZ – Head – b. 1833 Poland – aged 48- Tailor
Rosetta GLANTZ – Wife – b. 1839 Whitechapel – aged 42
Jessie GLANTZ – Daughter – b. 1863 Aldgate – aged 18 – Tailoress
Rebecca GLANTZ – Daughter – b. 1865 Aldgate – aged 16 – Tailoress

GLANTZ, Rosetta/Rose – B-11-36

Lewis GLANTZ – Son – b. 1870 Aldgate – aged 11 – Scholar
Herman GLANTZ – Son – b. 1874 Aldgate – aged 7 – Scholar
Jane GLANTZ – Daughter – b. 1875 Aldgate – aged 6 – Scholar
Silvia GLANTZ – Daughter – b. 1877 Aldgate – aged 4 – Scholar
Rachael GLANTZ – Daughter – b. 1880 Aldgate – aged 1

1871 Census

Address:

Ellison Street, Aldgate, London

Residents:

Benjamin GLANTZ – Head – b. 1832 London – aged 39
Rosetta S. GLANTZ – Wife – b. 1839 Middlesex – aged 32
Jesse GLANTZ – Daughter – b. 1863 Middlesex – aged 8
Rebecca GLANTZ – Daughter – b. 1865 Middlesex – aged 6
Sarah GLANTZ – Daughter – b. 1866 Middlesex – aged 5
Katie GLANTZ – Daughter – b. 1868 Middlesex – aged 3
Lewis GLANTZ – Son – b. 1870 Middlesex – aged 1
Mary Ann INCHY – Domestic Servant

Marriage:

Benjamin GLANZ - Q2 1862 LONDON CITY 1c 249. No indication of wife's name.

1901 Census

Address:

21 New Road, Mile End Old Town

Residents:

Benjamin GLANTZ – Head – Widower – b. 1833 Poland – aged 68 – Tailor
Jessie GLANTZ – Daughter – b. 1863 London – aged 38 – Tailoress
Sarah GLANTZ – Daughter – b. 1866 London – aged 35 – Housekeeper
Louis GLANTZ – Son – b. 1871 London – aged 30 – Agent for 'Singers' Machines
Herman GLANTZ – Son – b. 1873 London – aged 28 – Tailor's Cutter
Jane GLANTZ – Daughter – b. 1875 London – aged 26 – Machinist
Sylvia GLANTZ – Daughter – b. 1877 London – aged 24 – Hand Button Hole Maker
Ray GLANTZ – Daughter – b.1879 London – aged 22 – Feather Curler
Julia GLANTZ – Daughter – b. 1881 London – aged 20 – Tailoress
Solomon GLANTZ – Son – b. 1886 Mile End Old Town – aged 15 – Apprentice Tailor's Cutter

1911 Census

Address:

21 New Road, London E.

Residents:

Benjamin GLANTZ – Head – Widower – b. 1836 Poland – aged 75 – Coat Tailor
Jessie GLANTZ – Daughter – b. 1866 London – aged 45 – Coat Tailoress
Sarah GLANTZ – Daughter – b. 1868 London – aged 43 – Tailoress
Lewis GLANTZ – Son – b. 1870 London – aged 41 – General Traveller
Jane GLANTZ – Daughter – b. 1890 London – aged 21 – Coat Machinist
Julia GLANTZ – Daughter – b. 1881 London – aged 20 – Button Hole Maker
Solomon GLANTZ – Son – b. 1887 Stepney – aged 24 – Tailor's Cutter
Mary MACKENZIE – Domestic Servant

Death:

Benjamin GLANTZ – Q2 1917 [86] MILE END 1c 377
Buried at Plashet Cemetery – L-20-31 on 07 Jun 1917.

Jewish Chronicle – 08 Jun 1917

GLANTZ – On the 5th of June, at 21, New Road, E., Benjamin Glantz, dearly beloved grandfather of Harry, Ben, Lew and Isidore Sprengers, of 10, Rutland Street, Stepney. May his soul rest in peace.

GOLDBERG, Deborah – B-9-37

Died: **23 Jul 1900**
Buried: **24 Jul 1900**
Parents: **Solomon & Betsy Goldberg**
Aged: **20th year**

Jewish Chronicle – 27 Jul 1900

GOLDBERG – On the 23rd of July, at 6, Booth Street, Brick Lane, after a brief illness, Deborah, dearly beloved daughter of Mr and Mrs S. Goldberg, in her 20th year. Deeply mourned by her sorrowing parents, brother, sisters, grandfather, uncles, aunts, and friends. May her dear soul rest in peace.

Jewish Chronicle – 28 Dec 1900

The tombstone in loving memory of our dear daughter and sister, Deborah Goldberg, of 6a, Booth Street, Spitalfields, will be set at Plashet Cemetery, on Sunday next, December 30th, at 2 p.m. Relatives and friends please accept this, the only intimation.

GOLDBERG, Deborah – B-9-37

Death:
Q3 1900 [19] WHITECHAPEL 1c 179.

1891 Census

Address:
26 Booth Street, Spitalfields

Residents:
Solomon GOLDBERG – Head – b. 1851 Poland – aged 40 – Tailor
Betsy GOLDBERG – Wife – b. 1853 Poland – aged 38
Myer GOLDBERG – Son – b. 1876 Spitalfields – aged 15 – Tailor's Apprentice
Rose GOLDBERG – Daughter – b. 1878 Spitalfields – aged 13 – Tailor's Apprentice
Deborah GOLDBERG – Daughter – b. 1879 Whitechapel – aged 12 – Scholar
Annie GOLDBERG – Daughter – b. 1880 Spitalfields – aged 11 – Scholar
Lily GOLDBERG – Daughter – b. 1882 Spitalfields – aged 9 – Scholar
Annie RENNEWICK – Domestic Servant

1881 Census

Address:
17 Booth Street, Spitalfields

Residents:
Solomon GOLDBERG – Head – b. 1852 Poland – aged 29 – Tailor
Betsy GOLDBERG – Wife – b. 1852 Poland – aged 29
Myer GOLDBERG – Son – b. 1875 Spitalfields – aged 6 – Scholar
Rosie GOLDBERG – Daughter – b. 1877 Spitalfields – aged 4
Deborah GOLDBERG – Daughter – b. 1878 Spitalfields – aged 3
Annie GOLDBERG – Daughter – b. 1880 Whitechapel – aged 1

Marriage:
Solomon GOLDBERG to Betsy Dinah RENEWICH – Q4 1873 LONDON CITY 1c 210.

1901 Census

Address:
6a Booth Street, Spitalfields

Residents:
Solomon GOLDBERG – Head – b. 1853 Poland – aged 48 – Tailor
Betsy GOLDBERG – Wife – b. 1855 Poland – aged 46
Myer GOLDBERG – Son – b. 1877 Spitalfields – aged 24 – Tailor Machinist
Annie GOLDBERG – Daughter – b, 1881 Spitalfields – aged 20 – Fancy Bazaar Assistant
Lily GOLDBERG – Daughter – b. 1883 Spitalfields – aged 18

1911 Census

Address:

9 Nicholas Street, Mile End, London E.

Residents:

Soloman GOLDBERG – Head – b. 1851 Ry Grot, Poland – aged 60 – Gents Tailor
Betsy GOLDBERG – Wife (38 years) – b. 1852 Litta, Russia – aged 59 – working at home.

GOLDBERG, Kitty – D-19-6

Died: **14 Feb 1900**
Buried: **15 Feb 1900**
Partner: **John Goldberg (d. 1890)**
Age: **38th year**

Jewish Chronicle – 16 Feb 1900

GOLDBERG – On the 14th of February, at 1, Ridley Road, Dalston, after a long and painful illness, Kitty, widow of the late John Goldberg, in her 38th year, beloved daughter of Mrs Julia and the late Mr A. Cohen, 63, Middlesex Street, Aldgate. May her soul rest in peace.

Jewish Chronicle – 13 Jul 1900

The tombstone in memory of the late Kitty Goldberg, daughter of Mrs Cohen, 63, Middlesex Street, will be set on Tuesday next, the 17th inst., at 3.30 p.m., at Plashet Cemetery. Relatives and friends will kindly accept this intimation.

Death:

Q1 1900 [38] HACKNEY 1b 431.

1891 Census

Address:

1 Ridley Road, Hackney

Residents:

Kate GOLDBERG – Head – Widow – b. 1863 Whitechapel – aged 28 – Grocer
Julia GOLDBERG – Daughter – b. 1886 Kensington – aged 5
Morris GOLDBERG – Son – b. 1887 Kensington – aged 4
Margaret BINNS – General Servant

Marriage:

Solomon GOLDBERG to Kitty COHEN – Q1 1885 LONDON CITY 1c 139.

GOLDBERG, Kitty – D-19-6

1901 Census

Address:

273 Brunswick Buildings, Whitechapel

Residents:

Isaac BLOM – Head – b. 1849 Holland – aged 52 – Cigar Maker
Eva BLOM – Wife – b. 1855 Spitalfields – aged 46
Julia GOLDBERG – Niece – b. 1886 N. Kensington – aged 15 – Feather Curler

Address:

1 Princes Block, St. Botolph Without Aldgate

Residents:

Charles LEO – Head – b. 1859 Poland – aged 42 – Waiter
Elizabeth LEO – Wife – b. 1861 London – aged 40 – Dressmaker
Morris GOLDBERG – Nephew – b. 1887 Notting Hill – aged 14 – Printer Boy

Death:

John (Jacob) GOLDBERG – Q1 1890 [25] WHITECHAPEL 1c 282.
Buried at West Ham Cemetery – K-20-8 on 16 Jan 1890.

GROUSE, Charles – B-8-22

Died: 28 Apr 1900
Buried: 30 Apr 1900
Partner: Kate Grouse (d. 1906)
Aged: 72 years

Jewish Chronicle – 04 May 1900

GROUSE – On the 28th of April, at 62, Mayfield Road, Dalston, after a long and painful illness, Charles Grouse, beloved husband of Kate Grouse (nee Samuels), and dearly beloved father of Louis and Jacob Grouse, and beloved brother of Mrs Mark Simmons, 6, Elgin Avenue, aged 72. God rest his dear soul. Shiva at 2, Albion Road, Dalston.

Death:

Q2 1900 [72] HACKNEY 1b 312.

1891 Census

Address:

38 Middleton Road, Hackney

Residents:

Charles GROUSE – Head – b. 1827 Poland – aged 64 – Job Buyer
Kate GROUSE – Wife – b. 1829 Manchester – aged 62
Louis C. GROUSE – Son – b. 1857 Soho – aged 34 – Tutor/Teach of Languages
Jacob L. GROUSE – Son – Married - b.1866 St. James – aged 25 – Boot Clicker
Pauline GROUSE – Daughter-in-law – b. 1867 New York – aged 24
Charles GROUSE – Grandson – b. 1889 Finsbury – aged 2

1881 Census

Address:

1 West Street, St. James Westminster

Residents:

Joseph GROUSE – Head – b. 1821 Poland – aged 60 - Woollen Merchant
Rebecca GROUSE – Wife – b. 1821 Poland – aged 60
Deborah GROUSE – Daughter – b. 1851 Poland – aged 30
Lewis GROUSE – Son – b. 1855 St. James – aged 26 – Woollen Merchant
David GROUSE – Son – b. 1857 St. James – aged 24 – Woollen Draper
Jacob GROUSE – Son – b. 1859 St. James – aged 22 – Actor

1871 Census

Address:

West Street, St. James Westminster

Residents:

Joseph GROUSE – Head – b. 1817 Poland – aged 54 – Piece Broker

Rebecca GROUSE – Wife – b. 1817 Poland – aged 54
Deborah GROUSE – Daughter – b. 1851 Poland – aged 20
Lewis GROUSE – Son – b. 1855 Middlesex – aged 16
David GROUSE – Son – b. 1857 Middlesex – aged 14
Jacob GROUSE – Son – b. 1860 Middlesex – aged 11

1861 Census

Address:
1 West Street, St. James Whitechapel
Residents:
Joseph GROUSE – Head – b. 1817 Poland – aged 44 – Cloth Dealer
Rebecca GROUSE – Wife – b. 1821 Poland – aged 40
Miriam GROUSE – Daughter – b. 1845 Poland – aged 16
Solomon GROUSE – Son – b. 1848 Poland – aged 13
Deborah GROUSE – Daughter – b. 1850 Poland – aged 11
Lewis GROUSE – Son – b. 1855 Westminster – aged 6
David GROUSE – Son – b. 1857 Westminster – aged 4
Jacob GROUSE – Son – b. 1859 Westminster – aged 2

Death:
Rebecca GROUSE – Q2 1882 [64] WESTMINSTER 1a 319.
Place of burial unknown.

Kate GROUSE – Q2 1906 [61] SHOREDITCH 1c 53.
Buried at Plashet Cemetery – G-12-6 on 24 Apr 1906.

HART, Sylvia - B-12-12

Died: 29 Nov 1900
Buried: 02 Dec 1900
Partner: Ezekiel Hart (d. 1877)
Aged: 85th year

Jewish Chronicle – 02 Dec 1900

HART – On the 29th of November, at her residence, 9, Lincoln Street, Bow, Sylvia Hart, relict of the late Ezekiel Hart, for many years at Clare Court, Drury Lane; sister of Aaron Green, 71, Middlesex Street, in her 85th year. Deeply lamented by her sorrowing children, grandchildren, great-grandchildren, and brother. May her soul rest in peace.

HART – On the 29th of November, 1900, at her residence, 9, Lincoln Street, Bow, Sylvia Hart, relict of the late Ezekiel Hart, mother of Mrs Isaac Levy, of 50, Russell Square, W.C., in her 85th year. Deeply lamented by her sorrowing children,

grandchildren and great-grandchildren. May her dear soul rest in peace. Amen.
HART – On the 29th of November, 1900, at her residence, 9, Lincoln Street, Bow, Sylvia Hart, relict of the late Ezekiel Hart in her 85th year, mother of Mrs H. Shuter, of 53, Aldham Street, King's Cross. Deeply mourned by her sorrowing children, grandchildren, and great grandchildren. May her dear soul rest in peace. Amen.
HART – On the 29th of November, 1900, at her residence, 9, Lincoln Street, Mile End Road, Sylvia Hart (relict of the late Ezekiel Hart) and mother of Leah, Ray, Hyam, Abraham, Lewis, and Henry Hart. Deeply mourned by her sorrowing children and a large circle of friends. May her soul rest in peace.
HART – On the 29th of November, 1900, at her residence, No. 9, Lincoln Street, Mile End Road, Sylvia Hart, relict of the late Ezekiel Hart, and mother of Mrs David Shuter, of the "Admiral Keppel", High Street, Shoredeitch. Deeply mourned by her grandchildren. May her soul rest in peace.

Jewish Chronicle – 19 Apr 1901

The setting of the tombstone in memory of the late Mrs Hart, of 9, Lincoln Street, Bow, will take place at Plashet on Sunday next, at 4 p.m. Relatives and friends will please accept this, the only intimation.

Death:

Q4 1900 [85] MILE END 1c 298.

1891 Census

Address:

76 Lincoln Street, Mile End Old Town

Residents:

Sylvia HART – Head – Widow – b. 1819 Tower Hamlets – aged 72
Leah HART – Daughter – b. 1864 Tower Hamlets – aged 27

1881 Census

Address:

108 Drury Lane, St. Clement Danes

Residents:

Sylvia HART – Head – Widow – b. 1821 Whitechapel – aged 60 – Fishmonger
Leah HART – Daughter – b. 1851 Whitechapel – aged 30 – Fishmonger
Rachel HART – Daughter – b. 1852 Whitechapel – aged 29 – Fishmonger
Abraham HART – Son – b. 1857 Westminster – aged 24 – Fishmonger
Louie HART – Son – b. 1859 Westminster – aged 22 – Fishmonger
Henry HART – Son – b. 1860 Westminster – aged 21 – Fishmonger

1871 Census

Address:

1 Clare Court, St. Clement Danes

Residents:

Ezekiel HART – Head – b. 1816 Middlesex – aged 55 – Fishmonger
Sylvia HART – Wife – b. 1826 Middlesex – aged 45
Leah HART – Daughter – b. 1845 Middlesex – aged 26
Rachel HART – Daughter – b. 1846 Middlesex – aged 25
Sylvia HART – Daughter – b. 1853 Middlesex – aged 18
Amelia HART – Daughter – b. 1854 Middlesex – aged 17
Abraham HART – Son – b. 1855 Middlesex – aged 16
Louis HART – Son – b. 1857 Middlesex – aged 14
Henry HART – Son – b. 1859 Middlesex – aged 12

1861 Census

Address:

1 Clare Court, St. Clement Danes

Residents:

Ezekiel HART – Head – b. 1814 Whitechapel – aged 47 – Fishmonger
Sylvia HART – Wife – b. 1821 Whitechapel – aged 40
Rachel HART – Daughter – b. 1844 Whitechapel – aged 17
Benjamin HART – Son – b. 1846 Whitechapel – aged 15
Hyam HART – Son – b. 1847 Whitechapel – aged 14 – Scholar
Sarah HART – Daughter – b. 1849 Westminster – aged 12 – Scholar
Silvya HART – Daughter – b. 1853 Westminster – aged 8
Abraham HART – Son – b. 1854 Westminster – aged 7 – Scholar
Lewis HART – Son – b. 1855 Westminster – aged 6 – Scholar
Henry HART – Son – b. 1858 Westminster – aged 3

1851 Census

Address:

1 Clare Court, St. Clement Danes, Westminster

Residents:

Ezekiel HART – Head – b. 1803 Whitechapel – aged 48 – Fish Salesman
Sylvia HART – Wife – b. 1811 Whitechapel – aged 40
Rachel HART – Daughter – b. 1844 Whitechapel – aged 7
Benjamin HART – Son – b. 1845 Whitechapel – aged 6
Hyman HART – Son – b. 1847 Westminster – aged 4
Sarah HART – Daughter – b. 1848 Westminster – aged 3
Silvya HART – Daughter – b. 1850 Westminster – aged 1
Hannah ISRAEL – Domestic Servant

Marriage:

Ezekiel HART to Sylvia GREEN – Q4 1841 LONDON CITY 2 158.

Death:

Ezekiel HART – Q3 1877 [65] STRAND 1b 338.
Place of burial unknown.

HYAMS, Esther – B-8-44

Died: 17 May 1900
Buried: 20 May 1900
Parents: Joseph & Hannah Hyams
Aged: 25 years

Jewish Chronicle – 25 May 1900

HYAMS – On the 17th of May, at 16, Newnham Street, Great Alie Street, after a period of intense suffering borne with fortitude and resignation, Esther, dearly beloved daughter of Mr and Mrs Hyams, aged 25 years. Deeply mourned by her sorrowing parents, sisters, brothers and intended husband, relatives and a large circle of friends. May her dear soul rest in peace.

Jewish Chronicle – 31 Aug 1900

The tombstone in memory of my loving daughter, Esther Hyams, of 16, Newnham Street, E., will be set at Plashet Cemetery, on Sunday, September 2nd, at 4.30 p.m. Relatives and friends please accept this, the only intimation.

Death:

Q2 1900 [24] WHITECHAPEL 1c 219.

Birth:

Esther HYAMS – Q1 1876 WHITECHAPEL 1c 379.

1901 Census

Address:

16 Newnham Street, Whitechapel

Residents:

Joseph HYAMS – Head – b. 1849 Whitechapel – aged 52 – Cigar Maker
Hannah HYAMS - Wife – b. 1850 Whitechapel – aged 51
Sarah HYAMS – Daughter – b. 1874 Whitechapel – aged 27 – Cigar Maker
Maria HYAMS – Daughter – b. 1877 Whitechapel – aged 24 – Cigar Maker
Betsy HYAMS – Daughter – b. 1879 Whitechapel – aged 22 – Cigar Maker
Millie HYAMS – Daughter – b. 1881 Whitechapel – aged 20 – Cigar Maker
Kate HYAMS – Daughter – b. 1884 Whitechapel – aged 17 – Cigar Maker
Samuel HYAMS – Son – b. 1885 Whitechapel – aged 16 – Fret Cutter#
Sophy HYAMS – Daughter – b. 1887 Whitechapel – aged 14
Solomon HYAMS – Son – b. 1890 Whitechapel – aged 11
Julia HYAMS – Daughter – b. 1893 Whitechapel – aged 8
Harry HYAMS – Son – b. 1895 Whitechapel – aged 6
Betsy HART – Niece – b. 1889 Whitechapel – aged 12

1891 Census

Address:

5 Bull Court, Spitalfields, London, Whitechapel

Residents:

Joseph HYAMS – Head – b. 1847 Spitalfields – aged 44 – Cigar Maker
Hannah HYAMS – Wife – b. 1849 Spitalfields – aged 42
Sarah HYAMS – Daughter – b. 1874 Spitalfields – aged 17 – Cigar Maker
Esther HYAMS – Daughter – b. 1876 Spitalfields – aged 15 – Cigar Maker
Maria HYAMS – Daughter – b. 1877 Spitalfields – aged 14 – Cigar Maker
Betsy HYAMS – Daughter – b. 1880 Spitalfields – aged 11 – Scholar
Minnie HYAMS – Daughter – b. 1882 Spitalfields – aged 9 – Scholar
Elizabeth HYAMS – Daughter – b. 1884 Spitalfields – aged 7 – Scholar
Samuel HYAMS – Son – b. 1885 Spitalfields – aged 6 – Scholar
Sophie HYAMS – Daughter – b. 1888 Spitalfields – aged 3 – Scholar
Solomon HYAMS – Son – b. 1890 Spitalfields – aged 1
Sophia PARITTS – Wife's aunt – b. 1827 Spitalfields – aged 64 – Clothes Dealer

1881 Census

Address:

1 Bulls Court, Spitalfields

Residents:

Joseph HYAMS – Head – b. 1848 Spitalfields – aged 33 – Cigar Maker
Hannah HYAMS – Wife – b. 1850 Spitalfields – aged 31 – Housekeeper
Sarah HYAMS – Daughter – b. 1873 Bow – aged 8 – Scholar
Esther HYAMS – Daughter – b. 1875 Spitalfields – aged 6 – Scholar
Maria HYAMS – Daughter – b. 1877 Spitalfields – aged 4 – Scholar
Betsy HYAMS – Daughter – b. 1880 Spitalfields – aged 1
Samuel JONAS – Lodger – Head – b. 1835 London – aged 46 – Druggist
Sarah JONAS – Wife – b. 1847 London – aged 34 – Housekeeper
Lazarus JONAS – Lodger's son – b. 1879 London – aged 2

Marriage:

Joseph HYAMS to Hannah HART – Q4 1872 LONDON CITY 1c 205.

1911 Census

Address:

3 Alderney Road, Mile End Old Town

Residents:

Joseph HYAMS – Head – b. 1847 Whitechapel – aged 64 – Cigar Maker
Hannah HYAMS – Wife (40 years) – b. 1850 – aged 61
Elizabeth HYAMS – Daughter – b. 1884 Whitechapel – aged 27 – Cigar Maker
Solomon HYAMS – Son – b. 1890 Whitechapel – aged 21
Julia HYAMS – Daughter – b. 1893 Whitechapel – aged 18 – Undergarment Maker
Harry HYAMS – Son – b. 1896 Limehouse – aged 15 – Tailor's Assistant

ISAACS, Jessie Gaby – B-7-3

Died: 20 Feb 1900
Buried: 22 Feb 1900
Hebrew Name: Masha bat Michael
Partner: Moses Isaacs (d. 1880)
Aged: 84 years

Jewish Chronicle – 23 Feb 1900

ISAACS – On the 20th of February, 1900, at 117, White Horse Lane, Mile End, after a long and painful illness, Leah Gaby Jessie Isaacs, late of Royal Mint Street, aged 84. The dearly beloved mother of Sam Isaacs, 103, Murray Street, New North Road, George Isaacs, 9, Buckland Street, Hoxton, Mrs Morris Moses, of Brooklyn, New York, Mrs J. Cohen, 1, Newman Street, Goodman's Fields, Mrs N. Romain, Skidmore Street, Mile End, Mrs A. Jacobs, 269, Kingsland Road, Mrs M. Levy, late of Kingsland Gate, Mrs M. Levy, 56-1/2, Royal Mint Street, and the beloved sister of Mr Henry Pollock, of 13, Grafton Street, Mile End. Deeply regretted by her children, grandchildren, and great grandchildren, and a large circle of friends. God rest her dear soul in peace. Gone, but not forgotten. Shiva at above addresses.

Jewish Chronicle – 19 Oct 1900

The tombstone in loving memory of our dear mother, the late Jessie Gaby Isaacs, of Royal Mint Street, will be set at Plashet Cemetery on Sunday next at 3 o'clock. Relatives and friends kindly accept this, the only intimation.

Death:

Q1 1900 [83] MILE END 1c 355.

1891 Census

Address:

56½ Royal Mint Street, St. Mary Whitechapel, London

Residents:

Jessie ISAACS – Head –Widow - b. 1818 Spitalfields – aged 73 – Fishmonger
Samuel JACOBS – Grandson – b. 1868 Whitechapel – aged 23 – Fishmonger
Rebecca COHEN – Niece – b. 1855 Aldgate – aged 36 – Hat and Cap Maker
Barney JEOL – Servant – b. 1875 Stratford – aged 16 – Fishmongers Assistant
Annie WOODCOCK – General Servant
Alfred CARL – Cook
Moses LEVY – Lodger – b. 1877 Whitechapel – aged 14 – Carmans Boy

1881 Census

Address:

56½ Royal Mint Street, St. Mary Whitechapel

ISAACS, Jessie Gaby – B-7-3

Residents:

Jessie ISAACS – Head – Widow – b. 1819 Spitalfields – aged 62 – Fishmonger
George ISAACS – Son – b. 1860 Whitechapel – aged 21 – Fishmonger
Frederick CORNELL – Lodger – b. 1853 Ottery – aged 28 – Carman
Samuel ISAACS – Grandson – b. 1869 Whitechapel – aged 12 – Scholar

1871 Census

Address:

Royal Mint Street, St. Mary Whitechapel

Residents:

Moses ISAACS – Head – b. 1815 Surrey – aged 56 – Fishmonger
Jesse ISAACS – Wife – b. 1818 Middlesex – aged 53
Samuel ISAACS – Son – b. 1857 Middlesex – aged 14
Bella ISAACS – Daughter – b. 1855 Middlesex – aged 16
George ISAACS – Son – b. 1860 Middlesex – aged 11
Henry ISAACS – Son – b. 1862 Middlesex – aged 9
Henry ISAACS – Grandson – b. 1859 – aged 12
Samuel ISAACS – Father – b. 1781 Middlesex – aged 90
Ezekiel ISAACS – Brother – b. 1831 Middlesex – aged 40
Thomas MURSTON – Lodger – b. 1854 Middlesex – aged 17

1861 Census

Address:

34 Tenter Street, Spitalfields

Residents:

Moses ISAACS – Head – b. 1810 Strand – aged 51 – Fish Dealer
Jessy ISAACS – Wife – b. 2829 Spitalfields – aged 42
Frances ISAACS – Daughter – b. 1839 Spitalfields – aged 22 – Domestic Servant
Sarah ISAACS – Daughter – b. 1841 Spitalfields – aged 20 – Tailoress
Rachel ISAACS – Daughter – b. 1842 Spitalfields – aged 19 – Waist Coat Maker
Phoebe ISAACS – Daughter – b. 1844 Spitalfields – aged 17 – Dressmaker
Matilda ISAACS – Daughter – b. 1846 Spitalfields – aged 15 – Tailoress
Rebecca ISAACS – Daughter – b. 1848 Spitalfields – aged 13
Samuel ISAACS – Son – b. 1857 Spitalfields – aged 4
Betsy ISAACS – Daughter – b. 1856 Spitalfields – aged 5
George ISAACS – Son – b. 1859 Spitalfields – aged 2
Henry ISAACS – Grandson – b. 1859 Whitechapel – aged 2
Rachel ISAACS – Mother – Widow – b. 1787 Aldgate – aged 74
Millery COHEAN – Boarder – b. 1843 London – aged 18 – Waistcoat Maker

1851 Census

Address:

34 Tenter Street, Christchurch, Tower Hamlets

Residents:

Moses ISAACS – Head – b. 1811 London – aged 40 – Dealer in Fish
Jesse ISAACS – Wife – b. 1819 London – aged 32
Frances ISAACS – Daughter – b. 1839 London – aged 12 – at School
Sarah ISAACS – Daughter – b. 1840 London – aged 11 – Scholar
Rachel ISAACS – Daughter – b. 1842 London – aged 9 – Scholar
Phoebe ISAACS – Daughter – b. 1845 London – aged 6 – Scholar
Matilda ISAACS – Daughter – b. 1847 London – aged 4 – Scholar
Rebecca ISAACS – Daughter – b. 1849 London – aged 2 – Scholar
Amelia COHEN – Lodger – b. 1843 London – aged 8 – Scholar
Moses COHEN – Lodger – b. 1813 London – aged 38
Moses DACOSTA – Lodger – b. 1775 – aged 76

Marriage:

Moses ISAACS to Jessy POLACK – Q3 1837 LONDON CITY 2 451.

Death:

Moses Isaacs – Q4 1880 [72] LONDON CITY 1c 20.
Buried at West Ham Cemetery – M-3-19 buried on 07 Nov 1880.

JACOBS, Joseph – D-23-17

Died: **09 Nov 1900**
Buried: **11 Nov 1900**
Hebrew Name: **Yosef ben Itzhak**
Partner: **Harriet Jacobs (d. 1910)**
Age: **60th year**

Jewish Chronicle – 16 Nov 1900

JACOBS – On the 9th of November, 1900 – Heshvan 17th, 5661, at 5, Hutchison Street, Aldgate, E.C., Joseph Jacobs, in his 60th year. Deeply lamented by his sorrowing wife, sons, daughters, brother and sister, and a large circle of friends. His end was peace. God rest his dear soul.

Jewish Chronicle – 11 Nov 1910

JACOBS – The tombstones in loving memory of our dear parents, the late Mr and Mrs Joseph Jacobs, of 5, Hutchison Street, Aldgate, will be consecrated at Plashet Cemetery, on Sunday, November 13th, at 3 o'clock. Relatives and friends kindly accept this, the only intimation.

Death:

Q4 1900 LONDON CITY 1c 3.

JACOBS, Joseph – D-23-17

1891 Census

Address:

5 Hutchinson Street, Aldgate, London

Residents:

Joseph JACOBS – Head – b. 1843 Southwark – aged 48 – General Dealer
Harriet JACOBS – Wife – b. 1844 Bishopsgate – aged 47
Esther JACOBS – Daughter – b. 1868 Aldgate – aged 23 – Tobacconist
John JACOBS – Son – b. 1870 Aldgate – aged 21 – Harness Maker
Maria JACOBS – Daughter – b. 1871 Aldgate – aged 20
Phoebe JACOBS – Daughter – b. 1876 Aldgate – aged 15 – Cigarette Maker
Judah JACOBS – Son – b. 1878 Aldgate – aged 13 – Errand Boy
Rachel JACOBS – Daughter – b. 1880 Aldgate – aged 11 – Scholar
Frances JACOBS – Daughter – b. 1882 Aldgate – aged 9 – Scholar
Harry P. JACOBS – Son – b. 1884 Aldgate – aged 7 – Scholar

1881 Census

Address:

5 Hutchinson Street, St. Botolph Without Aldgate

Residents:

Joseph JACOBS – Head – b. 1841 Southwark – aged 40 – General Dealer
Harriett JACOBS – Wife – b. 1844 London – aged 37
Esther JACOBS – Daughter – b. 1869 London – aged 12
John JACOBS – Son – b. 1871 London – aged 10
Maria JACOBS – Daughter – b. 1872 London – aged 9
Phoebe JACOBS – Daughter – b. 1875 London – aged 6
Judah JACOBS – Son – b. 1878 London – aged 3
Rachel JACOBS – Daughter – b. 1880 London – aged 1

1871 Census

Address:

5 Hutchinson Street, Aldgate, London

Residents:

Joseph JACOBS – Head – b. 1844 Surrey – aged 27 – Dealer
Harriett JACOBS – Wife – b. 1845 Middlesex – aged 26
Esther JACOBS – Daughter – b. 1868 London – aged 3
John JACOBS – Son – b. 1870 London – aged 1
Maria JACOBS – Daughter – b. 1871 London – aged 0

Marriage:

Joseph JACOBS to Harriet HART – Q2 1867 LONDON CITY 1c 215.

1901 Census

Address:

5 Hutchinson Street, St. Botolph Without Aldgate

Residents:

Harriett JACOBS – Head – Widow – b. 1844 Bloomsbury – aged 57
Maria JACOBS – Daughter – b. 1872 Aldgate – aged 29
Frances JACOBS – Daughter – b. 1882 Aldgate – aged 19 – Tailoress
Henry JACOBS – Son – b. 1884 Aldgate – aged 17 – Pianoforte Maker
Philip ABRAHAMS – Son-in-law – b. 1864 Coventry – aged 37 – Pianoforte Maker
Leah ABRAHAMS – Mother-in-law – Widow – b. 1820 London – aged 81
Esther ABRAHAMS – Daughter – b. 1878 London – aged 32 – Tailoress
Esther WEINBAUM – Visitor – b. 1856 London – aged 45 – Mantle Maker
Nellie AARONS – Visitor – b. 1882 London – aged 19 – Typist

Death:

Harriet JACOBS – Q2 1910 [66] CAMBERWELL 1d 386
Buried at Plashet Cemetery – I-17-18 on 17 May 1910.

Jewish Chronicle – 20 May 1910

JACOBS – On the 15th of May, at her daughters, Maria and Mrs Phoebe Rosenbaum's residence, 53, Station Road, Camberwell; Harriett Jacobs, of 5, Hutchinson Street, Aldgate, beloved wife of the late Joseph Jacobs, who after a short illness, passed peacefully away in her 67th year. Deeply mourned by her sorrowing sons and daughters, Esther, John, Maria, George, Phoebe, Rachel, Francis and Henry, brother, Harty Hart, sons and daughters-in-law, grandchildren, and a large circle of friends. May her dear soul rest in peace. Shiva at above address, also Mrs Esther Benjamin at her address, 96, Bridge Street, Burdett Road; John, at his residence, 23, Rectory Square, Stepney; George and Mrs Rachel Levy, at her residence, 11, Rathbone Street, Canning Town; Henry and Mrs Francis Silver, at 53, Station Road, Camberwell. American papers please copy.

JACOBS, Polly – D-21-1

Died: **07/05/1900**
Buried: **09/05/1900**
Hebrew Name: **Miriam bat Michael**
Partner: **Solomon Jacobs (d. 1899)**
Age: **70 years**

Jewish Chronicle – 11 May 1900

JACOBS – On the 7th of May, at 14, Louisa Street, Mile End, Polly, aged 70, the relict of the late Solomon Jacobs, formerly of Cobb's Yard, the beloved mother of Barnett Jacobs, of 19, Court Street, Whitechapel; Michael Jacobs, of 156, Brunswick Buildings, Goulston Street, E.; John Jacobs, of Melbourne; Mrs Alf.

JACOBS, Polly – D-21-1

פ"ט
מ' מרים בת מיכאל
אלמנת שלמה בר ברוך
נפטרה ח' אייר תר"ס ל'
ת'נ'צ'ב'ה

In Memory
of
POLLY,
WIDOW OF
SOLOMON JACOBS,
WHO DEPARTED THIS LIFE
MAY 7TH 1900, IVAR 8TH 5660,
AGED 70.
BENEATH THIS STONE IN DEATH'S COLD ARMS RECLINED.

Pollock, of 81, Whitehorse Lane, Mile End; and Mrs I. Marks, 91, Leather Lane, Holborn; Miss Sophia, Angel Jacobs, and sister of Mrs Lewis Isaacs, 288, Mile End Road. Deeply lamented by her sorrowing children, grandchildren, brothers, sisters, and a large circle of friends. May her dear soul rest in peace. Australian and Cape papers please copy.
JACOBS – On the 7th of May, at 14, Louisa Street, Beaumont Street, Mile End, Polly, relict of the late Sol Jacobs and sister of Dave Jones, 58, Southboro' Road and Solomon Jones, 92 Lauriston Road, South Hackney. God rest her dear soul in peace. Shiva at 92, Lauriston Road.
JACOBS – On the 7th of May, at 14, Louisa Street, Mile End, Polly, relict of the late Solomon Jacobs, formerly of Cobb's Yard, sister of Mrs Marks, of 16, Carter Street, Cutler Street, Houndsditch. Deeply lamented. May her soul rest in peace. Shiva at Carter Street.

Jewish Chronicle – 29 Jun 1900

The tombstones in memory of the late Solomon (D-16-1) and Polly Jacobs, of 14 Louisa Street, Beaumont Street, E., formerly of Cobb's Yard, Middlesex Street, will be set at Plashet Cemetery, on Sunday next, July 1st, at 4.30. Relatives and friends please accept this, the only intimation.

Death:
Q2 1900 [71] MILE END 1c 293.

1891 Census

Address:
21 Cobbs Yard, Spitalfields, Whitechapel

Residents:
Solomon JACOBS – Head – b. 1833 Spitalfields – aged 58 – General Dealer
Mary JACOBS – Wife – b. 1840 Spitalfields – aged 51
Lizzie JACOBS – Daughter – b. 1864 Spitalfields – aged 27
Sophia JACOBS – Daughter – b. 1868 Spitalfields – aged 23 – Tailoress
Nellie CALDEN – Domestic Servant

1881 Census

Address:
19 Cobbs Court, Spitalfields

Residents:
Solomon JACOBS – Head – b. 1831 Spitalfields – aged 50 – General Dealer
Mary JACOBS – Wife – b. 1830 Spitalfields – aged 51
Kate JACOBS – Daughter – b. 1862 Spitalfields – aged 19 – Tailoress
Elizabeth JACOBS – Daughter – b. 1864 Spitalfields – aged 17 – Feather Maker
Sophia JACOBS – Daughter – b. 1868 Spitalfields – aged 13 – Scholar
Angel JACOBS – Son – b. 1875 Spitalfields – aged 6
Harriett SMITH – Domestic Servant

1871 Census
Address:
19 Cobbs Yard, Christ Church
Residents:
Solomon JACOBS – Head – b. 1834 Aldgate – aged 37 – General Dealer
Mary A. JACOBS – Wife – b. 1833 Spitalfields – aged 38
Barnett JACOBS – Son – b. 1859 Spitalfields – aged 12 – Scholar
Michael JACOBS – Son – b. 1861 Spitalfields – aged 10 – Scholar
Kate JACOBS – Daughter – b. 1862 Spitalfields – aged 9 – Scholar
John JACOBS – Son – b. 1863 Spitalfields – aged 8 – Scholar
Elizabeth JACOBS – Daughter – b. 1864 Spitalfields – aged 7 – Scholar
Sophia JACOBS – Daughter – b. 1868 Spitalfields – aged 3
Harriet JOHNSON – Domestic Servant

1861 Census
Address:
19 Cobbs Yard, Spitalfields
Residents:
Solomon JACOBS – Head – b. 1832 Spitalfields – aged 29 – General Dealer
Mary JACOBS – Wife – b. 1831 Spitalfields – aged 30
Barry/Barnett JACOBS – b. 1859 Spitalfields – aged 2
Michael JACOBS – Son – b. 1860 Spitalfields – aged 1
Mary SAYES – General Servant

Marriage:
Solomon JACOBS to Mary JONES – Q2 1857 LONDON CITY 1c 277.

Death:
Solomon JACOBS – Q3 1899 [67] POPLAR 1c 455.
Buried at Plashet Cemetery – D-16-1 on 31 Aug 1899.

Jewish Chronicle – 01 Sep 1899

JACOBS – On the 29th of August, at his residence, 23, British Street, Bow, Solomon Jacobs, late of 19, Cobb's Yard, Middlesex Street, aged 67, the beloved husband of Polly Jacobs, and father of Sophie and Angel Jacobs, also of Barney Jacobs, of 19, Court Street, Whitechapel, Michael Jacobs, of Brunswick Buildings, Goulston Street, E., Mrs Alfred Pollock, of 81, Whitehorse Lane, Mile End, Mr John Jacobs and Mrs I. Marks, of 91, Leather Lane, Holborn, and brother of Henry and Hannah Jacobs. Deeply mourned by all who knew him. Shiva at above addresses. Australian and Cape papers please copy.

JEWELL, Julian/Jullien – B-7-1

Died: 20 Feb 1900
Buried: 22 Feb 1900
Hebrew Name: Uial bar Moshe
Partner: Kate Jewell (d. 1895)
Aged: 48th year

Jewish Chronicle – 23 Feb 1900

JEWELL – On the 20th of February, at 16, Tenter Street South, Aldgate, Lincolns Inn Fields, W.C., Julian Jewell, aged 48, brother of Mr S. Jewell, 38, Lloyd's Road, Clerkenwell. Mourned by his sorrowing daughters and brothers. Shiva 11, Sheffield Street, W.C.

Jewish Chronicle – 12 Sep 1902

The tombstone to the memory of our dear mother Kate, the wife of the late Jullien Jewell, of Sheffield Street, W.C., will be set at West Ham Cemetery on Sunday, September 21st at 4 o'clock. Also, the tombstone to the memory of our dear father, the late Jullien Jewell of the above address will be set at Plashet Cemetery, September 28th, at 4 o'clock. Relatives and friends kindly accept this, the only intimation.

Death:

Q1 1900 [47] ST. GILES 1b 496.

1891 Census

Address:

26 Kentish Town Road, St. Pancras

Residents:

Jullien JEWELL – Head – b. 1852 London – aged 39 – Waste Paper Dealer
Kate JEWELL – Wife – b. 1857 Whitechapel – aged 34
Sophia JEWELL – Daughter – b. 1882 Bermondsey – aged 9 – Scholar
Rose JEWELL – Daughter – b. 1883 Islington – aged 8 – Scholar

1881 Census

Address:

29 Ber New Road (Bermondsey New Road), Bermondsey

Residents:

Julian JEWELL – b. 1853 Marylebone – aged 28 – Rag Merchant
Kate JEWELL – Wife – b. 1857 Whitechapel – aged 24

Marriage:

Julian JEWELL to Kate BARNETT – Q4 1880 LONDON CITY 1c 184.

JEWELL, Julian/Jullien – B-7-1

Parents:

Julian's parents – Morris & Sophia JEWELL (1871 Census)
Kate's parents – Morris & Rose BARNETT (1871 Census)

Death:

Kate JEWELL – Q2 1895 [38] ST. GILES 1b 330.
Buried at West Ham Cemetery – A-5-11 on 09 May 1895.

KOSKI, Jacob – D-23-27

Died: **19 Nov 1900**
Buried: **21 Nov 1900**
Hebrew Name: **Yakob ben Shmuel**
Partner: **Rachel Koski (d. 1901)**
Age: **56th year**

Jewish Chronicle – 23 Nov 1900

KOSKI – On the 19th of November, corresponding with 27th Heshan, at 2, Hutchison Street, Aldgate, Jacob, the dearly beloved husband of Rachel Koski, in his 56th year. Peacefully went to sleep. Deeply mourned by his sorrowing wife, sons, daughters, grandchildren, and a large circle of friends. Gone from our sight but ever present in our hearts. God rest his soul, Amen. Shiva at 2, Hutchison Street, Aldgate.
KOSKI – On the 19th of November, at 2, Hutchison Street, Aldgate, after a short illness, Jacob Koski, brother of Mr Charles Koski, of 131, Grosvenor Road, Highbury New Park. May his soul rest in peace. Shiva at 131, Grosvenor Road.

Jewish Chronicle – 06 Sep 1901

The tombstone in loving memory of our darling husband and loving father, Jacob Koski, will be set at Plashet on Sunday next, September 8th, at 4 o'clock. Relatives and friends please accept this only intimation.

Death:

Q4 1900 [56] LONDON CITY 1c 4.

1891 Census

Address:

2 Hutchinson Street, Aldgate, London

Residents:

Jacob KOSKI – Head – b. 1843 Russia – aged 48 – Tailor
Rachel KOSKI – Wife – b. 1846 Russia – aged 45
Leah KOSKI – Daughter – b. 1870 Aldgate – aged 21 – Tailoress
Lewis KOSKI – Son – b. 1873 Aldgate – aged 18 – Fruit Dealer

KOSKI, Jacob – D-23-27

Daniel KOSKI – Son – b. 1874 Aldgate – aged 17 – Tailor
Kate KOSKI – Daughter – b. 1876 Aldgate – aged 15 – Scholar
Phillip KOSKI – Son – b. 1878 Aldgate – aged 13 – Scholar
Ada KOSKI – Daughter – b. 1879 Aldgate – aged 12 – Scholar
Charles KOSKI – Son – b. 1881 Aldgate – aged 10 – Scholar

1871 Census

Address:
6 Ebenezer Square, Aldgate, London

Residents:
Jacob KOSKI – Head – b. 1843 Poland – aged 28 – Tailor employing 3 hands
Rachel KOSKI – Wife – b. 1845 Poland – aged 26
Leah KOSKI – Daughter – b. 1871 St. Botolph – aged 0

Marriage:
Jacob KOSKI to Rachael LOBERMAN – Q3 1869 LONDON CITY 1c 181.

1901 Census

Address:
2 Hutchinson Street, St. Botolph Without Aldgate

Residents:
Rachel KOSKI – Head – Widow – b. 1849 Germany – aged 52
Lewis KOSKI – Son – b. 1876 London – aged 25 – Fruit Carman
Philip KOSKI – Son – b. 1879 London – aged 22 – Tailor's Machinist
Charles KOSKI – Son – b. 1881 London – aged 20 – Tailor's Machinist
Ada KOSKI – Daughter – b. 1882 London – aged 19 – Cigarette Maker

Death:
Rachel KOSKI – Q4 1901 [49] LONDON CITY 1c 4.
Buried at Plashet Cemetery – B-20-29 on 22 Dec 1901.

Jewish Chronicle – 27 Dec 1901

KOSKI – On the 20th of December, at 2, Hutchison Street, Aldgate, Rachel, widow of the late Jacob Koski, in her 49th year. Mourned by her sorrowing children and brother. May her dear soul rest in peace. Amen

Jewish Chronicle – 07 Feb 1902

The tombstone in loving memory of our darling mother, Rachel Koski, will be set at Plashet Cemetery, Sunday, February 9th, at 3 o'clock. Relatives and friends accept this intimation.

LEVY, Matilda – B-7-26

Died: 18 Mar 1900
Buried: 20 Mar 1900
Parents: Lewis & Jessie Levy (of Bedford)
Aged: 61 years

Jewish Chronicle – 23 Mar 1900

LEVY – On the 18th of March, Matilda, youngest daughter of the late Lewis and Jessie Levy, of Bedford, and sister of Mrs J.F. Stern and Miss Levy, of 7, Mount Grove Road, Green Lanes, N.

Jewish Chronicle – 22 Jun 1900

The tombstone in memory of the late Matilda Levy, daughter of the late Lewis and Jessie Levy, formerly of Bedford, will be set at the Plashet Cemetery, on Sunday, July 1st, at 12 o'clock. Relatives and friends please accept this, the only intimation.

Death:

Q1 1900 [61] ISLINGTON 1b 327.

1891 Census

Address:

24 Mountgrove Road, Islington, London

Residents:

Matilda LEVY – Niece – Single – b. 1849 Bedford – aged 42 – Companion

1881 Census

Address:

92 Englefield Road, Islington

Residents:

Marko BENTWITCH – Head – b. 1829 Poland – aged 52 – Jeweller
Rosa BENTWITCH – Wife – b. 1828 Bedford – aged 53
Norman J. HERTZBERG – Grandson – b. 1879 London – aged 2
Matilda LEVY – Niece – b. 1849 Bedford – aged 32
Sara Jane WEST – General Servant

1871 Census

Address:

7 Offa Street, St. Peter, Bedford

Residents:

Lewis LEVY – Head – b. 1814 Bedfordshire – aged 57
Jessy LEVY – Wife – b. 1813 Middlesex – aged 58
Catherine LEVY – Daughter – b. 1845 Bedfordshire – aged 26
Matilda LEVY – Daughter – b. 1849 Bedfordshire – aged 22

Jacob STERN – Grandson – b. 1869 Middlesex – aged 2
George LEVYNE – Nephew – b. 1861 United States – aged 10
Eliza JEFFERY – Domestic Servant

1851 Census

Address:
Offa Street, St. Peter Martin, Bedford

Residents:
Lewis LEVY – Head – b. 1814 Bedford – aged 37 – Watch & Clock Maker
Jessy LEVY – Wife – b. 1812 London – aged 39
Betsy LEVY – Daughter – b. 1843 Bedford – aged 8
Catherine LEVY – Daughter – b. 1845 Bedford – aged 6
Matilda LEVY – Daughter – b. 1849 Bedford – aged 2
Godfrey LEVY – Father – Widower – b. 1773 London – aged 78 – Jeweller
Lavina ROSE – Domestic Servant

1841 Census

Address:
Conduit Street, St. Paul, Bedford

Residents:
Godfree LEVY – Head
Lewis LEVY – b. 1816 Bedfordshire – aged 25
Cathrine LEVY – b. 1818 Bedfordshire – aged 23
Frances LEVY – b. 1821 Bedfordshire – aged 20
Jane LEVY – b. 1826 Bedfordshire – aged 15
Sarah LEVY – b. 1827 Bedfordshire – aged 14
Lemul LEVY – b. 1828 Bedfordshire – aged 13

1901 Census

Address:
7 Mountgrove Road, Islington

Residents:
Betsy STERN – Head – Widow – b. 1843 Bedford – aged 58
Katherine LEVY – Sister – b. 1845 Bedford – aged 56
Louis SWITZENER – Boarder – Widower – b. 1813 Germany – aged 88

Death:
Jessy LEVY – Q4 1873 [67] BEDFORD 3b 198.
Lewis LEVY – Q3 1879 [65] WHITECHAPEL 1c 223.

LEWIS, Amelia (Milly) – B-11-48

LEWIS, Amelia (Milly) – B-11-48

Died: 03 Nov 1900
Buried: 05 Nov 1900
Hebrew Name: Malka bat Itzhak
Parents: Charles & Elizabeth Lewis
Aged: 24 years

Jewish Chronicle – 09 Nov 1900

LEWIS – On the 3rd of November, Milly, the only and dearly beloved daughter of Charles and Betsy Lewis, aged 23, of 289, Mile End Road, and fiancée of J. Fineberg, of 45, Gray's Inn Road. Deeply mourned by her sorrowing parents, brothers, fiancée, relatives and a large circle of friends. May her dear soul rest in peace. Amen.

Jewish Chronicle – 19 Jul 1901

The tombstone in loving memory of Amelia, the beloved daughter of Charles and Betsy Lewis, of 289, Mile End Road, will be set on Sunday, the 21st, at Plashet, at 5 p.m. Relatives and friends please accept this, the only intimation.

Death:

Q4 1900 [23] GREENWICH 1d 585.

1891 Census

Address:

3 Clapton High Road, Hackney, South Hackney

Residents:

Charles LEWIS – Head – b. 1844 Yorkshire – aged 47 – Fruiterer & Greengrocer
Elizabeth LEWIS – Wife – b. 1850 Aldgate – aged 41
Amelia LEWIS – Daughter – b. 1877 Shoreditch – aged 14
Louis LEWIS – Son – b. 1879 Shoreditch – aged 12
Barnet LEWIS – Son – b. 188- Shoreditch – aged 11
Mop LEWIS – Son – b. 1881 Shoreditch – aged 10
Joseph LEWIS – Son – b. 1884 Shoreditch – aged 7
Abraham LEWIS – Son – b. 1889 Shoreditch – aged 2
Laura FAGE – General Domestic Servant

1881 Census

Address:

141 East Road, Shoreditch

Residents:

Charles LEWIS – Head – b. 1845 York – aged 36 – Fruiterer
Elizabeth LEWIS – Wife – b. 1853 Whitechapel – aged 28
Amelia LEWIS – Daughter – b. 1877 Hoxton – aged 4

Lewis LEWIS – Son – b. 1879 Hoxton – aged 2
Barnet LEWIS – Son – b. 1880 Hoxton – aged 1
Moss LEWIS – Son – b. 1881 Hoxton – aged 0
Louisa WYATT – Domestic Servant
Rachael HARRIS – Monthly Nurse

1901 Census

Address:

289 Mile End Road, Mile End Old Town

Residents:

Charles LEWIS – Head – b. 1844 London – aged 57 – Fruiterer
Elizabeth LEWIS – Wife – b. 1851 London – aged 50
Louis LEWIS – Son – b. 1879 London – aged 22 – Printing Machine Minder
Barnett LEWIS – Son – b. 1880 London – aged 21 – Hairdresser Assistant
Moss LEWIS – Son – b. 1882 London – aged 19 – Packer
Joseph LEWIS – Son – b. 1884 London – aged 17 – Greengrocer
Abraham LEWIS – Son – b. 1889 London – aged 12
Mark LEWIS – Son – b. 1892 London – aged 9

1911 Census

Address:

96 Clinton Road, Mile End, London E.

Residents:

Louis LEWIS – Head – b. 1879 Shoreditch – aged 32 – Tailor's Cutter
Phoebe LEWIS – Wife (8 years) – b. 1878 London – aged 33
Charles LEWIS – Son – b. 1904 Woolwich – aged 7
John LEWIS – Son – b. 1906 Stepney – aged 5
Charles LEWIS – Father – Widower – b. 1844 York – aged 67 – Retired
Barnett LEWIS – Brother – b. 1879 Shoreditch – aged 32 – Hairdresser
Mark LEWIS – Brother – b. 1892 Clapton – aged 19 – Warehouse Porter
Matilda BAXTER – Domestic Servant
Nelson FRENCH – Boarder – b. 1889 Canterbury – aged 22 – Fitter

Death:

Elizabeth Lewis – Q3 1904 [55] WHITECHAPEL 1c 172.
Buried at Plashet Cemetery – E-20-14 on 22 Jul 1904.

Charles Lewis – Q2 1912 [67] MILE END OLD TOWN 1c 409.
Buried at Plashet Cemetery – N-3-21 on 18 Jun 1912.

LIPMAN, Rachel – B-8-35

Died: 06 May 1900
Buried: 08 May 1900
Partner: Jonas Lipman (d. 1887)
Aged: 81st year

Jewish Chronicle – 11 May 1900

LIPMAN – On the 6th of May, corresponding with the 7th Iyar, at her residence, No. 11, Queen's Block, Houndsditch, Rachel, relict of the late Jonas Lipman, of Bury Street, E.C., in her 81st year. Mother of Mrs B. Isaacs, Mrs S.A. Romain, Mr M. Lipman, Mr. S. Lipman, of Brooklyn, Mr L. Lipman, the late Mrs J.S. Myers, Mr Sol Lipman, and Mrs I. Belasco. Deeply mourned by her sorrowing children, grandchildren, relations and friends. God rest her soul in peace. Amen. American and Cape papers please copy.

Jewish Chronicle – 28 Dec 1900

The tombstone in affectionate memory of the late Rachel Lipman, late of 7, Bury Street, St, Mary Axe, will be set at Plashet on Sunday, December 30th, at two p.m. Relatives and friends please accept this, the only intimation.

Death:

Q2 1900 [80] LONDON CITY 1c 2.

1891 Census

Address:

7 Bury Street, St. Katherine Cree, London

Residents:

Rachel LIPMAN – Head – Widow – b. 1821 – aged 70 – Living on own means
Esther LIPMAN – Daughter – b. 1866 London – aged 25 – Feather Business

1881 Census

Address:

7 Bury Street, St. Katherine Cree

Residents:

Jonas LIPMAN – Head – b. 1826 Middlesex – aged 55 – General Dealer
Rachel LIPMAN – Wife – b. 1823 Middlesex – aged 58
Elizabeth LIPMAN – Daughter – b. 1853 Middlesex – aged 28
Lewis LIPMAN – Son – b. 1861 Middlesex – aged 20 – General Dealer
Rosey LIPMAN – Daughter – b. 1862 London – aged 19 – Fruit Shop Worker
Solomon LIPMAN – Son – b. 1864 London – aged 17 – General Dealer
Esther LIPMAN – Daughter – b. 1866 London – aged 15 – Apprentice Feather Curler
Ann HURLEY – General Domestic Servant

LIPMAN, Rachel – B-8-35

1871 Census

Address:

2 King Street, St. James Dukes Place, London

Residents:

Jonas LIPMAN – Head – b. 1826 Middlesex – aged 45 – Orange Merchant
Rachel LIPMAN – Wife – b. 1826 Middlesex – aged 45
Betsy LIPMAN – Daughter – b. 1853 Middlesex – aged 18
Michael LIPMAN – Son – b. 1855 Middlesex – aged 16
Mary LIPMAN – Daughter – b. 1856 Middlesex – aged 15
Samuel LIPMAN – Son – b. 1858 London – aged 13
Barnet LIPMAN – Son – b. 1859 London – aged 12 (d. 16/02/1876)
Rosetta LIPMAN – Daughter – b. 1860 London – aged 11
Lewis LIPMAN – Son – b. 1861 London – aged 10
Soloman LIPMAN – Son – b. 1863 London – aged 8
Esther LIPMAN – Daughter – b. 1865 London – aged 6
Anna LAWSON – Domestic Servant

1861 Census

Address:

13 Ebenezer Square, St. Botolph Aldgate, City of London

Residents:

Jonas LIPMAN – Head – b. 1825 Whitechapel – aged 36 – Fruiterer
Rachel LIPMAN – Wife – b. 1825 Whitechapel – aged 36 – General Dealer
Elizabeth LIPMAN – Daughter – b. 1852 Aldgate – aged 9 - Scholar
Mary LIPMAN – Daughter – b. 1853 Aldgate – aged 8 – Scholar
Michael LIPMAN – Son – b. 1857 Aldgate – aged 4 – Scholar
Samuel LIPMAN – Son – b. 1858 Aldgate – aged 3 – Scholar
Barnet LIPMAN – Son – b. 1859 Aldgate – aged 2
Rosetta LIPMAN – Daughter – b. 1860 Aldgate – aged 1

1851 Census

Address:

13 Ebenezer Square, St. Botolph Aldgate, London

Residents:

Jonas LIPMAN – Head – b. 1827 Spitalfields – aged 24 – General Dealer
Rachel LIPMAN – Wife – b. 1828 Aldgate – aged 23 – General Dealer
Sarah LIPMAN – Daughter – b. 1861 Aldgate – aged 3 months
Mary MURPHY – Domestic Servant

Marriage:

Jonas LIPMAN to Rachael JACOBS – Q3 1849 LONDON CITY 2 201.

Death:

Jonas LIPMAN – Q1 1887 [62] LONDON CITY 1c 43.
Place of burial unknown.

Jewish Chronicle – 14 Jan 1887

On the 10th of January, at his residence, 7, Bury Street, St. Mary Axe, E.C. Jonas Lipman, aged 62. May his soul rest in peace. Cape and American papers please copy.

MARKS, Esther – D-19-4

Died: **13 Feb 1900**
Buried: **15 Feb 1900**
Hebrew Name: **Ester bat Avraham**
Parents: **Solomon Marks (d. 1918)**
Age: **59th year**

Jewish Chronicle – 16 Feb 1900

MARKS – On the 13th of February, at 242, Pentonville Road, King's Cross, Esther, the dearly beloved wife of Solomon Marks, in her 59th year, mother of Harry Marks, 175, High Road, Kilburn, Mrs Sam Myers, 136, Bridge Street, Burdett Road, E., Mrs R. Silverston, 75, Kennington Park Road, S.E., Mrs Jack

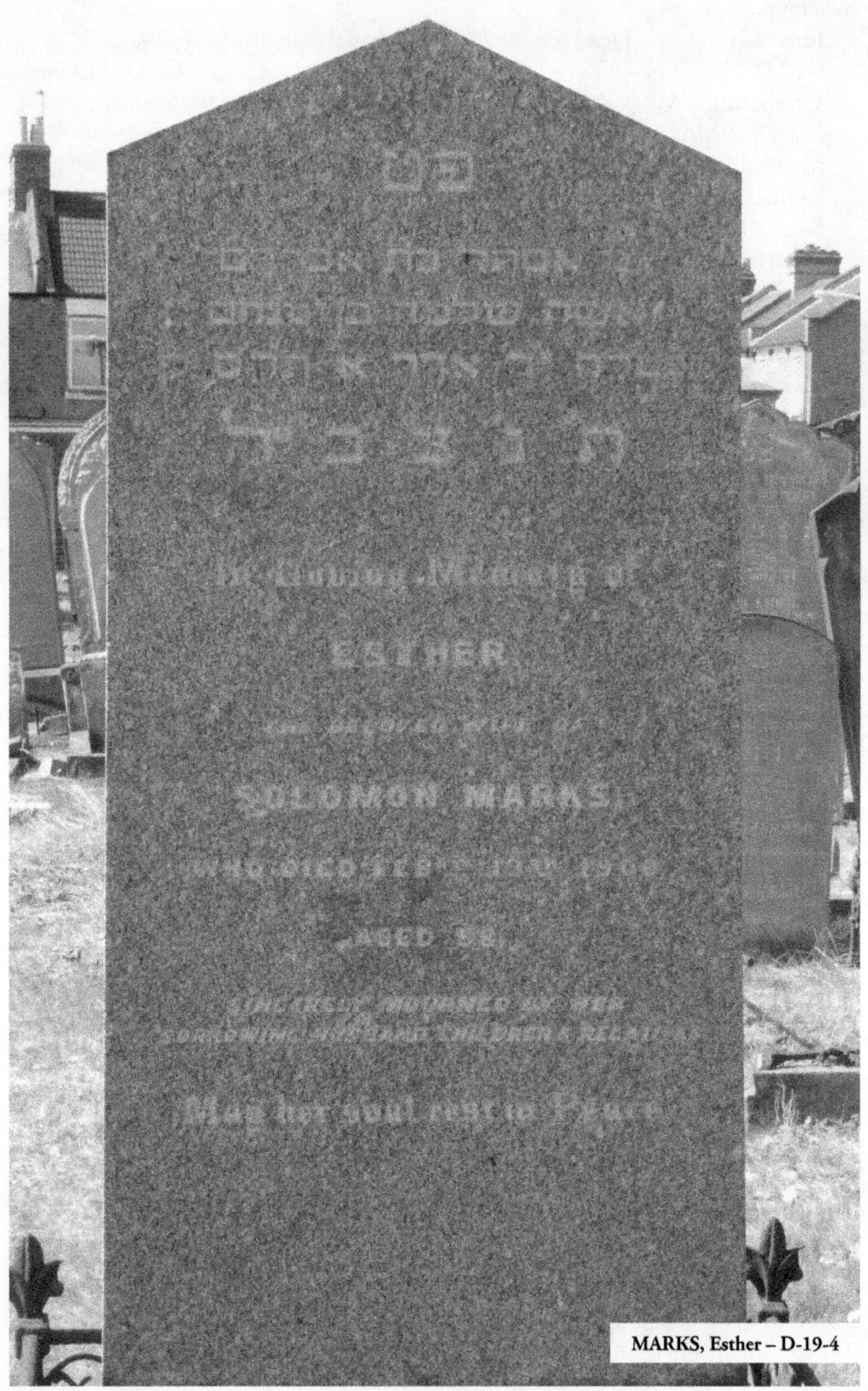

MARKS, Esther – D-19-4

Cohen, 4, Evelyn Street, Deptford, S.E., and Maurice Marks, 17, Steedman Street, Walworth, S.E. Shiva at 242, Pentonville Road. May her dear soul rest in peace. MARKS – On the 13th of February, at 242, Pentonville Road, King's Cross, Esther Marks, the dearly beloved sister of Isaac Abrahams, 136, Whitechapel Road, E., Miss Abrahams, 37, Shore Road, South Hackney, and Mrs Z. Cohen, 3, Turners Road, Burdett Road, E. Shiva at 136, Whitechapel Road.

Jewish Chronicle – 15 Jun 1900

The tombstone in memory of Esther, the dearly-beloved wife of S. Marks, 242, Pentonville Road, King's Cross, N., will be set at Plashet, Sunday next, June 17th at 12 o'clock. Relatives and friends please accept this, the only intimation.

Death:

Q1 1900 [58] HOLBORN 1b 570.

1891 Census

Address:

237 Boro High Street (Borough High Street), Newington, London

Residents:

Solomon MARKS – Head – b. 1839 Couben Poland – aged 52 – Clothier
Esther MARKS – Wife – b. 1842 London – aged 49
Julia MARKS – Daughter – b. 1872 London – aged 19
Ray MARKS – Daughter – b. 1873 London – aged 18
Harry MARKS – Son – b. 1874 Spitalfields – aged 17 – Tailors Assistant
Samuel MARKS – Son – b. 1875 Spitalfields – aged 16 – Tailors Cashier
Morris MARKS – Son – b. 1878 Spitalfields – aged 13 – Scholar
Dora MARKS – Daughter – b. 1880 Spitalfields – aged 11 – Scholar

1881 Census

Address:

8 Church Street, Spitalfields

Residents:

Solomon MARKS – Head – b. 1841 Poland – aged 40 – Tailor employing 48 hands
Esther MARKS – Wife – b. 1842 London – aged 39
Abraham MARKS – Son – b. 1866 Spitalfields – aged 15 – Apprentice Tailor
Rose MARKS – Daughter – b. 1868 Spitalfields – aged 13 – Scholar
Amelia MARKS – Daughter – b. 1870 Spitalfields – aged 11 – Scholar
Julia MARKS – Daughter – b. 1871 Spitalfields – aged 10 – Scholar
Rachel MARKS – Daughter – b. 1873 Spitalfields – aged 8 – Scholar
Harry MARKS – Son – b. 1874 Spitalfields – aged 7 – Scholar
Samuel MARKS – Son – b. 1876 Spitalfields – aged 5 – Scholar
Morris MARKS – Son – b. 1878 Spitalfields – aged 3
Dora MARKS – Daughter – b. 1880 Spitalfields – aged 1

Mary COLLINS – Nursemaid / Domestic Servant
Margaret PALMER – Housemaid / Domestic Servant

1871 Census

Address:

134 Commercial Street, Christ Church Spitalfields

Residents:

Solomon MARKS – Head – b. 1841 Russian Poland – aged 30 – Tailor
Esther MARKS – Wife – b. 1842 London – aged 29
Abraham MARKS – Son – b. 1866 London – aged 5 – Scholar
Rose MARKS – Daughter – b. 1868 London – aged 3
Amelie MARKS – Daughter – b. 1870 London – aged 1
Julia MARKS – Daughter – b. 1871 London – aged 0

Marriage:

Solomon MARKS to Esther ABRAHAMS - Q2 1865 LONDON CITY 1c 252.

1901 Census

Address:

242 Pentonville Road, Islington

Residents:

Solomon MARKS – Head – Widower – b. 1841 Poland – aged 60 – Tailor & Outfitter
Julia MARKS – Daughter – b. 1871 Spitalfields – aged 30
Samuel MARKS – Son – b. 1876 Spitalfields – aged 25 – Tailors Assistant
Dora MARKS – Daughter – b. 1880 Spitalfields – aged 21
Theresa – Domestic Servant

1911 Census

Address:

40 Grafton Road, Holloway, London N.

Residents:

Solomon MARKS – Head – Widower – b. 1841 Konin Poland – aged 70 – Tailor
Julia MARKS – Daughter – b. 1871 Spitalfields – aged 40
Dora MARKS – Daughter – b. 1880 Spitalfields – aged 31 – Bookkeeper

Death:

Solomon MARKS – Q2 1918 [78] ISLINGTON 1b 259.
Buried at Willesden Cemetery – BX-11-8 on 11 Jun 1918.

Jewish Chronicle – 14 Jun 1918

MARKS – On the 9th of June, at 40, Grafton Road, Holloway, N., Solomon

Marks, in his 79th year, the beloved father of Julia, Ray, Samuel, Dora and Morris. Deeply mourned.
MARKS – On the 9th of June, at 40, Grafton Road, Holloway, N., Solomon Marks, beloved father of Harry Marks, 48, Plympton Road, Brondesbury, N.W.6, and 9, Westbury Road, Watford (temporary address). Deeply mourned.
MARKS – On the 9th of June, at 40, Grafton Road, Holloway, N., Solomon Marks, beloved father of Rose Myers, 45, King Edward Road, Hackney and 2, Upper Lattimore Road, St. Albans (temporary address). Deeply mourned.

MILCH, Rudolf – B-12-48

Died: 21 Dec 1900
Buried: 25 Dec 1900
Partner: Fanny Milch (d. 1928)
Aged: 42 years

Jewish Chronicle – 28 Dec 1900

MILCH – On the 21st of December, at Marazion Hotel, Cornwall, Rudolf Milch, beloved husband of Fanny Milch, of 89, Petherton Road, Canonbury, London N., aged 42 years. Deeply mourned by his dear wife, children and family, and respected by all who knew him.

Jewish Chronicle – 06 Sep 1901

The tombstone in loving memory of the late Rudolf Milch, of 89, Petherton Road, Canonbury, will be set at Plashet Cemetery on Sunday next, 8th of September, at 3 o'clock. Relatives and friends please accept this, the only intimation.

Death:
Q4 1900 [42] PENZANCE 5c 146.

1901 Census

Address:
89 Petherton Road, Islington

Residents:
Fanny MILCH – Head – Widow – b. 1858 Whitechapel – aged 43 – Living on Own Means
Bessie MILCH – Daughter – b. 1896 Highbury – aged 5
Flora MILCH – Daughter – b. 1898 Highbury – aged 3
Morris MILCH – Son – b. 1900 Highbury – aged 1 year, 6 months
Blanche TOWEY – Domestic Servant

MILCH, Rudolf – B-12-48

Marriage:

Rudolph MILCH to Fanny LEK – Q2 1892 LONDON CITY 1c 115.

Marriage:

Fanny MILCH to Samuel GLUCKSTEIN – Q3 1907 ISLINGTON 1b 729

1911 Census

Address:

89 Leconfield Road, Highbury N.

Residents:

Samuel GLUCKSTEIN – Head – b. 1869 Mile End – aged 42 – Surveyors Clerk/Draftsman
Fanny GLUCKSTEIN – Wife (4 years) – b. 1861 Mile End – aged 50
Bessie MILCH – Step-daughter – b. 1896 Mile End – aged 15
Florence MILCH – Step-daughter – b. 1898 Mile End – aged 13
Morris MILCH – Step-son – b. 1900 Mile End – aged 11

Death:

Fanny GLUCKSTEIN – Q1 1928 [70] ISLINGTON 1b 204.
Buried at East Ham Jewish Cemetery – W-8-53 on 11 Jan 1928.

MOSES, Montague Henry – D-19-13

Died: 05 Feb 1900
Buried: 18 Feb 1900
Hebrew Name: Moshe ben Zvi
Partner: Caroline Moses (d. 1919)
Age: 65 years

Jewish Chronicle – 23 Feb 1900

MOSES – On the 15th of February, at 125, Petherton Road, Canonbury, after a long and painful illness, Montague Henry Moses, aged 65. May his dear soul rest in peace.
MOSES – On the 15th of February, at 125, Petherton Road, N. Montague H. Moses, brother of Sylvester Moses, of 44, Priory Road, N.W. Deeply lamented.

Jewish Chronicle – 24 Aug 1900

The tombstone in loving memory of our dear husband and father, the late Montague Henry Moses, will be set on Sunday next, August 26th, at Plashet Cemetery, at 4 o'clock – 125 Petherton Road, N.

MOSES, Montague Henry – D-19-13

Death:

Q1 1900 [65] POPLAR 1c 434 [Jehoiada Moses].

1891 Census

Address:

36 Houndsditch, Aldgate, London

Residents:

Montague H. MOSES – Head – b. 1841 London – aged 50 – Clothier
Caroline MOSES – Wife – b. 1846 London – aged 45
Henry B. MOSES – Son – b. 1866 London – aged 25 – Clothiers Salesman
Celia MOSES – Daughter – b. 1868 London – aged 23
Alfred C. MOSES – Son – b. 1872 London – aged 19 – Clothiers Salesman
Sydney B. MOSES – Son – b. 1871 London – aged 20 – Clothiers Cutter
Louise MOSES – Daughter – b. 1875 London – aged 16 – Scholar
Moss MOSES – Son – b. 1876 London – aged 15 – Scholar
Theresa E. MOSES – Daughter – b. 1879 London – aged 12 – Scholar
Annie ROONEY – General Servant

1881 Census

Address:

36 Houndsditch, St. Botolph Without Aldgate

Residents:

Montague H. MOSES – Head – b. 1838 London – aged 43 – Clothier
Caroline MOSES – Wife – b. 1846 London – aged 35
Celia MOSES – Daughter – b. 1868 London – aged 13
Sydney Joseph MOSES – Son – b. 1870 London – aged 11
Alfred Charles MOSES – Son – b. 1872 London – aged 9
Leopold Jonas MOSES – Son – b. 1873 London – aged 8
Evelyn Florata MOSES – Daughter – b. 1874 London – aged 7
Louise Rosalind MOSES – Daughter – b. 1875 London – aged 6
Moss MOSES – Son – b. 1877 London – aged 4
Theresa Ethel MOSES – Daughter – b. 1878 – aged 3
Julia BARNES – Domestic Servant

1871 Census

Address:

36 Houndsditch, Aldgate, London

Residents:

Montague H. MOSES – Head – b. 1836 Middlesex – aged 35
Caroline MOSES – Wife – b. 1845 London – aged 26
Henry B. MOSES – Son – b. 1866 London – aged 5
Alexander J. MOSES – Son – b. 1867 London – aged 4

Celia MOSES – Daughter – b. 1868 London – aged 3
Sidney B. MOSES – Son – b. 1870 London – aged 1
Alfred C. MOSES – Son – b. 1871 Middlesex – aged 0
Julia SAUNDERS – Servant
Elizabeth SAUNDERS – Servant
Anne SMITH – Servant

Marriage:

Montague Henry MOSES to Caroline WOOLF – Q3 1864 LONDON CITY 1c 233.

Death:

Caroline MOSES – Q3 1919 [74] PADDINGTON 1a 6.
Buried at Plashet Cemetery – L-3-20 on 22 Jul 1919.

Jewish Chronicle – 25 Jul 1919

MOSES (MORTON) – On the 19th of July, at 102, Elgin Avenue, Maida Vale, Caroline, relict of the late Montague Henry Moses, and dearly beloved mother of Celia Morton, Alfred Morton, and Theresa Stygall. God rest her dear soul.

MYERS, Rose – B-10-32

Died: **03 Sep 1900**
Buried: **04 Sep 1900**
Partner: **Philip Myers (d. 1910)**
Aged: **44 years**

Jewish Chronicle – 07 Sep 1900

MYERS – On the 3rd of September, at 14, Lincoln Street, Bow, Rose, the dearly beloved wife of Phil Myers, aged 44, and daughter of Lewis Levy, of 24, Rutland Street. Deeply mourned by her sorrowing husband, children, father, brother, and sisters. May her dear soul rest in peace.

MYERS – On the 3rd of September, at 14, Lincoln Street, Bow, Rose, beloved wife of Philip Myers, aged 44. Deeply mourned by her sorrowing husband, children, and friends. May her soul rest in peace.

MYERS – On the 3rd of September, at 14, Lincoln Street, Bow, Rose Myers, the dearly beloved sister of Mrs H. Cooper, of 43, Colvestone Crescent, Dalston, and Mrs H. Levy, of 54, Sandringham Road, Dalston. May her dear soul rest in peace.

Jewish Chronicle – 11 Oct 1901

The tombstones in loving memory of the late Louis Levy (B-14-29), of the "Sir Walter Raleigh", New Street, Houndsditch, and his wife, Sophia (A-13-68), also his daughter, Mrs Rose Myers, will be set on Sunday, the 13th of October, at 3 o'clock, at Plashet Cemetery. Relatives and friends kindly accept this invitation – 7, Station Road, Leyton.

Death:

Q3 1900 [44] MILE END OLD TOWN 1c 344.

1891 Census

Address:

171 Mile End Road, Mile End Old Town

Residents:

Phillip MYERS – Head – b. 1841 Borough – aged 50 – Traveller
Rose MYERS – Wife – b. 1856 Houndsditch – aged 35 – Tobacconist
Sarah MYERS – Daughter – b. 1867 Aldgate – aged 24 – Cigar Maker
Bella MYERS – Daughter – b. 1877 Mile End – aged 14 – Cigar Maker
Lewis MYERS – Son – b. 1885 Mile End – aged 6
Samuel MYERS – Son – b. 1887 Mile End – aged 4
Edward MYERS – Son – b. 1889 Mile End – aged 2
Susan MYERS – Daughter – b. 1891 Mile End – aged 3 months
Jessy MAY – Domestic Servant

1881 Census

Address:

66 Stepney Green, Mile End Old Town

Residents:

Philip MYERS – Head – b. 1841 Bermondsey – aged 40 – Commercial Traveller
Rebecca MYERS – Wife – b. 1842 Aldgate – aged 39
Kate MYERS – Daughter – b. 1860 Mile End – aged 21 – Tailoress
Rebecca MYERS – Daughter – b. 1862 Hoxton – aged 19 – Sewing Machinist
Judah MYERS – Son – b. 1864 Aldgate – aged 17 – Fruiterer
Abraham MYERS – Son – b. 1866 Aldgate – aged 15 – Fishmonger
Sarah MYERS – Daughter – b. 1868 Aldgate – aged 13 – Scholar
Solomon MYERS – Son – b. 1869 St. Lukes – aged 12 – Scholar
Betty MYERS – Daughter – b. 1876 Mile End – aged 5 – Scholar
Moses MYERS – Son – b. 1880 Mile End – aged 1
Elizabeth ISRAEL – Mother-in-law – Widow – b. 1817 Aldgate – aged 64
Elizabeth GUEST – Domestic Servant

1871 Census

Address:

146 Jubilee Street, Mile End Old Town

Residents:

Phillip MYERS – Head – b. 1841 Surrey – aged 30 – Traveller
Rebecca MYERS – Wife – b. 1843 Middlesex – aged 28
Kate MYERS – Daughter – b. 1861 Middlesex – aged 10
Rebecca MYERS – Daughter – b. 1863 Middlesex – aged 8
Judah MYERS – Son – b. 1864 Middlesex – aged 7
Abraham MYERS – Son – b. 1866 Middlesex – aged 5
Sarah MYERS – Daughter – b. 1867 Middlesex – aged 4
Solomon MYERS – Son – b. 1869 Middlesex – aged 2
Emily COBBINS – Domestic Servant

Marriage:

Phillip MYERS to Rose LEVY – Q2 1884 LONDON CITY 1c 128.

Phillip MYERS to Rebecca ISRAEL – Q4 1860 LONDON CITY 1c 265.

Death:

Rebecca MYERS – Q2 1881 [39] MILE END OLD TOWN 1c 379.
Burial place unknown.

Philip MYERS – Q4 1910 [69] WHITECHAPEL 1c 179.
Buried at Plashet Cemetery – J-21-39 on 02 Dec 1910.

Jewish Chronicle – 02 Dec 1910

MYERS – On the 30th of November, Phillip Myers, in his 70th year, of 31, Merchant Street, Bow. Dearly beloved father of Mrs M. Gompertz, 95, High Street, Stoke Newington; Mrs G. Bendon, 47, Flaxman Road, Camberwell; Mrs A. Jacobs, 75, Napier Road, Stratford. Deeply mourned by his loving daughters. May his soul rest in peace. Shiva at above addresses.

MYERS – On the 30th of November, at the London Hospital, Phillip Myers, in his 70th year, the beloved father of Mrs Michael E. Crabe, of 58, King Edward Road, and Susan Myers, of 18 Graham Mansions. Shiva at King Edward Road.

MYERS – On the 30th of November, Philip Myers, in his 70th year, of 31, Merchant Street, Bow, dearly beloved father of Jim Myers, 99, Lower Kennington Lane; Alf Myers, 11, Florestan Street, Mile End; Sol. Myers, 37, Drury Lane, W.C.; Moss Myers, 231, Navarino Mansions, Dalston; Lew Myers, 18, Graham Mansions, Graham Road, Dalston; Sam Myers, 31, Merchant Street, Bow; Edward Myers, 18, North Block, Stoney Lane, Houndsditch. Deeply mourned by his loving sons. May his soul rest in peace. Shiva at above addresses.

PARKER, Rachel Ada – D-22-6

Died: 29 Aug 1900
Buried: 31 Aug 1900
Partner: Henry Solomon Parker (d. 1911)
Aged: 48 years

Jewish Chronicle – 31 Aug 1900

PARKER – On the 29th of August, at Sandford House, 317, Green Lanes, N., Ada, the dearly beloved wife of Henry Solomon Parker (late of "The Swan", Islington). Deeply mourned by her sorrowing husband, daughter and sister, and a large circle of friends. May her dear soul rest in peace. Funeral leaves above address 2 o'clock to-day (Friday).

Death:
Q3 1900 [48] EDMONTON 3a 199.

1891 Census

Address:
3 Bow Road, Bow OR Stratford Le Bow, Bow & Bromley the Tower Hamlets

Residents:
Henry S. PARKER – Head – b. 1854 Spitalfields – aged 37 – Boot Maker
Ada R. PARKER – Wife – b. 1854 Spitalfields – aged 37
Jane PARKER – Daughter – b. 1887 Spitalfields – aged 4
Jane BAYLISS – Domestic Servant

Marriage:
Henry Solomon PARKER to Ada Rachel ABRAHAMS – Q3 1885 LONDON C 1c 168.

1901 census

Address:
317 Green Lanes, Stoke Newington

Residents:
Henry S. PARKER – Head – b. 1854 Hackney – aged 47 – Living on own Means
Isaac S. PARKER – Father – b. 1826 Bermondsey – aged 75
Sarah PARKER – Mother – b. 1833 Bermondsey – aged 68
Elizabeth PARKER – Sister-in-Law – b. 1861 Bermondsey – aged 40
Emma HART – General Domestic Servant
Alice LONG – General Domestic Servant

PARKER, Rachel Ada – D-22-6

1911 Census

Address:
26 West Street, Brighton

Residents:
Henry S. PARKER – Head – b. 1854 London – aged 57 – Private Means
Elizabeth PARKER – Wife (2 years) – b. 1860 London – aged 51
Solomon CROOK – Son-in-law – b. 1891 London – aged 20 – Tailor
Jennie CROOK – Daughter – b. 1887 London – aged 24
Henry CROOK – Grandson-in-law – b. 1911 Brighton – aged 0
Nellie FORD – Domestic Servant

Death:
Henry S. PARKER – Q4 1911 [57] BRIGHTON 2b 294.
Buried at Plashet Cemetery – D-22-7 on 19 Dec 1911.

Jewish Chronicle – 22 Dec 1911

PARKER – On the 16th of December, at 26, West Street, Brighton, after a very short illness, Harry, the devoted husband of Lizzie, father of Mrs S. Crook, in his 58th year. Deeply mourned by his sorrowing wife, daughter, son-in-law and grandchild. Shiva at above address. American papers please copy.
PARKER – On the 16th of December, at Brighton, Harry, brother of Coley Parker, of 15, Kyverdale Road, Stoke Newington, where Shiva is observed.
PARKER – On December the 16th, at 26, West Street, Brighton, Harry, the beloved brother of Mrs J. Goldstein. Deeply mourned by his sorrowing sister, brother-in-law and aunt Polly. Shiva at 46, Russell Square, Brighton.
PARKER – On Saturday, December 16th, Harry S. Parker, of 25, West Street, Brighton, brother of Mike Parker. God rest his soul. Shiva at "The Two Brothers", New Road, Battersea, S.W.

PHILLIPS, Abigail – D-18-22

Died:	**07 Jan 1900**
Buried:	**09 Jan 1900**
Parents:	**Isaiah/Isaac Phillips (d. 1929)**
Age:	45 years

Jewish Chronicle – 12 Jan 1900

PHILLIPS – On Sunday, the 7th of January, at 13, Bell Lane, Spitalfields, Abigail, wife of Isaiah Phillips, daughter of the late Mr and Mrs James Phillips, of 20, Sandy's Row, aged 45. May her soul rest in peace.
PHILLIPS – On Sunday, the 7th of January, at 13, Bell Lane, Spitalfields, Abigail Phillips, aged 45, sister of Mr H.J. Phillips, 10, St. Petersburgh Place, Mr E.J. and

Mr P.J. Phillips, 39, Pembridge Road, Mrs J. Lelyveld, 29, Pembridge Road, and Mrs H. Goldstein, 62, Victoria Park Road. May her soul rest in peace.

Jewish Chronicle – 09 Feb 1900

The tombstone in memory of the late Abigail Phillips, of 13, Bell Lane, Spitalfields, will be set at Plashet Cemetery on Sunday, the 11th inst., at 3.30 o'clock. A train will leave Liverpool Street for Manor Park at 2.52.

Death:

Q1 1900 [45] WHITECHAPEL 1c 204.

1891 Census

Address:

13 Bell Lane, Spitalfields, London

Residents:

Isaac PHILLIPS – Head – b. 1853 Spitalfields – aged 38 – Confectioner
Abigail PHILLIPS – Wife – b. 1854 Southwark – aged 37
Julia PHILLIPS – Daughter – b. 1880 London – aged 11 – Scholar
James PHILLIPS – Son – b. 1882 London – aged 9 – Scholar
Sarah PHILLIPS – Daughter – b. 1884 London – aged 7 – Scholar
Annie BIGGS – Domestic Servant

1881 Census

Address:

13 Bell Lane, Spitalfields

Residents:

Isaiah / Isaac PHILLIPS – Head – b. 1853 Middlesex – aged 28 – Pastry Cook
Abigail PHILLIPS – Wife – b. 1854 Southwark – aged 27
Julia PHILLIPS – Daughter – b. 1879 Middlesex – aged 2

Marriage:

Isaiah PHILLIPS to Abigail PHILLIPS – Q3 1878 LONDON CITY 1c 175.

1871 Census

Address:

Sandy's Row, Christ Church, Spitalfields

Residents:

James PHILLIPS – Head – b. 1825 Newington – aged 46 – Broker / General Dealer
Sarah PHILLIPS – Wife – b. 1831 Westminster – aged 40
Humphrey PHILLIPS – Son – b. 1852 Southwark – aged 19 – Warehouseman
Abigail PHILLIPS – Daughter – b. 1854 Southwark – aged 17 – Pupil Teacher
Elizabeth PHILLIPS – Daughter – b. 1859 Southwark – aged 12 – Dressmaker
Edward PHILLIPS – Son – b. 1863 Artillery Ground – aged 8 – Scholar

PHILLIPS, Abigail – D-18-22

Phillip PHILLIPS – Son – b. 1866 Artillery Ground – aged 5 – Scholar
Ella PHILLIPS – Daughter – b. 1869 Spitalfields – aged 2
Mary Ann PHILLIPS – Daughter – b. 1871 Spitalfields – aged 0
Elizabeth HODGES – Domestic Servant

1911 Census

Address:

4 Mount Street, Whitechapel, London E.

Residents:

Isaiah PHILLIPS – Head – Widower – b. 1852 Whitechapel – aged 59 – Journeyman Baker
James Isaac PHILLIPS – Son – b. 1882 Whitechapel – aged 29 – Market Porter

Death:

Isaiah PHILLIPS – Q4 1929 [77] BETHNAL GREEN 1c 134.
Buried at East Ham Cemetery – Z-6-37 on 26 Nov 1929.

POSNER, Julia – B-8-25

Died: 01 May 1900
Buried: 04 May 1900
Partner: Benjamin Posner (d. 1903)
Aged: 32 years

Jewish Chronicle – 04 May 1900

POSENER – On the 1st of May, Julia, the beloved wife of Ben Posener, of 10, Edward Street, St. Peter's Road, and beloved sister of Hyam, Mark and Mick Goldstein, of Cape Town, and sister of the Misses Goldstein. Shiva at 128, Jamaica Street, Stepney. May her dear soul rest in peace.

Jewish Chronicle – 31 Aug 1900

The tombstone in memory of the late Mrs B. Posner, will be set at Plashet, on Sunday, September 2nd, at 4 p.m.

Death:
Q2 1900 [32] BARNET 3a 166.

1891 Census

Address:
51 Hackney Road, Shoreditch, London

Residents:
Benjamin POSNER – Head – b. 1861 Poland – aged 30 – Cigarette Maker
Julia POSNER – Wife – b. 1868 Shoreditch – aged 23
Percy POSNER – Son – b. 1889 Shoreditch – aged 2
Alfred POSNER – Son – b. 1890 Lewisham – aged 1
Maria POSNER – Daughter – b. 1891 Shoreditch – aged 1 month

1871 Census

Address:
Scarborough Street, Whitechapel

Residents:
Abraham GOLDSTEIN – Head – b. 1840 Poland – aged 31
Maria GOLDSTEIN – Wife – b. 1841 Middlesex – aged 30
Julia GOLDSTEIN – Daughter – b. 1868 Middlesex – aged 3
Hyman GOLDSTEIN – Son – b. 1871 Middlesex – aged 0
Eliza KING – Domestic Servant

Marriage:
Benjamin POSNER to Julia GOLDSTEIN – Q1 1888 LONDON CITY 1c 82.

1901 Census

Address:

10 Edward Street, Mile End Old Town

Residents:

Benjamin POSNER – Head – Widower – b. 1861 Kalish Poland – aged 40 – Cigarette Maker
Alfred POSNER – Son – b. 1890 Lewisham – aged 11
Celia POSNER – Daughter – b. 1894 Bow – aged 7
Amelia POSNER – Daughter – b. 1896 Bow – aged 5
Mark POSNER – Son – b. 1897 Bow – aged 4
Jessie STEVENS – Domestic Servant

Death:

Benjamin POSNER – Q3 1903 [40] MILE END OLD TOWN 1c 266.
Buried in Plashet Cemetery – E-12-4 on 29 Sep 1903.

Jewish Chronicle – 02 Oct 1903

POSNER – On the 27th of September, Benjamin Posner, eldest son of Mrs and the late H.P. Posner, brother of Mrs P. Herman, Mrs F.N. Bloomberg, and Miss Rose Posner. Shiva at 186, Evering Road, Upper Clapton.
POSNER – On the 27th of September, at 164, Jamaica Street, Stepney, Benjamin Posner, aged 43,
POSNER – On the 27th of September, at 164, Jamaica Street, Stepney, Benjamin, brother of Mr Samuel Posner, of 30, Beresford Road, Canonbury, N. Shiva at 186, Evering Road, Upper Clapton, N.E.

Jewish Chronicle – 03 Jun 1904

The tombstone in loving memory of Benjamin Posner, late of 164, Jamaica Street, Stepney, will be set at Plashet Cemetery on Sunday, June 5th, at 3.30 p.m. Relatives and friends please accept this, the only intimation.

ROOS, Fanny – D-19-22

Died: 20 Feb 1900
Buried: 21 Feb 1900
Partner: Michael Roos (d. 1908)
Age: 72nd year

Jewish Chronicle – 23 Feb 1900

ROOS – On the 20th of February, at 1, Goring Street, Houndsditch, Fanny, the dearly beloved wife of Michael Roos, in her 72nd year. Mother of John Roos, 46, Shacklewell Lane, Dalston, Mrs A. Gluckstien, of Chicago, and Solomon Roos, of Melbourne. Shiva at 1, Goring Street, Houndsditch. May her dear soul rest in peace.

ROOS, Fanny – D-19-22

Jewish Chronicle – 04 May 1900

The tombstone to the memory of the late lamented Fanny Roos, of 1, Goring Street, Houndsditch, will be set on Sunday, May 6th, at 4 o'clock at Plashet Cemetery. Relatives and friends accept this, the only intimation.

Death:
Q1 1900 [71] LONDON C 1c 5.

1891 Census

Address:
1 Goring Street, Aldgate, London
Residents:
Michael ROOS – Head – b. 1832 Holland – aged 59 – General Dealer
Fanny ROOS – Wife – b. 1829 Holland – aged 62
John ROOS – Son – b. 1865 Holland – aged 26 – General Dealer

1881 Census

Address:
135 Middlesex Street, Whitechapel
Residents:
Michael ROOS – Head – b. 1832 Holland – aged 49 – General Dealer
Fanny ROOS – Wife – b. 1829 Holland – aged 52
Sophia GLUCK – Daughter – b. 1857 Holland – aged 24
Fanny GLUCK – Granddaughter – b. 1880 Whitechapel – aged 1

1871 Census

Address:
127 Middlesex Street, Whitechapel
Residents:
Maykel ROOS – Head – b. 1832 Holland – aged 39 – General Dealer
Fannie ROOS – Wife – b. 1828 Holland – aged 43
Betzi OESTERMAN – Mother – b. 1807 Holland – aged 64
Sophia ROOS – Daughter – b. 1857 Holland – aged 14 – Tailoress
Hyman ROOS – Son – b. 1859 Holland – aged 12 – Butcher
Solomon ROOS – Son – b. 1860 Holland – aged 11 – Scholar
Joseph ROOS – Son – b. 1864 Holland – aged 7 – Scholar

Death:
Michael (Machiel) Roos – Q4 1908 [76] LONDON CITY 1c 2.
Buried at Plashet Cemetery – I-10-27 on 22 Nov 1908.

Jewish Chronicle – 27 Nov 1908

ROOS – On the 20th of November, at 118, Houndsditch, Michael Roos, aged 76, beloved husband of Mrs V. Roos, and father of John Roos, 124, Stoke Newington Road, and Mrs S. Gluckstein, of Mobile, USA. Respected by all who knew him. May his dear soul rest in peace.

ROSENTHAL, Rebecca – B-11-10

Died: **05 Oct 1900**
Buried: **07 Oct 1900**
Partner: **Jonah Rosenthal (d. 1909)**
Aged: **31st year**

Jewish Chronicle – 12 Oct 1900
ROSENTHAL – On the 5th of October, at "The African Chief", Ossulston Street, Euston Road, after a long and painful illness, Rebecca, the dearly beloved wife of Jonah Rosenthal, in her 31st year. Deeply mourned by her sorrowing husband and children. May her soul rest in peace.
ROSENTHAL – On the 5th of October, Rebecca Rosenthal, the beloved sister of Mrs Sam Rosenthal. God rest her soul in peace – "John O'Groat", Gray Street, Blackfriars.
ROSENTHAL – On the 5th of October, Rebecca Rosenthal, the beloved sister of George, Alfred and Raphael Alexander, and Mrs I.A. Rosenthal, of Johannesburg. God rest her soul in peace – 28, Tredegar Square, Bow.

Jewish Chronicle – 28 Jun 1901
The tombstone to the memory of Rebecca, the beloved wife of Jonah Rosenthal, of "The African Chief", Ossulston Street, will be set on Sunday next, at Plashet Cemetery, at 4.30. Relatives and friends please accept this intimation.

Death:
Q4 1900 [31] PANCRAS 1b 53.
Marriage:
Jonah ROSENTHAL to Rebecca FUNK – Q1 1894 LONDON CITY 1c 92.

1891 Census
Address:
28 Tredegar Square, Mile End
Residents:
Nicholas FUNK – Head – b. 1832 Naturalised – aged 59 – Gentleman
Rosa FUNK – Wife – b. 1847 Naturalised – aged 44
Amelia FUNK – Daughter – b. 1868 London – aged 23
Rebecca FUNK – Daughter – b. 1870 London – aged 21
Miriam FUNK – Daughter – b. 1872 London – aged 19
Alfred FUNK – son – b. 1874 London – aged 17 – Fine Art Publisher

ROSENTHAL, Rebecca – B-11-10

1891 Census

Address:

3 Church Street, Spitalfields, London, Tower Hamlets

Residents:

Joseph ROSENTHAL – Head – b. 1849 London – aged 42 – Tailor
Julia ROSENTHAL – Wife – b. 1843 London – aged 48
Deborah ROSENTHAL – Daughter – b. 1869 London – aged 22 – Tailoress
Jonah ROSENTHAL – Son – b. 1870 London – aged 21 – Tailor
Leah ROSENTHAL – Daughter – b. 1872 London – aged 19 – Tailoress
Jeannette ROSENTHAL – Daughter – b. 1875 London – aged 16 – Teacher
Hannah ROSENTHAL – Daughter – b. 1877 London – aged 14

1901 Census

Address:

69 Ossulston Street, St. Pancras

Residents:

Jonah ROSENTHAL – Head – Widower – b. 1871 Mile End – aged 30 – Licensed Victualler
Elizabeth ROSENTHAL – Daughter – b. 1895 Bow – aged 6
Hannah ROSENTHAL – Daughter – b. 1897 Bow – aged 4
Rose WYALL – Domestic Servant
Louisa WYALL – Domestic Servant
Ernest BARKET – Visitor
Arthur HEARN – Barman
George H. WATSON – Barman

Death:

Jonah (Joel) ROSENTHAL – Q4 1909 [40] ST. GEORGE IN THE EAST 1c 202.
Buried at Plashet Cemetery – J-14-39 on 30 Nov 1909.

SHINBERG, Abraham L. – B-8-30

Died: **05 May 1900**
Buried: **07 May 1900**
Hebrew Name: **Avraham ben Yehuda Yakov**
Partner: **Nancy Shinberg (d. 1934)**
Aged: **37 years**

Jewish Chronicle – 11 May 1900

SHINBERG – On the 5th of May, at his residence, 71, Great Prescot Street, Goodman's Fields, Abraham, the dearly beloved husband of Nancy Shinberg, aged

SHINBERG, Abraham L. – B-8-30

37. Deeply mourned by his sorrowing wife, children, relatives and friends. May his soul rest in peace.
SHINBERG – On the 5th of May, at 71, Great Prescot Street, Abraham Shinberg, dearly beloved brother of Mrs Mark Bloomberg, 288, New Cross Road, S.E. Deeply regretted. God rest his soul.
SHINBERG – On the 5th of May, at 71, Great Prescot Street, Abraham Shinberg , only brother of Mrs Henry Friedlander, of 37, Mecklenburgh Square, and Mrs J. Forrest, 43, Great Prescot Street. Deeply lamented. Rest in peace.

Jewish Chronicle – 28 Sep 1900

The tombstone in loving memory of the late Abraham Shinberg, of 71, Gt. Prescot Street, Goodman's Field, will be set on Sunday next, September 30th, at 3.30 p.m., at Plashet Cemetery. Relatives and friends accept this, the only intimation.

Death:

Q2 1900 [37] WHITECHAPEL 1c 218.

1891 Census

Address:

9 Tenter Street North, St. Mary Whitechapel, London, Tower Hamlets

Residents:

Abraham L. SHINBERG – Head – b. 1863 Whitechapel – aged 28 – Tailor
Nancy SHINBERG – Wife – b. 1865 Whitechapel – aged 26
Gertrude SHINBERG – Daughter – b. 1889 – aged 2
Rebecca SHINBERG – Daughter – b. 1890 – aged 1
Mary Ann WHITE – Domestic Servant

Marriage:

Abraham Lewis SHINBERG to Nancy COHEN – Q3 1887 LONDON CITY 1c 130.

1901 Census

Registered as SHINEBERG

Address:

71 Great Prescott Street, Whitechapel

Residents:

Nancy SHINBERG – Head – Widow – b. 1866 London – aged 35 – Tailoress
Gertrude SHINBERG – Daughter – b. 1889 London – aged 12
Rebecca SHINBERG – Daughter – b. 1890 London – aged 11
Walter SHINBERG – Son – b. 1894 London – aged 7
Nathan SHINBERG – Son – b. 1896 London – aged 5

1911 Census

Address:

71 Great Prescott Street, Goodman's Fields, Whitechapel

Residents:

Nancy SHINBERG – Head – Widow – b. 1866 Whitechapel – aged 45 – Trouser Maker
Gertrude SHINBERG – Daughter – b. 1889 Whitechapel – aged 22 – Tailoress
Rebecca SHINBERG – Daughter – b. 1890 Whitechapel – aged 21 – Tailoress
Walter SHINBERG – Son – b. 1894 Whitechapel – aged 17 – Tailors Cutter
Nathan SHINBERG – Son – b. 1896 Whitechapel – aged 15 – Junior Clerk
Esther COHEN – Sister – b. 1871 Whitechapel – aged 40 – Tailoress
Jeannette COHEN – Sister – b. 1874 Whitechapel – aged 37 – Tailoress
Julia COHEN – Sister – b. 1876 Whitechapel – aged 35 – Tailoress
Annie JOHNSON – General Domestic Servant

Death:

Nancy SHINBERG – Q4 1934 [69] STOKE NEWINGTON 1b 324.
Buried at East Ham Cemetery – XC-4-307 buried 04 Oct 1934.

Jewish Chronicle – 05 Oct 1934

SHINBERG – On the 2nd of October, Nancy (relict of the late Abraham Shinberg), of 40, Albion Road, Stoke Newington, beloved mother of Gertie, Walter and Nat (Shirley), sister of Mrs Spyers, 73, Bow Road, Mrs Toff, Julia and Nat, of 12, Bearsted House, Middlesex Street. Deeply mourned by her daughters-in-law, grandchildren, sisters-in-law, brothers-in-law, nieces, nephews, and a large circle of friends. God rest her dear soul.

SIMMONS, Sarah – D-22-1

Died: 25 Aug 1900
Buried: 27 Aug 1900
Hebrew Name: Sarah bat Itzhak Halevi
Parents: Simon & Hannah Simmons
Age: 45 years

Jewish Chronicle – 31 Aug 1900

SIMMONS – On Saturday, the 25th of August, at 17, Middlesex Street, Aldgate, Sarah, the second daughter of Simmy and Hannah Simmons, aged 45. Deeply mourned by her parents, brothers and sisters. Shiva at above address.

Jewish Chronicle – 19 Jul 1901

The tombstone in memory of Sarah Simmons, the beloved daughter of Simon and

SIMMONS, Sarah – D-22-1

Hannah Simmons, of 17, Middlesex Street, Aldgate, will be set on Sunday next at Plashet Cemetery at 3 o'clock. Relatives and friends accept this, the only intimation.

Death:

Q3 1900 [45] LONDON C 1c 2.

1891 Census

Address:

17 Middlesex Street, Aldgate, London

Residents:

Simon SIMMONS – Head – b. 1822 London – aged 69 – General Dealer
Anna SIMMONS – Wife – b. 1826 Brighton – aged 65
Sarah SIMMONS – Daughter – b. 1855 London – aged 36
Jane SIMMONS – Daughter – b. 1863 London – aged 28
Abigail SIMMONS – Daughter – b. 1866 London – aged 25

1881 Census

Address:

20 Carter Street, St. Botolph Without Aldgate

Residents:

Simon SIMMONS – Head – b. 1822 London – aged 59 – General Dealer
Hannah SIMMONS – Wife – b. 1827 Brighton – aged 54
Esther SOLOMONS – Daughter – b. 1861 – aged 20
Sarah SIMMONS – Daughter – b. 1855 – aged 26
Jane SIMMONS – Daughter – b. 1862 – aged 19
Abigail SIMMONS – Daughter – b. 1865 – aged 16
Phoebe SIMMONS – Daughter – b. 1867 – aged 14
Miriam SIMMONS – Daughter – b. 1869 – aged 12
David SOLOMONS – Grandson – b. 1878 – aged 3
Hannah SOLOMONS – Granddaughter – b. 1879 – aged 2

1871 Census

Address:

35 Heneage Street, Stepney

Residents:

Simon SIMMONS – Head – b. 1822 Spitalfields – aged 49 – General Dealer
Hannah SIMMONS – Wife – b. 1827 Houndsditch – aged 44 – Cook
Esther SIMMONS – Daughter – b. 1851 Aldgate – aged 20 – Cook
Samuel SIMMONS – Son – b. 1853 Aldgate – aged 18 – Clothes Dealer
Sarah SIMMONS – Daughter – b. 1855 Aldgate – aged 16
Betsy SIMMONS – Daughter – b. 1857 Aldgate – aged 14 – Tailoress
Amelia SIMMONS – Daughter – b. 1860 Aldgate – aged 11
Jane SIMMONS – Daughter – b. 1862 Aldgate – aged 9

Julia SIMMONS – Daughter – b. 1864 Whitechapel – aged 7
Abigail SIMMONS – Daughter – b. 1866 Whitechapel – aged 5
Phoebe SIMMONS – Daughter – b. 1868 Mile End – aged 3
Miriam SIMMONS – Daughter – b. 1870 Mile End – aged 1

1861 Census

Address:
4 Providence Place, St. Botolph Without Aldgate, London

Residents:
Simon SIMMONS – Head – b. 1822 Aldgate – aged 39 – General Dealer
Hannah SIMMONS – Wife – b. 1827 Aldgate – aged 34
Lewis SIMMONS – Son – b. 1859 Aldgate – aged 2
Sophia SIMMONS – Daughter – b. 1851 Aldgate – aged 10 - Scholar
Samuel SIMMONS – Son – b. 1853 Aldgate – aged 8 – Scholar
Sarah SIMMONS – Daughter – b. 1855 Aldgate – aged 6 – Scholar
Elizabeth SIMMONS – Daughter – b. 1857 Aldgate – aged 4 – Scholar
Amelia SIMMONS – Daughter – b. 1861 Aldgate – aged 8 months

1851 Census

Address:
7 Angel Court, Saint Botolph Aldgate, London

Residents:
Simon SIMMONS (SIMONS) – Head – b. 1822 Spitalfields – aged 29 – General Dealer
Hannah SIMMONS – Wife – b. 1824 Spitalfields – aged 27
Louis SIMMONS – Son – b. 1848 Spitalfields – aged 3
Esther SIMMONS – Daughter – b. 1851 Spitalfields – aged 3 months

Marriage:
Simon SIMMONS to Hannah MOSS - Q2 1848 ST. LUKES 2 283.

Death:
Simon SIMMONS – Q3 1910 [90] MILE END OLD TOWN 1c 217.
Buried at Plashet Cemetery – I-18-21 on 17 Jul 1910

Hannah SIMMONS – Q3 1912 [87] MILE END OLD TOWN 1c 411.
Buried at Plashet Cemetery – K-33-16 on 31 Jul 1912.

STOKVIS, Isaac – B-9-22

Died: 09 Jul 1900
Buried: 12 Jul 1900
Partner: Amelia Stokvis (d. 1936)
Aged: 49 years

Jewish Chronicle – 13 Jul 1900

STOKVIS – On the 9th of July, through a terrible accident, Isaac Stokvis. Dearly beloved and deeply mourned by his sorrowing wife, son and daughter. May his soul rest in peace. Continental papers please copy. Shiva at 3, Wellesley Villas, Clapham Road, S.W.

Jewish Chronicle – 14 Sep 1900

The tombstone in loving memory of the late Mr Isaac Stokvis will be set at Plashet Cemetery on Sunday next, September 16th, at 2.30 p.m. Relatives and friends kindly accept this, the only intimation.

Death:

Q3 1900 [49] ST. OLAVE SOUTHWARK 1d 100.

1881 Census

Address:

16 Wood Street, Spitalfields

Residents:

Isaac STOKVIS – Head – b. 1851 Amsterdam – aged 30 – Cigar Manufacturer
Amelia STOKVIS – Wife – b. 1855 Sedan – aged 26
Lucian STOKVIS – Son – b. 1879 Spitalfields – aged 2
Sara S. STOKVIS – Daughter – b. 1881 Middlesex – aged 0
Anna HALSWORTH – Domestic Servant

London Gazette – 11 February 1876

NOTICE is hereby given, that the Partnership heretofore subsisting between the undersigned, Isaac Stokvis and Barnett Stokvis, carrying on business as Cigar Manufacturers and Importers, at 16, Wood-street, Spitalfields, in the county of Middlesex under the style or firm of J. and B. Stokvis and Co., has been this day dissolved by mutual consent. And that the said business will henceforth be carried on by the said Isaac Stokvis alone, by whom all debts owing to and by the said late firm will be received and paid.
—Dated this 1st day of February, 1876.
Isaac Stokvis.
Barnett Stokvis.

Post Office Directory - 1899

Isaac Stokvis is listed as the Publican of the Star & Garter, and lived at 62 Poland Street, W1.

Death:

Amelia STOKVIS – Q4 1936 [83] WANDSWORTH 1d 570.
Place of burial unknown.

TURNER, Leon Drayer – D-19-2

Died: **11 Feb 1900**
Buried: **13 Feb 1900**
Hebrew Name: **Ariah ben Aahron**
Partner: **Sarah Drayer Turner (d. 1939)**
Age: **37 years**

Jewish Chronicle – 16 Feb 1900

DRAYER TURNER – On the 11th of February, 1900, at 44, Burma Road, Green Lanes, after a long and painful illness, Leon, dearly beloved husband of Sarah Drayer Turner, aged 37. Deeply mourned by his sorrowing wife, children, relatives and large circle of friends. May his dear soul rest in peace.

Jewish Chronicle – 13 Jul 1900

The tombstone in loving memory of Leon Drayer Turner, late of 44, Burma Road, Green Lanes, will be set at the Plashet Cemetery on Sunday next, July 15th, at 5 o'clock, prompt. Relatives and friends will please accept this intimation.

Death:

Q1 1900 [37] HACKNEY 1b 359 – registered under TURNER, Leon Drayer.

1891 Census

Address:

19 St. Marks Street, St. Mary Whitechapel, London, Tower Hamlets

Residents:

Jacob LUSTIG – Head – b. 1842 Poland – aged 49 – Meat Dealer
Jane LUSTIG – Wife – b. 1829 Holland – aged 62
Henrietta LUSTIG – Daughter – b. 1872 Sheffield – aged 19 – Button Hole Hand
Priscilla LUSTIG – Daughter – b. 1870 Sheffield – aged 21
Leon DRAYER – Son-in-law – b. 1864 Holland – aged 27 – Musician
Sarah DRAYER – Daughter – b. 1865 USA – aged 26
Aaron DRAYER – Grandson – b. 1887 London – aged 4
Jennie DRAYER – Granddaughter – b. 1889 London – aged 2

TURNER, Leon Drayer – D-19-2

Marriage:

Leon DRAYER to Sarah LUSTIG – Q4 1885 LONDON CITY 1c 133.

1881 Census

Address:

2 Tenter Street North, Whitechapel

Residents:

Aaron DRAAYER – Head – b. 1820 The Netherlands – aged 61 – Diamond Polisher
Judith DRAAYER – Wife – b. 1820 The Netherlands – aged 61
Esther DRAAYER – Daughter – b. 1856 The Netherlands – aged 25 – Housemaid
Samuel DRAAYER – Son – b. 1856 The Netherlands – aged 25 – Cigar Maker
Leon DRAAYER – Son – b. 1863 The Netherlands – aged 18 – Musician
Abraham ENSEL – Boarder – b. 1858 The Netherlands – aged 23 – Tailor

1901 Census

Address:

41 Mildmay Grove, Islington

Residents:

Raphael LUSTIG – Head – b. 1865 Holland – aged 36 – Butcher
Ethel LUSTIG – Wife – b. 1878 Birmingham – aged 23
Jennie LUSTIG – Daughter – b. 1887 Islington – aged 14
Jack LUSTIG – Son – b. 1888 Islington – aged 13
Edward LUSTIG – Son – b. 1889 Islington – aged 12
Jennie TURNER – Niece – b. 1889 Islington – aged 12
Florence SIMS – Domestic Servant
Tryphena TARRIS – Domestic Servant

1911 Census

Address:

26 Chapel Street, Islington N.

Residents:

Sarah TURNER – Head – Widow – b. 1864 American – aged 47
Ernest TURNER – Son – b. 1887 Aldgate – aged 24 – Butcher
Jeannie TURNER – Daughter – b. 1889 Aldgate – aged 22 – Cashier
Julia TURNER – Daughter – b. 1892 Aldgate – aged 19
Priscilla TURNER – Daughter – b. 1894 Aldgate – aged 17 – Cashier
Henrietta TURNER – Daughter – b. 1895 Aldgate – aged 16 – Fancy Goods
Clara Harriet NOAKES – General Servant

Death:

Sarah TURNER – Q1 1939 [78] FULHAM 1a 429.
Buried at East Ham Cemetery – XA-21-27 on 12 Feb 1939.

WALDMAN, Rosa / Rose – B-10-21

Died: 21 Aug 1900
Buried: 22 Aug 1900
Partner: Michael Waldman (d. 1903)
Aged: 74 years

Jewish Chronicle – 24 Aug 1900

WALDMAN – On Tuesday, the 21st of August, at 251, Hackney Road, N.E., the dearly beloved wife of Michael Waldman, and mother of M. Waldman. May her soul rest in peace. Shiva at above address. Aged 74.

Jewish Chronicle – 23 Aug 1901

The tombstone to the memory of the late Mrs Mike Waldman, of 251, Hackney Road, will be set at Plashet Cemetery on Sunday next, the 25th inst., at 4. Friends accept this, the only intimation.

Death:

Q3 1900 [74] SHOREDEITCH 1c 81.

1891 Census

Registered as WALLMAN

Address:

15 Hoxton Square, Shoreditch, London

Residents:

Michael WALDMAN – Head – b. 1829 Russia – aged 62 – Boot Machinist
Rose WALDMAN – Wife – b. 1832 Russia – aged 59
Kate WALDMAN – Daughter – b. 1862 London – aged 29 – Machinist
Eva WALDMAN – Daughter – b. 1876 London – aged 15 – Tailoress
Leon WALDMAN – Grandson – b. 1887 London – aged 4
Nellie PORTER – Domestic Servant

1881 Census

Registered as WALDEMAN

Address:

15 Hoxton Square, Shoreditch

Residents:

Michael WALDMAN – Head – b. 1832 Russia – aged 49 – Boot Machinist
Rosetta WALDMAN – Wife – b. 1834 Russia – aged 47
Sarah WALDMAN – Daughter – b. 1856 Poplar – aged 25 – Boot Machinist
Kate WALDMAN – Daughter – b. 1858 Poplar – aged 23 – Boot Machinist
Golder WALDMAN – Daughter – b. 1860 Poplar – aged 21 – Boot Machinist

WALDMAN, Rosa / Rose – B-10-21

Leah WALDMAN – Daughter – b. 1863 Shoreditch – aged 18 – Boot Fitter
Elizabeth WALDMAN – Daughter – b. 1865 Shoreditch – aged 16 – Scholar
Amelia WALDMAN – Domestic Servant

1871 Census

Address:
111 Wellington Row, Bethnal Green

Residents:
Michael WALDMAN – Head – b. 1829 Germany –aged 42 - Boot Machinist
Rosey WALDMAN – Wife – b. 1831 Germany – aged 40
Moses WALDMAN – Son – b. 1853 Middlesex – aged 18
Sarah WALDMAN – Daughter – b. 1855 Middlesex – aged 16
Jane WALDMAN – Daughter – b. 1857 Middlesex – aged 14
Kate WALDMAN – Daughter - b. 1859 Middlesex – aged 12
Golder WALDMAN – Daughter – b. 1861 Middlesex – aged 10
Leah WALDMAN – Daughter – b. 1865 Middlesex – aged 6
Betsy WALDMAN – Daughter – b. 1867 Middlesex – aged 4
Lewis BARNET – Brother-in-law – b. 1833 Germany – aged 38 – Tailor
Sarah DAVIS – Niece – b. 1856 Middlesex – aged 15 – Boot Fitter
Julia GOODALL – Domestic Servant

1861 Census

Address:
13 Lamb Street, Spitalfields

Residents:
Michael WALDMAN – Head – b. 1829 – Russian Poland – aged 32 – Cap Maker
Rosa WALDMAN – Wife – b. 1831 Russian Poland – aged 30
Moses WALDMAN – Son – b. 1853 Spitalfields – aged 8 – Scholar
Sarah WALDMAN – Daughter – b. 1855 Spitalfields – aged 6 – Scholar
Jane WALDMAN – Daughter – b. 1857 St. George East – aged 4
Catherine WALDMAN – Daughter – b. 1860 Whitechapel – aged 1
Abby POORE – Domestic Servant

Marriage:
Michael WALDMAN to Rose LEVENSTONE – Q2 1852 ST LUKE 1b 753.

1901 Census

Registered as WALDEN

Address:
251 Hackney Road, Shoreditch

Residents:
Morris WALDEN – Head – b. 1854 London – aged 47 – Leather Dealer

Emily WALDEN – Wife – b. 1869 London – aged 32
Albert WALDEN – Son – b. 1879 London – aged 22 – Boot Machinist
Eva WALDEN – Daughter – b. 1877 London – aged 24 – Tailoress
Hyam WALDEN – Son – b. 1880 London – aged 21 – Boot Machinist
Leon WALDEN – Son – b. 1887 London – aged 14
John WALDEN – Son – b. 1889 London – aged 12
Michael WALDMAN – Father – Widower – b. 1828 Russia – aged 73
Lily STEDMAN – General Domestic Servant

Death:

Michael WALDMAN – Q1 1903 [76] SHOREDITCH 1c 61.
Buried at Plashet Cemetery – D-41-21 (date unknown).

Jewish Chronicle – 23 Jan 1903

WALDMAN – On the 16th of January, at 251, Hackney Road, Michael Waldman, aged 76, the beloved father of Morris Waldman, of the above address, Mrs L.B. Newman, of Johannesburg, Mrs H. Davidson of East London, Cape Colony, Mrs H. Isaacs, 247, Hackney Road, and Mrs H.S. Isaacs, of 41, Great Queen Street, Holborn. May his dear soul rest in peace.

WINKEL, Dinah - B-11-17

Died: **08 Oct 1900**
Buried: **10 Oct 1900**
Hebrew Name: **Dinah bat Ephraim**
Partner: **Abraham Winkel (d. 1903) (Avraham ben Asher)**
Aged: **51 years**

Jewish Chronicle – 12 Oct 1900

WINKEL – On the 8th of October, at 139, Stepney Green, Dinah, the dearly beloved wife of Abraham Winkel, and sister of Mrs S. De Winter, of 1, Maria Terrace, Beaumont Square. Deeply mourned by her sorrowing husband and children. Dutch papers please copy.

1891 Census

Registered as WINKLE

Address:

139 Stepney Green, Mile End Old Town

Residents:

Abraham WINKEL – Head – b. 1850 Holland – aged 41 – Engraver
Dinah WINKEL – Wife – b. 1850 Holland – aged 41
Amelia WINKEL – Daughter – b. 1874 Whitechapel – aged 17 – Dressmaker
Rebecca WINKEL – Daughter – b. 1876 Whitechapel – aged 15 – Cigar Maker

Sophia WINKEL – Daughter – b. 1876 Whitechapel – aged 15 – Cigar Maker
Betsey WINKEL – Daughter – b. 1880 Whitechapel – aged 11 – Scholar
Rose WINKEL – Daughter – b. 1882 Stepney – aged 9 – Scholar
Alfred WINKEL – Son – b. 1886 Stepney – aged 5 – Scholar
Eva WINKEL – Daughter – b. 1886 Stepney – aged 5 – Scholar
Harriet WINKEL – Daughter – b. 1890 Stepney – aged 1
Sophia WINKEL – Sister – b. 1861 Whitechapel – aged 30 – Tailoress

1881 Census

Registered as WINKE

Address:

115 Redmans Road - Shop, Mile End Old Town

Residents:

Abraham WINKEL – Head – b. 1850 Netherlands – aged 31 – Engraver & Dealer
Dinah WINKEL – Wife – b. 1850 Netherlands – aged 31
Amilla WINKEL – Daughter – b. 1874 Spitalfields – aged 7 – Scholar
Rebecca WINKEL – Daughter – b. 1876 Spitalfields – aged 5 – Scholar
Sophia WINKEL – Daughter – b. 1878 Stepney – aged 3
Elizabeth WINKEL – Daughter – b. 1880 Stepney – aged 1
Leon WINKEL – Father – Widower – b. 1818 Netherlands – aged 63 – Tobacconist
Sophia WINKEL – Sister – b. 1861 Spitalfields – aged 20 – Tailoress
Elizabeth SCHAAP – Sister-in-law – b. 1857 Spitalfields – aged 24 – Tailoress
Elizabeth MOORE – Domestic Servant

1871 Census

Address:

34 Tenter Street, Christ Church

Residents:

Leon WINKEL – Head – b. 1817 Holland – aged 54 – Shop Keeper
Mary WINKEL – Wife – b. 1821 Holland – aged 50 – Dress maker
Abraham WINKEL – Son – b. 1850 Holland – aged 21 - Engraver
Joseph WINKEL – Son – b. 1852 Holland – aged 19 – Bootmaker
David SARLUIS – Lodger – b. 1793 Holland – aged 78

Marriage:

Abraham WINKEL to Dinah SCHAAP – Q4 1873 LONDON CITY 1c 217.

Death:

Abraham WINKEL – Q1 1903 [53] MILE END 1c 269.
Buried at Plashet Cemetery – B-11-18 on 15 Feb 1903.

WINKEL, Dinah - B-11-17

Jewish Chronicle – 20 Feb 1903 – p. 25 – Obituary

"The East London Synagogue has sustained a severe loss by the death of Mr Abraham Winkel, who had held the office of Beadle and Collector of the Synagogue for a period of twenty-three years. The deceased had been confined to his bed for some five weeks with influenza, but his condition was not regarded as serious till within a few days of his death, which was due to heart failure, and occurred on Friday morning last. The deceased was a native of Holland, his material great grand-father being the Rev. J.A. Lehmans (Rabbi Lemel), Rabbi of the Hague, who was succeeded in the Rabbinical office by his son, the Rev. I. Lehmans. Mr Winkel's parents settled in London early in life, and although as a lad he received no special training in Synagogue procedures and custom, his religious upbringing and regular attendance at public worship gave him a thorough knowledge of the duties attaching to the office to which he was elected while still a young man. During the early years of the history of the East London Synagogue, when the congregation gained an unenviable notoriety in the community on account of the internal dissensions which divided the members into rival factions and seriously retarded the success of the synagogue, the Beadle by his tact and courtesy towards every member of the congregation was the only official who steered clear of the unpleasant conditions of affairs that arose within the synagogue, and from which such strong and capable communal leaders as the late Dr. Asher and Mr Lionel L. Cohen were unable to extricate it. During the past fifteen years that the synagogue has run its course in peace and harmony, and has thereby almost doubled its membership and considerably improved its financial position, Mr Winkel was recognised as one who played not the smallest part in promoting its prosperity. He was devoted to the interests of the congregation, and spared himself no effort to be of service to those responsible for its management and to the members individually. No one was more cordially welcomed in the homes of the seat-holders, on occasions of joy or sorrow, than he, and no one was more ready with the timely tactful word, or more eager to render any personal service that the circumstances of the moment demanded. He combined the best qualities of the familiar Shamash of a bygone age with the business aptitude and readiness of resource of the modern Beadle. There was nothing in Shool life that was foreign to him, nothing to be done in his department of activity that was beyond him. He was possessed of good common-sense, and of many qualities of heart and mind that would not be sought for in a man occupying his position. He could decorate the Synagogue and the Succah as artistically as any skilled florist, and he delighted to show how pleasing an effect he could produce with that minimum expenditure of money which is so rigorously insisted upon by those who control the communal coffers, in connection with a synagogue that is successful in producing an annual deficit altogether disproportionate to the surplus of good work it accomplishes in many directions of public usefulness. And he readily volunteered his service in many varied capacities, because he loved the synagogue and was proud of being regarded as its indispensable factotum. When his son was Barmitzvah he presented a Mantle for the Scroll of Law in celebration of the occasion, and he encouraged his children to follow his example in perpetrating the memory of their mother, who predeceased him some two years since. His loyalty and helpfulness to the minister under whom he served during the past fifteen years, and his scrupulous integrity in all things, were qualities which endeared him to the rite, who knew his worth and endeavoured to make his appreciation of it whenever the occasion arose. In 1899, when he celebrated his silver wedding, the members of the congregation marked the occasion by the presentation of an address and a cheque, to which even the humblest members readily contributed their mite. Although his synagogue duties occupied practically all his time, he rendered much useful service to the societies to which he belonged. He was Vice-President of the Sisterhood (a women's confined mourning society) for fifteen years, the Secretary of his Friendly Sick Lodge for ten years, a member of the Ancient Order of Foresters, a Life-Governor of the Jews' Hospital and Orphan Asylum through the medium of the East London Orphan Aid Society and a subscriber to many communal charities. His sympathy with the poor of the district was very real, and his inability to refuse an application for help may be set down as the exception that proved the practicality of the man. His inherent good nature made him give first and consider afterwards, and he was unable to think of his own tomorrow when the needs of his poorer brother pressed today.

The large concourse of people that gathered at his funeral on Sunday, both at his home adjoining the Synagogue in Stepney Green, and at the Plashet Cemetery, testified to the respect in which the late Beadle was held by all classes. Among those who attended, in addition to the Honorary Officers and members of the Board of Management of the Synagogue, were Mr Lewis Levy, a former Warden of the Synagogue, the Rev. S. Bronkhorst, representing the Sandys Row Synagogue, of which the deceased was for some years an active member, representatives of the societies to which he belonged, and the Rev. J.F. Stern, who officiated at the funeral service. Mr Winkel leaves a large family of children, three of whom are still of school age. Their grief will be shared by every member of the synagogue, which their father served with an ability, zeal and fidelity that won for him the good name he has bequeathed to them, and that "grace and good understanding in the sight of God and man" to which the lowliest can aspire and need not fail to win." [J.F.S.]

Jewish Chronicle – 07 Aug 1903

The tombstone to the memory of the late Abraham Winkel (late Beadle of the East London Synagogue), will be set on Sunday, the 9th inst., at Plashet Cemetery, at 4 o'clock. Relatives and friends kindly accept this, the only intimation.

WOOLF, Jane – D-19-8

Died: 17 Feb 1900
Buried: 19 Feb 1900
Partner: Henry Woolf (d. 1875)
Age: 81st year

Jewish Chronicle – 23 Feb 1900

WOOLF – On the 17th of February, at 43, Pyrland Road, Canonbury, N., Jane, widow of the late Henry Woolf, of Tooley Street, S.E., in her 81st year. Dearly loved mother of Abraham H. Woolf, and of Meyer Woolf, of 17, Finsbury Square. Shiva at 43, Pyrland Road, Canonbury. God rest her darling soul.
WOOLF – On the 17th of February, at Canonbury, Jane, widow of the late Henry Woof, of Tooley Street, S.E., in her 81st year. Dearly loved mother of Mrs L. Van Boolen, of 26, Sandringham Road, Dalston. God rest her dear soul.
WOOLF – On the 17th of February, at Canonbury, London, Jane, widow of the late Henry Woolf, of Tooley Street, S.E. in her 81st year. Dearly loved mother of Lewis Woolf, of 1, Brunswick Square, Brighton. May her soul rest in peace.

Jewish Chronicle – 04 Jan 1901

The memorial to the memory of our late dear mother, Mrs Jane Woolf, of 48, Pyrland Road, Canonbury, will be set on Sunday next, January 6th, at one o'clock, at Plashet Cemetery. The only intimation.

Death:
Q1 1900 [80] ISLINGTON 1b 319.

1891 Census

Address:
65 Balfour Road, Islington

Residents:
Jane WOOLF – Head – Widow – b. 1819 Holland – aged 72 – Retired Pawnbroker
Meyer WOOLF – Son – b. 1863 Southwark – aged 28 – Surveyor
Minnie ELFORD – General Domestic Servant
Ellen WORDING – General Domestic Servant

1881 Census

Address:
42 Addington Road, Bow aka St. Mary Stratford-le-Bow

Residents:
Jane WOOLF – Head – Widow – b. 1820 Holland – aged 61 – Retired Pawnbroker

WOOLF, Jane – D-19-8

Meyer WOOLF – Son – b. 1863 Hasley Down – aged 18 – Auctioneer's Clerk
Hannah SILVER – Niece – b. 1863 Spitalfields – aged 18
Sarah Ann HILL – Servant / Nurse

1871 Census

Address:
168 Tooley Street, St. John, St. Olave Southwark

Residents:
Henry WOOLF – Head – b. 1823 Bavaria – aged 48 – Pawnbroker
Jane WOOLF – Wife – b. 1821 Amsterdam – aged 50
Priscille WOOLF – Daughter – b. 1850 Middlesex – aged 21
Hannah WOOLF – Daughter – b. 1853 Middlesex – aged 18
Lewis WOOLF – Son – b. 1855 Middlesex – aged 16 – Scholar
Abraham WOOLF – Son – b. 1857 Middlesex – aged 14 – Scholar
Charles WOOLF – Son – b. 1858 Middlesex – aged 13 – Scholar
Mayer WOOLF – Son – b. 1864 Surrey – aged 7 – Scholar
Jane SMART – Domestic Servant

Marriage:
Henry WOOLF to Jane SILVER – Q2 1848 ST. LUKE 2 285.

Death:
Henry WOOLF – Q3 1875 [52] ST. OLAVE SOUTHWARK 1d 137.
Place of burial unknown.

WOOLF, Lewis – D-19-10

Died: 17 Feb 1900
Buried: 19 Feb 1900
Partner: Rose Woolf (d. 1917)
Aged: 49 years

Jewish Chronicle – 23 Feb 1900

WOOLF – On the 17th of February, at 83, Myrdle Street, Commercial Road, E., after a long and painful illness, Lewis, the dearly beloved husband of Rose Woolf, aged 49. Deeply mourned by his sorrowing wife, children, relatives, and a large circle of friends. May his dear soul rest in peace.

Jewish Chronicle – 03 Aug 1900

The tombstone in loving memory of Lewis Woolf, of 83, Myrdle Street, Commercial Road, E., will be set at Plashet Cemetery on Sunday, August 12th at 4 o'clock. Relatives and friends will please accept this, the only intimation.

Death:

Q1 1900 [49] MILE END OLD TOWN 1c 353.

1891 Census

Address:

83 Myrdle Street, Mile End Old Town

Residents:

Lewis WOOLF – Head – b. 1852 Spitalfields – aged 39 – General Dealer Shop
Rose WOOLF – Wife – b. 1858 Mile End – aged 33
Michael WOOLF – Son – b. 1877 Stepney – aged 14 – Bootmakers Apprentice
Abraham WOOLF – Son – b.1878 Stepney – aged 13 – Scholar
Benjamin WOOLF – Son – b. 1880 Stepney – aged 11 – Scholar
Lewis WOOLF – Son – b. 1882 Stepney – aged 9 – Scholar
Rachael WOOLF – Daughter – b. 1884 Stepney – aged 7 – Scholar
Jacob WOOLF – Son – b. 1887 Stepney – aged 4 – Scholar
Amelia WOOLF – Daughter – b. 1889 Stepney – aged 2

Marriage:

Lewis WOOLF to Rose MYERS – Q2 1875 LONDON CITY 1c 161.

1901 Census

Address:

83 Myrdle Street, Mile End Old Town

Residents:

Rose WOOLF – Head – Widow – b. 1852 Stepney – aged 49
Michael WOOLF – Son – b. 1877 Stepney – aged 24 – Boot Laster
Abraham WOOLF – Son – b. 1878 Stepney – aged 23 – Second Hand Clothes Dealer
Benjamin WOOLF – Son – b. 1879 Stepney – aged 22 – Ironmongers Porter
Lewis WOOLF – Son – b. 1881 Stepney – aged 20 – Assistant in Clothes Shop
Rachel WOOLF – Daughter – b. 1884 Stepney – aged 17 – Cashier
Jacob WOOLF – Son – b. 1886 Stepney – aged 15 – Tailors Cutter Apprentice
Amelia WOOLF – Daughter – b. 1890 Stepney – aged 11
Hyman WOOLF – Son – b. 1891 Stepney – aged 10

1911 Census

Address:

22 Coborn Road, Bow, London E.

Residents:

Rose WOOLF – Head – Widow – b. 1853 London – aged 58
Mike WOOLF – Son – b. 1877 London – aged 34 - Motor Cab Driver
Abraham WOOLF – Son – b. 1879 London – aged 32 – Wardrobe Dealer
Ray WOOLF – Daughter – b. 1886 London – aged 25 – Cashier

Jacob WOOLF – Son – b. 1888 London – aged 23 – Cloth Cutter
Amelia WOOLF – Daughter – b. 1890 London – aged 21
Hyman WOOLF – Son – b. 1892 London – aged 19 – Optician
Lewis MYERS – Brother – Widower – b. 1849 London – aged 62 – Sponge Traveller

Death:

Rose WOOLF – Q2 1917 [64] WHITECHAPEL 1c 295.
Buried at Plashet Cemetery – P-2-31 on 21 Jun 1917.

NAME INDEX

NAME	CEM. REF.	DIED	PHOTO	PAGE
ABRAHAMS, Emanuel	B-6-16	1900	336	337
ABRAHAMS, Jane	A-12-2	1898	94	95
ABRAHAMS, Kate	A-11-20	1898	98	97
ABRAHAMS, Louisa	A-7-28	1897	12	13
ABRAHAMS, Rebecca	A-6-27	1897	-	14
ANGEL, Coleman	A-14-12	1898	100	99
BARDER, Hannah	A-13-25	1898	-	103
BARNETT, Aaron	B-7-46	1900	339	338
BARNETT, Eva	D-11-31	1899	-	196
BARNETT, Nancy	A-13-4	1898	105	104
BARNETT, Simon John	B-9-34	1900	342	341
BARNETT, Solomon	B-5-29	1899	198	197
BENJAMIN, Hyman	B-3-1	1897	17	16
BENJAMIN, Maria	B-8-38	1900	344	345
BERLINSKY, Israel Joseph	B-1-19	1896	2	3
BLOM, Lewis Reginald	C-13-27	1899	-	200
BOSS, Gumpert	A-8-6	1897	18	19
BRESLAR, Raphael	B-6-1	1900	347	346
BRIGMAN, Simon	B-2-43	1897	-	21
BUCKS, Michael	A-14-53	1899	-	202
CASSELL, Bennett	D-16-2	1899	204	203
CITROEN, Cosman	D-20-1	1900	-	350
COHEN, Elias	A-12-7	1898	109	108
COHEN, George	D-9-12	1899	-	206
COHEN, John	A-14-57	1899	208	207
COHEN, Joseph	D-15-1	1899	-	210
COHEN, Michael	D-10-33	1899	-	212
COHEN, Saul	B-7-5	1900	-	351
COOK, Fanny	A-6-6	1897	23	22
COWEN, Rose	D-22-2	1900	-	353
COWEN, Samuel	A-11-62	1898	112	111
DAVIDS, Rachel	D-13-25	1899	216	215
DAVIS, Leah	A-13-8	1898	114	113
DAVIS, Sarah Queenie	C-2-33	1897	26	25

NAME	CEM. REF.	DIED	PHOTO	PAGE
DE FRIEND, Clara	D-19-17	1900	355	354
DE FRIES, Hannah	D-6-15	1898	-	117
DE HAAS, Bertha	B-6-36	1900	358	357
DE SMITH, Dinah	D-13-8	1899	218	219
FRANKEL, Joseph A.	B-11-29	1900	361	360
FRANKELL, Sophie	D-23-4	1900	-	363
FREIWALD, Fanny	D-9-26	1899	221	220
FRESCO, Levy	D-5-23	1898	-	119
FRIEDEBERG, Hyam Solomon	C-17-5	1900	366	365
FUNK, Nicholas	B-9-23	1900	368	369
GELBERG, Abraham	D-7-1	1898	122	123
GLANTZ, Rosetta	B-11-36	1900	372	371
GLENSNICK, Augusta	A-7-3	1897	30	31
GOLDBERG, Deborah	B-9-37	1900	375	374
GOLDBERG, Kitty	D-19-6	1900	378	377
GOLDBERG, Morris	A-6-59	1897	34	33
GOLDSMID, Kate	B-4-5	1899	-	223
GOLDSTEIN, Simeon	A-14-26	1898	125	124
GOODMAN, Rose/Rosa	A-14-14	1898	128	127
GREEN, Rose	D-18-1	1899	-	226
GROUSE, Charles	B-8-22	1900	-	379
GUTTENBERG, Henry	D-16-15	1899	228	227
HARRIS, Augustus Henry	D-13-22	1899	231	230
HARRIS, Lewis	D-10-4	1899	234	233
HARRIS, Moss	D-16-14	1899	-	236
HART, Gershon	B-2-26	1897	-	35
HART, Sarah	D-17-35	1899	238	237
HART, Sylvia	B-12-12	1900	-	380
HENDRICKS, Jane	D-11-3	1899	-	241
HESS, Alice	D-10-1	1899	244	243
HOSE, Esther	A-13-24	1898	132	131
HOUTMAN, Judah	A-11-24	1898	134	135
HUMPHREYS, Rosetta	D-7-2	1898	137	136
HYAM, David	B-2-16	1896	-	5
HYAMS, Esther	B-8-44	1900	-	383
HYAMS, Joseph Mitchell	B-5-7	1899	-	246

NAME	CEM. REF.	DIED	PHOTO	PAGE
HYAMS, Kate	D-15-9	1899	-	248
ISAACS, Alexander	D-15-4	1899	251	250
ISAACS, Amelia	B-5-16	1899	-	252
ISAACS, Asher	A-14-43	1899	-	254
ISAACS, Jessie Gaby	B-7-3	1900	386	385
ISAACS, Joseph	B-3-6	1897	39	38
ISAACS, Michael	A-8-32	1897	42	41
ISAACS, Sarah	D-8-1A	1899	258	257
ISRAEL, Caroline	A-11-43	1898	-	139
ISRAEL, Lazarus	A-13-36	1898	142	141
ISRAEL, Nancy	A-14-16	1898	145	144
ISRAEL, Rachel	A-14-23	1899	262	261
ISRAEL, Rebecca	B-1-44	1896	7	8
ISRAEL, Samuel	A-14-39	1899	-	264
JACOBS, Abigail	B-5-1	1899	267	266
JACOBS, Joseph	D-23-17	1900	389	388
JACOBS, Polly	D-21-1	1900	392	391
JACOBS, Solomon	A-7-40	1897	44	43
JEWELL, Julian/Jullien	B-7-1	1900	396	395
JOEL, Harry	B-3-8	1897	-	47
JONAS, Esther	A-9-13	1897	49	48
JOSEPH, Mary	A-8-12	1897	-	50
JOSEPH, Myer	A-14-21	1898	148	147
KAUFMAN, Elias	A-14-49	1899	-	270
KING, Nathaniel	A-10-43	1898	150	149
KLEIN, Moses	D-11-2	1899	-	272
KOSKI, Jacob	D-23-27	1900	398	397
LANCASTER, Polly	D-13-7	1899	-	274
LEAPMAN, Lewis	A-14-35	1899	276	277
LEVY, Dinah	D-13-6	1899	-	279
LEVY, Harriet	A-12-27	1898	152	153
LEVY, John	D-13-21	1899	-	281
LEVY, Matilda	B-7-26	1900	-	400
LEVY, Minnie	A-7-19	1897	54	53
LEVY, Newman	A-14-36	1898	155	154
LEWIS, Amelia (Milly)	B-11-48	1900	402	403

NAME	CEM. REF.	DIED	PHOTO	PAGE
LEWIS, Bernard	C-9-25	1899	284	283
LIMBURG, Abraham	B-3-7	1897	-	55
LIPMAN, Rachel	B-8-35	1900	406	405
MAGNUS, Eliza	B-3-46	1898	-	157
MANHEIM, Catherine	B-3-28	1897	59	58
MARKS, Esther	D-19-4	1900	408	407
MARKS, Josiah	A-14-5	1898	159	158
MARKS, Solomon	D-15-20	1899	-	286
MARTIN, Esther Rachel	A-6-27	1897	60	61
MELLER, Abraham	A-11-10	1898	163	161
MILCH, Rudolf	B-12-48	1900	412	411
MORDECAI, Mark	D-13-1	1899	288	289
MORRIS, John K.	A-12-15	1898	-	164
MORRIS, Rachel	D-9-1B	1899	293	292
MORRIS, Sarah	A-13-18	1898	166	165
MOSES, Emanuel Frederick	A-9-35	1897	63	62
MOSES, Montague Henry	D-19-13	1900	414	413
MYERS, Abraham	A-9-5	1897	66	65
MYERS, Leah	A-11-18	1898	168	167
MYERS, Rose	A-12-16	1898	171	170
MYERS, Rose	B-10-32	1900	-	416
NASCH, Augusta Esther	A-9-21	1897	70	69
NATHAN, Esther	A-7-5	1897	-	71
NATHAN, Matilda	A-6-37	1897	74	73
NATHAN, Sarah	B-4-47	1899	-	294
PARKER, Rachel Ada	D-22-6	1900	420	419
PHILLIPS, Abigail	D-18-22	1900	423	421
PIZER, Yetta	A-11-12	1898	173	172
POSNER, Julia	B-8-25	1900	-	424
POZNER, Abraham L.	A-11-19	1898	176	175
RAPHAEL, James	D-16-18	1899	298	297
ROOS, Fanny	D-19-22	1900	426	425
ROSENTHAL, Isaac	B-2-32	1897	-	75
ROSENTHAL, Rebecca	B-11-10	1900	429	428
SACKSHIVER, Betsy	A-14-51	1899	300	299
SAMPSON, Rose/Rosetta	A-11-1	1897	-	77

NAME	CEM. REF.	DIED	PHOTO	PAGE
SAMUEL, Henry	D-7-1A	1899	-	302
SAMUEL, Samuel	C-9-1	1898	179	178
SAUNDERS, Annie	B-2-31	1897	81	80
SCHREIBERG, Woolf	B-1-19	1896	-	10
SEIGENBERG, John K.	D-8-1	1898	182	181
SHINBERG, Abraham L.	B-8-30	1900	431	430
SHINBERG, Rebecca	D-15-2	1899	306	305
SHOCK, Solomon	B-4-2	1899	308	307
SHUTER, Esther	D-13-31	1899	-	310
SILVER, Solomon	D-13-3	1899	314	312
SIMMONS, Annie	A-13-6	1898	185	184
SIMMONS, Sarah	D-22-1	1900	434	433
SOLOMONS, Fanny	B-2-29	1897	84	83
SOLOMONS, Michael	A-14-25	1898	188	187
SOMERS, John Isaac	D-16-4	1899	-	316
STOKVIS, Isaac	B-9-22	1900	-	437
SYMONDS/SYMONS, Elizabeth	D-14-12	1899	318	317
TURNER, Leon Drayer	D-19-2	1900	439	438
VAN BOOLEN, Flora	D-11-1	1899	322	320
VAN GELDER, Lydia	A-12-1	1899	324	323
VAN LEER, Elias	D-10-31	1899	327	325
VAN PRAAGH, Moses	A-11-3	1897	86	85
VANDERSLUIS, Julia	D-12-18	1899	-	328
WALDMAN, Rosa	B-10-21	1900	442	441
WEINRABE, Esther	B-2-28	1897	-	88
WESTHEIMER, Ivan Isaac	C-9-4	1899	-	330
WHITE, Jacob	D-16-34	1899	331	330
WINKEL, Dinah	B-11-17	1900	446	444
WOOLF, Jane	D-19-8	1900	450	449
WOOLF, Joel	A-13-11	1898	-	189
WOOLF, Lewis	D-19-10	1900	-	451
WOOLF, Sarah	A-9-7	1897	-	90
ZEFFERT, Sarah	A-11-9	1898	-	191

MARRIAGE INDEX - GROOM

GROOM	BRIDE (MAIDEN NAME)	MARRIED	PAGE
ABRAHAMS, Jack	JOEL, Louisa	1891	13
ABRAHAMS, Isaac	LEVY, Jane	1866	95
ABRAHAMS, Harry	SAMUELS, Kate	1885	97
ANGEL, Coleman	SAMUELS, Jane	1856	99
BARNETT, Joshua	BENJAMIN, Nancy	1844	104
BARNETT, Solomon	GOLDBERG, Amelia Leah	1871	197
BARNETT, Simon John	HUMPHREYS, Mary Ann	1848	341
BENJAMIN, Hyman	WOOLF, Jane	1875	16
BENJAMIN, Joseph	LEVY, Maria	1897	345
BERLINSKY, Israel Joseph	VAN PRAAG, Clara	1876	3
BRESLAR, Raphael	LYONS, Rebecca	1861	346
BRIGMAN, Simon	MORRIS, Annie	1878	21
BUCK, Michael	RAILTON, Hannah	1856	202
CASSEL(L), Bennet(t)	NATHAN, Dinah	1862	203
CITROEN, Cosman Jacob	VOORZANGER, Rosa Levie	1855	350
COHEN, Elias	LEVY, Catherine	1859	108
COHEN, Joseph	DAVIS, Rachel	1889	210
COHEN, Michael	SOLOMONS, Bloomah	1847	212
COHEN, Saul	LEVY, Leah	1885	351
COOK, Barnett	ROSENBERG, Fanny	1888	22
DAVIS, Solomon	GREEN, Sylvia	1877	25
DAVIS, Morris	CHURCH, Leah	1859	113
DE FRIEND, Lewis	SILVER, Clara	1864	354
DE FRIES, Henry	HARRIS, Hannah	1849	117
FRANKELL, Michael	JACOBS, Sophia	1882	363
FUNK, Nicholas	ALEXANDER, Rosalie	1871	369
GOLDBERG, Solomon	COHEN, Kitty	1885	377
GREEN, Samuel	MORTON, Rose Anna	1865	226
GUTTENBERG, Henry	POSNER, Rachel	1879	227
HARRIS, Augustus H.H.	RENDLE, Florence Edgcumbe	1881	230
HARRIS, Lewis	HART, Jane	1866	233
HARRIS, Moss	WILKS, Clara	1896	236
HART, Gershon	HYAMS, Rosetta	1869	35
HART, Moses	MOSES, Sarah	1841	237

GROOM	BRIDE (MAIDEN NAME)	MARRIED	PAGE
HART, Ezekiel	GREEN, Sylvia	1841	380
HESS, Samuel	CANTOR, Alice	1854	243
HOSE, Joseph Barnett	JACOBS, Esther	1885	131
HYAMS, Joseph	DE YOUNG, Jeanette	1879	246
ISAACS, Joseph	EMANUEL, Mary	1856	38
ISAACS, Michael	JACOBS, Amelia	1874	41
ISAACS, Alexander	BARNETT, Henrietta Sarah	1896	250
ISAACS, Asher	DAVIS, Esther	1847	254
ISAACS, Angel	MOSES, Sarah	1862	257
ISAACS, Moses	POLACK, Jessy	1837	385
ISRAEL, Abraham	ISRAEL, Rebecca	1869	8
ISRAEL, Elkin	LYONS, Caroline	1850	139
ISRAEL, Lazarus	JOSEPH, Mary Ann	1867	141
ISRAEL, Joseph	HYAMS, Catherine (Rachel)	1870	261
JACOBS, Solomon	JOSEPH, Rachel	1856	43
JACOBS, Abraham	NATHAN, Abigail	1868	266
JACOBS, Joseph	HART, Harriet	1867	388
JACOBS, Solomon	JONES, Mary / Polly	1857	391
JEWELL, Julian	BARNETT, Kate	1880	395
JOEL, Henry	HULBERT, Amelia Sarah	1863	47
JONAS, Samuel	DE ROSE (nee) SOESAN, Esther	1888	48
JOSEPH, John (Jacob)	JACOBS, Mary	1868	50
KAUFMAN, Elias	HYMAN, Esther	1856	270
KING, Nathaniel	LORD, Mary	1880	149
KOSKI, Jacob	LOBERMAN, Rachel	1869	397
LEAPMAN, Lewis	JOEL, Miriam	1858	277
LEVY, Aaron	BLUMENTHAL, Minnie	1870	53
LEVY, Michael	LEVY, Harriet Reta	1894	153
LEVY, John L.	MAGNAY, Mary	1840	281
LIMBURG, Abraham	GOLDSTEIN, Sophia	1859	55
LIPMAN, Jonas	JACOBS, Rachael	1849	405
MAGNUS, Lewis	RAPHAEL, Eliza	1854	157
MARKS, Josiah	BERLINER, Fanny	1854	158
MARKS, Solomon	COLE, Hannah	1867	286
MARKS, Solomon	ABRAHAMS, Esther	1865	407
MELLER, Abraham	SAKMAN(N), Hannah	1861	161

GROOM	BRIDE (MAIDEN NAME)	MARRIED	PAGE
MILCH, Rudolph	LEK, Fanny	1892	411
MORRIS, John	LEAPMAN, Louisa	1889	164
MORRIS, Moses	LEVY, Sarah	1889	165
MORRIS, Henry	BARNETT, Rachel	1859	292
MOSES, Emanuel Frederick	KISCH, Esther	1849	62
MOSES, Montague Henry	WOOLF, Caroline	1864	413
MYERS, Samuel	LYONS, Leah	1858	167
MYERS, Solomon	LIPMAN, Rose	1885	170
MYERS, Phillip	LEVY, Rose	1884	416
NATHAN, Nathan	ISAACS, Sarah	1866	294
PARKER, Henry Solomon	ABRAHAMS, Ada Rachel	1885	419
PHILLIPS, Isaiah	PHILLIPS, Abigail	1878	421
POSNER, Benjamin	GOLDSTEIN, Julia	1888	424
POZNER, Abraham Lazarus	JACOBS, Julia	1859	175
RAFHAEL, James	BENJAMIN, Caroline	1858	297
ROSENTHAL, Isaac	MAISONPIERRE, Evaline	1858	75
ROSENTHAL, Jonah	FUNK, Rebecca	1894	428
SAMPSON, Nathan	LEVY, Rosetta	1872	77
SAMUEL, Henry	LEVY, Sarah Deborah	1860	302
SAUNDERS, Nathan	NEWMAN, Annie	1882	80
SEIGENBERG, John	JACOBS, Julia	1865	181
SHINBERG, Abraham Lewis	COHEN, Nancy	1887	430
SHOCK, Solomon	LEWIS, Flora	1877	307
SHUTER, Samuel	WOOLF, Hannah	1850	310
SILVER, Solomon	ABRAHAMS, Simney	1857	312
SIMMONS, Joseph	JOSEPH, Annie	1887	184
SOMERS, John Isaac	GRANT, Emily	1889	316
SYMONS, Isaac	LEE, Elizabeth	1876	317
TURNER, Leon Drayer	LUSTIG, Sarah	1885	438
VAN BOOLEN, Reuben	CITROEN, Flora	1884	320
VANDERSLUIS, Isaac	KASNER, Julia	1862	328
WALDMAN, Michael	LEVENSTONE, Rose	1852	441
WEINRABE, Abraham Maurice	SIMONDS, Esther	1875	88
WHITE, Jacob	MYERS, Rachel	1861	330
WINKEL, Abraham	SCHAAP, Dinah	1873	444
WOOLF, Raphael	LAZARUS, Sarah	1878	90

GROOM	BRIDE (MAIDEN NAME)	MARRIED	PAGE
WOOLF, Joel	SOLOMONS, Helen	1851	189
WOOLF, Henry	SILVER, Jane	1848	449
WOOLF, Lewis	MYERS, Rose	1875	451

MARRIAGE INDEX - BRIDE

BRIDE (MAIDEN NAME)	GROOM	MARRIED	PAGE
ABRAHAMS, Esther	MARKS, Solomon	1865	407
ABRAHAMS, Ada Rachel	PARKER, Henry Solomon	1885	419
ABRAHAMS, Simney	SILVER, Solomon	1857	312
ALEXANDER, Rosalie	FUNK, Nicholas	1871	369
BARNETT, Henrietta Sarah	ISAACS, Alexander	1896	250
BARNETT, Kate	JEWELL, Julian	1880	395
BARNETT, Rachel	MORRIS, Henry	1859	292
BENJAMIN, Nancy	BARNETT, Joshua	1844	104
BENJAMIN, Caroline	RAFHAEL, James	1858	297
BERLINER, Fanny	MARKS, Josiah	1854	158
BLUMENTHAL, Minnie	LEVY, Aaron	1870	53
CANTOR, Alice	HESS, Samuel	1854	243
CHURCH, Leah	DAVIS, Morris	1859	113
CITROEN, Flora	VAN BOOLEN, Reuben	1884	320
COHEN, Kitty	GOLDBERG, Solomon	1885	377
COHEN, Nancy	SHINBERG, Abraham Lewis	1887	430
COLE, Hannah	MARKS, Solomon	1867	286
DAVIS, Rachel	COHEN, Joseph	1889	210
DAVIS, Esther	ISAACS, Asher	1847	254
DE ROSE (nee) SOESAN, Esther	JONAS, Samuel	1888	48
DE YOUNG, Jeanette	HYAMS, Joseph	1879	246
EMANUEL, Mary	ISAACS, Joseph	1856	38
FUNK, Rebecca	ROSENTHAL, Jonah	1894	428
GOLDBERG, Amelia Leah	BARNETT, Solomon	1871	197
GOLDSTEIN, Sophia	LIMBURG, Abraham	1859	55
GOLDSTEIN, Julia	POSNER, Benjamin	1888	424
GRANT, Emily	SOMERS, John Isaac	1889	316

BRIDE (MAIDEN NAME)	GROOM	MARRIED	PAGE
GREEN, Sylvia	HART, Ezekiel	1841	380
HARRIS, Hannah	DE FRIES, Henry	1849	117
HART, Jane	HARRIS, Lewis	1866	233
HART, Harriet	JACOBS, Joseph	1867	388
HULBERT, Amelia Sarah	JOEL, Henry	1863	47
HUMPHREYS, Mary Ann	BARNETT, Simon John	1848	341
HYAMS, Rosetta	HART, Gershon	1869	35
HYAMS, Catherine (Rachel)	ISRAEL, Joseph	1870	261
HYMAN, Esther	KAUFMAN, Elias	1856	270
ISAACS, Sarah	NATHAN, Nathan	1866	294
ISRAEL, Rebecca	ISRAEL, Abraham	1869	8
JACOBS, Sophia	FRANKELL, Michael	1882	363
JACOBS, Esther	HOSE, Joseph Barnett	1885	131
JACOBS, Amelia	ISAACS, Michael	1874	41
JACOBS, Mary	JOSEPH, John (Jacob)	1868	50
JACOBS, Rachael	LIPMAN, Jonas	1849	405
JACOBS, Julia	POZNER, Abraham Lazarus	1859	175
JACOBS, Julia	SEIGENBERG, John	1865	181
JOEL, Louisa	ABRAHAMS, Jack	1891	13
JOEL, Miriam	LEAPMAN, Lewis	1858	277
JONES, Mary / Polly	JACOBS, Solomon	1857	391
JOSEPH, Mary Ann	ISRAEL, Lazarus	1867	141
JOSEPH, Rachel	JACOBS, Solomon	1856	43
JOSEPH, Annie	SIMMONS, Joseph	1887	184
KASNER, Julia	VANDERSLUIS, Isaac	1862	328
KISCH, Esther	MOSES, Emanuel Frederick	1849	62
LAZARUS, Sarah	WOOLF, Raphael	1878	90
LEAPMAN, Louisa	MORRIS, John	1889	164
LEE, Elizabeth	SYMONS, Isaac	1876	317
LEK, Fanny	MILCH, Rudolph	1892	411
LEVENSTONE, Rose	WALDMAN, Michael	1852	441
LEVY, Jane	ABRAHAMS, Isaac	1866	95
LEVY, Maria	BENJAMIN, Joseph	1897	345
LEVY, Catherine	COHEN, Elias	1859	108
LEVY, Leah	COHEN, Saul	1885	351
LEVY, Harriet Reta	LEVY, Michael	1894	153

BRIDE (MAIDEN NAME)	GROOM	MARRIED	PAGE
LEVY, Rose	MYERS, Phillip	1884	416
LEVY, Rosetta	SAMPSON, Nathan	1872	77
LEVY, Sarah Deborah	SAMUEL, Henry	1860	302
LEWIS, Flora	SHOCK, Solomon	1877	307
LIPMAN, Rose	MYERS, Solomon	1885	170
LOBERMAN, Rachel	KOSKI, Jacob	1869	397
LORD, Mary	KING, Nathaniel	1880	149
LUSTIG, Sarah	TURNER, Leon Drayer	1885	438
LYONS, Rebecca	BRESLAR, Raphael	1861	346
LYONS, Caroline	ISRAEL, Elkin	1850	139
LYONS, Leah	MYERS, Samuel	1858	167
MAGNAY, Mary	LEVY, John L.	1840	281
MAISONPIERRE, Evaline	ROSENTHAL, Isaac	1858	75
MORRIS, Annie	BRIGMAN, Simon	1878	21
MORTON, Rose Anna	GREEN, Samuel	1865	226
MOSES, Sarah	HART, Moses	1841	237
MOSES, Sarah	ISAACS, Angel	1862	257
MYERS, Rachel	WHITE, Jacob	1861	330
MYERS, Rose	WOOLF, Lewis	1875	451
NATHAN, Dinah	CASSEL(L), Bennet(t)	1862	203
NATHAN, Abigail	JACOBS, Abraham	1868	266
NEWMAN, Annie	SAUNDERS, Nathan	1882	80
PHILLIPS, Abigail	PHILLIPS, Isaiah	1878	421
POLACK, Jessy	ISAACS, Moses	1837	385
POSNER, Rachel	GUTTENBERG, Henry	1879	227
RAILTON, Hannah	BUCK, Michael	1856	202
RAPHAEL, Eliza	MAGNUS, Lewis	1854	157
RENDLE, Florence Edgcumbe	HARRIS, Augustus H.H.	1881	230
ROSENBERG, Fanny	COOK, Barnett	1888	22
SAKMAN(N), Hannah	MELLER, Abraham	1861	161
SAMUELS, Kate	ABRAHAMS, Harry	1885	97
SAMUELS, Jane	ANGEL, Coleman	1856	99
SCHAAP, Dinah	WINKEL, Abraham	1873	444
SILVER, Clara	DE FRIEND, Lewis	1864	354
SILVER, Jane	WOOLF, Henry	1848	449
SIMONDS, Esther	WEINRABE, Abraham Maurice	1875	88

BRIDE (MAIDEN NAME)	GROOM	MARRIED	PAGE
SOLOMONS, Bloomah	COHEN, Michael	1847	212
SOLOMONS, Helen	WOOLF, Joel	1851	189
VAN PRAAG, Clara	BERLINSKY, Israel Joseph	1876	3
VOORZANGER, Rosa Levie	CITROEN, Cosman Jacob	1855	350
WILKS, Clara	HARRIS, Moss	1896	236
WOOLF, Jane	BENJAMIN, Hyman	1875	16
WOOLF, Caroline	MOSES, Montague Henry	1864	413
WOOLF, Hannah	SHUTER, Samuel	1850	310

BIBLIOGRAPHY

Arnold, Catherine. *Necropolis London and its Dead.* (2006) Simon & Schuster UK, Ltd, London, UK.

Bard, Robert. *Graveyard London: Lost and Forgotten Burial Grounds.* (2008) Historical Publications Ltd, London, UK.

Berger, Doreen. *The Jewish Victorian: Genealogical Information from the Jewish Newspapers 1871-1880.*
(1999) Robert Boyd Publications, Witney, UK.

Black, Gerry. *Jewish London: An Illustrated History.* (2007) Breedon Books Publishing Co Ltd., Derby, UK.

Brook, Stephen. *The Club: The Jews of modern Britain.* (1989) Constable & Co. Ltd, London, UK.

Brooks, Chris. *Mortal Remains: The History and Present State of the Victorian and Edwardian Cemetery.*
(1989) Wheaton Publishers Ltd., Devon, UK.

Cesarani, David, *The Jewish Chronicle and Anglo-Jewry 1841-1991.* (1994) Cambridge University Press, UK.

DeVilliers, John, *My Memories.* (1931) Grant Richards, London, UK.

Endelman, Todd M. *The Jews of Britain 1656 to 2000.* (2002) University of California Press, Los Angeles, USA.

Francis, Doris, Kellaher, Leonie & Neophytou, Georgina. *The Secret Cemetery.* (2005) Berg, London, UK

Glinert, Ed. *London's Dead: A Guided Tour of the Capital's Dead.* (2008) Harper Collins Publishers, London, UK.

Kolatch, Alfred J. *The Jewish Book of Why.* (1981) Jonathan David Publishers, New York, USA.

Massil, Stephen W. (ed), *The Jewish Year Book.* (2002) Vallentine Mitchell, London, UK.

Meller, Hugh & Parsons, Brian. *London Cemeteries: An Illustrated Guide & Gazetteer* (4th Edition). (2008)
The History Press, Stroud, UK.

Menachemson, Nolan, *A Practical Guide to Jewish Cemeteries.* (2007) Avotaynu Inc., Bergenfield, USA.

Newman, Aubrey, *The United Synagogue 1870-1970.* (1977) Routledge & Kena Paul Ltd, London, UK.

Roth, Cecil, *The History of the Jews.* (1963) Schocken Books, New York, USA.

Roth, Cecil. *A History of the Jews in England.* (1941) Clarendon Press, Oxford, UK.

Schwartzman, Arnold. *Graven Images: Graphic Motifs of the Jewish Gravestone.* (1993) Harry N. Abrams, Inc., New York, USA.

Segal, Joshua L. *A Field Guide to Visiting a Jewish Cemetery: A Spiritual Journey to the Past, Present and Future.* (2005) Jewish Cemetery Publishing, Nashua, USA.

Taylor, Mark C. & Lammerts, Dietrich Christian. *Grave Matters.* (2002) Reaktion Books Ltd., London, UK.

ACKNOWLEDGEMENTS

The number of people to be acknowledged for their help is long indeed. Many would say that they were just doing their jobs, while others went out of their way to provide me with good advice and help. Some people were also responsible for telling me to go away – and to those people I say a loud 'thank you' for making me stick to my guns.

People who should be mentioned include the staff of the United Synagogue's Burial Society. Thanks go to Melvyn Hartog (Head of Burial), Leonard Shear (IT Manager), Marcia Wohlman (Burial Office Manager), Ruth Shorrick (Office Assistant), and most importantly, Roy Marney (Groundsman) who supported my ideas from the beginning.

My principal supporter has been my darling husband, Fred, who has put up with me talking about Plashet cemetery for years, rather than cooking his dinner and looking after him. He has been totally supportive, even to the point of taking out his camera and taking photos at the cemetery for me.

My family have been very supportive and therefore need to be acknowledged, especially my darling mother, Ruth, and my step-father, Professor Michael McIntyre, of Cambridge. Other members of the family who have helped with the production of the book include my half-sister, Aviva, and her husband, Gil, my brothers Jonathan (Saha) and Peter, and their wives, Rose and Estelle.

I have also been supported by a group of people inside and outside genealogical circles. Rieke and Peter Nasch of the Australian Jewish Genealogical Society have supported me, not only with proof-reading skills, but in the production of the Preface. Charles Tucker, the Archivist of the London Beth Din, generated ideas that led to creation of this book.

Friends including Karen and Philip, and Mark and Jackie, both of London, supported me with information about the history of the Burial Society and the names of people involved in London's Jewish community. Francine and Philip, of Amsterdam, showed me how the Dutch community had produced books about Jewish cemeteries, and finally, Lida Lopes Cardozo Kindersley from Cambridge, who generously gave of her valuable time and knowledge about stones.

To all of the above people I say a big 'thank you'.

www.ingramcontent.com/pod-product-compliance
Lightning Source LLC
Chambersburg PA
CBHW020330270326
41926CB00007B/118

* 9 7 8 0 9 8 7 5 6 1 0 1 5 *